MW00830409

GOLIATH
of Panama

GOLIATH
of Panama

The Life of Soldier and Canal Builder
WILLIAM LUTHER SIBERT

ROBERT W. DICKEY

For Colonel Steve & June Stevenson —
Great memories of PANAMA
and the 33rd Regimental Combat Team!

Robert Dickey

AP™
Acclaim Press
MORLEY, MISSOURI

Acclaim Press
—— *Your Next Great Book* ——
P.O. Box 238
Morley, MO 63767
(573) 472-9800
www.acclaimpress.com

Publishing Consultant: Keith Ellebrecht
Editor: Charles A. Francis
Book Design: Rodney Atchley
Cover Design: Kevin Williamson, *Kevin Willamson Design*

ISBN-13: 978-1-938905-91-9
ISBN-10: 1-938905-91-1

Library of Congress Control Number: 2014922395

First Printing: 2015
Printed in the United States of America
10 9 8 7 6 5 4 3 2 1

This publication was produced using available information.
The publisher regrets it cannot assume responsibility for errors or omissions.

CONTENTS

This book is dedicated to the men and women filling the ranks of the U.S. Army Corps of Engineers–dedicated builders in peace and war and first-class warriors when war-making is necessary to protect the United States of America and its citizens.

ACKNOWLEDGMENTS

Wish I could list all who helped me paint General Sibert's portrait but I can't due to lost notes and such. However, those not specifically mentioned below are no less appreciated. My deep appreciation for all the help and encouragement received is extended (in no particular order) to the following:

Janie Daugherty at the Mobile Public Library's Local History and Geneology Division; Deborah L. Braden, Anastasia Island Branch of St. Johns County (Florida) Public Library; the staff of the Kentucky Library at Western Kentucky University; the staff of the Houston Cole Library, Jacksonville (Alabama) State University; Jessica Lacher Feldman, curator of W.S. Hoole Special Collections at University of Alabama Libraries; Kip A. Lindberg, director, U.S. Army Chemical Corps Museum, Ft. Leonard Wood; Paul Losch, curator of Panama Canal Museum Collection at George A. Smathers Libraries, University of Florida; Kathy Egolf of the Panama Canal Society; Luther W. Tolton, former principal of Duck Springs (Alabama) School; Danny K. Crownover, president, Etowah Historical Society and Heritage Museum, Gadsden, Alabama; the Alabama Department of Archives and History; the late author/historian Leland R. Johnson of Westmoreland, Tennessee, who knew all about navigation on the Ohio River, and his co-conspirator, Charles "Chuck" Parrish, Army Corps of Engineers author/historian; and Jane Gruver, the "Mola Lady", a veteran Panama hand with the San Blas mission to the Kuna Indians.

In Bowling Green: Ex-WKU professor/historian Nancy D. Baird, who expertly critiqued the manuscript: Ray Buckberry, Jr., Dr. Jerry Cohron and XV Club member Carroll Hildreth helped, as did Rotarians Dr. Larry Pack and Hugh David Roe, Cora Jane (Mrs. Robert) Spiller and the Colonel, and Ken Hines. The Butler County crew includes actor Andy Stahl and his mother, Antoinette "Toni" Stahl, who oversee the extant portion of General Sibert's personal library, and Mary Alice Motley Black and her Green River friends.

It would have been impossible to understand General Sibert's collision with General Pershing in World War I without the guidance of Edward M. "Mac" Coffman, professor-emeritus, University of Wisconsin, an expert on the American generals in the Great War. My research began with Anne Sibert, great granddaughter of General Sibert and world-class economist. Her father, the late Edwin Sibert, the General's grandson, furnished indispensable information, along with his wife, "Maggie", when interviewed at their home on Martha's Vineyard.

Engineer Colonel Alan M. Dodd, just returned from hazardous duty in Afghanistan and now commanding the Jacksonville District, Corps of Engineers, was kind enough to read the manuscript and reflect on the battlefield dangers daily experienced by engineers, regardless of which war is being fought. Colonel Dodd said General Sibert always met the high standards—in courage as well as engineering expertise—of the U.S. Army Corps of Engineers.

I enthusiastically applaud my editor, Charlie Francis of Acclaim Press, for his patience and skill in smoothing the rough edges of the manuscript. And last but not least, wife and friend Joy Dickey, ex-University of Louisville linguistics professor, among other things, again earns the Most Valuable Player award for critical proofing and unflagging support of the General and me. And Helen of Danville would be quick to point out, that any lingering mistakes are, of course, mine alone.

Robert W. Dickey
December 8, 2014

Prologue

A GRANDSON'S VIEW OF A LEGEND

Sometimes you get lucky and encounter a fellow human being who not only has vital information unavailable from any other living source, but who turns out to be an absolute delight. Edwin Sibert is an absolute delight—the kind of fellow you would choose to spend a day with fishing, hunting, sailing, canoeing, or simply sharing a quiet lunch and easy talk without TV blaring in the background. It is altogether likely that the bloodlines directly connecting him to his grandfather, with whom he shares a middle name, explain a lot.

Edwin Luther Sibert, when interviewed in his historic home on Martha's Vineyard in November 2011, constituted one of the few—perhaps the only living link—who actually knew Major General William Luther Sibert (1860-1935), a builder of the Panama Canal.

You notice the shift to past tense. As if to confirm November fears of family and friends, this vital man died in the spring of 2012 at age 91. The grandson of a legend, but so intimately acquainted with his grandfather that he never regarded him as such. Also, being the son of another major general—all told there were three generals in the family—probably had something to do with his matter-of-fact appraisal of his grandfather:

"I first remember my grandfather from a visit he made to Ithaca, New York, where, at the time, my father was serving as an instructor in ROTC (Reserve Officers Training Corps) at Cornell University," Edwin recalled. His most vivid memories, however, are from family visits to his grandfather's Barren River home and farm in Kentucky and to the Government Street house Sibert rented while working in Mobile.

During the last half of the 1920s, Edwin, his younger brother, and their mother, actually joined Sibert's Mobile household for the better part of a year while his father attended the Army's field artillery school at Fort Sill, Oklahoma. At the time, only bachelor officers' quarters (BOQ) were available at the post, prompting his grandfather (who knew all about the vagaries of housing on Army posts) to invite the younger Sibert's family for an extended visit in Mobile.

"My grandfather had employed this black lady as his cook in Mobile, and I shall never forget her name, Centennial Chastain," Sibert said, explaining that the lady earned the name honestly, having been born in 1876. As it turned out, Ms. Chastain took on added duties when the Sibert brothers joined the household. When Evelyn, the general's wife, and their mother were not around, the cook filled in as unofficial governess and teacher in the school of life. That, according to Edwin, is where the fun began.

"Centennial loved to go crabbing in Mobile Bay and, to their everlasting delight, she always took along her young charges," Edwin recalled. "Although we mostly got in her way, we learned about crabbing, and she was good at it. Centennial never failed to return with an abundance of crabs for the general's table."

Although the boys were content to spend all of their time with Centennial, their mother and grandfather planned a kindergarten program offered by a private school convenient to the Sibert home in Mobile. The boys enrolled, and the family looked forward to their first encounter with organized education. For the pair, kindergarten soon ended a fleeting experience. Even at the tender age of 5, the Sibert boys understood all about discipline as practiced and preached by their West Pointer father and grandfather and were developing good manners to match. School, or so it seemed to the boys, was an altogether different matter where other rules or, perhaps, no rules applied.

"All of the children (in the kindergarten) were well behaved except," Edwin smiled and mischievously admitted, "the Sibert boys!" There were a growing series of incidents where the brothers ran counter to the rules of the school, an institution, said Sibert, "with a reputation for excellent discipline." The structured atmosphere challenged the pair who preferred crabbing with Centennial.

"I don't know what caused us to do this, but we would jump up on top of the desks, and our behavior was unacceptable. The other children saw us do some crazy things, so some of them started to do what we did, which was quite naughty," the retired banker explained, "and (the other children) called it playing Sibert!" Punctuated by a hearty laugh, he concluded the story: "We were not invited to come back to that school." The general was a little gruff that night but the twinkle in his eyes suggested he meant the demeanor to benefit their mother. The end result, so far as the boys were concerned, was highly acceptable— more time to go crabbing with Centennial.

Even the children recognized that the general regarded his cook as a key member of the household. Back in Bowling Green, another cook ruled the kitchen and, in the table of organization, stood second only to the keeper of their grandfather's hounds in Kentucky. At his first and last permanent address since leaving Gadsden, Alabama, for Tuscaloosa, as a student, Sibert's cook practiced the culinary arts to perfection. "Food was an important thing to General Sibert, and he always had a table loaded with good things," according to his grandson. When his father was traveling between duty stations, the family always spent several days at the river farm where the dining room table groaned under its burden of food at suppertime—the evening meal at which his grandfather insisted that everyone be present and accounted for. Edwin recalled the pie incident.

"In addition to my grandfather and his wife and my own family, several guests were around the table, and everyone seemed to have enjoyed the meal. When it came time for dessert, the cook served pie and, as it was passed around, a mistake was made: They gave me the general's piece of pie, and it was huge!"

Seated next to Edwin, his younger brother regarded his own piece of pie with disappointment. When compared to the general-size portion received by Edwin, the wedge seemed even smaller, a mere sliver, and that was too much for the younger child. Upset by his brother's bonanza and his own shabby treatment, the younger boy burst into tears. That is when the general stepped in and took charge, ordering a supplementary slice of pie for the unhappy brother, a partial remedy to the bad scene. He completed the double play faultlessly, his grandson recalled, allowing Edwin to keep the big piece and ordering a second helping of pie for himself.

Edwin turned 13 in 1933, the first year of Roosevelt's New Deal, and had acquired a wider appreciation of his grandfather and his many accomplishments. "I had a pretty positive view of the general and, most of all, I respected him," said his grandson, pointing out that his grandfather had a presence that commanded respect. "I can't recall him being addressed as anything but general, and I never heard of anybody calling him Bill."

According to his grandson, Sibert impressed adults without even trying. "He did pretty well with his contemporaries, but I didn't get the impression that he related too well with the children. Maybe I should have asked my father about that." Edwin had no problem communicating with the general who often devoted time to him at the farm. "I remember taking a walk across the farm with the general to inspect his oil well, only one of his wide variety of interests."

Edwin remembered seeing his grandfather's prize foxhounds in Kentucky and, with some ceremony, being introduced to the black man who was in charge of the kennel. Although the keeper of the hounds was respectful, discussions concerning the care of the dogs took place between a pair of equals with General Sibert sometimes deferring to his employee regarding management of the pack. The grandson quoted the general as later explaining: "That man is in full charge of the hounds, and he has my full trust." What a marvelous thing, Edwin thought at the time, to enjoy the general's full trust.

Aunt Evelyn also enjoyed the full trust of William Luther Sibert. That is how the Sibert boys addressed their grandfather's third wife, the only one they ever knew, their grandmother, Mamie, having died many years before. Evelyn Sibert deeply impressed Edwin: "I recall her very well. She was what I would call a raw-boned Scot who made her presence felt. To us, she was Aunt Evelyn, and I really can't recall whether we especially liked her or disliked her."

"She was just there and she ran the show," Edwin added, not without a significant degree of genuine admiration. Himself being the son of a general-in-waiting for World War II, Edwin confided that a general, even a retired one, really needed someone to run the show, a sort of civilian chief of staff or aide de camp. He thought Aunt Evelyn perfect for the job.

General Sibert never bored companions reciting his accomplishments, being much more likely to express disappointment over missing a war or two. Still, Edwin picked up the story of the canal adventure and World War I and details of Sibert's clashes with Goethals and Pershing, when listening to the general and his father swap stories. Edwin Sibert never knew General George Washington Goethals, sometimes his grandfather's antagonist in the Canal Zone, and vice versa. And it was not until the retirement years that the paths of the banker Sibert and the Goethals family crossed on a tiny island with little chance of escape.

"I never met Goethals, but his children and grandchildren settled in Martha's Vineyard in their retirement years," said the retired banker. "I knew them all, and we got along quite well. In fact, General Goethals' grandson is a good friend of mine, and we have talked about their differences (between the respective grandfathers)."

"I think their differences were mostly about the construction of the canal," mused Edwin. "For example, at Mira Flores, there was a question of whether there would be one or two sets of locks. My grandfather wanted one set as he built at Gatun, but Goethals wanted two. As senior man, Goethals prevailed and two sets were installed (on the Pacific side), one at Mira Flores, the other at St. Miguel."

The ex-banker, like his father and grandfather, also had a military background and understood the chain of command and the primacy of seniority in the Armed Forces. Yet, being somewhat of a rebel, perhaps dating from the Mobile kindergarten scene, Edwin forsook the Army, graduating from the U.S. Naval Academy in 1942. He saw service as a gunnery officer on the U.S.S. *Pringle* (DD 477) and a quartet of other destroyers in World War II.

By then, the young naval officer had heard all the details of his grandfather's career: chasing insurgents and building railroads in the Philippines, concreting hydraulic stairways from ocean to ocean in Panama, organizing and training the Big Red 1 infantry division while enduring Pershing's barbs in France, and organizing the Army's first Chemical Warfare Service.

At age 91, within months of his death, Edwin Sibert had pardonable pride in the accomplishments of his grandfather, recalling stories of his prowess as a horseman and hunter, and as a good storyteller before his literary club audience. "He wore glasses, sported a mustache, and always appeared to be in good physical condition even as his physical capabilities were in decline in the 1930s, but I guess it was his cigar that was distinctive and never seemed to be lit," said Edwin. "It was almost like a trade-mark. He always had that cigar."

"I remember as he was approaching the end of his life, when we visited him at the farm in Bowling Green, his eyesight had deteriorated to the point where he couldn't read anymore. My father would sit on the porch and read the newspaper to him. The general never lost interest in current events, education progress, and the world in general," Edwin recalled. A son reading newspapers to his father, Edwin explained, was a very Sibert kind of thing to do. Typical, he said, of a close-knitted family group that managed to stay close over the years, even when separated by thousands of miles. An inclusive and cohesive outfit demonstrated by the brothers and their mother bunking in for an extended stay with the general in Mobile.

All of this and more from the cherubic mouth of Edwin Luther Sibert made one want to know the Siberts—especially Major General William Luther Sibert, U.S. Army Corps of Engineers (1860-1935). [1]

GOLIATH
of Panama

The Life of Soldier and Canal Builder
WILLIAM LUTHER SIBERT

Chapter One

ABOARD THE TUGBOAT *GATUN*

L ieutenant Colonel William Luther Sibert dominated the deck of the vessel. It was an exciting event for the Army engineer—being lifted almost 65 feet from an arm of the Atlantic Ocean (Caribbean Sea) into Gatun Lake. He was aboard the workboat for the short but memorable voyage—more akin to a first ascent of an alpine giant than what it was—the maiden passage into the Panama Canal.

(The Gatun Locks and Dam—and Sibert—were way ahead of schedule. Predicted by experts to be the last part of the gigantic construction project to be completed, it was first. Formal canal opening, signaled by a full transit of the waterway by the *S.S. Ancon*, did not occur for almost another year—August 15, 1914.)

Aptly named the *Gatun*, the seagoing tug measured 101 feet from stem to stern. With a beam of 22 feet and a draft of 12-1/2 feet, she was built by Neafie & Levy at Philadelphia and originally named the *H.B. Chamberlain*. The first Isthmian Canal Commission purchased the vessel and brought her to Panama in 1906 where she was renamed and put to work.

The tug was neither showy nor big, its lines low, bulky, squared, and configured with work in mind. Strictly a blue collar boat, she reflected the strength and determination exhibited by the Americans in undertaking the isthmian canal construction and, in doing so, constructing the grandest set of locks ever envisioned by man. It was altogether fitting that the *Gatun* was chosen for the initial trip through the first workable locks of the still uncompleted Panama Canal.

For more than seven years the *Gatun* had served without adornment, except this one day—September 26, 1913. An overly large Stars and Stripes waved from the stern, and the bow boasted the nation's naval ensign, now sporting 48 stars with the recent admission of the state of Arizona. A dozen or more colorful pennants fluttered from rigging in further salute to the historic transit upward through the Gatun locks into Gatun Lake, newly formed from the waters of the Chagres River impounded behind Gatun Dam. [1]

Everything around it dwarfed the tug, beginning with the dam, a full one-half mile wide at its base and stretching 1-1/2 miles across the valley before bonding with the triple-decked locks. Designed to permit simultaneous two-way traffic, each of the six lock chambers was capable of accommodating a vessel almost 1,000 feet in length, so long as its beam did not exceed 110 feet. Laid out below the hundreds of spectators lining the locks' topmost ramparts, the scene was breathtakingly concrete. Long, smooth guide walls and flared approaches led to the sea gates and the lowest tier of locks, and then another, and finally a third lock. Yet, even from the commanding heights, the enormous scale of the locks was incomprehensible. It was only from the deck of the *Gatun*—looking up from water level into the towering manmade canyons of concrete—that its passengers caught the full breathtaking impact from upturned heads clear down to their toes. Alive with excitement, the scene from the deck of the *Gatun* quickened the pulse. [2]

Captain F.F. Stewart commanded the tug and, along with the usual crew, there was a small and select group of passengers aboard, more than ready to witness the trio of steel gated locks lift the vessel vertically almost 65 feet. The precise elevation gain is 64.70 feet—from the tide of the Caribbean to the crest of Gatun Lake, its waters holding steady behind the elongated and uniform eminence of Gatun Dam.

Ever thoughtful of colleagues, Sibert—the officer in charge of the mammoth locks and dam construction project—had moved the date forward so that two of his key assistants might participate in the truly—and literally—uplifting ceremonial cruise. September 26 was the very last day Major James P. Jervey, who had overseen masonry work on the locks, and Major George M. Hoffman, who had bossed dam construction, were available before their ordered departure from the Canal Zone. It was also fitting that Lieutenant Colonel Harry F. Hodges was aboard. Under the reorganization plan, he had completed design work on the locks and assumed responsibility for the design and erection of the huge lock gates. Smiling broadly, Sibert made sure all were aboard the *Gatun* before joining Mrs. Sibert and their younger children. What emotions the event must have stirred deep within the Army engineer as he gazed upward at all of that concrete and the enormous array of spectators! [3]

They included Colonel George Washington Goethals, the Army bird colonel in charge of building the American canal across Panama—and his superior officer with whom Sibert had clashed on several key aspects of the Gatun construction. All were looking down, and some were wondering if the poured concrete triplets really could lift the *Gatun*, much resembling a toy boat when viewed from the top of the locks, into the immense lake now securely impounded behind the dam. [4]

As for Sibert, Hodges, and the majors, they had absolutely no doubt that the sea gates on the lower lock would open properly, and they did. With the *Gatun*'s whistle loudly blowing a salute never to be forgotten by those in attendance, Captain Steward and W.G. Comber, his chief navigator, expertly maneuvered the tug into the lock chamber. Then the sea gates closed without a squeak or creak. Water from Gatun Lake was introduced into the chamber through huge conduits punctuating the lock floor to effortlessly (or so it seemed) raise the *Gatun* exactly 11.2 feet. This put the tug at the same elevation as the lake water remaining trapped within the middle lock.

Next, the lower gates of the middle lock opened and admitted the tug before closing and sealing the middle chamber, now ready to receive additional lake water, enough to buoy the boat upward another 23.7 feet to the same level as water impounded in the upper lock. When the lower gates of the upper lock opened, the process repeated at the higher level and the tug steamed into the third and highest lock. After the lower gates closed, resealing the upper lock chamber, even more lake water entered, enough to float the tug upward a final 29.8 feet to a level identical to the expansive waters of Gatun Lake. Engineers had only to open the lock's upper gates, the lake gates, to admit the *Gatun* into its namesake lake.

The system worked perfectly as Sibert knew it would. It was a personal and professional triumph for the 52-year-old officer. The entire Atlantic side of the canal had been his bailiwick since July 1, 1908, when Goethals, a fellow Army Corps of Engineers officer, who was also the chairman and chief engineer of the Isthmian Canal Commission (ICC), reorganized the command structure and prepared to build the canal *the army way*. And build it they did. [5]

Strength in simplicity could well have been the motto of the new administrative setup. Canal Zone geography governed responsibility, the Atlantic Division being Sibert's command. Relatively short on mileage, the Atlantic and Pacific divisions each contained locks, the mechanical keys which facilitated coupling of two mighty oceans, and dams to harness the waters to make the locks work. The Central Division covered approximately 32 miles, by far the longest sector, and contained the infamous Culebra Cut. [6]

Because the Atlantic Division involved construction of the gigantic Gatun Dam and the largest, most sophisticated set of locks ever designed by engineers, Sibert had been the logical choice to shoulder the task. The complexity and sheer size of the undertaking prompted engineers to realistically project that it would be the last segment of the canal to be completed.

For more than five long years William Luther Sibert had had his hands full dealing with the daily turmoil attendant to reaching the Atlantic Division's ambitious construction goals. And then, suddenly, the product of his toil confirmed its worth as that unpretentious tugboat steamed sedately from the perfectly functioning locks into the lake Gatun Dam had created. September 26, 1913, was not just another hot, humid day under Panama's unrelenting sun. It was a unique Sibert Day! And what a day for Sibert! And for the United States of America!

Chapter Two

THE SIBERT LEGACY

Siberts began populating America more than 130 years before the *Gatun* made its historic transit from ocean to lake through the Gatun Locks. And when John David Sibert, a 26-year-old South Carolinian, ventured almost due west from his father's home in Abbeville in 1819—only 44 years had lapsed since the shots fired at Lexington and Concord were heard around the world. Crossing north Georgia, he penetrated almost 60 miles into Alabama, deep in pioneer territory, where he purchased land and built a house near Ashville in St. Clair County. Known as David among family and friends, Sibert was a long way from home and, it seems, smack dab in the middle of pursuing long range plans. Once the house was completed, those plans called for him to immediately make the arduous return trip to Abbeville.

His plans centered on Miss Elizabeth Cook, at age 28, well past the customary age for brides in the frontier settlements—the indispensable party to David's future. She was a native of County Downs, Ireland, the daughter of Henry Philip Cook and Margaret Susanna Lightfoot Cook. Elizabeth had continued to live in South Carolina with her mother, by then the widow of her second husband, Henry Clark, during Sibert's extended expedition.

The families of David and Elizabeth were well acquainted, and in all likelihood the couple had been keeping company before David's trek into Alabama. It can be safely assumed that the lady was not at all surprised by David's prompt proposal when he returned. More likely than not, she had been an early and active participant in planning the westward migration. Without delay, the couple married November 29, 1820.

The fact that David Sibert was betrothed, in addition to his bride, to a ready-made family, appears to confirm the couple's careful, advanced planning, plus recognition of the bride's family ties and duties, obligations not easily abandoned or broken. Not only had David assembled cattle and wagons loaded with household goods and the basic tools required to farm and sustain pioneer life, but his train also included human cargo, all with hands that would prove helpful on the expedition. Along with his new wife, making the trip to Alabama were his mother-in-law, Margaret Clark, and his bride's half sister, Martha Clark, who, by those same frontier standards that had threatened Elizabeth with the dreaded spinsterhood, had just reached marrying age.

David Sibert was named for his father, the Rev. John David Sibert, who, along with his wife (whose first name is unknown and only identified in family genealogical records by her maiden name: Miss Wilmore of Virginia), stayed behind in Abbeville in the care of David's younger brother, George Sibert. It was David's rather formidable father who first planted Sibert roots, at least this particular branch of the family tree, in America. He had emigrated from the Alsace region, an area just to the north of the Swiss border and considered to be either a part of France or of Germany in the 19th Century, depending upon which country triumphed in their latest war. The area had been historically contested by the neighboring states, the German conquerors, from time to time, managing to liberally sprinkle the predominantly French speaking population with the likes of the Siberts.

There is no documentation to suggest what impelled a young John David Sibert to quit Alsace and take his chances in America, whether it was lack of local economic opportunity, or friction generated by his Lutheran beliefs colliding with those of the Catholic faith, or his youthful outlook and taste for new experiences, even adventure, or most likely of all, a combination of causes. What is known is that his surname was unmistakably German-sounding and sometimes spelled Sybert in the New World.

Lacking a treasure trove of those documentary links genealogists are forever seeking, the Sibert canvas on the European side of the Atlantic is not just murky, not at all. But for mention in a rather obscure book written in the 20th century by a Sibert of northeast Alabama origin, several generations removed from his German ancestors, it would be entirely blank. The book seems to connect some of the dots:

—⚏—

For John David Sibert, the original John David so far as is known and the one who is generally given credit for establishing the Sibert family on the American side of the ocean, a run of ill luck began early. His initial misfortune was not being the first born son, the son who would inherit whatever lands and fortunes his father had managed to accumulate. Bluntly stated, the second son was generally on his own economically, not always a bad thing. The English witnessed a legion of second sons fashion the mighty British Empire of the 19th century while seeking their fortunes around the globe. For the individual second sons, however, English or otherwise, it was usually a difficult journey.

His second son ranking did not deter 17-year-old John David I from becoming hopelessly infatuated with Hulda Offa, the daughter of a neighbor, thereby casting the pair as principal players in a Germanic variation of Shakespeare's *Romeo and Juliet* theme. Their families had been fast friends in the past, but something had happened to ignite a feud, a conflict which seemed to have no end. It was against this disagreeable and entirely negative background that John David and Hulda somehow managed not only to meet but to fall in love, much to the consternation of both families. Details of their devotion to each other and whatever steps the families may have been taken to cool their ardor are lacking. The untimely death of Hulda wrought a tragic end to the romance with the circumstances of the teenager's death also remaining a mystery.

There was certainly no mystery about how the heart-broken boy friend felt—angry and bitter to the core—to such an extent that he blamed his sweetheart's father for her death. His anger and bitterness soon festered into hatred, this deeply felt emotion interfering with and temporarily overcoming John David's normally rational train of thought. Dusk was rapidly approaching when young Sibert left home with one goal in mind, the death of Hulda's father. Sibert's intention was to kill Herr Offa! In his oppressive and overwrought emotional state, he believed that by causing the father's death, he would somehow avenge the death of the daughter.

Fortunately for all concerned, it took some time to reach the Offa home, precious time to allow John David's inflamed emotions to cool down, time for the rational thought processes to return and prevail. Revenge was put aside and forgotten, perhaps some sort of epiphany occurring as the young man realized that he had almost become a part of the family of the man he intended to kill, and that made no sense to him whatsoever. Instead of returning home, he continued on to the Offa home, but in an entirely different frame of mind.

In the last quarter of the 18th century in Alsace, regardless of which country may have owned it at the time, homeowners were reluctant to open their doors after dark, especially to strangers. And it was dark when Sibert arrived at the Offa homestead, a place he had never been before because of the feud; the families never spoke (except for John David and Hulda) because of the conflict, making the visitor almost a stranger to Hulda's family.

There was a pause after John David identified himself as a Sibert, then the door opened and Herr Offa invited the young man in with a proper but cool reception. What followed is a matter of conjecture, but communications were established, and the unexpected visitor got along well with his hosts. Shared sadness over Hulda's death was most likely the catalyst that gradually warmed the meeting and blunted past hostilities, which were submerged if not forgotten. As a result, Sibert ended up feeling much better about himself and his relations with the Offa family, particularly Herr Offa, who hours before was destined to be his target. With his emotions still running high, John David finally took leave of the Offa family, but did not go directly home, instead taking the darkened path to his sweetheart's grave.

As he stood silently to the side, it is written that the moon cast his shadow across Hulda's final resting place, prompting him to move to the opposite side where he knelt and cried aloud, trying mightily to release all of his pain and anguish into the night air. We are not told how successful that was, but the exercise was loud enough and long enough to wake the neighborhood, including the Offa family. The beneficial side effect of John David's emotional tribute to the departed Hulda marked the termination of the Sibert-Offa feud and restored peace between the families. Much later, after John David Sibert was established in America, he received a letter from his mother remarking that ever since that fateful night at Hulda's grave, the Offa and Sibert families had referred to John David as the peacemaker.

John David Sibert's life next took on a martial air as he sought to solve two problems that would not go away: the death of his sweetheart and his position as the family's second son. This is when the young man's odyssey really began, first to an adjoining German state and from there to America. Within that journey he hoped to find a solution to both of his problems.

It was not far from the Sibert homestead in Alsace to the adjoining German principality of Rhein Hessen, a distance that could be covered in a few days riding double with his older brother on a family horse. The reputation of the Hessian military was well known, and it is likely that young Sibert had heard rumors of the hiring of Hessian regiments by George III for service in America. The English king needed additional troops to help in policing those unruly colonials who had the audacity to mount a rebellion in America against the British crown.

A trip to America and the promise of a new life, assuming he survived the police action against the colonials, was what attracted Sibert to the Hessian border. As his brother turned the horse around for the trip back to the Sibert estates, the younger of the two quietly slipped across the Hessian frontier. The fact that the young man had no official papers of introduction or identity would have made no difference to the recruiting sergeant. He would appraise Sibert, who could speak the language and appeared to be in excellent physical condition, as a prime recruit. The sergeant would also confirm that those rumors Sibert had heard were altogether true and that he would soon find himself aboard a ship bound for America. At that point, both time and distance went to work on John David Sibert's pair of problems: his lost love for Hulda and the loss of the Sibert estates.

Nothing is known about his career as a Hessian mercenary except that he managed to survive and somehow separated himself from his fellow soldiers. There is no indication that he had been wounded and left behind when his regiment embarked for the return trip to Germany. Of course, his enlistment could have expired while in America and he chose not to return to Germany. Or he could have simply taken French leave and deserted the Hessian ranks when the opportunity arose, taking a major and irrevocable step toward a new life in America.

Although not out of the question, it would be difficult to ascribe political motivation to the teenager's departure from Hessian ranks. It would be even more difficult to classify him as a true mercenary—a soldier of fortune—just because he next joined the ranks of the rebels and pointed his musket at those troops still fighting for the English king. Yet, in a fashion, he remained a mercenary: Thanks to the victory of the fledgling United States, John David Sibert, now a genuine patriot in his brand new country, was ultimately rewarded for his services in the Revolutionary War with a grant of land in Georgia.

It is written that those services included a hitch under a General Marion, with no additional identification of either the American general or the unit he commanded. If Francis Marion, the Swamp Fox, could be identified as Sibert's general, it would put a finer point on the story. The Swamp Fox would neatly fit because his area of operations in the southern states would place young Sibert very close to the land he was ultimately granted in the State of Georgia and to the State of South Carolina where he made his home in later years. The narrator recounts one perilous incident which occurred while Sibert was soldiering under the mysterious Marion's command: Having been cut off from his unit and surrounded by British troops, the soldier hid in a hollow log, all well and good until the English decided to make camp on that very spot. Trapped in his hiding place without food and water, there was nothing to do but wait. Just when Sibert thought he would starve, the English broke camp a couple of days later, allowing him to complete his escape.

And that is how John David Sibert, a Hessian mercenary, came to America, became a patriot in the War for Independence, and established the Sibert family which has since produced more than its share of generals and officers for the U.S. Army, even a naval officer or two.

So the story goes. [1]

—✦—

Building on the Hessian story, it can be easily speculated that, while still a Hessian, the campaign took Sibert into Virginia where it would have provided the soldier from Alsace the rare opportunity to meet the Miss Wilmore of Virginia, who was otherwise a long way off, separated from Georgia and South Carolina by many hard miles of difficult roads and trails.

Turning to hard facts, there is nothing speculative about John David Sibert being discharged from his service on behalf of the brand new United States at Savannah, Georgia, where he was paid for those services with a grant of 300 acres in Burke County, Georgia. With Miss Wilmore now Mrs. Sibert, the couple homesteaded in Burke County where the family resided before, according to the 1790 Census, relocating in the Orangeburg District of South Carolina. The family later moved west to Abbeville, not far from the Georgia border, where the elder Sibert purchased a farm on Hard Labor Creek.

In addition to working his farm and rearing his family at Abbeville, the elder Sibert took on additional chores as pastor of St. George's Lutheran Church, its sanctuary being a pioneer log structure, chinked with mud and located conveniently near the Sibert farm. Later, Sibert made a denominational swing from Lutheran to Methodist and thereafter served as pastor of the Tranquil Methodist Church which had been built about a mile northwest of the Lutheran structure. [2]

In his role as pastor, the farmer was not easily forgotten by anyone with eyesight. When preaching, he was clad in long hose and knee breeches with silver buckles at the knees, attire not often seen in the western settlements. Although that was enough to deeply engrave the memory of a youngster who had witnessed Sibert's Sunday sartorial splendor, the child found Sibert's sermons were equally arresting and difficult to understand thanks to the pastor's heavy German accent, which strongly suggested fire and brimstone.

Again leaving his father's powerful preaching behind, the younger Sibert found progress along the crude Carolina and Georgia roads and trails exceedingly slow. This time he was responsible for heavily laden wagons, which required continuous maintenance and frequent stops to rest the pulling teams. The small herd of valuable livestock being driven with the wagons had to be constantly monitored to prevent straying, keeping the extended family busy throughout the trip. In Georgia, David called a long halt during the 1821 growing season where, by necessity, he planted and harvested crops of hay, grain, and vegetables to replenish the larder. It was not until early 1822 that the party arrived in St. Clair County where they occupied the house Sibert had erected during the earlier visit.

The dwelling may have been a little crowded by 1830 when, according to the Census, the family had expanded with the birth of eight children, five boys and three girls. Also counted in the Census was one female slave, a young woman likely retained to share household duties with Elizabeth. Mrs. Sibert's half sister, Martha Clark, was no longer part of the household, having fallen in love with a neighbor's son, Curtis G. Beeson, soon after arriving in St. Clair County. Their wedding on July 29, 1822, took place at the Sibert home. Sibert's mother-in-law is not identifiable in the 1830 Census, strongly suggesting that she was no longer living.

The final move for David Sibert's family was, compared to the original exodus from South Carolina, a relatively short haul northward to DeKalb County where David settled his family on Wills Creek in Big Wills Valley, the valley being located about two miles west of present-day Keener. This area eventually became a part of Etowah County, a new county created in 1868.

Being a farmer (often identified as a planter) by trade, David Sibert must have recognized a need for a flourmill in the vicinity of the valley, an obvious boon to area farmers who would no longer be required to haul grain long and torturous distances for milling. The ultimate question, equally obvious to the pragmatic Sibert: were there reasonable prospects for economic success if such a mill were built? After long and careful consideration, Sibert concluded that the mill venture was a good opportunity for the family and proceeded in 1836 to purchase land from the Cherokee Indians, including 80 acres already cleared for cultivation and the site of an abandoned Indian village in Big Wills Valley.

The centerpiece of the Indian village was a large log house with thatched roof into which the expanded Sibert family moved and resumed pioneer life. At the same time, David and his two oldest sons, John W. and Henry, set to work building the first mill in the valley with plans to capture the waters of Big Wills Creek as its source of power. That required the construction of a modest dam and millrace, marking, so far as is known, the Sibert family's first personal encounter with a dam and the effects it can visit on the adjacent riparian scene and its populace.

The millstones for processing corn were fashioned from what was described as grit rock found on nearby Lookout Mountain. The finer millstones required to produce wheat flour were purchased, along with bolting cloth, in France. The imported stones arrived in the valley after a long sea passage to Mobile, then up the Alabama River to Wetumpka from where the heavy cargo was loaded aboard wagons for the final 150-mile journey into the valley.

While awaiting the millstones, Sibert's oldest sons fashioned the large turbine wheels for their father's mill, a two-story structure of hewn timber that was sided with split laths. (Among the Sibert children who were at the time too young to work on actual construction of the mill was the youngest of David Sibert's five sons, William Joshua Sibert, born October 17, 1833.)

Once in operation, the mill proved to be an economic success for the Sibert family. During peak activity following harvests, it was often in operation around the clock and frequently on Sundays. The attention David Sibert and his sons gave to the business, always making an extra effort to accommodate those hard scrabble farmers who accounted for the vast majority of their customers, established David Sibert and his family as hard-working entrepreneurs who never cheated on the milling charges. Reflecting the high regard the farmer turned miller had earned among valley citizens, David Sibert followed in his father's footsteps, being active in church affairs and serving as pastor of the Methodist Church in Big Wills Valley.

Reared on his father's farm and furnished with a common school education, David's youngest son, William Joshua Sibert, by all accounts, matured into an enterprising, hard-working farmer, and responsible citizen. He was destined to sire a future general in the Army of the United States and thereafter survive the Civil War as a Confederate soldier.

On September 28, 1856, less than three weeks short of his 23rd birthday, William Joshua Sibert and Marietta (also referred to as Mary E.) Ward appeared before Justice of the Peace W.D. Petty to secure the State of Alabama's blessing on their union. She would turn 15 on her next birthday, November 28. Less than two years after the birth of William Luther Sibert, the couple's second child, William Joshua Sibert left the children with their mother on the farm to enlist on May 10, 1862, as a private in the Army of the Confederate States of America.

While serving in Company G of the 48th Alabama Infantry Regiment, William first saw action on August 9, 1862, during the battle of Cedar Run (also called the battle of Slaughter's Mountain) in Culpepper County, Virginia. Part of General Taliaferro's brigade, the 48th suffered heavy casualties while repelling the federal assault on General Stonewall Jackson's left flank. Sibert escaped injury only to be seriously wounded later that month at 2nd Manassas (2nd Bull Run); he survived the Wilderness Campaign in early May 1864, before his wounds forced him to retire from the field at Petersburg, Virginia. No longer able to serve on the firing line, Sibert joined the quartermaster's department where he served the Confederacy until the end of the war. Being mounted, he never formally surrendered; instead horse and rider simply hightailed it for Alabama.

Both Sibert and his horse made it home from the war although neither was in good condition. Both were hungry, and the soldier was bothered by his wounds. As for the horse, it had lost an eye and part of an ear to Yankee gunfire. Family legend says that the horse was never hungry again and lived a long and comfortable life on the Sibert farm. As for his master, William never fully recovered from the war injuries although he lived until July 29, 1909. Death occurred at Gadsden, and his wife's death quickly followed on August 15, 1909.

Although William Joshua Sibert had been a vigorous and successful farmer prior to the outbreak of hostilities, his postwar agricultural career was severely curtailed by the lingering effects of the war wounds which effectively prevented him from meeting the daily physical demands of 19th century farming. While managing to retain the family farm, Sibert's solution was to enter the hotel business in Gadsden, the county seat of Etowah County, in 1867, a pursuit he continued until 1879. Then, with a partner named Barnett, he became engaged in the mercantile business under the firm name, Barnett and Sibert. The business continued after Mr. Barnett's retirement in 1882, with only the name being changed to Sibert & Ward, the Ward portion of the name honoring Mrs. Sibert's maiden name. With another partner, Sibert formed a second company, Sibert & Blair, a retail and wholesale distributor of hardware that primarily catered to the needs of the agricultural community. Agriculture was the name of the game in Etowah County. [3]

For the farmer-merchant, it was a good and bad news combination: the good news was the growing success of his agriculturally-oriented mercantile ventures; the bad news was the lingering effects of his wounds which were never compatible with the manual labor required of a farmer. Still, the Sibert farm continued in operation, its owner sensing that it was good business—good for his mercantile enterprises which catered primarily to farmers—to continue to be one himself.

While growing food for his family, the merchant also learned to use the farm as a bridge, a means to keep in touch with fellow farmers, the very people he depended on to buy his wares. The ups and downs of his own farming operation furnished insight into the wants, needs, aspirations, even the fears, of his customers, a valuable aid to marketing the products Sibert sold. As the years passed, more and more responsibility for the farm's operation, together with its demanding physical labor, was shouldered by another William—William Luther Sibert—his father's eldest son.

Chapter Three

THE MATHEMATICAL FARM BOY

William Luther Sibert, born October 12, 1860, the second child of William and Marietta, joined his 18-month-old sister, Charlsie Eledora Sibert, in the Sibert household. In all, ten Sibert children were born between 1859 and 1882 in Big Wills Valley where the family received its mail at the Duck Springs post office. As his father's oldest male and heir, the younger William held a special place in the family structure and in the agrarian society of northeast Alabama. [1]

A first son is a very important person with much expected of him, assuming he survived the rigors of childhood, not easily done in the 1860s. At an early age, he milked the cow, slopped the hogs, helped mend fences, and learned to plow a straight furrow with expectations of succeeding his father as the hard-working farm manager. His father's sub-par health and preoccupation with his mercantile business accelerated the process for William Luther Sibert, notwithstanding other equally important considerations.

Because of the loss of family records by fire in South Carolina, little is known of the intellectual achievements of young Sibert's forebears, but there are some clues, the most pronounced being the identification of his great grandfather as a minister who pastored churches in western South Carolina. Generally speaking, at least before the *Great Awakening* produced a bumper crop of uneducated clergy in the early 1800s, a preacher, minister, priest—regardless of church affiliation— was usually better educated than his flock, even along America's rough and tumble ever westward moving frontier.

The typical community's preacher could usually read and write, and some had been exposed to formal theological training. The educational background of the Rev. John David Sibert is unknown, but the German speaker learned to speak heavily accented English—fluent enough for the pulpit—after arriving in America. With little else to go on, his interest in theology at least suggests some educational attainment (limited though it may have been) and an accompanying appreciation of its value. From him, the educational thread is undocumented and indistinct until his grandson, William Joshua Sibert, received a common school education while being reared on his father's farm in Big Wills Valley.

Already infected with this early educational germ, it is likely that William Joshua Sibert's experience in transitioning from farming into hotel operations, and then into the mercantile field, underscored the value of education as something worth passing along to his children. For his oldest son, the process began at age 5 when he daily walked two miles to a country school at Duck Springs. At age 7, when the family moved into Gadsden where the hotel was located, young Sibert attended a town school, still of the one-room variety with a single teacher responsible for teaching all grades. Reading and writing were taught but there were no classes covering the third leg of the generally recognized stool of American basic education—arithmetic.

During the school day, and in the normally accepted sense of the term, the teacher did not teach any classes in mathematics. That is not to imply that mathematics could not be learned at the Gadsden schoolhouse; it could, but the process involved a unique system of independent study at the most elementary level. The student was required to invest a great degree of personal initiative in the process before there could be any hope of success, and only if the pupil could already read well and possessed the intellectual capacity to absorb mathematical knowledge in the abstract. How did it work?

A student interested in mathematics, Sibert in this case, received one of the school's mathematics books with directions to begin at page one and work his way through the problems it contained. As the pupil progressed at his own speed, the teacher offered oversight. Young Sibert's questions were periodically answered and his errors in computations corrected, while receiving appropriate expressions of approval for correct answers. From all indications, Sibert made the teacher's task an easy one because he usually got it right.

Where mathematics was concerned, the son of the hotelkeeper demonstrated a propensity for reading and understanding abstract mathematical concepts, and then applying them to correctly answer concrete problems. The source of his ability to understand numbers is unclear, whether from natural aptitude or the product of serious study by a youngster who found himself genuinely interested, even fascinated by the subject. A combination of the two is the likely answer, with encouraging words from the teacher lighting the way.

Regardless of how it came about, William Luther Sibert had not only mastered arithmetic, but could also comfortably solve elementary algebra problems by age 11. Little is known about his performance in other subjects offered at the Gadsden school, except through his own self-deprecating comments. In a nutshell, he seems to have had passing grades in the other subjects, but nothing to brag about. Based upon his later academic performances and professional attainments, Sibert's lackluster record in subjects other than mathematics may be chalked up to disinterest.

Conditions in the South conspired to end Sibert's formal education in 1874 with the region still in free fall from the lingering effect of being on the losing end of the Civil War. Romantically referred to as *The Lost Cause*, the economy in northeast Alabama was anything but romantic—going from bad to worse. With few travelers capable of paying for lodging for a night, breaking even in the hotel business was extremely difficult. However, as landowners, the Siberts' economics were far superior to the lots of sharecroppers and former slaves, although that was faint praise. Even so, the land proved to be their salvation and continued to be a factor in the family's economy even after the elder Sibert made the transition from innkeeper to successful merchant in 1880.

By 1874, the ex-mathematics student comfortably roamed the woods, mountains, and fields of northeast Alabama, absorbing outdoor lore with the same intensity once devoted to the well-worn books of mathematics. Little escaped Sibert's notice as he honed his skills as an outdoorsman and hunter, determined that he would be a worthy successor in woods craft to the Cherokee braves who once called the Sibert farm home.

Even after a strenuous day of farm labor—sun baked in summer and chilled by winds sweeping down from Lookout Mountain in winter—the young farmer eagerly returned to the fields and surrounding woods. After work, a rifle replaced the hoe, all to the accompaniment of a pair of spirited hounds, now awake and ready for a chase after sleeping most of the day away. The quarry varied, anything from rabbit to raccoon, occasional deer, or, most dangerous to the hunter, a wild pig gone feral. The thrill of the hunt always seemed to perk up the tall slender youth who reveled in the sport it offered while not losing sight of the opportunity to add meat to the larder.

For four years, young Sibert, the farmer, worked every bit as hard as the occasional hired hand his father provided during planting and harvesting seasons. And young Sibert, the hunter, continued to stalk game in the forests and along the streams draining into the valley from the nearby highlands. He sometimes hunted with a companion, but more often he was alone except for the hounds. And, regardless of the season, the demands of the farm never ceased; tasks varied but there was always something that needed to be done.

Most of Sibert's labors—ranging from plowing and chopping wood for his mother's big cast iron range to fence mending and caring for the farm animals—fell in the strenuous category. Mixed with his forays into the woods along the higher elevations of northeast Alabama—either mountains on the small side or extremely tall and rugged hills—the physically demanding farm work naturally regulated the teen's life. Not unexpectedly, he slept like a baby under the tin roof of the Sibert farmhouse, ate like the horse he had followed down countless furrows, and grew like those weeds he was required to hoe lest they overrun the family garden. The net result was a man, much taller than his peers and, at first, slender to a fault. After that came the muscles and tendons and even more height.

Sibert's predictable and basically happy existence had its share of anxieties, bundled for the most part around the more disagreeable and sometimes disastrous antics worked upon the farming community by a capricious Mother Nature. The farm boy-man, no stranger to adult level responsibility, comfortable with his role as the first son, and seemingly content with his lot in life, admittedly experienced those occasional dreams, always about numbers, formulae, and solutions which he could never quite solve. The young man wondered—was there a missing ingredient—something important missing from his life even though it seemed most orderly and complete? [2]

And then something happened, perhaps a combination of events. Gradual improvement in family economics broadened his outlook and spurred a growing thirst for the logic he had found so naturally fulfilling in those never to be forgotten mathematics books. Sibert had little opportunity to exercise his skill and understanding of numbers behind the plow, yet he remained acutely sharp and altogether comfortable with his computations. Whether negotiating the sale of two hundred bushels of corn, or buying enough alfalfa seed to cover that ten-acre field down by the creek, or figuring how many rods of barbed wire were needed to complete the partnership fence, William Luther Sibert always seemed to get it right.

Older farmers were deferential to the youngster in matters of mathematics and that mattered to Sibert in two distinct ways: First, he was competitive and liked to be correct and quick with an answer; second, he sensed a certain respect many of his elders came to have of his mathematical ability. For the youngster, the down side to the equation involved both quantity and quality: As for quantity, too few problems came his way, hardly enough to whet his appetite. The quality was also deficient with problems always of the most basic variety: the conversion of fencing rods to feet, or the calculation of acreage from the dimensions of a cornfield. The absence of any challenge to his intellect, no true test of his ability to analyze and solve more complicated arithmetical riddles, left Sibert with a bland feeling.

The success of William Joshua Sibert's mercantile business finally paid off handsomely, due in part to Etowah County's growing population—from just over 10,000 recorded in the 1870 Census to 15,398, according to the 1880 Census. More and more farmers needed more and more implements for planting and harvesting the corn, cotton, wheat, and oats from more than 60,000 acres of land under cultivation in Etowah County by 1880. This expanded business made it possible for the merchant to engage the services of hired hands on the Sibert farm, or perhaps install a sharecropper family to carry the major load, thereby freeing the younger Sibert from farming chores. This was highly significant for the son, even more so for the father. The Confederate veteran, who had never ceased to struggle with his war wounds, at last had the opportunity to satisfy his longstanding curiosity about his first son. He unchained William Luther Sibert from the plow and his obviously unfulfilling agricultural pursuits to see, once and for all, just how far all those numbers swirling about within an otherwise stable Sibert brainpan might take him.

The big question was how to do it, a perplexing problem for a man much more comfortable negotiating the price of a farm implement with a neighbor than plotting his son's future education. The more the elder Sibert studied the problem, the more he became convinced that the answer was not in his own backyard, but lay to the southwest, almost all the way across the state at Tuscaloosa.

It is beyond doubt that when William Luther Sibert walked away from the plow on his father's Etowah County farm, his sights were set on the University of Alabama. However, before he could hope to enroll at the university, it was catch up time for Sibert, notwithstanding his knack for numbers. Sibert had not seen the inside of a schoolroom or been exposed to a teacher for more than three years when, at age 17, he carefully listened to his father's proposal—the opportunity for a university education. A grateful son endorsed his father's plan with enthusiasm despite every immediate indication that the process would not be easy.

Nor was it easy for the State of Alabama to get its university up and running. In 1818, the Alabama Territory established a township as a site for a "seminary of learning" with a second township added following Alabama's admission to the Union on March 2, 1819. The seminary, officially established on December 18, 1820, received the name: "The University of the State of Alabama". Because Tuscaloosa served as the state's capital, the town became the school's permanent home in 1827. Then followed a long wait for the inaugural ceremonies, which finally opened the university for business on April 18, 1831. [3]

The younger Sibert's first step toward Tuscaloosa required a pledge of diligent study under the direction of the Gadsden tutor his father hired with one goal in mind: qualify his son for admission to Alabama's seminary of learning at Tuscaloosa. Sibert's long absence from formal instruction and the rather strict time limits imposed by an otherwise supportive father resulted in a demanding academic assignment. Although the costs of instruction could not go on indefinitely, the elder Sibert's desire to quickly measure his son's abilities produced the greatest influence on the educational timetable. The merchant recognized his own problems of advancing age—accentuated by the old wounds that never ceased to nag—and hoped to prepare the farm boy to be his business successor with the best possible education. The father viewed university preparation as a serious matter and expected his son to do the same by concentrating on his studies.

William Luther Sibert made a rocky return to academic pursuits with major difficulties arising from the broad nature of the instruction itself. Subjects covered included English, history, penmanship, and other non-mathematical subjects, which tended to bore the student of numbers.

To devote all of his time and energy to the ambitious program of studies, the farm boy returned to Gadsden where he roomed at the hotel and tried to adjust to the task ahead. It wasn't an easy trade, even grossly unfair when seen from the new pupil's perspective. He viewed his situation as a totally one-sided concession to the learning process during those first weeks of study. He felt sacrificial, daydreaming of all of that open sky, woods, hills, and farm fields he had grown to love, now forfeited for day upon dreary day with a mountain of books in his tutor's parlor, sans rifle and without his loyal hounds.

Sibert's contemporaries would have argued in favor of his father's plan because it carried with it the opportunity to escape the farm and the backbreaking labor required to wrest a living from the soil. Sibert, too, knew his father was right and, able to draw upon that extra maturity he had gained through daily dealing with all those little problems he had routinely faced on the farm, Sibert gritted his teeth, shook off the momentary melancholy, and secretly applauded his father. Weekend visits to the Sibert farm helped, a run with the dogs into the surrounding hills serving to renew his spirits in preparation for another week of intensive study.

The study of mathematics always stimulated Sibert and was never a problem. Not wishing to disappoint his father, the first son tackled English, history, and his other studies with sufficient vigor to finally overcome the preexisting malaise. Discipline of the self-imposed variety paced Sibert's tutorial success. In little more than a year of concentrated effort, the farm boy overcame boredom and the feeling of isolation from the outdoors he loved, to master the equivalent of a high school education. The source of the monumental self-discipline is unclear, likely a mixture of Teutonic genes, the influence of an ex-Rebel soldier of the Methodist faith, and the patience ingrained from hours behind the plow or on the trail of an elusive buck. Whatever its origin, this discipline, wrapped unobtrusively in quiet determination, would serve him and his country well until his death. [4]

Even with today's modern highway system, it is quite a distance from Gadsden to Tuscaloosa. Interstate 59 rolls unerringly to the southwest, skirting Ashville—where David Sibert established the first

Sibert homestead in Alabama—and then crossing north of downtown Birmingham. The impressive Mercedes Benz complex is passed during the final third of the trip to the university town and former state capital—now better known as home base for the Crimson Tide football team. The entire 120 miles can be driven in the 21st century in two hours without doing violence to the speed limits.

When William Luther Sibert completed the journey in 1878, there were more miles to be counted due to the circuitous nature of the hodgepodge network of country roads, and those miles were often difficult for the traveler. Once the young man reached Birmingham, the railway station must have been a welcome sight because he could ride the train the final 58 or so miles to Tuscaloosa.

The budding mathematician must have been thrilled to arrive on the campus, figuring that those days spent controlling the Sibert's mule with a succession of gees and haws, while manhandling the plow and struggling to keep the furrows straight, might very well be ending. Sibert dreamed of success at the State of Alabama's citadel of higher learning; he had excelled during his limited exposure to the classroom and welcomed the challenge found in the study of mathematics.

Based upon his tutor's certification of the pupil's proficiency as a result of the intensive year of study and a penetrating interview by a member of the faculty, Sibert was admitted as a member of the freshman class at the University of Alabama in 1878. The school had evolved since its inception, even being transformed into a military school in 1860 by state leaders, a prelude to the unhappy events in 1865 which witnessed destructive Union troops razing the campus where only seven buildings were spared.

When Sibert arrived, the Crimson Tide was still in the future. The absence of football on the Alabama campus likely inured to the academic benefit of the new freshman. Without the temptation to play with the funny-shaped ball, the robust, highly competitive outdoorsman did what his father expected him to do—study and learn how best to apply all that knowledge of numbers to the greater success of the Sibert business enterprises. The father definitely wanted a fair return on the investment made in his elder son's college education.

Not only did the university lack a football team in 1878, it had no School of Engineering even though civil engineering classes had been offered under the auspices of applied mathematics as early as 1837.

Whether Sibert studied engineering while in Tuscaloosa is unknown, but his tackling engineering studies and their inherent mathematical bases would come as no surprise. [5]

Initially, thoughts of the U.S. Military Academy (West Point) played no part in Sibert's selection of courses although his fascination with numbers may have attracted him to engineering studies. Even though such studies provided excellent preparation for the military school, with its strong engineering component, the new college student concentrated on the goal he shared with his father: He intended not only to return to Gadsden, but to bring with him the ability to serve the Sibert business interests in a useful capacity.

Like most brand new college students, Sibert worried about his grades and his father's reaction should he fare badly. Not unexpectedly, from the very first he excelled in all courses concerned with higher mathematics—a diligent student, in tune with the numbers, and possessing an innate aptitude to absorb the underlying theories.

Also true to form, William Luther continued to experience difficulty keeping his mind on other studies that did not attract and hold his interest to the same degree as did the pursuit of mathematical knowledge. With some difficulty, he got by in a generally undistinguished fashion, except for superior marks in mathematics, and even learned a bit of Spanish along the way from a Professor Parker, who took an interest in the obviously bright but arithmetically preoccupied student.

After completing his freshman year, Sibert returned to Gadsden for a summer of work—a summer ripe with possibilities of major changes in the student's future. Things became unsettled because a Confederate war hero—and member of the U.S. House of representatives in 1879—desperately wanted a young man from his congressional district to graduate from the U.S. Military Academy at West Point, New York.

When the Alabama locals wrested control of state government from Reconstruction's Carpetbagger regime in 1875, William Henry Forney was elected to the United States 44th Congress from Alabama's Seventh Congressional District which included Gadsden. The former Confederate general managed to survive the Civil War while suffering an astonishing 13 wounds during combat. He held the Seventh District seat in the U.S. Congress until he retired in 1892.

With such a resume, it is understandable that Congressman Fortney wanted to sponsor a West Point appointment for a young man from his district with promise of graduating—a means to continue the area's military tradition which the congressman had helped fashion. But the Civil War had ended more than a decade earlier and the district was yet to claim a postwar military academy graduate. A search for an appointee who could succeed at West Point led Congressman Forney to the mercantile building presided over by William Joshua Sibert.

During summer recess from duties in Washington, the congressman met with the merchant in Gadsden and the subject of the discussion, William Luther Sibert, was probably in attendance. Regardless, it was a very private and frank discussion of the young man's future: Did a West Point education look attractive to the Sibert family and, perhaps more important to Forney, did the younger Sibert possess the intellectual skills required to meet the academy's stringent academic program? A glance at the strapping youth left no doubt that he was more than capable of coping with the physical demands of the already storied institution on the Hudson.

Thus, the Alabama congressman, still suffering from some of the 13 wounds he received at the hands of the U.S. Army—its sharpshooters often commanded by those gentlemen officers from West Point who had remained loyal to the Union—became the instrument by which William Luther Sibert was proposed for appointment to the U.S. Military Academy. The appointment came with the approval of a father who had also experienced firsthand the effects of the Federal Army's firepower. [6]

A tough decision for both father and son: While the young man's ability to meet the rigorous physical requirements never seemed in doubt, they worried about his rural, unsophisticated background where the one-room schoolhouse limited intellectual opportunities. Not only were these impediments to passing the academy's entrance examinations, but also represented possible barriers to academic success during the academy's full four-year course leading to graduation. To flunk out would be no disgrace, yet valuable time would be lost should he falter, time that could have been spent completing his degree at Tuscaloosa, time lost from assuming a leadership role in the family business enterprises.

And what of David Sibert's businesses if the first son graduated from West Point and embarked on a military career? Either way, application of William Luther Sibert's talents in furtherance of the Sibert business interests would be in serious jeopardy. In just such a situation, the advice and encouragement of Congressman Forney, thirsty for a worthy son from Alabama's Seventh Congressional District to graduate from West Point and win a commission in the U.S. Army, tipped the scales.

Meanwhile, young Sibert began his second year at Tuscaloosa, continuing to make an exceptional record in classes devoted to the study of mathematics in its several forms. Average best describes his other classroom pursuits although mediocre and indifferent would do as well. That had to change if Sibert hoped to successfully storm the ramparts of West Point where passing the initial entrance examination was a tall order for the product of a one-room schoolhouse. Potential trouble permeated those parts of the academic inquiry unconcerned with numbers. He needed another tutor, not any tutor, but a gifted teacher schooled in the classics and capable of grabbing the attention of the previously reluctant student.

Because 20th century Sibert family sources did not know the first name of this Parker fellow who taught Spanish, he was initially presumed to be some obscure journeyman pedagogue who happened to be passing through Tuscaloosa while William Luther was a student. To the contrary, Professor William A. Parker was a towering academic figure during his long career at the University of Alabama (1871-1908). Parker was among the initial set of instructors hired when, following the war, the Tuscaloosa campus first reopened to students in 1871. He was a Renaissance man, a professor of Greek, whose teaching expertise was put to the test as Sibert's second tutor.

Professor Parker immersed the student in subjects that were of little or no innate interest to the pupil. Rather relentlessly, he pounded home facts and nuances found within a classical education—groundwork for passing the entrance exam and succeeding in West Point's recitation halls. The role Parker played in Sibert's academic career at the University of Alabama, and beyond, cannot be overstated. All of his efforts faced stern testing at the U.S. Military Academy. [7]

Chapter Four
WEST POINT: DAVID AND GOLIATH

Much has been written about the U.S. Military Academy at West Point, New York—about both the institution and the young men it molds into leaders who time and again distinguish themselves in both war and peace. They are altogether serious about *Duty, Honor, and Country* on the plains above the Hudson River where William Luther Sibert's life was forever changed. Some of the transformation, from farm boy to military officer, was readily apparent while more subtle changes were not so obvious. For the 19-year-old Sibert, it all began during the early summer of 1880 after a long, hot train trip from Gadsden to the State of New York.

Immediately awaiting Sibert and his companions—all young male civilians—was arguably the most important academic exercise in which they would engage over the next four years. The academy's qualifications tests were exceedingly difficult, written examinations designed to reveal each candidate's academic capabilities. Based upon the results, the faculty decided whether the candidate possessed sufficient intellect to complete the demanding four-year curriculum in a satisfactory manner.

While struggling through the testing, Sibert must have wondered just exactly what Professor Parker might be doing on the Tuscaloosa campus when he was sorely needed by his protégé on the crenelated campus, a reminder of its first life as a key fort commanding the plateau above the Hudson River. Even without actually standing beside him, eager to whisper helpful clues to the answers to barrage after barrage of questions, the University of Alabama professor made his presence known to the candidate. The examination was no breeze for any of the candidates, some of whom had come from the finest of prep schools.

Nonetheless, Sibert assessed the testing from a slightly different point of view. With Parker's guidance, he knew that he had done everything he could possibly do to prepare for the testing. And, after answering the last question, he found himself imbued with a certain confidence that he had done well. With no time for second-guessing, and certainly no display of arrogance, all Sibert had was an unshakable sense of assurance. Directly attributable to the Sibert personality and intellect, as honed and fine-tuned by Professor Parker, this attitude allowed Sibert to relax and not sweat it, once the testing ordeal ended. Based on the testing, he believed they would keep him. They did.

The newly-accepted cadet next greeted an array of more upsetting thoughts with stoicism. He felt tremendous pressure to succeed at West Point—obligations, first to a father who believed in his son's ability. And never far from his thoughts were Congressman Forney and his hope for a West Point graduate. With those pressures and thoughts tucked safely away in the deep recesses of his psyche, where they would not be bothersome on a day-to-day basis, Sibert joined his fellow classmates as a member of the Fourth Year Class at the U.S. Military Academy and braced for the next challenge in the summer of 1880. (West Point counts and labels classes differently from other schools. Rather than freshmen, brand new cadets became members of the academy's Fourth Year Class—the bottom of the academic barrel.)

So it was that Sibert became a Plebe, the designated nomenclature for a member of the Fourth Year Class, and prepared to camp out for the first time as a student-soldier in Plebe camp, tents and all. It was his first taste of army life in the field, a full two months under canvas before the Plebes qualified for admittance within the solid stone walls of West Point's barracks, only slightly less Spartan than the camp. Observing the reactions of some Plebes to their first exposure to tent life, the cadet from Alabama began to appreciate his farm heritage. He was thankful for all of that deep woods hunting, camping, and exploring he had done, experiences which had made him comfortable and very much at home in the outdoors.

Whether by design or chance, two native-born Southerners ended up tent mates at Plebe camp. Tall and slender David DuBose Gaillard of South Carolina, like Sibert, was among the first from his state to attend the academy following the war. They were destined to be roommates and friendly competitors throughout their four years at the academy. Thereafter, differing army assignments parted them for more than 20 years before their epic reunion on the Isthmus of Panama, no longer pawns on the Army chessboard but full-fledged knights of the first order.

Much as Sibert hoped to be the first cadet from Alabama's Seventh Congressional District to graduate from West Point after the Civil War, Gaillard likely felt even more pressure. Besides being among the first from South Carolina to seek a West Point commission after the war, the Gaillard family already had a West Point pedigree. Prior to the war, other South Carolina Gaillards had proudly worn cadet grey before at least one felt obligated to trade it for the Confederate butternut. Understandably, Gaillard was expected to not only reestablish the family ties with the academy, but to do it in exemplary fashion.

A pair of Southerners appointed to the U.S. Military Academy in 1880 may be excused for being a bit sensitive about their regional heritage springing from former rebel states; their northern counterparts could likewise be pardoned for any lingering suspicions regarding loyalty of the Southerners to the United States. When Sibert and Gaillard arrived on the Hudson, however, they benefitted directly from a noticeable change for the better in attitudes regarding regional relations. Southerners were less likely to be treated as stepchildren at the academy following a conciliatory visit to West Point by ex-Confederate Lieutenant General James Longstreet, USMA Class of 1842, in order to attend graduation ceremonies five years earlier.

It didn't take the pair of roommates long to attract the attention of senior cadets, those First Classmen active and instrumental in the administration of discipline within Plebe camp. Notoriety among their seniors could be either good or bad for Plebes, usually bad, and there was much to commend keeping a low profile. Dating from their very first night in camp, the coveted anonymity was not to be for Gaillard and Sibert.

The newly acquainted pair hardly had time to drive the last tent peg and stretch the government-issue canvas taut, in hopes that their tent, located on a corner of The Plain, not far from the Kosciusko monument, would pass muster with their cadet overseers. The pair quickly organized their sparse belongings, looking forward to at least a few minutes to relax within the sheltering canvas, briefly out of sight of those watchful upperclassmen. And then the canvas flap popped open.

A First Classman lifted the flap while making the rounds and checking his charges, first seeing Gaillard standing near the front of the tent. Snapping to attention with apprehension born of not knowing what to expect, Gaillard was relieved when the upperclassman merely asked his given name.

"David, sir," was his answer. Evidently satisfied with the answer, the requisite sir being the second and far more important half of the response, the visitor turned his attention to the tent's second occupant who was standing at the rear, also stiffly at attention. There was a long and ominously silent pause as the ranking cadet took in the physical appearance of Plebe Sibert before answering Gaillard with a quick wit honed by his first three years at the academy.

"Oh, yes," the First Classman said, looking directly at Gaillard, "you are David," before returning his gaze to Sibert, exclaiming: "and this is Goliath!" The appellation acquired an authenticity and permanence usually reserved for official records and monuments of bronze. Ever after, throughout his 40-year military career, to those soldiers who knew him best, William Luther Sibert, whether a lowly cadet or a captain in command, was always called Goliath. And he would always answer because Goliath was his name—at least it had been since that summer in Plebe camp in 1880.

Standing a solid six-foot-four, Sibert stood out in any crowd of late 19th century males who, at the time, averaged well under six feet. This was true of the Corps of Cadets, circa 1880, where Sibert's height and muscular physique sometimes attracted unwelcome attention, especially during his first year on the Hudson. On one or more occasions, Fourth Classman Sibert found himself fighting battles not of his own making. It was a traditional thing.

Life at West Point was highly disciplined and regulated with all kinds of rules to be obeyed and responsibilities to be met. The highly demanding regimen and system worked well. Still, as might be expected, personal differences arose from time to time between members of the Corps of Cadets. In order to prevent such personality clashes from festering and escalating into more serious differences deemed harmful to the Corps of Cadets and future army service, tradition demanded that the question be settled once and for all on the field of honor.

By 1880, at least at West Point, old-fashioned dueling with pistols or swords had been junked as counterproductive, replaced by the All-

American fistfight. Cadets determined that a time-tested bare-knuckle brawl can settle practically any question while extracting honor enough for both combatants. Regardless of the origin of the ill feelings, whether a simple misunderstanding or a deeper conflict over ancestry, politics, religion, or some other highly controversial subject, the system demanded a very personal settlement between the two antagonistic cadets. Immediately!

The simple system gained credence from an equally plain theory: Resolving a dispute quickly lessens chances of any lasting detrimental effects on either the parties or the Army. Regardless of right or wrong in the controversy—and often right or wrong are impossible to define in such conflicts between extremely sharp and healthy young American males—once the battle concluded, the system demanded that the winner and loser shake hands. And mean it!

The handshake sealed a usually hard fought bargain, signifying that the issue was settled, dead, and buried forever. By the handshake, the loser conceded the fight, and the victor acknowledged the loser's game and gallant effort in a losing cause. The unwritten rule required friendship to blossom between the fledgling warriors, and foes usually became friends. After slugging it out, many contestants did in fact become best of friends.

None of this was part of the academy's official rules of conduct and its strict disciplinary system did not mention impromptu boxing matches. Yet, those officers in charge of the academy were well aware of the courts traditionally in session behind the barracks. They liked the way the cadets handled such problems because it worked. It wasn't broke!

Plebe Sibert soon encountered two interrelated problems: Like all Fourth Classmen, he was a member of the brand new class, lorded over by the upperclassmen, and required to be respectful of all upperclassmen. In addition, Sibert carried the burden of practically every big guy. There is always somebody, oftentimes bigger, who wants to provoke the big fellow into a fight for supremacy. Nothing unusual about it, and the reason behind many big boys, Sibert included, striving to be skillful diplomats. Sibert had learned, sometimes the hard way, that for a variety of reasons, those fistfights avoided were the best kind, thus the soft-spoken diplomatic approach which usually worked for him, even as a Plebe at the Point. Not always.

It fell Sibert's lot, much like his Biblical namesake, to defend the honor of a fellow Plebe and, by extension, the entire class. The details are not important, but hazing—another feature of cadet life not officially condoned by the academy—caused the confrontation. A Third Classman, a Yearling in cadet vernacular, had gone overboard in his relentless hazing of a Plebe—straying well beyond the acceptable limits of endurance. A substantial portion of the Plebe class shared this view, and there was unanimous agreement that the injustice demanded cadet-style atonement. There was a problem.

Slight in stature and lighter than David Gaillard—the Plebe found himself hopelessly mismatched against the overbearing Yearling who weighed in excess of 200 pounds, well distributed over a Sibert-sized frame. This prompted Plebe leaders to make an unusual request of their Yearling counterparts: They wanted the freedom to select from the Plebe class a champion to represent their slightly built classmate in challenging the oppressive Yearling. The request was granted, probably because a strong current of fair play coursed through the cadets' unofficial code of conduct, demanding that the unauthorized fistfights be fair, if nothing else. A physically well-endowed big man pitted against a much smaller adversary simply failed the litmus test for fairness. With the request granted, the Plebes needed a worthy champion, somebody to defend the class' honor, win, lose or draw.

They didn't have to look far to find the obvious choice: Goliath! And so the diplomatic Sibert signed on to do battle in the gymnasium, or more likely, behind the barracks with the bullying Yearling. The combatants came from far different backgrounds but were approximately the same size and weight. With an age and experience advantage, including intramural boxing while at the academy, his classmates declared the Yearling a heavy favorite. They knew Sibert's farm boy background, a big fellow but very likely unskilled in boxing and the manly art of self defense. Wrong! Unknown to the Yearlings, Sibert had recognized early that his size alone made him a potential target for bullies and had taken boxing lessons in Tuscaloosa.

At the appointed time, the farm boy wasted no time in carrying the challenge to the Yearling, quickly demonstrating that he knew the difference between a left cross and a right uppercut and knew how to use them to great effect in a fistfight. The Plebe soundly thrashed the Yearling, indeed a rare occurrence. At the bout's conclusion, the Yearling conceded, and Sibert graciously accepted the surrender. Thereafter, the Yearling patched it up with the Plebe he had abused while the boxers shook hands and parted as friends. Once again, the system had worked, helped along by Goliath.

Sibert preferred avoiding boxing performances, especially when not personally involved in the spat. Regardless, when his classmates appealed for his services, the cadet from Gadsden cheerfully issued the challenge on behalf of his smaller classmate. Ironically, his decisive demonstration of fighting ability saved the big cadet from numerous similar encounters while at the academy. Very few wished to take on the farm boy in a fair fight.

Sibert was, however, often called upon to referee when two cadets, both being his friends, decided to settle their differences on the field of honor. Such appointments underscored Sibert's reputation for fairness as much as his knowledge of boxing. [1]

During West Point's first 43 years, physical education had been confined to military drills, sword exercises, and an early version of the game now known as football. This changed in 1858 when the scope of physical training expanded to include calisthenics, swimming, gymnastics, bayonet exercises, and fencing. The official program devoted one hour per day to developing the physical skills of cadets. Unrecorded is the amount of time devoted to unsanctioned fistfights.

Although the unique and colorful way cadets settled disputes added to the mystique of the academy, there was much, much more. The military arena required mastery of marching, weaponry, field training, and tactics. On the academic side, a cadet received a well-rounded classical education, with heavy emphasis on mathematics and engineering, both military and civil. The professors took names and issued grades based on merits, treating the education of cadets as serious work.

The United States Military Academy annually publishes the *Official Register of the Officers and Cadets of the U.S. Military Academy*. Issued in June of each year, it recorded class details as another contingent of newly-minted second lieutenants departed for active duty with the Army. The 1881 edition is the first in which William Luther Sibert's name appears with the other Fourth Class members, a total strength of 69 cadets.

Army reports, even concerning academic matters, are never short on details and, for example, by referring to the register, one can find out exactly what texts the Plebes read during that first arduous year on the Hudson. The books included Church's *Analytical Geometry*, Abbott and Seeley's *English Lessons for English People*, and Hart's *Manual of Rhetoric and Composition*. Lectures in ethics, began with the academy's famous honor code.

Books counted less beyond the lecture halls where regular Army sergeants relied on practical hands-on instruction. Cadets learned all about individual soldiering and how the Army functioned at the company and battalion levels. Exercises demonstrated the proper deployment and utilization of artillery as well as small arms instruction, fencing, and bayonet training. Overall, West Point required cadets to rapidly absorb instruction, much of it altogether foreign to the former civilians. For example, Sibert, the solitary hunter, moved easily, swiftly, and silently through Alabama forests, tracking game like a Cherokee, but experienced difficulty fitting into close order drill with hundreds of fellow cadets—uniformly moving as one—across the parade field.

With apologies to no one, the register contained considerable detail to establish each cadet's ranking at the completion of the Plebe year. Among the exceptional records was that of James C. Sanford, from New York, the overall class leader in what the academy calls the Order of general merit. In other categories he ranked first in discipline and second in mathematics, English studies, and French. Cadet Sanford did not receive a single demerit during the entire year. In second place overall, Horace I. Hale, appointed from Colorado, took first honors in the mathematics, English, and French courses, but was ranked only 22nd in discipline, having chalked up 62 demerits. A superior student, Hale's disciplinary shortcomings may have been indicative of a free spirit. Stiff competition prevailed among the class' 69 members, and the roommates from below the Mason Dixon Line were not far behind the leaders.

Goliath, the farm boy from Alabama, placed third overall in general merit, ranking fourth in mathematics, seventh in French, eighth in English studies, and ninth in discipline with 23 demerits. As a pair, the roommates did well with Gaillard ranked fifth overall with only eight demerits. In contrast, some cadets cracked the century mark with even more demerits to spare.

Where academic standings and overall ratings were concerned, the academy way of doing things recognized no such concept as a cadet's right to privacy. To the contrary: Records of each cadet's academic performance and his overall rating and position in the class decorated the register at the end of that first grueling year. West Point offered no comfort to shrinking violets.

Regardless of standing, each cadet immediately faced its long-range ramifications. God could be counted on to be totally forgiving, not so the Army hierarchy which, based largely on records accumulated by graduation time, assigned new officers to their first duty stations. Future commanding officers closely scrutinized the statistics and, in the nation's small standing army following the Civil War, seldom numbering more than 25,000 prior to the Spanish American War, word spread quickly about a new officer with an outstanding academy record.

In the most highly regulated environment imaginable, the roommates thrived on the spirit of competition within the Plebe community and, no doubt, between themselves. When the results of the 1881 annual examination were tabulated, Sibert, William L., was listed behind Sanford and Hale as third on the list of distinguished cadets among Fourth Classmen. Gaillard, David Du B. was just behind in fifth position. Their relative positions soon reversed.

By way of comparison, in that first year on the Hudson, Gaillard's eight demerits were outstanding and Sibert's 23 demerits looked very good when compared, for example, with the 206 owned by a cadet from Louisiana, with an unforgettable first name, Powhatan. No sectional bias here, another Plebe appointed from New York had even more demerits.

Gaillard not only overhauled his roommate, but vaulted over every other Third Year Classman except Hale to rank second. Sibert ranked ninth among Yearlings, their number reduced by the academy's rigid standards to 42. Powhatan was among the survivors, and Gaillard was again named as a distinguished cadet, an honor he repeated during his final two years at West Point.

On the military side, both roommates were appointed corporals in the Corps of Cadets, corporal being the highest rank obtainable by a Yearling. As Second Classmen the following year, Sibert was appointed sergeant and Gaillard was one of the four first sergeants in the Corps of Cadets. During Sibert's third year at West Point he proved to be an outstanding student of philosophy while continuing to hold the ninth position in class standing, a model of consistency.

By graduation time, in addition to the continuing array of academic subjects, ranging from engineering and history to philosophy and law, First Classmen had received intensive instruction in tactics, ordnance, and gunnery. Between roommates, Gaillard took the prize in ordnance and gunnery while Sibert was the superior student of tactics. Overall, the graduating roommates scored consistently high with Gaillard, perhaps at some advantage with his family lineage to West Point, winning the competition between roommates.

Gaillard held on to fifth, and Sibert had pulled up to seventh in the final ranking of the Class of 1884. Even at that, Sibert had plenty of bragging rights, having posted scores superior to Gaillard's marks in mathematics, English, philosophy and tactics. The South Carolinian bested him in foreign languages and history. It came as no surprise to either cadet that Gaillard bettered Sibert in the discipline category, Goliath receiving 26 demerits during his final two years at the academy while his roommate incurred not a single one—zero demerits. Usually only a few points separated the roommates, regardless of who was on top.

Both David and Goliath made it. Only 37 of the 69 Plebes listed in the June 1881 register successfully completed the rigorous four-year trial in the arts—both of warfare and of the liberal variety—strongly flavored with engineering studies and close order *esprit de corps*. Because they had chosen arguably the toughest and most demanding institution of higher learning America had to offer, those graduating cadets bringing up the rear earned full rights to the pride that goes with West Point graduation. The Louisianan, Powhatan, made it as no. 37 on the list of graduates.

Sibert and Gaillard continued to lead as First Classmen, being among the 14 cadets appointed as lieutenants in the Corps of Cadets. Gaillard also served as quartermaster. For the two Southerners, it couldn't have been much better when they received their West Point diplomas on June 14, 1884. Along with graduation came an oath seriously taken to serve as 2nd lieutenants in the U.S. Army, and an equally serious promise to serve their country as a commissioned army officer for at least four years.[2]

Sibert was on post-graduation leave in Gadsden when he signed the oath of office on July 14, 1884, and did "solemnly swear that I will support and defend the Constitution of the United States against all enemies, foreign and domestic. ..." L.E. Hamlin, Etowah County's probate judge, witnessed Sibert's signature. Then there were the orders. [3]

Both Sibert and Gaillard accepted assignments to the Corps of Engineers, such appointments reserved for the top echelon of the graduating class. It made sense because the pair had graduated from West Point, arguably the nation's best engineering school. The appointment carried with it an assignment for postgraduate engineering studies at the Army's Engineering School of Application at Ft. Totten, New York. Although Sibert and Gaillard were now army regulars, commissioned as lieutenants of Engineers, they were yet to break out of school.

Back in Tuscaloosa, Professor Parker could not have been prouder of his protégé's performance at the military academy, prompting him to take a second look at the educational future of his own son.

Chapter Five
TEXAS BELLE AND KENTUCKY RIVER

Thoughts of bridge building fundamentals, surveys by triangulation, and the best way to build coastal fortifications—and all other engineering concepts pounded home at the Army's Engineering School of Application—were temporarily banished during the long trip south from New York. Sibert received congratulations for successfully completing the Army's postgraduate engineering course—and parental blessings for their son's next endeavor—at the Gadsden stopover. His appointment in Texas was strictly personal, with plenty of time left for the Army over the next 33 years.

Galveston was located in excess of 200 miles to the northeast of the lieutenant's destination, the small town of Brownsville, which sits on the American side of the Rio Grande just across from the Mexican border town of Matamoros. Since the glory days of the Republic of Texas, the Mexican War, and the Civil War, military leaders considered Brownsville's location strategically important. It is less than 20 miles from Brazos Island and Boca Chica, where the boundary river fans out to meet the Gulf of Mexico. The U.S. Army concluded that it was important enough to deserve a fort.

Even by 19th century Texas standards, Galveston was a long way off, but close enough for the *Galveston Daily News* to be more than a little bit interested in a wedding that took place in Brownsville on the evening of September 18, 1887. Quoting the September 19, 1887, edition of the Galveston daily:

"Miss Mamie Cummings, youngest daughter of the late Judge Franklin Cummings and a belle of Brownsville, was married here last night to Lieutenant W.S. (sic) Sibert, Corps of Engineers, United States army, in the Episcopal Church."

Everyone in Brownsville and, apparently, Galveston, knew Mamie, the Brownsville belle, to be Mary Margaret Cummings, so no real necessity to identify her by her proper name in the news account of the wedding. Nobody in Texas had ever heard of the lieutenant and, as a consequence, the paper failed to correctly record his middle initial. The journalistic error affected neither the legitimacy nor the altogether happy and glittering aura surrounding the border town nuptials.

With a fair complexion, blue eyes and brown hair, the Brownsville belle stood five feet two, appearing both feminine and tiny by her strapping bridegroom in his Army dress blue uniform, complete with saber. Even more sabers tented the couple as they emerged from the church, courtesy of the officer corps then stationed at Fort Brown. The bride was given away by her brother, Joseph Franklin Cummings, himself a West Pointer and former cavalry officer. The officers' corps from Fort Brown, along with their ladies, was in attendance. So much for the military flavor.

More attention was directed toward the bride in her "white satin en train with pearl ornaments, the bodice V shaped, with point lace border and other decorations." Her bridesmaids, Mary More, Irene Dalzell, and Lizzi Wilman, were, according to the news account, "elegantly attired" and attended by groomsmen, W.J. Russell, Jessie Thornham, and Lt. Ives of the U.S. Army.

Presided over by the Rev. H.C. Graybell, the newspaper described the wedding as "one of the most brilliant affairs of the kind that has been witnessed in this city. ... " [1]

At West Point, Cadet Sibert managed to avoid any of those entangling alliances, often promoted by Flirtation Walk on the academy's campus. Later, while attending the Army's advanced engineering school at Fort Totten, the new lieutenant met the belle from Brownsville. The future bridegroom must have made an impression, towering over the future bride and obviously a very eligible bachelor.

Thanks to Army obligations and the geographical separation of western Long Island from as far south as you can go in Texas, the long distance courtship featured numerous letters at a time when writing a proper letter was regarded as an essential art for the more cultured of the species. Regardless, by the time Sibert had successfully completed the post graduate engineering studies and was ready for his first posting—his first *real job* with the U.S. Army—he was also ready to launch on the sea of matrimony. He was less than a month shy of his 27th birthday when vows were exchanged in Brownsville.

It is a little difficult to understand why the vivacious Mary Margaret Cummings, known to family and friends as Mamie, had remained still single, having been born August 16, 1862, and just turning 25 when she wed. From all reports, the bride had never been short of suitors. Perhaps it was because the selection of suitable mates had been severely limited by the size and isolated location of her hometown. Putting it another way, she had patiently waited until the right one came along and that was Sibert. From the very first, the couple had a lot going for them.

Both were from the Old South, from states where the Confederacy's customs, mores, history—and myths—continued to strongly influence the populace long after Appomattox. Their fathers fought in the Civil War on the losing side. And both backgrounds were solidly anchored to pioneer people who were both ambitious and industrious and who had an appreciation for benefits to be derived from a sound education.

Franklin Cummings, Mamie's father, was born in 1823, and died of consumption in Brownsville in 1874. A native of Maine and son of a Methodist minister, he held a law degree from Wesleyan University. Cummings married Ann Mildred Jones in April 1850 and moved with his bride to Brownsville where he was a partner of Stephen Powers, who established the first law office in Brownsville. The lawyers had a monopoly on the Brownsville postmaster's job with Cummings being appointed to succeed Powers in 1851; he held the office for seven years. Active in politics, he was one of the early mayors of Brownsville, served as judge, and at one time was a Cameron County commissioner. During the Civil War, he served with Texas state troops at Fort Brown; he also served on the Committee of Public Safety after the Cortina raid in 1859. [2]

Following her husband's death, Mrs. Cummings took on the task of rearing her 12-year-old daughter.

Possibly going well beyond his duty to give the bride away on behalf of the family, Mamie's brother accompanied the couple when they departed Brownsville on their wedding trip, the first leg of which was aboard the *Arkansas*, a steamer bound for Galveston. Now retired from the army after serving during the Indian wars as an officer in the Third Cavalry Regiment, Joseph Franklin Cummings was not needed as a chaperone for the newly-weds. School business is the more likely reason for the trip; the ex-officer taught school in Galveston before returning to Brownsville in July 1888 to organize the local school system. He is acknowledged as the founder of the public school system in Brownsville.

In Galveston, the Siberts took leave of Mamie's brother and were at last on their own. A leisurely cruise for a few days along the Gulf shore was not a bad way to begin life as a married couple. At some port with good rail connections, either New Orleans or Mobile, the Siberts abandoned ship in favor of trains. The honeymoon continued and included "certain points in Georgia" before turning north to Cincinnati and their new home, the Galveston paper reported. [3]

So it was that, after the wedding and honeymoon, Lieutenant Sibert and his bride used the remainder of his leave to set up housekeeping in the Queen City, probably in sight of the Ohio River, a stream destined to play a major role in the officer's career.

After leave expired, Sibert complied with Special Order No. 152, dated July 2, 1887, by reporting in person to Major Amos Stickney at the Corps of Engineers offices in Louisville, Kentucky, about 80 miles downstream from Cincinnati. Even the newest Corps of Engineers officers knew that meant working on the mighty Ohio River and its tributaries. Acting through the adjutant general, famed Union cavalry leader, Phil Sheridan, now Army chief of staff, signed off on Order No. 152, assigning Sibert his first real engineering job as a 2nd Lieutenant of Engineers.

Sibert thought it was about time for the Army to put him to work in a bona fide and meaningful job. He welcomed the posting after all the schooling at West Point and Fort Totten. Although Sibert had served as an engineer company officer at Fort Totten, the emphasis had been on study. In sharp contrast, Sibert saw an Ohio River system replete with a variety of brawny and very real navigation problems, the kind of things hard to duplicate in classroom exercises. This exciting and diverse engineering arena welcomed the officer who firmly believed that the Corps of Engineers could fix practically anything, given the resources to complete the job. The important river system begged for improvements—and experimentation—to make it better.

The Ohio River, generally regarded as a major line of demarcation between the Southeast and the rest of the nation, is a most imposing stream that, along with its numerous tributaries, bound the Eastern Seaboard to the nation's midsection in the 19th century. The river furnished early pioneers with a nautical path west, a relatively easy route when compared to walking or driving oxen-powered wagons. With the advent of steam propulsion, the river grew in importance as a reliable avenue of ever increasing commerce, although it was not without its problems.

The Ohio's capricious, not always gentle, navigational nature can be experienced full bore at the Falls City. Aptly nicknamed, Louisville owes its birth and early growth in large measure to the Falls of the Ohio, a most formidable barrier to navigation. The resulting slow, labor-intensive portaging of river freight and passengers around the rocky obstacle and its imposing fossil beds, and the services required by both passengers and freight, spurred Louisville's development.

Once people and cargoes portaged safely around the falls and transferred to downstream boats, the Ohio resumed its imperative penetration of America's western frontier. As a bold alternative to portage, a daring riverboat pilot might occasionally succeed in shooting the falls with the river in flood. Regardless, the falls had been a continuing challenge to the Army Corps of Engineers while pursuing its mission: the maintenance and improvement of the Ohio River's slack water navigation system.

The Kentucky River part of the navigation system served citizens and businesses scattered along a lengthy corridor from Beattyville in east Kentucky, west into the Bluegrass Region and, after passing through Frankfort, the state capital, turning north to unite with the Ohio at Carrollton. The Kentucky provided Sibert with his first authentic workshop—or laboratory—devoted to studying, building, and maintaining the locks and dams of a slack water system. The officer's first engineering job was a learning process and, even if he didn't always get it right, he learned from the experience.

When originally ordered to the Louisville District, it is likely that the lieutenant received advance notice of his assignment on the Kentucky River and that the river was only temporarily within the Louisville office's jurisdiction. This would explain his bride's plans to establish the couple's first home at Cincinnati; Louisville was no closer to the Kentucky River action than Cincinnati, which sat on the Ohio side of the river, directly across from the North Kentucky apex. Besides,

Cincinnati was larger than Louisville and may have seemed a bit more sophisticated to Mrs. Sibert.

The home choice looked even better when the Kentucky River—and Lieutenant Sibert—were officially reassigned to the command of Captain D.W. Lockwood at Cincinnati on April 17, 1888, with Sibert's duties on the Kentucky River remaining the same. Before the year was finished, Lockwood, having been promoted to major, tapped Sibert for a difficult task which sent him steaming up the Green and Barren rivers to Bowling Green in December 1888, an assignment which would take almost four years to complete.

Before receiving orders for Bowling Green, Sibert devoted most of his energy to the Kentucky River, a busy time for the lieutenant with plenty of work to superintend and his Texas lady to entertain in Cincinnati. There was also an important trip to New York City in the spring of 1888 when he was ordered to the Army Building, located at 39 Whitehall Street in Manhattan. Once there, he faced a Board of Engineer Officers, presided over by a bird colonel, and convened for the express purpose of examining Sibert to determine his fitness for promotion to first lieutenant.

The members of the board of examiners questioned Sibert about anything and everything associated with the *Profession of Arms*, as enunciated within the dogma and doctrine of the U.S. Army. Particular emphasis was placed on both military and civil engineering. It is difficult to imagine anyone better prepared for a good grilling by senior officers.

Consider that Sibert had graduated in the upper echelon of West Point's Class of 1884 and had devoted the next three years to advanced engineering studies while assigned to the Engineer Battalion at Fort Totten. The academics were followed by the large dose of real world engineering problems that challenged Sibert's initiative on the locks, dams, and channels of the Kentucky.

Sibert completed the examination on April 12, 1888. When Colonel Thomas L. Casey issued the board's findings, by letter dated May 11, 1888, to the army's adjutant general, as properly channeled through the Chief of Engineers, there were no frills attached, no ruffles and flourishes, none whatsoever. The letter merely confirmed that "Lieutenant Sibert is approved for promotion". Never swift, the army's promotion documents arrived in time for William Luther Sibert to take the oath of office as a first lieutenant in the Corps of Engineers before Homer F. Jordan, a notary public for Hamilton County (Cincinnati), Ohio, on June 12, 1888. [4]

Was Sibert in suspense over the outcome of the examination as his train cleared New Jersey on the return trip to Cincinnati and a resumption of his regular duties on the Kentucky? That is doubtful, even if a board member or two did not smile and wink their impending approval at the conclusion of the interrogation. Always confident of his abilities, it is likely that the officer sensed his successful performance. Regardless, he returned to duty on the Kentucky River just in time to witness the change in his immediate superior from Major Stickney to Captain Lockwood.

Under Sibert's direction, much activity along the Kentucky centered on the reconstruction of the lock and dam at Beattyville and the installation of a new lock and dam (No. 6) on the Kentucky. The badly deteriorated existing dam at Beattyville had been "cut down and floored over", the old foundation left in place after being pronounced sound and capable of supporting a new top. Meanwhile, with the dam crest and two upper steps removed pending completion of the new lock, boat traffic could safely cross the structure's reduced profile when there was an adequate flow of water.

The availability of stone to reconstruct the Beattyville lock and top off the dam became a problem when, on March 3, 1888, Major Stickney rejected, as being too high, the only bid received for supplying the stone. The order granting Stickney the authority to procure the stone directly (without using a civilian contractor), in essence, put Lieutenant Sibert in the quarry business for the first time. Within the collective experience of the Corps of Engineers, it was just another routine complication, not unexpected, when working on locks and dams in Eastern Kentucky in 1888. For Sibert, it was a valuable learning experience.

Fortunately, the engineer located some construction grade limestone very near the river and only four miles downstream from the dam. The landowner agreed to make it available for a royalty of 10 cents per cubic yard—if the corps did its own quarrying. In addition, the Army leased a five-acre site with river frontage, a third of a mile upstream from the quarry, for use as a cutting and storage yard. A tramway, one-half mile in length and capable of transporting the heavy rough cut quarried stone, linked the quarry to the cutting yard. Workers in the cutting yard shaped the stone to usable dimensions before it was barged to the construction site. Add quarry operations and the construction and operation of the mini-railway to Sibert's repertoire of engineering experience.

Despite unusually low water delaying until mid-April the arrival of the quarry plant by steamer, actual stone cutting was underway by mid-May. Although the quarry began operations "under circumstances far from favorable", it soon produced the finest building stone yet found on the Kentucky River. After the shortage of stone initially stalled construction, Captain Lockwood happily predicted rapid and uninterrupted delivery of enough quality stone to finish the lock.

In his contribution to the annual report of the Corps of Engineers, the captain emphasized the importance of the Kentucky River navigation system to the region: "As the people on the Upper Kentucky are for a portion of each year entire dependent upon the river to obtain supplies, and ship and receive whatever freight there may be, owing to the utter lack of roads that can be used for these purposes, it would appear advisable to make such improvements between Ford and Beattyville as may be necessary to insure the low-water navigation of that portion of the river." There was room for all sorts of improvements on the Kentucky River, and Sibert had made a good start.

Still, setbacks occurred as when construction fell behind schedule at the new lock and dam. Lack of stone was not the problem, the contractor having permission to quarry stone on government land immediately adjacent to the construction site, a distinct advantage. Never one to mince words, the problem, according to Lieutenant Sibert, resulted from poor management on the contractor's part. In March 1888, the officer predicted that the contractor would be unable to meet the August 31, 1888, deadline for completion of the work. At any rate, Lieutenant Sibert kept the pressure on, pushing the contractor in an effort to reduce the delay. [5]

Lockwood's first opportunity to observe his still new lieutenant came with the end of Stickney's temporary command, a chance to gauge his proficiency and potential. From his headquarters in Cincinnati, Lockwood immediately reviewed the Kentucky River projects in detail, subjecting Sibert's work to intense scrutiny. It was the kind of examination reserved for an officer being considered for a position of trust and a heap of additional responsibility.

After examining Sibert's meager records, mainly academics, the captain gave special attention to the new man's work habits and the results they had produced on the Kentucky River. As for the lieutenant's current performance, Sibert's launching of the independent quarrying operation in support of the Beattyville lock and dam construction deeply impressed Lockwood. There was nothing spectacular, but work on the Kentucky River system progressed steadily, notwithstanding adverse conditions. Flashes of initiative accented the lieutenant's performance, prompting Lockwood, newly promoted to major, to take a fairly large gamble with Sibert.

Why not place 1st Lieutenant William L. Sibert in charge of the Corps of Engineers' brand new stepchild? The Army was scheduled to inherit the problem-plagued slack water navigation system on Green and Barren rivers, no longer a problem for its former owner, the Commonwealth of Kentucky. In December 1888, official responsibility for the Green and Barren rivers shifted to Army engineers and one in particular—Sibert.

The major bet that Sibert's enthusiasm would trump his thin veneer of practical experience. He discovered that his subordinate was a quick learner on the Kentucky River and could think of no better place for the lieutenant's practical education to continue than the lock and dam disaster spread along the waters of the Green and Barren.

In his mind, the major downplayed the risk of his gamble with the inexperienced Sibert because, no matter what the lieutenant might try to do and regardless of the outcome, the navigation system could get no worse. His analysis of the existing situation led him to believe that, so far as the newly acquired locks and dams were concerned, the only way to go was up. And he sensed that the energetic Sibert had the capacity to do the necessary heavy lifting to get the job done.

His decision was dictated by circumstances and the necessity of utilizing available personnel to the best possible advantage, rather than some overriding belief that his new subordinate was an engineering diamond in the rough. Still, he thought Sibert capable of handling what could be considered a sort of independent command. The Corps of Engineers had a clear-cut goal on the Green and Barren rivers, one which could be precisely, almost scientifically, measured. Its execution promised to test the mettle of William Luther Sibert, Lieutenant of Engineers.

Chapter Six

THE WATERS OF GREEN RIVER VALLEY

An icy wind from the southwest swept and chilled the Texas deck of the sternwheeler, keeping most passengers snug within their cabins as the vessel made way against a moderately swift current. Thanks to abundant late autumn gulley washers throughout the valley reaching far into Kentucky, at the moment, Green River looked anything but green. Regardless of color, the river moved with authority unimaginable in early August when an extended dry spell sapped most of its current, inducing a lake-like calm.

The river was nowhere near flood stage, being only five feet or so above normal pool and well within normal fluctuations as pre-winter weather cycled out of the turbulent southwest. The precipitation it carried—rain, bone-chilling sleet, and even some early snow—inseparably joined all of that other transient river water, some draining from faraway Greensburg in South Central Kentucky, and from Kentucky's southernmost counties bordering Tennessee. Reddish-brown particulates from clay-based bottoms bordering the stream stained the crystalline rain to only a shade or two lighter than the wet, raw earth girding the river's flanks. Once dry, it awaited the mules and early spring plowing to begin another season. [1]

The captain of the *Evansville*, one of the packets to bear the name of the Indiana river town, had seen the polychromatic river in all its moods and colors, ranging from its namesake emerald green to a study in brown when the water looked substantial enough for walking. The waterway's rich caramel hue did not concern the riverman who was giving his full attention to another byproduct of fall rains: the increased velocity of the current, which relentlessly propelled the clay-colored torrent downstream. Much like headwinds that impede modern-day aircraft, the rain reinforced current reduced the riverboat's upstream rate of progress to a sedate four miles per hour, sometimes less.

Rank has its privileges: A valid concept in the U.S. Army in 1888, likewise a keenly enforced pecking order on the *Evansville* and every other packet plying America's inland waterways. Military privileges or not, the big fellow's size commanded attention. More than just big—physically imposing best described him—but without the excessive girth that marked many successful, gout-prone American businessmen of the period. At six-foot-four, he soared above the average American male of the day. Early farm labor in Alabama, topped off by the physical demands of four years at West Point, kept the 29-year-old trim and fit. Only to a practiced eye would his posture and self-assured bearing betray the military concealed beneath his civilian attire.

Yet, without pulling rank, the stranger discretely managed an invitation from the captain for a peaceful military incursion into the pilot house. Mounted well forward and above the Texas deck where the passenger normally belonged, the pilot's station gave the passenger a better view of the two rivers destined to occupy a significant portion of his professional and private life for almost half a century. Although riverboat captains, as a group, were zealous of their high station in life along America's western waterways in 1888, they were also reasonably good judges of character because their responsibilities required them to be, and the captain of the packet was no exception.

The character analysis began with a handshake, measured by the captain as firm but not overpowering, when he greeted the passenger boarding from the Evansville wharf. Recently arrived on an Ohio River steamer bound downstream from Cincinnati, his attire and quiet demeanor suggested literacy and the good manners of a gentleman. After a quick glance at the passenger manifest, the master of the *Evansville* failed to associate the unfamiliar name with any of the myriad business interests with which he was familiar in Bowling Green, the tall passenger's destination.

Once underway, the packet briefly retraced the stranger's previous route by churning upstream a short distance on the Ohio River, covering about 10 miles before finding the familiar mouth of the Green River. As the Ohio swerved gently to the left toward Three Mile Island, the packet tacked to the right, crossing to the south (or east) side of the river, and lining up for entry into the Green. Once the boat had safely completed the passage into the Green, the captain turned the wheel over to a trusted mate and relaxed a bit.

So far his guest had been quietly alert, and the time had come to engage him in conversation and determine whether it had been a mistake granting the stranger's request for admittance to the pilot house. (When rarely admitting a civilian to his *sanctum sanctorum*, the captain could tolerate a scoundrel if his stories were entertaining, but a bore quickly found himself back on a lower deck.) The big fellow beat him to it.

He thanked the captain for allowing him access to the pilot house, the nerve center of the riverboat, before unobtrusively pulling a packet of papers from his overcoat. Next he handed a letter, written on Army Corps of Engineers stationery, and a copy of his orders to his host. Without doubt, those orders installed him as the undisputed master of navigation on the Green and Barren rivers. And the captain knew it.

The river pilot's expression did not change as he inwardly congratulated himself on his ability to distinguish men of true importance and, hopefully, worth, from among the host of pretenders he routinely spotted among his passengers. Now the captain's turn, he took full advantage of being the first Green River riverboat captain to meet the officer, graciously welcoming him to the valley and tendering the best cigar he had to offer. It, the cigar, was the right thing to do.

Although the captain of the packet kept his thoughts to himself, he instinctively regarded the stranger as another boss with whom to contend and wondered how it would all come out, this new idea of putting the U.S. Army in charge of navigation on the Green and its major tributary, the Barren River. While willing to give the Corps of Engineers a fair chance, he recalled his own military days and was skeptical. As a 15-year-old in the waning days of the war, he had survived a nasty dose of what brand new lieutenants can do to make an awful situation even worse.

With a slight, involuntary shudder, the veteran river man could only speculate just exactly what this officer might do to make matters even worse than they already were for the packet trade on the Green and Barren rivers. Playing a key role in the navigation system, Barren River served the town of Bowling Green, 180 miles upstream from the Ohio and the mouth of the Green. The town was a principal reason, if not *the* principal reason, for initial development of the navigation system.

Although Bowling Green's upper wharf—called the boatlanding—marked the head of navigation on the Green River system, it had been a long 10 months since a trip from Bowling Green to Evansville (and vice versa) was possible without changing boats. That was not good for the river trade, both passenger and freight, at a time when railroads were making their presence felt.

Besides being a good judge of character, the captain was also somewhat of a diplomat who knew when it was prudent to roll out the red carpet and let nature take its course, hoping that a pattern would arise containing clues to guide his future conduct. That is why the tall stranger was invited to revisit the windy environs of the pilot house, as often as he wished, rather than share the steamer's Texas deck with fellow passengers. The stranger was grateful because there was no better place to view his newly acquired domain. Had the Army Corps of Engineers had such a rank within its table of organization, the captain knew he was in on the coronation of the King of the Green River Valley.

The lieutenant impressed the captain, however, as being down-to-earth rather than regal. Even if he wanted to, the officer found it difficult to flaunt his rank and status as a newly minted and most junior 1st lieutenant. Besides, blowing his own bugle was not his style. Rather than dominating the easy conversation between the two, the soldier in mufti politely listened, letting the older man do most of the talking. The officer seemed genuinely interested in hearing the captain's personal opinions of the river trade, its bad features as well as good. He was just as interested in what the older man could tell him about the game a skilled hunter might stalk among the forests of west Kentucky. Besides all of that, the captain grudgingly admitted to himself that he had experienced an instant liking for his new acquaintance.

First Lieutenant William Luther Sibert took it all in with utmost concentration, the same kind of interest he had exhibited in West Point's lecture halls and at the Army's post graduate engineering school on Long Island. He smiled slightly, reflecting on the distance he had covered, both geographically and culturally, since leaving his father's Etowah County farm in northeast Alabama.

An instant later his face brightened with a broad and genuine grin as he gazed upstream, perhaps appreciating his unique position for the first time: He was standing firmly on the threshold of his first real opportunity to exercise all of that newly-gained knowledge—on his own—(more or less) since completing the schooling the Army had so generously bestowed. Sibert gained his first practical river engineering experience on the Kentucky River where, understandably, his activities had been carefully monitored. It had also been his first exposure to the Commonwealth of Kentucky and its people. He liked both the work and the people and, far removed from headquarters in Cincinnati, he was elated at the opportunity to be his own boss in the Green River Valley. At least as much as his silver lieutenant's bar would allow. [2]

A lot of water flowed over the dams on the Green and Barren before the Army assumed control in 1888—the rivers turned turbulent and alien by petty politics and monopolistic greed as much as spring floods.

With cessation of hostilities following surrender of Confederate forces in 1865, things quickly returned to normal in Frankfort where the General Assembly of the Commonwealth of Kentucky wrestled with a perennial problem—insufficient funds for public works deemed beneficial to Kentuckians. And, not unlike most legislative bodies, policies and projects were often skewed to better serve the influential and politically powerful instead of the citizenry at large. On some occasions, however, it was possible to serve both constituencies equally well. Upgrading the slack water navigation system on the Green and Barren rivers—damaged and neglected during the war—was one of those happy occasions.

A workable navigation system on the rivers obviously benefited some special interests, such as the owners of the boats engaged in the packet trade. And, by extension, river trade bestowed a multitude of other benefits throughout the valley. Some tended to be nonessential, such as the ladies' shopping excursions to the big town of Evansville, while others were economically vital. A relatively cheap and dependable navigation system, capable of transporting people, products, and produce in and out of the valley, transformed the rivers into an economic aorta.

Without funds to initiate repairs and improvements the system sorely needed, the Legislature passed the buck and the risks and the financial burden of operating the navigation system to private enterprise. By offering a franchise to private investors who would be responsible for repairing, maintaining, and operating the system of locks and dams, Frankfort looked forward to a fiscal hand washing while hoping things would turn out in the best interests of the people of the valley.

A group of investors—including steamboat owners, businessmen, bankers, and merchants, mainly centered in Bowling Green (the up-river town with the most to lose through isolation should the river navigation system fail completely), was successful bidder for the navigation system franchise. They called themselves the Green and Barren Rivers Navigation Company. The company's aim was to keep the river system open for commerce—including all the freight and passengers the navigation company's packets could carry—and in the process ring up substantial profits.

It worked, at least for awhile, and may have gone on indefinitely but for what critics perceived as palpable overreaching by those enterprising riverine rascals who wanted all, or at least most of the river commerce for themselves. Other boat owners had little choice: they either paid the navigation company's tolls for locking through the system, or their packets left to find another river to run. Meanwhile, the navigation company's packets plied the Green and Barren free of charge, a big competitive advantage. The added costs of lockage soon drove competing packets from the river, creating a stern-wheeling monopoly for the navigation company.

That monopoly splashed over farmers, loggers, merchants, and the ladies bound for Evansville, all of whom had to pay the company's tariffs for freight and passengers—or walk. Still, the navigation company may have successfully steamed into the early 20th century but for the power wielded on Capitol Hill by an ex-Union general, Don Carlos Buell. During the Civil War, Buell proved himself to be one of the more able Union commanders in the West and was credited with securing Kentucky, a hotly contested border state, for the Union. He also saved Grant by his 11th hour arrival at Shiloh.

Based on his wartime experiences, Buell recognized what he perceived to be a golden opportunity to make his mark as a captain of industry in the Bluegrass State. Because of its close proximity to mammoth coal deposits, Buell proposed to establish an iron foundry at Airdrie, a Green River village in Muhlenberg County. The second part of the equation was the presence of the slack water navigation system and its promise of cheap, efficient hauling. Low transportation rates were essential in the iron industry, which consumed heavy, bulky raw materials before transporting its equally heavy and often cumbersome finished products to market. But there was a problem.

Operators of barges and packets, which would otherwise serve the iron works, faced high tolls for using the navigation company's locks, charges that had to be passed on to shippers. Meanwhile, the navigation company's own boats were exempt, but the freight charges excessive. The resulting monopoly on water-borne commerce, presided over by the Green and Barren Rivers Navigation Company, hit the ex-Union general where it hurt most—his wallet. Like all shippers requiring water transportation, Buell's iron enterprise had only two options, both of which required him to do costly business with the navigation company. He could either operate his own boats and pay exorbitant tolls for use of the company's locks, or pay the equally forbidding freight charges for shipping on vessels owned by the navigation company.

The former Union general, unaccustomed to being economically abused, mounted a campaign which soon turned into a crusade to unseat the navigation company from its franchised position of power and restore competition to the river trade. It took a long time, but he succeeded even though he never smelted, much less shipped, that first pig of unforged iron.

Making a long and sometimes bitter story short, Congress provided the final solution by throwing money at the problem. After Uncle Sam bought out the holders of the franchise for $135,000 in 1888, the Commonwealth of Kentucky turned the slack water navigation system on Green and Barren rivers over to the Army.

Actually, when the U.S. House of Representatives and Senate passed the Rivers and Harbors Bill, the appropriation set aside to finance transition of the existing system from private ownership into the jurisdiction of the Army Corps of Engineers was in a total amount of $150,000. After buying out the navigation company, the remaining $15,000 financed the Army's first efforts to survey the system's deteriorated condition and begin to fix it.

The Civil War, labeled The War Between the States by those with Confederate sympathies, had been unkind to the slack water navigation system serving the Green and Barren rivers. The effects of damage inflicted by Confederate raiders lingered and the neglected maintenance of the system, both during the war and the years thereafter, was even more devastating. William Luther Sibert's orders were clear: Fix it! [3]

Lieutenant Sibert had been thoroughly briefed and was well aware of the recent history of commerce on the Green and Barren rivers before he boarded the steamer with a ticket to Evansville. At the busy Indiana river town, he changed boats, walking up the gangplank of the *Evansville*, the town's namesake packet. The officer was prepared for trouble, not with pistol and saber—only a common sense approach to remedies for some acute river problems.

He knew there were potential hornet nests, the understandable residue of the rivers' change in management. Even before leaving the Ohio River's table top flat shoreline, as the captain lined up the packet for the long graceful approach across the Ohio, and into the mouth of the not so Green River, the officer secretly vowed to avoid the hornets with diplomacy whenever possible. If not, he would rely on truth and candor for his shield.

The Green, shoreline to shoreline, is a smaller river than the Ohio, born a heavyweight at Pittsburgh, the often unruly progeny of the turbulent marriage of the Allegheny and the Monongahela. Still, lots of deep holes interspersed along the Green's main channel lent some credence to early claims by Kentuckians (always on the lookout for bragging rights) that the Green was the deepest little river in North America. [4]

Regardless of depth, and oftentimes in spite of it, the Green, like the Kentucky River, became an early and extremely vital economic link between Kentucky's farmers and foresters and the string of markets scattered along America's western frontier, New Orleans in particular. That was before locks and dams were built in the mid-19th century, creating a slack water navigation system reaching from the Ohio as far east as Bowling Green. On the eve of the Civil War, the town's boatlanding was the head of navigation on Big Barren River, one of numerous reasons for the town's strategic importance in the war.

Sibert planned to establish the Engineer Office, the administrative and engineering headquarters from which the Army Corps of Engineers would commence operating the Green and Barren rivers navigation system, at Bowling Green, 180 rambling river miles upstream from the Ohio. Located at the extreme eastern edge of navigation, the town served as the county seat of Warren County.

As the packet moved smartly from the Ohio into Green's broad mouth, Sibert knew that a series of five separate lock and dam systems stood between Evansville and Bowling Green, each with a set of problems begging for solutions. Even before the Engineer Office officially opened, Sibert worried over his limited budget. The frugal officer managed to turn the trip to his brand new duty station into an unofficial initial inspection of facilities he was now charged with maintaining, operating and, where possible, improving, all in the interest of commerce. Despite its unofficial nature, the young lieutenant's firsthand sortie upriver confirmed earlier reports to the Corps of Engineers which described the system as dilapidated. As he journeyed farther and farther upstream, Sibert began to think that the description may have been highly charitable.

The sternwheeler chugged all of five and a half miles up the Green while, except for one sweeping bend, the smaller river ran roughly parallel to the Ohio. Then, the Green seemed to break its flood plain embrace with the larger river and turn seriously south on about as straight a course as it ever gets, another three miles to the village of Spottsville. In passing, the officer observed Negro Creek, Race Creek, and Opossum Creek offering their modest contributions to the Green.

The relatively straight stretch gave Sibert his first glimpse of navigational facilities already officially entrusted to his care and soon to be subject to much closer scrutiny. Green River Lock and Dam No. 1 gradually grew larger, looming over the packet, which had slowed to a standstill. The lock itself hugged the western side of the river, the accompanying dam extending from the lock across the river where it was anchored into the Green's eastern shore. [5]

With no boats locking through from upstream, Sibert and the *Evansville* had the river all to themselves. The lower lock gate opened—hand powered by a capstan that furnished the lockkeeper and his assistant at least a little mechanical advantage. As they bent to their task, pushing against the distal ends of long wooden levers, they circled the pivoting capstan, looking much like a two-man carousel.

Attached to the capstan was a huge iron gear. It sprouted formidable teeth and was part of the proximal end of a long iron wand attached to the gate. As the teeth bit into the capstan gear, ever so slowly, the wands pushed open the downstream gate, inviting the steamer to carefully enter. Once the gate fully opened, the captain deftly maneuvered the craft into the lock chamber where lines secured the boat while the men turned and reversed the capstan, closing the gate just as slowly as it had opened. The process never varied and set the stage for part two of upstream lock passage. Spillways were opened to admit water from the upstream pool to the lock chamber.

For those passengers aboard a riverboat for the first time, the locking experience proved interesting, even exciting, especially for children. From a steamer's main deck, one had to tilt his head upward to see the top of the lock walls which were not far removed from the craft's port and starboard rails. The captain (and Sibert) saw things differently from the elevated wheelhouse where a splendid view beyond lock wall was possible, if they looked in that direction.

The captain normally directed his attention downward—at water level—making sure proper tension was maintained on the lines so that the packet did not scrape lock walls. And if any passengers tended toward the claustrophobic, those moments at the lower pool level could be trying with lock walls seeming to press inward from a few uncomfortable feet away before the welcome ascent began.

If those passengers traveling the inland waterways for the first time were thinking in scholarly terms, they immediately recognized passage through Lock No. 1 on Green River as a primer, if not a mini-seminar. It taught, by actual performance, just exactly how a slack water navigation system worked while playing a key role in linking the eastern seaboard with the developing west, as well as binding the industrial North with the agrarian South—not a bad thing to do only 23 years after Appomattox.

Manpower alone levered open the spillway, thereby introducing water from the higher upper pool into the lock chamber at a measured rate. The lieutenant, of course, knew all about locks and slack water navigation, and was not alarmed when major whirlpools began to bubble down the flanks of the boat. Barely perceivable at first, the 120-foot sternwheeler rose slowly within the confines of the lock chamber without benefit of steam and certainly not electrical power. Neither was available—or needed—at Spottsville in 1888, where garden variety gravity and the wondrous power of the water were routinely capable of raising 150 tons of riverboat almost 11 feet from the lower pool to the next level.

Water in the lock chamber soon reached the precise level of Lock No. 1's upper pool, prompting the pair of lock men to close the spillway and direct their energy to manning the upstream capstan and opening the lock's upper gate. With a wave to the lock crew, the captain ordered the roustabouts to cast off the lines as the driveshaft engaged and steam slowly began to turn the big paddle wheel at the stern. It furnished just enough push to permit a gingerly exit from the tightly confining lock walls.

First time passengers, including a young salesman from Evansville with a roundtrip ticket to Bowling Green, may have wondered how that lock would work on the return downstream, going downhill on the Green, so to speak. He had heard stories of packets shooting the dams when floodwaters topped the structures, providing ample depth above the barrier for the boats to cross over safely. Usually. Woe to the pilot who read the river wrong and holed the wooden bottom of his craft on the unyielding stone cap of a dam. He could only hope the boat would not hang on the dam and that he could maneuver the craft into shore and shallow water to take some of the sting out of the sinking sure to follow.

Had he been asked by a fellow passenger, Sibert would explain that a downstream trip through Lock No. 1, and any other lock for that matter, was exactly the same mechanically, only in reverse order. A steamer bound downstream entered the lock chamber after a spillway filled it level with the upper pool. After the upper gate closed, the lower spillway opened, evacuating water from the lock chamber until it reached the level of the downstream pool. Then, the lower gate opened for the steamer's exit. The system was again gravity operated with an assist from the lock crew manually opening and closing the gates and spillways.

Without a basic understanding of the river's profile and the physics and mechanics involved, strangers to river transportation often wondered why locks and dams were necessary in the first place. To the uninformed, they looked like another government boondoggle or worse. When quizzed by a passenger, Sibert explained that all boats, and particularly the larger commercial vessels, require a channel deep enough to allow travel from one place to another without running aground, without striking rock formations, gravel bars, mud banks, and other obstructions hidden beneath the water's surface. At best, striking an underwater hazard impeded travel and could result in sinking the packet. And on naturally shallow stretches along this very deep river, rapids openly advertised their obvious dangers.

Dams, according to the engineer, are designed to capture and back up water, storing it in pools to increase the river's depth. The dams marshaled sufficient water to cover obstructions and create a defined channel within which commercial craft could operate with reasonable safety. Sibert often relied on analogy, describing locks as river-style stair steps designed to allow vessels to rather effortlessly go up or down between river pools (created by dams) at different elevations.

In theory, so long as the rivers had ample water and a few men to open and close the gates and spillways, the slack water system on Green and Barren worked within the limits imposed by Mother Nature. That is, barring unforeseen calamities, such as the Civil War and other altogether foreseeable problems caused by a combination of poor initial construction, shoddy maintenance, and a large measure of entrepreneurial greed.

At least, the officer thought, the Spottsville facility worked, and the lockmaster knew what he was doing, a real plus. Another plus was the Green's continuation on a relatively straight and generally southern course, tacking ever so slightly to the east for more than five miles before abruptly lurching due east; east that is, if you straightened a series of bends, the sharpness of each a challenge calculated to keep river pilots alert.

Mason's Bend, the first, sharpest, and most demanding turn, required the packet to literally double back or run aground. The Birk City landing, another seven miles upstream, afforded northeast Daviess County access to river trade. The final bend in the series involved an acute turn to the right, more doubling back before the Green straightened a bit and adjusted its course to the southwest.

The same Green River carried the same brown water, only the bends so recently short and sharp, tended to be long and gentle and, for a river which refused to go straight, it at least tried as the packet made landings at the mouth of Panther Creek, at Delaware, at the mouth of Deer Creek, and at Ashbyburg. The huge bend between Delaware and Ashbyburg measured 30 miles upstream, shifting eastward so gradually and regularly that passengers unfamiliar with the river thought the passage had been charted with a straightedge. Offloading freight and a few passengers occurred at numerous landings—Rangers, Quinn, and Steamport among them.

Roustabouts loaded a fresh wood supply for the packet's boiler at Ashbyburg landing, only a mile downstream from the mouth of the Pond River. The master of the *Evansville* noted that they were less than 10 miles to Lock and Dam No. 2, shared by Calhoun on the north bank (the county seat of McLean County) and smaller Rumsey on the south shore. [6]

Both good news and bad news greeted Sibert's arrival at Calhoun where he again witnessed the captain expertly guide the boat into the lock chamber and the lockmaster direct a flawless operation of gates and spillways to raise the steamer another 14 feet to the upper pool. On the positive side, the packet had covered 63 miles upstream from the mouth of the Green. However, the bad news could not be concealed from the engineer, still in transit to his yet to be established headquarters in Bowling Green.

Just an eyeball inspection, of course, but it mesmerized Lieutenant Sibert. He found it extremely difficult to remove his gaze from the landside wall of the lock chamber where masonry was badly cracked and threatening to fall. Only makeshift anchorages to stone-filled cribs delayed the imminent collapse of the wall. With some effort, the officer shifted his attention to the riverside wall of the lock, finding its condition no better and perhaps worse: The wall bowed out, encroaching on the lock chamber, and like its companion on the landside, threatened a catastrophic failure at any time. [7]

Because the boat entered from the downstream pool and buoyed slowly upward on water flooding the lock chamber from the upstream pool, the engineer got a good bottom-to-top look at the chamber walls. Certainly not a pretty sight, but the infirmed lock worked surprisingly well. The transiting steamer had only one immediate problem: Avoid clipping the outward bow in the riverwall. Even a slight bumping, Sibert feared, would trigger an avalanche of stone into the lock chamber and onto the steamer's deck.

Ever observant, he noted how the boat avoided the bow by steering extremely close to the landwall. The lieutenant immediately commended the captain on his piloting skills and the ability to steer the boat within inches of the landwall without a scratch and with no room for error. The officer's newly found friend smiled indulgently, explaining that hugging the landwall had become the normal way to handle Lock No. 2; the bowed riverwall had long been a hazard and was getting worse. Only half joking, the captain expressed hope that the moment had not yet arrived for the wall's plunge into the lock.

Carefully measuring the inches to avoid lock walls and adjusting rudder angles and speed to safely negotiate Mason's Bend and similar knotty stretches where the Green reversed itself were among the more visible signs marking a truly skilled river pilot. Other skills, produced by the melding of good eyesight, precise handling of wheel and throttle, and an abundance of experience, were paramount, particularly on the Green during the fall and winter of 1888-89. There was a reason.

The purely manmade assets of the navigation system, the locks and dams and their appurtenances, were not the only objects of neglect dating back to damages sustained during the war. The river itself had been largely ignored, paid court by its operators only when absolutely necessary, and sometimes not even then. A rising population of highly dangerous obstacles to river traffic resulted throughout its 180 miles of navigable water. Some objects were overt with many, many more covert: Snags, gravel bars, and wrecks of unlucky riverboats were major offenders.

With no more neglected locks and dams to pique his interest over the next 45 miles, Sibert witnessed Rough River merging with the Green at Livermore where a ferry crossed both streams. From there, it was 20 miles south to South Carrollton landing where the Green turned southeast and a sequence of usually long, lazy bends, a good stretch of water for a person new to the river, like Sibert, to quietly contemplate. Eager to learn of its often hidden nuances, he observed how the captain piloted the boat, first near one shoreline, then to the opposite bank, and at other times pushing straight up the middle of the liquid carpet magically moving the packet upstream. [8]

The snags seemed easiest to understand: large tree trunks randomly stuck along the river with one end projecting above the surface, a menace to steamboats. The captain explained that a concealed snag, not visible above the surface after a rise in the river level, became an even more dangerous lance, fully capable of holing a wooden hull without warning. Long segments of the shoreline sprouted snags of all sizes and descriptions, even though the water was running high. Not even the captain could guess what was just beneath the surface of the Green.

The navigation channel must be kept clear of impediments to freely moving boat traffic in order for the system to properly function. Water must be deep enough to keep boats from running aground and all obstructions, snags for the most part, must be removed. Because snags qualified as a major problem on the inland waterways, a special boat evolved, specifically outfitted to remove the hazards and unimagina-

tively classified as a snag boat. A snag boat is equipped to pull inva-
sive logs and trees from the river and store them on deck. When fully
loaded, the boat transports the debris to dry land for disposal without
harming the navigation system. Boat crews daily faced difficult and
dangerous work while removing snags.

The Army engineer continued to mentally catalog countless snags
on both banks of the river—a clear indication that the river had not
seen the services of a snag boat in a long time. The captain chimed in
occasionally, voicing great concern for the safety of the boat, unhappy
with the palisades of snags, any of which could cause a disaster. The veteran river man's genuine apprehension deeply impressed Sibert, who
would waste no time awarding a contract for construction of a suitable
snag-boat. Once the new boat was in operation, he estimated it would
take from two to three years, working during low water seasons, to
remove all of the existing snags on the Green and Barren rivers.

The pilot at the helm of the *Evansville* had no choice but to rely upon
his experience and familiarity with the rivers when seeking the course
of the channel through the long-neglected waters. Depth was the big
question and the captain kept his own mental chart as current as possible. It had to be up-to-date because the river never ceased changing
and, during high water periods, the muscular Green was capable of
forming a gravel bar to block a channel almost overnight. The successful captain earned his considerable pay by knowing when and where
an unadvertised obstacle was likely to occur.

Both the Green and Barren rivers had depth problems—their channels often reduced by shifting gravel and sand bars and the natural
accumulation of silt. Sibert knew what was required to maintain a
channel consistently deep enough for the traffic—a boat even more
specialized than a snag boat. The system sorely needed a dredge, a
vessel especially designed to deepen navigation channels by scooping
mud, sand, and gravel from the riverbed and eventually depositing it
ashore. Sibert discovered an old dredge once used by the navigation
company, and now Army property. Inspection revealed that the dredging apparatus was in working order but the boat was no longer seawor-
thy, forcing Sibert to improvise: During his first six months on the job,
the engineer had a new hull constructed to accommodate the salvaged
dredging machinery and then began an aggressive dredging program
to keep the channels open.

Boats required for reconstruction of the damaged locks—two decked barges to transport building stone and two derrick boats to hoist materials—soon joined Sibert's navy. An ungainly lot, all were needed if Sibert had any hope of restoring and improving the navigation system during his tutelage. [9]

Although the *Evansville* was slowed by the swift current, the high water bestowed important benefits on the steamer. The river deepened from shoreline to shoreline, adding a few extra feet to channel depth to safely cover gravel bars and hundreds of snags. Along parts of the river where nature's silt had trimmed precious inches from channel depth, the extra water made the pilot's job easier.

The packet was 99 miles upstream from the mouth of the Green when the veteran pilot pointed in the direction of Airdrie Hill on the river's west bank. An abandoned iron furnace sat silent, having never produced any iron for its owner, Don Carlos Buell. It did, however, spur the ex-Union general's final and successful campaign to break the grip of the navigation company on the valley's river-borne commerce. But for Buell's efforts, the Green and Barren navigation system would not be an Army Corps of Engineers endeavor, nor would Lieutenant Sibert be riding a steamer upstream to Bowling Green. [10]

When the captain asked Sibert if he had ever seen paradise, the younger man answered with a quizzical look directed at the man behind the wheel. The pilot responded with a grin and pointed to starboard, the west side of the river, the location of another nondescript river landing less than a mile upstream from the abandoned furnace. It didn't look like much but played a key role in the economy of eastern Muhlenberg County and southern Ohio County just across the river. The name of the landing: Paradise. Its identification, the captain explained, never failed to register a smile.

At any given point, the river's eclectic collection of turns and bends might send the steamer north or south and, the captain noted, its bow even pointed west for a half mile or so just upstream from Davenport Landing. All the while, the Green steadily progressed eastward even though it sometimes seemed to be taking one step forward and two steps back along its serpentine course. [11]

Thus far, Lieutenant Sibert considered the trip a positive experience, even as he took note of the numerous problems facing him. Sibert intended to fully master the Green and the Barren rivers so that the streams might better serve the people of the valley. He had gotten along well with his fellow passengers and had found in the captain a kindred spirit who was all wrapped up in the future of river commerce. The quality of that future, to a great degree, depended upon the officer's success (or failure) in managing 180 miles of sometimes treacherous water.

Optimism ebbed and smiles vanished when the steamer pushed another three miles past Davenport Landing and, for the first time, Sibert saw Lock and Dam No. 3 on Green River. The captain warned Sibert to expect no smooth lifting of the packet from the lower pool almost 17 feet to the upper pool because Lock No. 3 didn't work. It choked off river traffic, a fact covered in the officer's briefing. Since the previous January 2, when a wall of the lock collapsed, the *Evansville's* skipper always terminated his trips upstream by making a landing immediately downstream from Lock No. 3. [12]

For almost a year the lock had posed an impenetrable barrier to navigation. Regardless of his skill and the worthiness of the packet, the captain could go no farther upstream. The closed lock gates barred all river traffic, regardless of size and, even if opened, debris from the collapsed wall filled and effectively blocked the lock chamber. With no other choice, all passengers disembarked and, while most of them rode carriages along the bank to the upper pool where another packet awaited, Sibert turned and strolled toward the lock and its land wall.

The officer briskly reconnoitered the entire length of the lock before returning to the downstream gate, only to repeat the route more slowly, lost in his thoughts. A careful observer noticed perceptible shakes of his head, one after another, measuring his deliberate march along the crest of the land wall. From there, the engineer viewed the lock's river wall, or at least that part still standing. The major portion of the masonry bulwark had loosened and plunged haphazardly into the lock chamber, a highly effective blockade to river traffic. The lieutenant grimaced, seeing his first major problem firsthand, a troublesome situation he had until then only read about.

In unprofessional and nontechnical terms, the lock at Rochester was a mess! An engineer's nightmare! This was the chokepoint on river commerce and transportation in the valley. Whether steaming upstream or downstream, it made no difference: When a packet reached Rochester—located 108 miles upstream from the Ohio and 72 miles

81

downstream from Bowling Green on the Barren—the boat had to stop, tie up, and be completely unloaded—every passenger and all of the freight. Then, river men depended on horse or mule drawn freight wagons and carriages to join the parts of the now bifurcated navigation system. [13]

While the *Evansville* tied up and began unloading, another packet, the *Bowling Green*, namesake of the upstream town where the navigation system terminated, made landing in the upstream pool, likewise unloading cargo and passengers ticketed downstream. Once tied up, the two packets literally exchanged their burdens, both passengers and freight, then turned to retrace their respective routes from Rochester.

Even as the Rochester lock collapsed, luck crowned the navigation company when two of its steamers, the *Bowling Green* and the *Ida*, were trapped in the upstream pools. They remained free to run between Bowling Green and Rochester while the downstream boats covered Evansville to Rochester. The portage made it possible to ride the packets all the way from Evansville to Bowling Green and vice versa—except for the Rochester transfer and carriage ride.

From the masters of the packets on down to the roustabouts, favorable weather and on-time arrivals at Rochester answered prayers. Good weather and good timing reduced the problems associated with the exchange of cargoes. It remained, however, a laborious time-consuming process. Passengers always expressed relief when boarding the next boat beyond the Rochester Dam. Besides the expense and lost time, the portage involved additional hazards to passengers and cargo alike, depending on such variables as the weather, the skill of the drovers and cargo handlers, and the stage of the river. The river trade could ill afford an irritating delay as it faced growing competition from the railroads and a slowly improving network of roads.

Lieutenant Sibert was not the first army officer to encounter problems at Rochester. In 1861, Confederate General Simon Boliver Buckner's orders were clear: Deny the invading Union Army the use of the Green and Barren navigation system. Before encamping 1,500 troops at Skilesville, just across the Green from Rochester, Buckner's troops jammed the lock at Greencastle—the only lock on Barren River—with huge rocks that would be difficult to remove.

Leaving nothing to chance, destruction of the Rochester lock, some 65 miles downstream on the Green, promised to put the final seal on the navigation system. The Rochester lock lay conveniently in range of Rebel artillery at Skilesville. A single cannon was trained on the locks and only three shots—all solid shot—boomed across the river. Highly accurate, the first ball tore several stone blocks from the lock, the second gouged another hole in the chamber wall, and the third struck one of the gates, damaging a hinge. The gate sagged but did not collapse. Meeting no resistance, the Confederates decided to save their precious cannon balls and finish the task with hand-set explosives. Engineers began drilling holes in the stone walls to accommodate the dynamite charges.

At that point, a Skilesville miller, fearing that blasting might also destroy the dam (the source of the water power used to operate his mills), arranged a parley. He found the Confederate general, a fellow Kentuckian from Hart County, sympathetic, yet bound by orders to render the lock useless to Union forces. Once he had secured a sympathetic ear, the miller, Silas House Brewer, pointed out a large raft of logs approaching the lock from upstream and proceeded to explain how the lock could be put out of commission without destructive blasting. General Buckner endorsed the idea and ordered his engineers to cease drilling.

Simple in concept, the plan required some genuine Johnny Reb sweat to implement. After first closing off the downstream gates, the locks were filled to capacity with the newly cut logs—still green and extremely heavy. Randomly jammed into the chamber in no discernible pattern, they formed a maze that would defy quick and easy dismantling by a shore party, if a Union gunboat steamed into the picture. Should that happen, Brewer explained to Buckner, the lower lock gate could be opened—triggering release of a torrent of logs capable of punching holes in the hull and sinking the gunboat. (So far as can be determined, this defensive system was never put to a test.)

The fact that the Rochester lock was spared from demolition was good news up and down the river, the logs being subsequently removed and the lock partially repaired when packet service resumed after hostilities ended. Regardless of origin—whether faulty initial construction, the Rebel bombardment, or slipshod postwar maintenance—the accumulated and chronic ills of the Rochester lock and dam became the exclusive responsibility of William Luther Sibert, Lieutenant of Engineers, U.S. Army, in December 1888. [14]

As he boarded the *Bowling Green* on the upstream side of the dam, Sibert knew he had just observed his most pressing problem, the ruined Rochester lock. In Rochester's upper pool, the trip returned to the routine, about 10 miles on a relatively straight eastbound course toward Mining City before a long graceful hook to the north around Little Bend. The journey continued north for another 10 miles, a relatively straight run, except for one prominent bend. Then, the river arced over, passing Cromwell Island, before plunging to the southeast, fairly straight except for a horseshoe bend at Logansport. Sibert counted more than 13 miles of river from Cromwell Island to Morgantown (county seat of Butler County), where he observed a busy wharf, even with trade slowed by the Rochester bottleneck.

Located less than six miles upstream from the Morgantown wharf, Lock and Dam No. 4 dominated the picturesque river village of Woodbury, being the final navigation facility in existence on Green River in 1888. Its pioneer builders strategically located it in 1839, but not for the purpose of extending navigation on the upper Green, even though it did no harm to that cause.

There was in 1839 a much bigger fish to fry and that was Bowling Green, by far the largest town in the region. Whether you labeled its location at the eastern edge of west Kentucky or in south central Kentucky, long before it had L & N Railroad service, Bowling Green became the region's predominant trading center. Located on Big Barren River (just Barren River in more modern times), it became home base for the most vocal supporters of the early slack water navigation system on Green and Barren rivers. For years, log rafts and flatboats hauling local products floated downstream, but that was not enough. For a nucleus of influential business and political leaders, the objective was nothing less than reliable steamboat connections between the town and the markets of New Orleans and all other landings and communities in between.

Current warts notwithstanding, the slack water navigation system and its five sets of locks and dams on the Green and Barren rivers furnished concrete evidence that those early Bowling Green captains of industry succeeded. From the 1840s, steamboats connected Bowling Green with New Orleans when war was not raging and the boiler didn't blow.

It was almost winter, with no leaves on the trees, when Sibert stood at the upper gate of the Woodbury lock, briefly off the *Bowling Green* to stretch legs and inspect the lock. He saw the mouth of Barren River, approximately one-half mile to the east, which daily poured thousands of gallons of water into Green River at the extreme northwestern tip of Warren County, not far from the Riverside community. The Barren is the Green's largest tributary although, based on volume, it could be forcefully argued that geographers got it backwards. In 1888, a short ferry ride would take a traveler from Warren County across Barren River to Butler County and vice versa. [15]

It was the nearby presence of Barren River that largely dictated the location of the lock and dam at Woodbury. The reason was simple: Big Barren led directly to Bowling Green and, like the Green, its waters had to be restrained and pooled if the channel was to reach Bowling Green. As for the upper reaches of the Green, they led into Edmonson County, past Brownsville and within a short walk of the historic natural entrance to Mammoth Cave. Lean budgets and the presence of shallows and rapids along its course through Edmonson County, even after the dam at Woodbury pooled water in that direction, barred navigation on the upper Green for another dozen years. [16]

Woodbury deserves more than a mere mention although the banks and stores are long gone from the river village. The view from Government Hill remains the same, the yellow brick houses built by the Corps of Engineers now housing a museum. Just up the road is the birthplace of Captain Thomas Henry "Behind the Lines" Hines, the most daring of Confederate raiders and spies who tried time and again to fight the Civil War on the Yankees' home turf.

It is uncertain if the old business building still standing near the waterfront once housed a store opened by an itinerant Jewish peddler who settled at Woodbury to rear his family, including Admiral Claude C. Bloch, commander of America's battleship fleet in 1935—a time when battleships still ruled the oceans and the relatively new aircraft carriers were more a curiosity than a decisive weapon of warfare. The village thrived for one simple reason: River trade was king and Green River Lock and Dam No. 4 made it possible for the packets to reach Bowling Green for about 125 years. Today, the lock and what is left of the dam at Woodbury are highly instructive and help immensely in fully understanding where Sibert began and the progress and contributions he made after 1888—when he first viewed the ruins of the Rochester lock on Green River. A bit of regression is required, but is worth it.

In the 40 years following 1888—including that significant long-term stopover (1907-1914) to pour concrete at Gatun in the Canal Zone—the mathematical schoolboy made enormous strides as did the engineering fraternity in general. Sibert posed the antithesis of that old adage suggesting extreme difficulty teaching old dogs—or engineers—new tricks. While treasuring past learning, he willingly learned any new tricks which might better prepare him for an uncertain future. This ingrained attitude—obsessive devotion to the ever-ascending learning curve—is graphically illustrated by Sibert's pilgrimage from log cabin dams forward to his championing of a new kind of structure built of steel-reinforced concrete.

Only 20 years after encountering the collapsed lock at Rochester, Sibert pored over final plans for the locks and spillways at Gatun in the Canal Zone—all to be built of steel-reinforced concrete. Also, it took Sibert's 1928 endorsement before construction was initiated on America's domestic monolith of concrete—Boulder Dam. Sibert's experience with such engineering began with work on structures best described as Abe Lincoln-style log cabins of the submerged variety.

Timber crib dams, the 19th century standard, were scattered along America's inland waterways, usually built to create deeper pools of water to aid steamboat navigation or to turn water wheels to power gristmills and sawmills. Surprisingly, numerous timber crib dams remain extant, some still serving their intended purposes. Most have been destroyed or retired from service into various stages of deterioration. Regrettably, some cases may soon be terminal. In Volume 15 of *Ohio Valley Historical Archaeology—the Journal of the Symposium on Ohio Valley Urban and Historical Archaeology* (2000)—Donald B. Ball of Louisville, wrote a comprehensive description and report on the conditions of Green River Dam No. 4 at Woodbury.

Construction of the Woodbury Lock and Dam was completed in 1839, only 30 years after Lincoln's birth in a crude log cabin near Hodgenville, Kentucky. With departure of the Indians, stockade forts were no longer necessary, but Kentuckians were well versed in the use of logs for all sorts of construction—homes, barns, bridges, etc.—as they burned uncounted cords of timber for cooking and heating their homes. Originally covered with forests, the abundant wood made fine building material. It was relatively easy to work wood into useful forms ranging from split shake shingles for cabin roofs to spoons when silver was in short supply.

The Woodbury Dam created a pool of water deep enough for steamboat traffic to navigate up Barren River about halfway to Bowling Green. The lock at Woodbury was capable of lifting Bowling Green–bound packets about 16 ½ feet from the downstream pool and that same lock could gently lower packets to the lower pool to continue a downstream course. The dam, of course, pooled the water and made it all possible.

From where it joins the river wall of the lock, the Woodbury Dam stretches 408 feet across the Green, according to Mr. Ball. It capped off the downstream pool originating at the Rochester dam, then pushed the upper pool deep into the Barren. When the Commonwealth of Kentucky built the original slack water navigation system from the Ohio River to Bowling Green, plans called for five timber crib dams to accomplish the task. All constructed between 1835 and 1841, their durability is surprising.

Green River Dam No. 1 at Spottsville, the original timber crib construction now topped off with a concrete cap, remains in service. At Calhoun (Dam No. 2), the original timber crib dam was finally removed and replaced by a concrete structure in 1956 that is still in operation. After Sibert reopened the Rochester lock in 1890, the facility remained in service until deactivation in September 1981. The Rochester Dam remains, but greatly altered by tons of large limestone blocks used to repair the structure.

Dam No. 1, at Greencastle on Barren River, is another timber crib design dating from 1841 and now capped with concrete. Although heavily damaged by time and floodwaters, it continues to contain its upstream pool reaching to the Bowling Green Boatlanding. The lock has not operated since failure of the Woodbury Dam robbed it of its downstream pool.

Study of the Woodbury Dam, victim of the 1965 breach (starkly visible) and stubbornly hanging on without any maintenance whatsoever over the past 48 years, furnishes a rare opportunity to observe and understand the way timber crib dams—the backbone of the slack water navigation system—were put together.

Imagine dozens of sets of king-size Lincoln Logs cabins strung end to end across Green River, and you can visualize the dam as it begins to take shape. These log cabins—cribs in engineers' jargon—are without the notches that make it easy for small fingers to assemble miniature versions of cabins and forts. These cabins—fashioned from logs cut locally—have neither roofs nor chinking, and each crib is interlocked with adjoining cribs. At Woodbury, they come in various rectangular sizes, two of which were measured by Mr. Ball: interior measurements of 8.75 feet by 6.5 feet for the smaller, and a larger size, 8.5 feet by 8.33 feet.

The first course of cribs sits on the stream bed and is 6.6 feet high, running from the river wall of the lock to the opposite shoreline. Additional rows of cribs—parallel to and interlocking with the rows already installed—parade across the river, as many as six lines in all. The lines of interlocking cribs widen the dam base to approximately 49 feet, as measured between the upstream and downstream toes of the structure. Sandstone rock originally filled the base cribs at Woodbury, with limestone added by later repairs.

Without the notches used to mate the logs of conventional pioneer cabins and the Lincoln Logs models, long iron spikes locked the dam logs together. Mr. Ball measured these retaining pins, which came in two lengths, 30-inch and 36-inch, each three-fourths of an inch in diameter. He was unable to identify the wood used in the cribs, but it would largely depend upon the species of locally available trees. The second course of cribs was centered on the base cribs and added 9.8 feet to the dam's height. As they ascended, these cribs narrowed uniformly—a rough-cut pyramid—also filled with rock. A cross section of the pyramidal structure produced by the stacked cribs covered about 563 square feet. With a length of 408 feet, the completed dam contained almost 230,000 cubic feet of rock fill. To finish off the structure, workers spiked wide wooden planking into place to form a sloping apron covering both the upstream and downstream sides of the pyramid.

Except for a concrete abutment installed on the bank opposite the lock (probably in the 1930s), Dam No. 4 remained basically unchanged from its original construction in 1839 until it washed out in 1965. Except for Sibert's extensive repairs, the Woodbury Dam endured with only routine maintenance—and sometimes not much of that—while serving the navigation system for approximately 126 years.

It was a long way from Woodbury to Panama, but at places like Woodbury, and Rochester, and Greencastle, as well as Calhoun and Spottsville, Lieutenant Sibert learned his trade well. When the time came, he was eminently prepared by these practical experiences to, at first, fully appreciate the majesty of the assigned task, and then proceed to actually construct Gatun Dam and Locks—functional engineering grandeur which made possible the operation of the Panama Canal. And still does. [17]

The prominence of Bowling Green business leaders in development of the navigation system and the town's location at the head of navigation on Barren River were sound reasons to locate the brand new Corps of Engineers' office in Bowling Green. To reach the site of his future office, Sibert's steamer exited Lock No. 4 and executed a 90-degree turn to starboard, entering the mouth of Barren River and pointed toward Bowling Green, only 30 river miles to the south. Eight miles upstream the packet passed Sally's Rock at the mouth of Gasper River and the short stretch known as the narrows. That is where the much smaller Gasper runs parallel with the Barren before emptying into the larger stream about five miles downstream from Greencastle. [18]

The pool created at Woodbury carried the packet safely to Greencastle, about half the remaining distance to Bowling Green. More help to safely cover a series of shoals, rocks, sand, and gravel bars south of Greencastle came in the form of Barren River Lock and Dam No. 1, located about 15 miles upstream from Woodbury at the Greencastle community in Warren County. Locally known as Brown's Lock—in recognition of entrepreneur William Brown's milling operations, powered over the years by water from Greencastle Dam's upper pool—the structure was the last before reaching Bowling Green. It was time for another lock and dam inspection or, as Sibert later reflected, a damned lock inspection.

Based on the lieutenant's firsthand observations, and after first describing the blocked lock at Rochester, Major Lockwood gave this assessment of the Greencastle situation in 1888: "Of the four other locks, No. 1 Barren was liable to fail at any time, as the lower end of the land-wall had cracked and opened near the upper end of the gate recess, and also at the junction of land and lower wing-wall. The detached portion inclined toward the lock-pit, and was anchored back to the lower wing-wall by iron straps bolted to the masonry." Certainly another mess which required some serious attention before a total collapse closed the lock. [19]

With a grimace, Sibert wondered how the land wall had managed to remain vertical. At least Barren No. 1 remained operational, capable of lifting the packet about 15 feet from the Woodbury pool into the system's final navigational pool. The dam trapped ample water to safely float the packet to the Bowling Green wharf although problems sometimes arose during dry seasons and the resulting low water.

As the river continued its southeasterly course, sweeping bends were less acute, the shoreline alternating between spacious bottomlands and picturesque river bluffs. Approximately eight miles upstream from Greencastle, the master of the *Bowling Green* pointed out Thomas' Landing, a location of utmost importance to Bowling Green's river trade. Located at the bottom of the *U* called Lock Bend, the river broadened enough to allow a packet, if necessary, to turn around without running aground. Of even greater significance, the gentle slope of the land to the river made it highly accessible, a good spot to land on the west side of the waterway, the same side as Bowling Green. Less than seven overland miles separated Thomas' Landing from Bowling Green's upper wharf—the head of navigation on the slack water system. [20]

During times of extremely low water, even with a mighty assist from the Greencastle pool, Thomas' Landing was as far as a packet could go upstream. Too shallow for steamers, the remaining water concealed too many gravel bars, most unfriendly to wooden keels. When water was extremely low, packets loaded with passengers and freight had only one choice at Thomas' Landing: Unload! From the landing, buckboards and wagons completed the final leg of the trip to Bowling Green. Mules and horses strained mightily to haul their burdens from the landing in the river bottoms up the unpaved country road, topping out on a line of high bluffs overlooking the river. The bluffs lost that extra elevation by the time the road crossed Jennings Creek on the approach to Bowling Green.

Only teamsters or farmers with sturdy wagons and dependable mules for hire welcomed a packet stymied by low water. Passengers considered it a nuisance, much preferring a less strenuous and more dignified homecoming by steamboat at the town wharf. Fortunately, Greencastle Dam usually maintained an adequate channel to Bowling Green, low water problems being an exception to the rule.

With plenty of water in the channel, Sibert's boat merely unloaded cargo ticketed for Thomas' Landing before reengaging the big stern paddlewheel that would push the packet upstream. Roustabouts had barely secured the *Bowling Green* to the Bowling Green wharf when Sibert left his perch to have a closer look at the wharf, commonly known as the boatlanding.

Now that he had seen the entire shopworn system firsthand—from the mouth of the Green to the boatlanding—for the first time he appreciated the enormity of the job his orders entailed. Still, Lieutenant Sibert had no reservations about his ability to open the Engineer Office, initiate work to remedy the ills of the neglected navigation system, and blend in with a business community that desperately needed his services. He might even make a friend or two along the way.

Chapter Seven
FIXING LOCKS AND MAKING FRIENDS

The inventory of the slack water navigation system on Green and Barren rivers looked dismal, downright depressing, even to laymen untrained in the science of engineering and the art of steamboat navigation on the nation's inland waterways. It only took that first voyage upstream by packets—two required because the broken lock barred the *Evansville's* progress at Rochester—to convince Sibert that he faced formidable problems with no easy solutions. Cheerless and disagreeable as it all was in December 1888, the lieutenant viewed the rivers and the decrepit and bisected navigation system from a unique and generally hopeful perspective.

Being realistic and painfully aware of his inexperience, the officer initially questioned the true nature of his new assignment. Perhaps, he thought, Major Lockwood had consigned him a task that was essentially cosmetic, short on honest engineering problems involving thoughtful decisions and real pick and shovel construction work. He feared a task designed to merely keep him busy and out of serious trouble while learning to deal with civilians and their myriad interests along America's rivers—such relations always a concern as the Army engineered the country's inland navigation system.

That first trip upriver to Bowling Green convinced him that the opposite was true and that he had been entrusted with a job involving a high degree of engineering skill and practical diplomacy and patience, lots and lots of patience. Sibert saw the potential of the rivers and the dreadful condition of the navigation system for what it was—a direct challenge, a true test of his merits as an engineer and officer in charge because he was in local—and total—control of an extensive navigation system of upmost importance to the people of the Green River Valley.

It was not a cosmetic assignment. Enough serious problems existed to keep Sibert busy. Another problem involved time—time enough, the officer hoped, to cure some major problems before they became catastrophes. With enough problems to go around, the decks of the Green River Valley packets were cleared for action by the U.S. Army. William Luther Sibert, Lieutenant of Engineers, had an auspicious but scary opportunity either to demonstrate his worth or fall flat on his face in failure.

It had always been easy for engineers—and promoters of construction projects—to take ignominious falls when especially speculative and unsound engineering practices were part of the picture. Exercising common sense and going by the book—adhering to proven engineering methods and standards—was, Sibert believed, the way to avoid such failures, as he took over management of the decrepit Green and Barren rivers system in 1888.

First things first best describes the lieutenant's approach to practically everything from engineering and tactics in the field to the family obligations of everyday life. Convinced it would be a lengthy campaign to put things right along the Green and Barren rivers, moving Mamie Sibert from Cincinnati to Bowling Green was a high priority, ranking just behind the opening of the first Corps of Engineers office in the county seat of Warren County. Rejecting the scenic river route, Mamie Sibert was finally delivered to Bowling Green by a passenger train operated by the Louisville & Nashville Railroad.

On the Green River itself, reactivation of the lock at the Rochester Dam (No. 3) held top priority by a wide margin. So long as the Rochester lock was tightly jammed by the collapse of the stone wall on the river side of the lock, there could be no through traffic between Evansville and Bowling Green. Packets upstream from Rochester remained trapped in the upper pools of Green and Barren unless a daring captain found enough water flowing over the Rochester dam to scrape across when the river was at flood stage.

Following the Army's acquisition of the system in December 1888, the lieutenant's first six months in west Kentucky were eventful, filled with preparation for the campaign to come. He devoted most of his time and effort to a deeper study of the various jobs to be done while purchasing the tools, appliances, and materials required to begin the mending process. The rivers flowed almost continuously at flood stage during the first months of 1889, thereby preventing significant repairs even if the equipment and supplies had been readily available. In a report covering the first half of 1889, Sibert clearly stated that, except for operating and caring for the locks and dams in order to maintain the *status quo*, high water had prevented the initiation of any renovation work until March 1889.

When repair and renovation work did get underway, Sibert managed to spend $46,557.77 on projects aimed at stalling further deterioration of the system before the fiscal year ended on June 30, 1889. This included removal of the remainder of the river wall, which had collapsed and blocked the Rochester lock since January 1888. Only after the stone left standing had been cleared from the lock could rebuilding the wall begin. At the same time, Sibert worked hard on other projects scattered along the navigation system, several of them only slightly less urgent than reconstruction of the Rochester lock.

Much resembling the Rochester problem, except that the land wall rather than the river wall was at risk, the lock at Greencastle (Barren River Dam No. 1) was in sad shape. The wall had buckled and was fast approaching total failure, a dangerous and destructive event that could drop tons of cut stone blocks within the lock. The end result would have been a blockage capable of closing the lock—exactly what had happened at Rochester. Not the cavalry, but Sibert arrived just in time to avert a repeat of Rochester. He supervised excavations at the rear of the defective land wall where 2,500 cubic yards of material was removed, the first step in stabilizing the wall and reconstructing the lock. The engineer planned construction of a crib to reinforce the defective river wall of Lock No. 2 (Calhoun-Rumsey Dam) on Green River. Sibert labeled this a temporary measure designed to prevent yet another Rochester failure until a permanent solution could be perfected. [1]

Like the legendary Dutch boy, Sibert experienced serious dike problems along the Green and Barren with not enough thumbs to stem the tide. Dike is basically synonymous with dam, both structures meant to contain water, with the latter's definition refined to more precisely reflect a barrier built across a waterway to control the flow or raise the level of water. A dam in a slack water system not only contains, raises the level, and regulates the flow of water, but also serves as an anchor on one side of the lock, the other side being wedded to the shoreline. The lock itself, with the capability of raising and lowering watercraft from one pool to another, is the system's indispensable mechanism.

But there are no structures more fundamental to a slack water system than the series of dams constructed to create within each succeeding pool of water sufficient depth for steamboats to safely navigate, while providing a strong, stable base to which locks can be fastened. Sibert found four of the five dams within the system to be in no better condition than the locks they served. He needed time, equipment, and manpower to bring them up to acceptable engineering standards.

By the standards of the day, expenditures in excess of $46,000.00 during his first six months at Bowling Green made it clear that Sibert was not bashful about committing financial resources, even with the budget-conscious Corps of Engineers hierarchy looking over his shoulder. (If funds were available, the lieutenant estimated he could easily spend in excess of $256,000 during the next fiscal year, ending June 30, 1890, in attacking the woes of the navigation system.) The line items cast the six months of expenditures in a favorable light, revealing the outline of a definite plan, a desperate attempt to get ahead of the rapidly crumbling curve of the navigation system. [2]

For example, construction of a suitable snag-boat, a necessity, explained Sibert, to restoring the navigation system, accounted for $18,400.00 of the total. He estimated that "working during low-water seasons, it will take two or three years to remove the snags, etc., that exist in the two rivers," an improvement of great importance to riverboat safety. No snag-boat was available when the Army took charge of the system.

While the Dutch boy analogy fit well into the officer's overall mission, he looked more like a juggler with daily schedules filled with office work—drafting plans, writing reports, hiring personnel, and balancing the books. The office duties always competed with field work—supervising construction, conducting new surveys, and continually inspecting the system's facilities in the search for problems and deficiencies. Without completely bogging down in the minutiae of the annual reports of the Corps of Engineers, calculated to account for and justify every penny spent as a basis for the next year's budget request, these varied items, not necessarily in order of importance, commanded Sibert's attention during that first six months:

He negotiated contracts with private companies to supply the stone necessary to repair the locks at Rochester and Greencastle. Sibert had counted on reusing most of the stone which fell into the Rochester lock before close examination found it to be too soft and friable and, therefore, unreliable for use in the reconstruction. Also, close inspection revealed that the cement used in the original construction of the locks was not as good as ordinary common lime.

Sibert also contracted for stone to construct dwellings for lockkeepers at each of the five locks with a second dwelling also planned at Spottsville.

At Rochester, the engineer directed installation of three derricks, first used to clear unusable stone from the lock and eventually employed to lift new stone into place along the lock's new river wall. Also, Sibert installed 80 feet of trestle to accommodate a tramway for moving building materials to and from the lock pit. The tramway was 200 feet long, with two tramway cars to carry materials. It was the second tramway built by Sibert, the first located at the quarry on the Kentucky River.

Sibert reported removal of 2,450 cubic yards of stone from the failed river wall at Rochester with another 250 cubic yards of stone and clay cleared from the crib below the river wall. He dispatched six barges downstream, all loaded with broken stone unsuitable for rebuilding the lock, but perfect for recycling as fill material for cribs supporting lock walls at the Calhoun facility.

With practically all of the debris from the failed river wall removed from the lock chamber at Rochester, Sibert positioned an old dipper-dredge, the only one at his disposal, in the upper pool to clear the site for construction of a coffer dam in anticipation of actual rebuilding of the locks.

In addition to executing the contract for constructing the new snag-boat, the engineer designed and supervised the building of two decked barges for transporting stone, two derrick-boat hulls, and one hull for a dredge, the dredging machinery to be salvaged from an old hull. He used hired labor for building the boats.

A multitude of smaller projects demanded attention before the old system qualified for the Army brand, some involving simple restoration of good order to the process, the improvement of appearances, and the establishment of a solid image. Among them, Sibert ordered bushes cut and old buildings removed at Spottsville, more undergrowth removed and the lockkeeper's dwelling fenced at Calhoun, the lockkeeper's residence rebuilt at Woodbury, and the federal property fenced at Greencastle. [3]

In addition to overseeing the ongoing construction projects, Sibert continued to closely observe and analyze the problems and conditions of the facilities entrusted to his care. As a result of intensive study, his contribution to Major Lockwood's annual report strongly recommended that the lock at Calhoun not be extensively repaired for two reasons: First, as a practical and monetary matter, its deteriorated foundation structure was beyond repair and, second, the original lock and dam were poorly and dangerously located at the head of a long rock shoal. The downstream pool contained too little water during the summer season to permit safe passage of loaded coal barges. At the lock's original site, it would be necessary "to blast out a channel between 200 and 300 yards in length below the lock" to remedy the situation, according to Sibert's calculations. Instead of that costly procedure, the lieutenant recommended pushing plans forward to relocate and rebuild Lock and Dam No. 2, before the original version collapsed. Major Lockwood concurred. The recommendation was a perfect blend of Sibert's pragmatism and his abhorrence of waste—he hated sending good money after bad.

For fiscal 1890, Sibert proposed, among other things, to complete rebuilding of the Rochester lock, continue repair work on the Greencastle lock and dam, and complete temporary cribs to support the lock's river wall at Calhoun. The work of the snag-boat and the dredges never ceased.

Unanticipated problems plagued the Rochester project and, as a result, Sibert failed to meet his self imposed deadline of June 30, 1890. Most of the complications were manmade, dating from the lock's original construction, enhanced by war damage, and compounded by years of neglected maintenance. Even the river exacted a toll, a flood halting the operations just as the cofferdam was completed and ready to be pumped dry so reconstruction work could begin. [4]

In removing the remainder of the old river wall, the engineer uncovered additional, previously concealed damage that included erosion of the lower course of masonry, the likely cause of the wall's final collapse. Before high water closed operations, workers managed to lay foundation courses of masonry for the new wall. After seasonal floodwaters receded in the spring of 1890, Sibert's efforts to evacuate the water from the cofferdam, so that Rochester reconstruction could proceed, were unsuccessful. Grudgingly but realistically recognizing that he didn't have a workable answer to the problem, the lieutenant made one of his rare requests for help and received assistance from one of the most knowledgeable and experienced waterways engineering experts then available. A civilian, Benjamin F. Thomas, was employed by the Corps of Engineers as assistant engineer on the Big Sandy River, the boundary stream between Kentucky and West Virginia.

Thomas, far more experienced than the lieutenant, had the answers when he was temporarily assigned to Rochester in May 1890. Under his experienced direction, the cofferdam was pumped dry in 10 days of feverish activity while Sibert carefully studied the methods employed. The lieutenant learned quickly and, when a similar problem arose, he would know what to do and how to do it. Once dry conditions were achieved, the new masonry was routinely installed, using the derricks and tramway Sibert had previously installed. As much needed repair work continued on the dam itself, Sibert completed reconstruction of the lock's river wall without additional setbacks. [5]

The Rochester lock reopened for navigation on November 10, 1890, a banner day welcomed by business, mining, timber, and agricultural leaders throughout the Green River Valley. Hundreds gathered at the river village to witness the first boat pass through the restored lock toll free! The reopened lock ended walking in the Rochester mud because of packets stymied by a lock that didn't work.

Economically speaking, it amounted to a commercial bonanza: Toll-free use of the entire liquid highway began for all crafts, ranging from johnboats and timber rafts to the packets with their diverse cargoes of freight, cattle, and passengers. Restoration of commercial river service from Evansville to Bowling Green, without the delay, expense, and inconvenience of changing boats at Rochester, also provided a psychological lift for valley citizens who no longer felt quite so isolated.

With restoration of through traffic, uninterrupted by portage, Lieutenant Sibert's name and rank, if not his serial number, entered the household lexicons throughout the Green River Valley. In this civilian world, he was the engineer, or the lieutenant, never Goliath as he was best known among army contemporaries.

Although the Rochester lock had been the top priority, Sibert never enjoyed the luxury of coping with one problem at a time. Instead, too many problems forever encroached on an acute shortage of time within which to fix the worst of them. While he hurried work along to reopen Rochester, the officer also pushed forward additional improvements, some as important to the system as the Rochester revival. They included:

At Greencastle, where the lock's land wall threatened imminent collapse akin to the Rochester disaster, the broken wall was removed and Sibert successfully installed a cofferdam on the downstream side prior to replacing the wall. Also, he directed rebuilding the lower portion of the dam and completed construction of two houses for lockkeepers.

At Spottsville, Sibert kept the lock at Dam No. 1 (on Green River) open by dredging both the upper and lower entrances after discovering that the system's prior operators had deposited dredged material on the banks of the lock approaches, only to have much of it wash back into the channel. Almost 1,000 cubic yards of dredged material and 300 cubic yards of common sawdust (the kind of stuff found around a sawmill) plugged some large leaks in the dam. On shore, two new dwellings for lockkeepers were built, the old ones razed and removed, and the grounds graded and fenced.

At Calhoun, dredging kept open the lock at Dam No. 2, Sibert having reported a year earlier that the dilapidated facility required nothing less than complete overhauling of the whole structure and even that might not be enough. He envisioned a brand new lock and dam at another location, the only logical answer for the poor location. Meanwhile, he discovered the primary cause of the land wall deterioration to be erosive waters from a millrace that increased pressure on the wall and disintegrated the poor quality cement.

The new snag-boat, the *William Preston Dixon*, which ended up costing $28,760.03, was launched and put into service on lower Green River, clearing snags in and near the navigation channel, thereby improving low water navigation and safety. More than 200 of the always dangerous snags were removed during the month of June 1890. When high water prevented snag removal activity, the boat was employed for towing, logging 1,181 miles up and down the Green and Barren.

In addition to reopening the lock, two new residences for lockkeepers were built at Rochester. Another lockkeeper's residence was completed at Woodbury while Sibert kept a close watch on the dam itself which he reported in need of extensive repairs.

It wasn't all about dredging and removing snags from the channel and repairing locks and dams although that was the final goal. There was much more, details which often looked insignificant viewed in isolation, while making a great deal of sense when seen as a part of the big picture. These details included construction of new quarters for lockkeepers and an aggressive program of work for what today would be called the buildings and grounds department. For numerous reasons, Sibert thought it essential for lockkeepers, usually on duty around the clock with few opportunities to leave the premises, to have modern and comfortable quarters. This projected a positive image for the Corps of Engineers and boosted morale. It also gave the officer an outlet for his abundant energy when high water interrupted reconstruction of the locks and dams.

Also, razing old dilapidated structures left over from the reign of the navigation company and fencing the new federal properties conveyed a positive impression. The ever observant and often critical public liked the order and authority subtly suggested by the new government quarters. It seemed to say the Army Corps of Engineers was in the Green River Valley to stay.

Reopening the Rochester lock, delayed by high water until November 1890, was logged in as a Corps of Engineers accomplishment in fiscal 1891. Of equal importance as a practical matter was completion of reconstruction of the lock at Greencastle on Barren River. By rebuilding the lock, Sibert prevented a repeat of the Rochester collapse and another blockage of the route between Evansville and Bowling Green. The Greencastle Dam also received much needed attention. In addition, measured progress was recorded in the repair and renovation of the other navigation facilities, and the *William Preston Dixon* continued the important work of clearing snags from the channel. Mundane but important improvement of the shore properties continued on schedule. [6]

Putting the navigation system back together kept the lieutenant busy on a daily basis, but not at the expense of some thoughtful consideration devoted to the future promise of the refurbished waterway. To test such thinking, Sibert led a survey party along the upper reaches of the Green, that part of the river above the mouth of Barren River.

After forming the north boundary of Warren County, Green River entered Edmonson County, passing the county seat of Brownsville. Edmonson County contained known mineral deposits, the development of which would benefit from a slack water navigation system's cheap and reliable transportation. But the existing system did not reach that far, with shoals, rapids, gravel and sand bars, and generally shallow water accurately describing the Green upstream from Woodbury. There was, however, one unique factor that made all of these navigational nightmares worth solving.

Mammoth Cave!

Often described in the latter half of the 19th century as the eighth wonder of the world, the natural phenomenon drew curious visitors from the world over, including sophisticated travelers from as far away as Europe. Once he became a part of the community, Sibert recognized Mammoth Cave's economic and cultural potential, which had been barely scratched, and lightly at that. Transportation to the cave site had always been a problem, and Sibert believed he could fix that.

Based on the results of his survey, the officer engineered a plan for development of the upper Green which would open the river to steamboats, allowing packets to transit the forbidding shoals, rapids, and bars and safely dock on the river's south bank—less than a half-mile from the natural entrance to the world's most famous cave system.

Sibert proposed construction of a new lock and dam at Glenmore, approximately 20 miles upstream from Woodbury, just downstream from the mouth of Bear Creek. The engineer located a second lock and dam, necessary to float packets the remaining distance to Mammoth Cave, about a half-mile or so upstream from Brownsville. The officer estimated costs at $361,346.40, as measured by 1891 dollars.

Buttressed by the information contained in the survey, Sibert found Major Lockwood receptive to the proposal, which subsequently received the endorsement of Colonel O.M. Poe, chief engineer for the Northwest Division. Grounded upon the facts and findings contained in Sibert's survey, Lockwood and Poe concluded that "this locality is worthy of improvement." The locality was, of course, Mammoth Cave. Unfortunately, funds were unavailable for the extension of the navigation system in the foreseeable future and Sibert's survey gathered dust, at least for a while. [7]

For the second full year in a row, Lieutenant Sibert came in under the system's projected budget for fiscal 1891, expending a total of $143,113.39, almost $16,000 below the budget estimate. In contrast to fiscal 1890 when an abnormal amount of high water curtailed construction activity and reduced expenditures proportionately, there was no high water factor in 1891 when much was accomplished. In the absence of other influences, it is likely that the lieutenant's frugal management of available resources played a key role in balancing the books.

An indication of the improved condition of the slack water navigation system on the Green and Barren rivers is contained in Sibert's estimated budget for fiscal 1892. The engineer earmarked a total amount of $93,980.77 for operating and improving the river system, strongly suggesting that much of the expensive reconstruction and repairs had been accomplished. Although the reduced numbers didn't help bolster the annual budget request by the Corps of Engineers, the modest estimate demonstrated the improved health of the Green River system and reflected favorably on Sibert's management skills.

When the Green and Barren rivers system came under Sibert's care in December 1888, time was precious in the extreme—success of the Army's restoration program depending to a great degree on Sibert's ability to expedite before more locks collapsed. With miles of river to cover, he saved valuable hours by often using the snag boat as a floating and highly portable command post. A snag boat works best at its appointed task—removing dangerous trees and logs from the rivers—when water is extremely low. At other times, the *William Preston Dixon* served as a most unlikely flagship for Sibert's ungainly but capable navy—a flotilla of dredges, derrick boats, transport barges, and, from time to time, ubiquitous johnboats.

Captain William Snoddy Overstreet, a veteran riverman and hold-over from the navigation company, commanded the snag boat. Now a civilian employee of the Corps of Engineers, his non-military title identified him as master of the *Dixon*. Not without authority, rivermen credited Overstreet with knowing every shoal, bar, rock, rapid, and eddy on the two rivers, perfect for providing Sibert an accurate picture of his new domain. A character in his own right, Overstreet's booming voice required no megaphone when he issued orders from the pilot house. The volume and tone of his commanding voice compared favorably with that of foghorns.

Overstreet's voice and lung capacity, in Sibert's view, qualified him to be an excellent sergeant major. From the professional point of view, the pair meshed from the very first, perhaps because both were strong willed and brooked little nonsense while on the job and because each sensed that the other was knowledgeable and competent in his trade. That produced mutual respect, and there was more.

Captain Overstreet was a hunter!

A native of Barren County, Kentucky, Overstreet served in the Confederate Army as a teenager before being captured and paroled. He returned to work on the family farm near present day Cave City, hunting in the rugged country now within Mammoth Cave National Park—mainly to put food on the table—although he loved the sport of it. Despite the age differential—Overstreet almost old enough to have been Sibert's father—their shared interests in hunting and the outdoors ripened mutual respect into lifetime friendship. All kinds of hunting followed, from raccoon to deer and everything in between. It included Captain Overstreet's favorite, soon to become the focus of the lieutenant's woodland pursuits—fox hunting. [8]

Meanwhile, on the domestic front, Mamie inaugurated the next generation of Siberts. Following her husband's reassignment, she arrived in Bowling Green with just enough time to get comfortable before William Olin Sibert was born October 23, 1889, the first of five consecutive sons before a daughter filled out the half dozen children Mamie and William Luther ushered into the world. While in Bowling Green, two more Army brats joined the Sibert family: Franklin Cummings Sibert, born January 3, 1891, and Harold Ward Sibert, born May 9, 1892. Each of the trio, like the two brothers yet to follow, had (to a greater or lesser degree) "Army" indelibly etched on their psyches.[9]

With his firstborn's arrival, Lieutenant Sibert found himself engaged in learning curve skirmishes on three separate fronts, including adapting his first-class education as an engineer to the taming and full utilization of Green and Barren rivers as productive avenues of commerce.

With the valley dominated by heavily wooded hills sheltering game of every description, the off-duty officer refined his riding skills, adding Kentucky style deer and fox hunting to his repertoire, and learned all there was to know about foxhounds and those Kentuckians who obsessively followed them. The obvious excitation and joys of the hunt notwithstanding, Sibert's greatest delight blossomed from the more genteel role of an apprentice father learning his trade.

The domestic lieutenant belied the gruff nature he sometimes assumed while making an unforgettable impression on a careless contractor or attracting the attention of a stubborn river pilot or chastising a worker who failed at his task. Regardless of the problems he faced on the rivers, Sibert managed to maintain a kind and gentle countenance around the house and the woman he adored. When those Sibert babies began to arrive on a fairly regular basis, the officer in charge proceeded to honey coat it all.

William Olin Sibert was baptized at Christ Episcopal Church on New Year's Day 1890. Next came Franklin Cummings Sibert, baptized at Christ Episcopal on January 3, 1891. The former Brownsville belle changed her church affiliation from the Episcopal Church in Brownsville, Texas, to Christ Episcopal, a sure sign of settling in for an indefinite stay. Indefinite always defined the length of Army postings. [10]

While seriously engaged in resurrecting the navigation system, the engineer and Mamie, equally busy as a mother and housewife, plunged into the social side of life in Bowling Green—and loved it. Their calendar included ice cream suppers, traveling theatrical shows, church events, and more. The congenial couple easily made friends; ample dinner engagements to host and attend followed. Perhaps because of the small town backgrounds they shared, Bowling Green life appealed to the Siberts; they felt a part of it and wanted to stay.

Initially and, of course, understandably, the local leadership viewed the lieutenant through jaundiced eyes, most apprehensive about the Army once again intruding into the life of the community, especially its economic life. The Bowling Green experience with military invasions, by both Confederate and Union armies, left a bitter taste for practically all concerned. Nothing seemed to work right during the war, and now they openly worried about the lieutenant's ability—to not only turn the ailing navigation system into an economic asset, but to do it in a hurry.

Early in his tour, Sibert overcame much of the entrenched opposition to the Army takeover through a generally calm and diplomatic demeanor. At the same time, the more truculent opponents, those given to shouting and ranting rather than reasoned deliberations, came to fear the Sibert temper. Usually held in check, the officer unleashed it, without hesitation, when diplomacy failed. The smart advice soon made its way up and down the rivers: Don't push the mild-mannered lieutenant too far or you just might be on the receiving end of a verbal 21-gun salute—a little rough on the ears. Most chose the easier course, and the Sibert family soon found themselves not only accepted but downright comfortable in Bowling Green.

The Alabama native, in the space of a few months short of four years, managed to bond with a diverse group of Kentucky contemporaries including a salty and experienced riverman old enough to be his father, skilled river pilots and roustabouts, rough-and-tumble contractors, hunters, and outdoorsmen of every stripe, and even the elite members of Bowling Green's first men's literary society. Throughout the valley, Sibert managed to blend with the locals. Mutual respect, if not downright friendship, eventually broadened to include those once disgruntled former owners of the Green and Barren River Navigation Company.

The ex-owners of the navigation company, regardless of the lucrative federally funded buyout, had an excuse for their river-induced melancholy. They lost positions of enormous political and economic power when stripped of the navigation system and were brim full of anger and resentment when Sibert first arrived. Why not blame the Army Corps of Engineers and the most accessible target: Sibert! That attitude didn't last long, only long enough to see that the lieutenant meant business—the restoration of a healthy river economy—and that he knew how to do it. The displaced lords of the Green and Barren waterways soon realized that Sibert's river savvy translated into new business opportunities for valley entrepreneurs. They were entrepreneurs—not dummies!

The community's leadership, the main movers and shakers within the political, economic, and social structure, soon realized the Army's personable representative was quite different from what they had expected. Clearly multi-dimensional, Sibert the soldier wasted no time demonstrating his engineering expertise. Literate, they agreed, best described the off duty civilian side of Sibert's third dimension. Accompanied by his agreeable personality, Sibert gained admission to the upper stratum of the community's male-dominated leadership.

A little bit like the Army.

Sibert got a number.

In February 1892, the lieutenant became No. 3, but only after accepting an invitation to join the ranks of the XV Club, which continues today as the oldest men's literary club in Bowling Green. John L. Caldwell, minister of the First Presbyterian Church, had the idea and is credited with organizing the XV Club on September 23, 1879, along with the other original members. From its inception, XV's group of men dedicated thoughtful consideration to society's problems, whether local, national, or international in scope, while enjoying urbane companionship and the finest of food. Article 4 of the group's constitution mandated that each meeting "shall culminate in a good supper." Libations, if any, were discretely administered out of respect for members who might be opposed to John Barleycorn on religious or moral grounds.

Organizers of the elegant and exclusive group chose to limit membership at any one time to 15—symbolized by the Roman numeral name. When initiated into XV, each member was assigned his personal number—always between one and 15—exclusively his so long as he was a member. Under the club's constitution, until one of the 15 slots became vacant (by resignation or death of a member), it was impossible to induct a new member. This explains why the bright, obviously talented, and well-educated lieutenant of engineers did not receive his invitation until February 18, 1892.

Although it sounds elite, never could the organization be accused of adhering to the snobbish and pretentious stereotypes often associated with elitism. For example, it was impossible for the richest man in the community to buy his way in. Likewise, the most erudite and fashionable gentleman, a worthy candidate in every respect, waited in vain for an invitation while all 15 chairs remained occupied. And when a vacancy did occur, a prospective member had to survive the sternest of all tests, the black ball ballot. The equivalent of a congeniality test, the secret plebiscite required nothing less than unanimous approval.

When the Reverend Caldwell left Bowling Green to pastor a church in New Orleans, his No. 3 slot opened for the first time for a new member. All that was needed was agreement among the remaining 14 members on a worthy—and congenial—candidate. They unanimously agreed and William Luther Sibert accepted the invitation and assumed the mantle of No. 3 upon Caldwell's departure. Sibert's selection was based on the sum of his personality, going well beyond mere intellect in choosing a companion with diverse interests in several disciplines— a true Renaissance man. The product was as much a tribute to his Gadsden tutor and the guidance of Professor Parker at the University of Alabama as it was to his superior engineering and military education at West Point and Fort Totten.

Many years later, when members reviewed the XV minutes covering the meeting held on February 18, 1892—the date Sibert became a member—they chuckled with amazement at the omen which went unrecognized at the time. A portent of big things to come in the life of the new No. 3, the evening's program centered on "Interoceanic Communication", those oceans being the Atlantic and Pacific. Although emphasis fell squarely on the proposed route across Nicaragua, the discussion also touched on canal possibilities across the Isthmus of Darian (Panama).

Sibert's thoughts on the canal question in 1892 are unrecorded, but he would not have hesitated to express his opinion. In all likelihood, he pointed out that a slack water navigation system can work in Central America, just as it did on the Green and Barren rivers, only with bigger locks and dams—much bigger. Of course, Lieutenant Sibert had no inkling of his future involvement in construction of the world's greatest canal. [11]

Meanwhile, Harold Ward Sibert arrived on May 9, 1892, a little late for christening ceremonies in Bowling Green in view of his father's orders to report on August 28, 1892, to his next duty station—Detroit, Michigan. The lady from Texas sighed wistfully, then took it all in stride and prepared to move to Michigan. But that was only after she experienced a great time with new friends in Bowling Green where she hoped to return. And her husband had no choice but to submit his resignation from the XV Club, barely seven months after his induction as the new No. 3.

Sibert greeted orders requiring a move from the Green River Valley with considerable sadness—even more so than Mamie. The valley agreed with him, its climate, geology, fauna, and flora reminding him of Duck Springs except that the Alabama highlands were measurably higher than the hills along Green and Barren rivers. Entranced by the open and wild geography within the valley, the lieutenant of engineers sadly contemplated leaving behind its abundance of game. While finding it difficult to leave Kentucky friends, forests, and rivers, Lieutenant Sibert welcomed another challenge in 1892 after fixing about everything that could be fixed on the Green and Barren navigation system.

When ordered north to the Great Lakes Division of the Corps of Engineers, headquartered in Detroit, Michigan, only the location surprised Sibert since periodic relocations were a normal feature of Army service. The transfer to Michigan and the staff of Colonel O.M. Poe afforded the officer the opportunity to work under Colonel Poe, one of the recognized leaders among the more experienced officers of the Corps of Engineers. And the change in assignments catapulted Sibert from the backwaters of Kentucky into an extensive waterways system already in the national spotlight.

The officer's new job involved working on the necklace of American waters extending hundreds and hundreds of miles eastward from Duluth, Minnesota, to the St. Lawrence River, and south to Chicago, Detroit, and Cleveland. The Soo Canal was the most famous splice within the Great Lakes slack water navigation system but canalization of the Detroit and St. Clair rivers at Detroit—connecting Lake Huron with Lake Erie—was equally important. Sibert worked at both locations.

Upgrading the St. Claire and Detroit rivers waterways offered Sibert an assignment both choice and challenging. With some degree of professional satisfaction, he recognized the high profile assignment thrust in his direction. The work directly affected the rapidly increasing commercial traffic on the Great Lakes and, Sibert concluded, would not be entrusted to a less promising officer. For that opportunity, he welcomed the trek north to Michigan.

Chapter Eight
GREAT LAKES, LITTLE ROCK
AND WILLET'S POINT

The Great Lakes are just that. Great! The undefended necklace of water separating the United States from the Dominion of Canada played an early and important role in exploration and westward expansion, helping turn 13 fragile coast-hugging colonies into the Lower 48. They provided broad avenues for boats capable of floating American pioneers westward. Early fur traders, followed by miners and lumberjacks, welcomed the free flowing lake route—an efficient and practical conveyor of their products to the markets of the East. Well, at least the route was free flowing, efficient, and practical for 99% of the way, and then there was this problem.

Ante-dating the voyageurs, the Ojibway Indians first became aware of a major obstruction and the greatest of bottlenecks—the rapids or falls on the St. Mary's River. Leading downstream from Lake Superior into the other greats in the chain of lakes, the falls later hampered the passage of settlers and their commerce. In their own backyard, the Ojibways handled the impassable rapids the only way they knew how: Canoes were portaged, always a physically demanding and time consuming task.

The Indians routinely unloaded canoes, packed to the gunnels with a hundred pounds or so of beaver furs, carried cargo and canoes around the falls, then reloaded for the remainder of the downstream trading trip. Because of the portage, the falls gained importance, a place where Indians met to exchange stories and information, and where fishing was exceptional. The Ojibway depended heavily on the spring catch of whitefish for valuable protein when other food sources were scarce at winter's end. Indian life revolved around the river, but even the most venerated of their 18th century medicine men could not foretell the activity spawned by the St. Mary's falls a few short years later.

As a consequence of being the only water connection between Lake Superior and Lake Huron, the St. Mary's River was vital to the fur trade. Its falls were a lock of the lock-and-key variety, barring rapid transit into Lake Huron, the gateway lake to Lakes Erie and Ontario, knifing toward East Coast markets. The falls also blocked the way south into Lake Michigan and the American midsection. The lock had to be picked.

The Northwest Fur Company took the plunge by building a navigation lock in 1797. The lock, 35 feet long, skirted the falls on the Canadian side of the river and eliminated the portage for small boats, very small boats. Building the frontier lock was a substantial undertaking on the company's part and suggests just how lucrative the fur trade was at the dawn of the 19th century. The wise and aged Ojibway medicine man had to be amazed, watching canoes safely and effortlessly pass the falls barrier, going in either direction, without portage.

The lock served the company's needs until it was destroyed during the War of 1812—relocking the St. Mary's as a promising commercial river until the middle of the 19th century. Then, government and business (spurred by enlightened self-interest) teamed up to tame the falls with a pair of locks. In 1852, Congress approved legislation granting 75,000 acres of public land to a private company in exchange for building a substantial lock system to circumvent the falls. Fairbanks Scale Company, with extensive mining interests in Michigan's Upper Peninsula, undertook the project in 1853.

It was a major construction project, two locks in tandem, each 350 feet long, were built at a cost just under $1,000,000, three times greater than the estimate. Finished within the two-year deadline set by the State of Michigan, the state took possession on May 31, 1855, and the canal serving the locks opened on schedule in June 1855. Toll was four cents per ton until 1877 when it was reduced a penny. The locks and canal boosted Michigan's fledgling mining industry, and the traffic it generated propelled the facilities into national economic importance.

Success bred success, attracting more and more traffic, much more than the locks could efficiently handle. The first boatload of iron ore passed through the new Michigan State Locks in August 1855, all 132 tons; in the aggregate, 1,447 tons of iron ore traveled the locks in 1855. By 1860, the annual tonnage of ore reached 120,000 tons and Michigan needed a new lock system, but the state declined to take on the job. Instead, Michigan ceded ownership and responsibility for operation of the locks to the federal government in 1881. Since that date, the locks have been operated toll free by the Army Corps of Engineers. [1]

So it was when Lieutenant Sibert journeyed north from Bowling Green to Detroit and another change for his Army wife and children. While Mamie regretted parting with Bowling Green friends, the opportunity to make new friends brightened her outlook. The Sibert children were too young for school transfers to be a problem.

Although visions of the Green River Valley lingered comfortably in the background, Lieutenant Sibert radiated unrestrained enthusiasm to begin work on the lakes when he appeared before Colonel Orlando M. Poe, a proven engineer of the fighting kind. Poe was cited and promoted for bravery during the Civil War while serving the Union in both the Eastern and Western theaters. He impressed William Tecumseh Sherman while supporting the Yankee general's legendary march through Georgia to the Atlantic. When peace returned, Sherman selected Poe to serve as his aide de camp after the general was named Army chief of staff, before Poe returned to his regular duties with the Corps of Engineers. [2]

Poe was in charge of the Detroit offices of the Corps of Engineers when Sibert reported to divisional headquarters, located at 34 West Congress Street. Indeed a busy place, engineers were working to keep the Great Lakes navigation system apace with the rapidly developing manufacturing industries around their perimeter.

When Lieutenant Sibert got his first official look at the existing charts and the plans for immediate improvements to the Great Lakes navigation system, he found that not all of the lakes were great and that often it is the little things that count. In the public's eyes, practically all attention seemed focused on the historic chokepoint—the St. Mary's dangerously turbulent and scenic passage between Lake Superior to the west and Lake Huron and Georgian Bay to the east. The St. Mary's River and its improvements, the Soo Canal and Locks, were classified by engineers as connecting waters, aptly named for their mission: connecting the lakes. Sibert worked on the Soo Canal and Locks. [3]

While not as picturesque and historically dramatic, there were other equally important connecting waters, without which there would be no navigation system. As it turned out, a major part of Sibert's Great Lakes tour involved improving the connecting waters between Lake Huron and Lake Erie in the vicinity of Detroit (and Windsor on the Canadian side). The goal: Increase channel depth to accommodate the fleet of ore boats and other freighters which kept heavy industries humming along the northern tier of states. As the demand for iron ore and other raw materials from the west increased, the size of transports increased proportionately. The bigger ships not only needed more elbow room for maneuvering, but required deeper and deeper channels.

Back in Kentucky, Sibert managed 180 miles of navigable waters, including five sets of locks and dams. His new responsibilities included the St. Clair River and Canal and, immediately downstream, Lake St. Clair, forming the water route from Lake Huron to Detroit, a distance of approximately 65 miles. At Detroit, the St. Clair's waters join the Detroit River, flowing south from the city and completing Huron's only connection with Lake Erie.

The channel through the St. Clair waters, both lake and river, would fit into the Green River system with 100 miles or more to spare. While Sibert shouldered responsibility for the entire Kentucky system, including repairs, reconstruction, and daily operation of locks and dams, his Detroit mission centered on deepening the existing navigation channel and widening it to provide safe passage for ships bound in opposite directions. The generally tedious and unglamorous work involved checking and rechecking the work of the civilian contractors. Specifications had to be followed as work progressed on schedule.

The engineers planned to increase the depth of the existing 16-foot channel to a minimum depth of 20 feet and, in some locations, to 21 feet. At other locations, such as Section 5 of the St. Clair project, plans required the existing channel leading from the south end of Lake Huron to be both deepened and widened. The additional width provided ample space within the channel for the most inept helmsman to safely pass an oncoming ore boat. Sibert presided over completion of Section 5, except for routine cleanup work, before being ordered to his next duty station in August 1894. [4]

Section 6 required excavation of 950,000 cubic yards of clay and sand in order to deepen the channel from the St. Clair River, through the St. Clair flats canal, and into St. Clair Lake. By June 1894, it had been dredged to the required 20-foot depth throughout its length and was nearing completion. [5]

Much to Sibert's consternation, the contractors responsible for extending the 20-foot channel across St. Clair Lake, and dredging a 21-foot channel through the bar at the mouth of the Detroit River, lagged behind schedule. None of their excuses satisfied the lieutenant, who remained deeply concerned about the lack of progress until the day he departed Detroit. As for Colonel Poe, he recognized that Sibert had done everything possible to expedite the work and that the problem was solely due to the shortcomings of the two contractors. Impressed by his subordinate's competence and industry, the colonel gave Sibert high marks for efficiency and recommended him for a higher station in the Corps. Poe's report carried weight even though the officer remained a first lieutenant. [6]

Leaving Detroit in 1894, Sibert took with him two years of experience working on the St. Clair segment of the huge navigation system requiring 20 and 21-foot channels. He also worked on the new lock chamber on the Soo Canal, which was 800 feet long and a full 100 feet wide. By comparison, the Soo facilities made the Green River system, with lock chambers 140 feet in length and 36 feet wide, seem tiny indeed. And the budget for Great Lakes projects involved millions of dollars, whereas Sibert had been accustomed to scraping by and making do with a comparatively few thousand dollars earmarked for the Green River system. Sibert's exposure to the larger and highly successful Great Lakes system produced a decidedly positive and expansive effect on Sibert's thinking as an engineer.

The Great Lakes experience under Colonel Poe's watchful eyes increased the lieutenant's professional boldness and self-confidence, as if the big soldier needed that. It led Sibert to fervently believe that there was no imaginable construction project so large, complicated, and costly that it could not be planned, designed, and engineered to a successful conclusion by the officer-engineers of the Army Corps of Engineers.

First Lieutenant William Luther Sibert left Michigan in total agreement that the Great Lakes were indeed great. Those huge bodies of precious fresh water were in a class by themselves, demanding that Sibert think big! They furnished the engineer with a grand opportunity to distinguish himself while working on a system which had captured the interest, if not the imagination, of those powers on the Potomac, the holders of the purse strings in the District of Columbia.

Given the opportunity, Sibert was ready to think big! He remained optimistic about his future with the Corps of Engineers, but knew that there had to be some adjustments when he received Special Order No. 179, one of those blanket orders reassigning numerous Army officers to new duty stations, in August 1894.

A posting to Little Rock, Arkansas? On the banks of the usually sluggish, sometimes turbulent, and most often muddy Arkansas River? Correct on both counts, according to Order No. 179, directing Sibert to take command of the Arkansas District for the Corps of Engineers on August 15, 1894. The new assignment sounded mundane, trading majestic lakes for a muddy river—even if the Arkansas was a big river and a major tributary of the Mississippi. Not at all a professional set-back, to the contrary, Lieutenant Sibert scored a highly significant pro-motion—an independent command! He was to be the officer in charge of the Arkansas District, Army Corps of Engineers. For the lieutenant, a first!

At his previous posts, Sibert served as a subordinate, an assistant to a superior officer in charge of and ultimately responsible for the work in which Sibert was engaged. He answered to Major Stickney, then to Major Lockwood on the Kentucky River system. Even after Lockwood placed Sibert in local charge of the Green and Barren rivers system, it remained Major Lockwood's ultimate responsibility in the eyes of the Corps of Engineers.

When the lieutenant relieved Captain Carl F. Palfrey as officer in charge of the Arkansas District, he filled a position beyond his rank and grade. Although the post of district commander called for a cap-tain, as in the case of his predecessor, Sibert took over, becoming the only lieutenant to command an engineering district within the Corps of Engineers table of organization. [7]

Had the Siberts wanted a change from Great Lakes scenery, the Ar-kansas delta qualified. Arkansas and its namesake river proved to be different, interesting if not exotic, and marked a milestone in the career of Lieutenant Sibert—responsibility for an independent command. His jurisdiction reached beyond the State of Arkansas, pursuing the meandering Arkansas River into the Indian Nation. It also covered the Arkansas' tributaries flowing south out of Missouri. This mere lieuten-ant acquired an inordinate amount of responsibility by the stroke of a War Department pen. Dating back to his early days of service on Kentucky's rivers, the junior officer counted a wealth of experience managing river navigation, but nothing comparable in scope to his new command.

The Arkansas River watershed dwarfed Kentucky's Green River drainage system and had its own unique character. Sibert's desk in Little Rock became the destination of every imaginable problem along the Arkansas, the place where the buck stopped and responsibility and decision making took over. The independent command meant much freedom in the operation of the vast slack water navigation system, and an equal amount of responsibility should things go wrong. Now the lieutenant of engineers answered directly for all engineering work—both successes and failures—throughout the district.

Sibert's job required skillful juggling of work boats, personnel, projects, and budgets to keep superiors and citizens—from the Arkansas to the Potomac—happy. Boosting his career required far more than engineering expertise: Dealing with the varied and often conflicting interests of citizens within the district demanded diplomatic skills worthy of a Franklin or Jefferson. And his superiors expected timely, accurate, and tactfully written reports of activity within the district. Even higher on the priority list were all of those other people in Washington, ranging from Congress to the White House, with control over appropriations for river improvements—the lifeblood of waterways improvements.

Beyond the problems forever surfacing along the waters of the Arkansas and its tributaries, Sibert began working diligently to blend the Army's way of doing things with the totally civilian world of Arkansas at peace during the final decade of the 19th century. When he arrived, the officer faced no overriding problem worthy of a white knight's attention, giving him time to settle in, catch his breath, and get his feet on the ground. But with no threat of a major catastrophe along the Arkansas—akin to the collapsed lock wall at Rochester on the Green—spontaneous celebrations of his engineering acumen were out of the question. Without a problem of star magnitude, Sibert vowed to win his spurs in the eyes of Arkansas citizens and their leaders in some less dramatic way—maybe by concentrating on doing the best possible job. Future appropriations for river projects in the district depended on it and, in turn, such fiscal matters figured prominently in the evaluations and promotions of Corps of Engineers officers.

The new assignment also challenged Mamie Sibert as she reestablished her household in Little Rock, her fourth home to punctuate her seven years of marriage to William Luther Sibert. Although she gave no hint of how the more extreme winter weather along the Great Lakes affected her growing family and herself, there can be little doubt that the ex-Texan welcomed a return to a more temperate climate. Being next door to Texas was another positive feature of Arkansas, shortening trips to visit her mother in Brownsville. The Sibert boys adapted quickly to the new environment. Although the older brothers were a little young for Tom Sawyer and Huckleberry Finn adventures on the muddy Arkansas, they managed to be barefoot and as full of mischief as any other six and eight-year-olds. The youngest lad was still a toddler.

When measured against the rivers the lieutenant cut his teeth on in Kentucky, the Arkansas was a giant. It flowed more than 1,400 miles from its source in the Colorado Rockies east and southeast to its juncture with the Mississippi at Napoleon, Arkansas. Along this course, it changed: From a mountain torrent of white water, it spilled into the Great Plains, spreading between low banks in Kansas, a wide and shallow stream subject to seasonal flooding. These characteristics remained fairly constant during its passage through the northeast quarter of the Indian Territory and across Arkansas. Some of its tributaries flowed south out of Missouri.

The Arkansas District included only that portion of the river within the Indian Territory and the State of Arkansas, but the engineer in charge could never ignore events occurring upstream in the Colorado Rockies. The geography, geology, and the resulting upstream hydrology directly impacted the character and condition of the downstream portion of the river. From its Rocky Mountains birth, the Arkansas River ran downhill, powered by an elevation drop of more than 11,000 feet between its source near Leadville, Colorado, and its merger with the Mississippi in delta country.

Sibert was grateful that the most abrupt drop in the river's elevation (4,000 feet) took place in Colorado, picturesque with rocks and rapids, but no place for a steamboat. At a slower rate, the Arkansas steadily lost elevation on the long trek across three-quarters of the southern tier of the State of Kansas, then south into the Indian Nation, now the State of Oklahoma. Finishing its bisection of the State of Arkansas, the river broadened and spread to form delta country with elevations to match.

When Sibert arrived on the scene, the Corps of Engineers maintained a six-foot navigation channel from Little Rock to the Mississippi. This provided sufficient water to accommodate most steamboats, barges, and other craft using the Arkansas during the last decade of the 19th century. Upstream from Little Rock to Ft. Smith and into the Indian Territory, shallow water limited the channel to a modest two feet—sufficient for flatboat traffic and capable of moving other shallow draft vessels. In addition, farmers and business firms depended on numerous tributaries for movement of produce to markets and products to consumers.

At times, measures taken to open tributaries for commercial purposes seemed simple, even primitive. Yet they were highly effective in facilitating shipping which was vital to economic growth in the absence of a dependable all-weather road system. In July 1895, farmers along the Cache River welcomed Sibert's plan to clear a navigation channel of snags from the mouth of the river to James Ferry, a distance of 79 miles. This simple measure opened a smooth running river highway where flatboats, loaded with produce, could navigate. The river provided a relatively easy trip to market compared to the rutted wagon trails available along the land route!

The St. Francis River received Sibert's attention to determine what, if any, improvements should be initiated from Sunk Land (just upstream from the St. Francis' juncture with the Little River) northward to Greenville, Missouri. The officer decided to clear a channel of snags as far as Poplin, Missouri, but not to Greenville, 40 or so miles to the north. He repeated this same exercise in judgment numerous times throughout the region influenced by the Arkansas River, netting additional, inexpensive water transportation on a widespread basis.

To make the entire system work, Sibert directed most of his attention to the Arkansas itself. Like most 19th century travel, certain hazards to passengers and cargo accompanied riverboat travel. Numerous wrecked and sunken boats offered mute testimony of the dangers interspersed along the banks and beneath the waters of the Arkansas. Submerged or not, each wreck added an additional hazard to be confronted by the next steamboat around the bend. For the fiscal year ending June 30, 1896, Sibert recorded substantial progress in wreck removals—a priority along with clearing snags and other navigation obstructions.

Sibert's domain included dikes, and there were many of them protecting flat, low-lying lands and communities, especially along the river's route through the delta region. Constant erosion often dissolved the river's extremely low banks and promoted channel blockage. The numerous bank collapses kept Sibert's work boats constantly on the job.

While construction of permanent locks and dams remained unapproved on a stretch of river, Sibert employed other devices to yield extra inches of water for floating the flatboats. For example, the officer devised methods of controlling, protecting, and deepening navigation channels with low dams or spur dikes constructed from available, budget friendly material. These makeshift structures blocked all but one chute around troublesome shoals and diverted vital water into the open chute. Augmented by the additional water, the open chute furnished a safe channel around the shoals. Armed with all of the most advanced engineering expertise the Army could confer, Sibert often employed more ancient methods to construct the spur dikes. In an annual report, the officer furnished details of spur dike construction:

First, a series of poles, four to eight inches in diameter, were driven into the riverbed to form pilings extending across the chute or channel to be closed. Spaced six to eight feet apart, the pilings were then joined by horizontal stringers made of poles that were wired or nailed securely in place. Bundles of brush (fascines) were next placed against the framework of pilings and stringers, their tops weighted with sandbags, to produce a barrier or dam capable of closing the chute. When river conditions prevented workers from wading and placing the brush, mattresses of the material were woven and installed from a barge.

Sibert used five small barges to build spur dikes, each vessel 30 feet in length with a beam of 18 feet and drawing less than 20 inches of water. A hand-driven pile driver graced one of the barges. The engineer's fleet also included one larger work barge, 60 feet in length (requiring three feet of water), and a 35-foot living boat on which were placed two tents "for use of the white persons in the working party. Colored labor was used, being paid at the rate of $1 per day and raw rations furnished them prior to October 17, after which time the wages were increased 25 cents per day."

While not spectacular and rarely exceeding five feet in height above the surface of the river, spur dikes worked well until funding permitted construction of permanent locks and dams. Minimal by any standard, the dikes kept open a two-foot channel on the upper reaches of the Arkansas and its tributaries—a boon of great worth to farmers, merchants, and rivermen in the region.

On at least one occasion, Sibert conducted a study of the Arkansas River to determine if dikes constructed in 1889 and 1894 contributed to erosion of the river's banks in the vicinity of Dardanelle, Arkansas. Completed in October 1897, the study concluded that instead of promoting erosion, the dikes were instrumental in slowing the process, protecting the banks from caving in along two miles of the river upstream from the town. New projects, surveys, and investigations followed, with another always awaiting Sibert just around the next bend in the Arkansas. [8]

In the normal course of managing and expanding the slack water navigation system, the officer ruffled a few civilian feathers, but not a lot. For the most part, his efforts to improve river navigation pleased the citizens of Arkansas. Rivermen and the general business community recognized the boost river improvements gave to the state's economic development. If that were not enough, the Sibert family was doing fine, and the officer found good companions with whom to enjoy the region's excellent hunting. Nevertheless, he welcomed an order directing him to journey east for an appearance before a board of officers in New York City in early 1896.

When an officer in the Army Corps of Engineers was under consideration for promotion during the last quarter of the 19th century, it seemed to always involve a trip to New York City. More specifically, the Army Building with a Manhattan Island address, 39 Whitehall Street, was the destination. Its location was so well known within Army circles that a street address was deemed unnecessary on orders announcing such meetings.

In the small peacetime Army, and probably more so within the somewhat elite Corps of Engineers, promotions came slowly, usually geared to natural attrition—when retirement or death left a position open within the service. Promotion of a higher-ranking officer could also leave an opening. When a candidate gained approval for promotion to the next grade, a standard part of the notice he received contained a disclaimer of sorts. After notifying the officer that the examining board had recommended him for promotion, and that the recommendation had been approved by no lesser personage than the Secretary of War, the document concluded by soberly reciting that "you will be promoted to the grade to which you will next be eligible whenever a vacancy occurs."

That was the way it worked when Lieutenant Sibert appeared at the Army Building on February 25, 1896, to be examined by a board of senior Corps of Engineers officers, plus high ranking medical personnel. The tribunal's mission: Determine Sibert's fitness to serve his country as a captain in the Corps of Engineers. The visitor from Arkansas first encountered the two-member medical team.

Conducted by Colonel C.T. Alexander, Assistant Surgeon General, U.S. Army, assisted by Captain W.B. Davis, Assistant Surgeon, the medical examination revealed that the lieutenant had a divergent strabismus of his right eye and a slight stiffness in his right knee, said to have resulted from an injury received while a cadet at West Point.

However, medical officers concluded that neither the stiff knee nor the eye condition was a serious matter and that William Luther Sibert "has no physical defects which unfit him at present or in the near future for the performance of his duties." With the medical questions resolved in the lieutenant's favor, the three-member board of senior engineers got down to more important business: Could Sibert stand muster not only as an engineer, but as an Army engineer skilled in the profession of arms and capable of commanding troops in combat should the occasion arise?

The comprehensive and exhaustive inquiry included problems ranging from seacoast defense and submarine mines to various facets of the art of war, as illustrated by military history, military administration, field fortifications, permanent fortifications, astronomy, electricity, guns, armor, and carriages. These were not the kind of problems or subjects that had concerned Sibert in Kentucky, on the Great Lakes, and currently in Arkansas. The board also inquired about a number of subjects about which Sibert had a wealth of practical experience to back up his book knowledge. They included the use of explosives, the mechanics of engineering and surveying, the utilization of building materials, and the improvement of rivers and harbors, including canals.

Near the close of the examination, the board requested that the candidate prepare plans for the defense of the ports along the Penobscot River at Fort Knox, Maine. At that point, the lieutenant was asked to retire while the board deliberated his fate behind closed doors. When reconvened, and after Lieutenant Sibert certified that he had not received unauthorized assistance during the examination, the board announced its finding that "Lieut. William L. Sibert, Corps of Engineers, has the physical, moral and professional qualifications to perform efficiently all the duties of the grade to which he will next be eligible, and recommend him for promotion thereto."

Along with the surgeons, the three engineers signed off on the order recommending promotion, including the president of the board, Colonel Henry M. Roberts, who would later be elevated to command the Corps of Engineers. Notwithstanding his success as an engineer and army officer, Colonel Roberts gained wider fame as the author of *Roberts' Rules of Order*, which remains the Bible of orderly procedure in the conduct of meetings ranging from the lodge halls of America upward to the higher echelons of local, state, and federal governments.

Although Colonel Roberts was not personally acquainted with Sibert before being assigned the task of presiding over the promotion board, in 1895 he had served as chief engineer for the Southwest Division of the Corps of Engineers, of which the Arkansas District was a subdivision. Just prior to Sibert's appearance before the board, Brigadier General W.P. Craighill, Chief of Engineers, had requested the opinion of Colonel Roberts in respect to Sibert's "character, attainments, efficiency, and fitness for promotion." Colonel Roberts answered General Craighill by letter dated January 19, 1896, in part stating:

"Lieutenant Sibert was in charge of the Arkansas District with offices at Little Rock, Ark., during which time he made a number of examinations, surveys and projects which I was obliged to look into carefully, and it resulted in giving me a very favorable opinion of this officer's good judgment and efficiency as an Engineer officer. ... I am free to say that, judging from the knowledge obtained of him as Division Engineer, he is fitted for promotion to the grade of Captain in the Corps of Engineers."

Not to suggest that Sibert managed to bag Roberts' vote even before the promotion board was convened, but at the very least, he had favorably impressed the colonel with his handling of business in the Arkansas District. Having never met Colonel Roberts, Sibert was unaware that Roberts had formed an opinion as to his proficiency as an officer, much less expressed that opinion in a letter to the Chief Engineer.

A letter from the adjutant general dated March 5, 1896, officially informed Lieutenant Sibert that the promotion board's favorable conclusion had wound its way to the top of the Washington brass heap where the Secretary of War added his stamp of approval. There was also the infamous caveat reminding the lieutenant that his second bar would be added "whenever a vacancy occurs." Fortunately for Sibert, a slot for a captain of engineers soon opened, and the actual promotion became official March 31, 1896. On May 16, 1896, he proceeded to sign the oath of office as a captain in the Army Corps of Engineers at his office in Little Rock. [9]

The promotion changed little except his pay scale when Captain Sibert returned to Little Rock where he continued to preside with distinction over the Arkansas and its tributaries. It is likely that the captain's increased salary prompted the Siberts to consider another child, and a fourth brother was welcomed into the household with the birth of Edwin Luther Sibert in Little Rock on March 2, 1897. Eighteen months later, after having endured three months of discouraging professional disappointments, Captain Sibert's morale immeasurably improved with the arrival of Martin David Sibert, born on September 11, 1898.

With the fifth brother, Mamie and the captain now counted two Arkansans to go with their trio of Kentuckians, thereby completing the Siberts' male progeny. As for their father, he derived enormous enjoyment from all of the boys while continuing to attend to the navigational needs of the Arkansas River system. Through his efforts, it remained in good working order and continued to furnish a reliable avenue of commerce. That fact made Sibert a favorite of the Little Rock business community, and he should have been happy. He was not.

Three months of disappointments preceding the birth of his fifth son in September 1898 are easily explained. During that time span, the United States went to war, blaming Spain for a deadly explosion that sank the U.S.S. *Maine* in Havana harbor. Unprepared for the conflict, Washington appealed for volunteers to beef up the tiny peacetime Army; thousands of men answered the call, swelling the ranks of volunteer regiments. Soon, practically all of Sibert's Army colleagues were in Cuba, leading the volunteers and remembering the *Maine* on the firing line!

Meanwhile, Captain William Luther Sibert, a soldier well-trained for his profession at West Point, continued to manage Corps of Engineer interests on the Arkansas River. The West Pointer considered himself a warrior, first and foremost, and as he sat on the sidelines in Arkansas, he was indeed a sad and frustrated warrior.

Not much of a war, historians concluded after reviewing the casualty lists, strictly a lightweight affair when compared with America's wasteful Civil War. That seems to be the consensus of those latter day experts who give only minimal credit to the Americans for defeating the weakened and rapidly receding global empire of Spain. But the families of soldiers cut down by Spanish bullets never dreamed of sloughing off the hostilities which they regarded as a most important war. After all, their soldiers were as dead as any son, brother, father, or sweetheart who had paid the ultimate price at Gettysburg or Chickamauga. Their view of the Spanish-American War was also shared by some long-range, strategic thinkers who credit the conflict with establishing the upstart Americans as a world power to be reckoned with.

Although the war was relatively short, only 112 days before Spanish capitulation, it was long enough to have lasting effects on American politics, including the formidable undergirding it furnished Theodore Roosevelt, one of the volunteers who mustered to "remember the *Maine*." After returning to civilian life following the war, many other volunteers also entered the political arena, always making sure the electorate knew they had been among those gallant volunteers who whipped the forces of Spain in '98.

Likewise, career officers and men of the U.S. Army looked fondly on the war, perhaps having in mind the traditional toast offered each Thursday by the officers of England's Royal Navy: A bloody war and quick promotion. Gallows humor notwithstanding, if America went to war—any war, any time, any place—the dedicated, serious, and ambitious regular officer wanted nothing so much as to be in the thick of it! Sibert was no exception, recognizing that active service in combat was a career builder, even for an officer of engineers as opposed to infantry, artillery, or the more glamorous cavalry. It was not to be.

In a hand-written letter addressed to the Adjutant General and dated June 9, 1898, Captain Sibert applied for a commission as a lieutenant colonel "in one of the U.S. Volunteer Infantry regiments. ... The 7th Regiment is to be raised in Missouri and Arkansas and a portion of Tennessee. I am acquainted in the above section and could be of some assistance in raising a regiment in that locality." (In line with the Army's plan to use regulars to command volunteer regiments, Sibert's proposal made geographic sense, the engineer being well known in the area for his work within the Arkansas River's watershed.) A second letter followed, this one typed and dated June 15, 1898, in which Sibert cast his net as wide as possible in quest of a combat command. His sights lowered, the letter simply requested "assignment to duty with troops in the field." Other letters followed, not all from Sibert.

Little Rock businessmen rallied to Sibert's cause, at least by mail, the first letter dated June 13, 1898, and addressed to W.L. Terry, a congressman, with a copy of the letter directed to U.S. Senator James K. Jones, both being from Arkansas. Allen N. Johnson, secretary of the Chas. F. Penzel Grocer Company, incorporated of Little Rock, writes that if Sibert were appointed as an officer of a volunteer regiment, "it would please me and hundreds of others of your friends here, beyond expectations." With some precision, Mr. Johnson explained why Sibert was the people's choice and why his appointment would be "an agreeable act for the Government":

"Capt. Sibert is one of the strongest characters I ever met in my life. He is modest, unassuming, and his real ability is not thoroughly recognized except by those who know him intimately. He is possessed of extraordinary mental attainments, of fine physique and a magnificent specimen of a Southerner. He is from Alabama and his relatives, who were old enough, attained marked distinction in the Confederate Army. ... I venture the assertion that no army officer has ever made a better impression or more sincere friends in Little Rock than Capt. Sibert. ..."

The chairman of the Arkansas Republican State Committee, Henry M. Cooper, took the practical approach, reminding the Secretary of War in a letter dated June 15, 1898, that the Rivers and Harbors Bill was not passed due to the war effort, leaving Captain Sibert in Little Rock with "practically nothing to do and he is chaffing under this inactivity, and has this day made application for assignment to duty in the field." While agreeing with the letter's purpose, the officer knew there was always plenty to do merely to keep the Arkansas River open for navigation. He just wanted somebody else to do it while he fought a war.

John T. Morgan, Alabama's senior U.S. senator, penned a four-page letter to President McKinley, endorsing Sibert's request for combat duty and the state's junior senator, Edmund Winston Pettus, agreed, describing Sibert as "a man of courage, brains, will-power, and most excellent character as an officer and as a man" in his own letter to the president. Congressman Stephen Brundidge, Jr., representing Arkansas's 6th Congressional District, added his voice. (He was well acquainted with Sibert through their shared interest in development of the White River, an important tributary to the Arkansas.)

Recognizing much earnest effort to put Sibert in harm's way, Brigadier General John M. Wilson, Chief of Engineers, signed a document dated June 20, 1898—hardly half a loaf. While holding some promise of future action, there were contingencies:

"In case the assignment of Capt. W.C. Langfitt, Corps of Engineers, as Major of the 2d Volunteer Engineer Regiment will prevent him from accompanying Company A, Battalion of Engineers, to the Philippines, it will be necessary to assign another Captain to that Company, and if the Secretary of War so directs arrangements will be made to have Captain Sibert transfer his present duties to some other officer so that he may be assigned to command Company A." [10]

Too many *ifs*! Even if he got command of Company A, the Philippines remained far from the war's important land operations in Cuba and Puerto Rico—an unlikely place to garner glory and possibly a promotion. The Army had not done much shooting in the Philippines where Commodore Dewey routed the Spanish fleet in Manila Bay. The short and sharp naval engagement—a smashing American victory—forced an early Spanish surrender in the Philippines. Strictly a naval war so far, future Army duty sounded like minor police work while politicians sorted things out in the newly acquired territory. The captain of engineers considered the Philippines an ugly—and much too quiet—stepsister, a wallflower compared with Cuba where the Army was heavily engaged. Still, if engineers needed a company commander in the Philippines, it meant a troop command and that was what his four years at West Point had been all about. While his ability to command troops remained untested, as a politician, Captain Sibert remained conspicuously unsuccessful.

Not that he didn't try.

Finally, however, a real order, dated September 1, 1898, directed Sibert to vacate the district engineer's office at Little Rock and report to Fort Totten for service as an instructor in civil engineering at the post-grad school for Army engineers. Not the order he had hoped for; it failed to soothe a nagging irritant: Sibert's chronic discomfort brought about by missing a war and the chance to lead troops in combat. American land and naval victories in the Caribbean brought an unexpectedly quick end to hostilities with Spain, apparently ending the captain's combat opportunities.

In addition to his appointment as an instructor at the army's premier school of engineering, Sibert took command of Company B of the army's engineering battalion based at Fort Totten. His family welcomed the geographical change while Professor Sibert, with 10 years of engineering experience, ranging from Kentucky to Arkansas with the Great Lakes in between, began instructing the next generation of Army engineers. He passed on a wealth of practical advice, unavailable in textbooks, based on his experience in dealing with a variety of thorny construction problems. The officer's genuine interest in passing along hard won knowledge stamped him as an exceptionally fine teacher.

Free time for the Sibert family helped brighten the scene on the northwest shore of Long Island. And Sibert enjoyed the social side of peacetime garrison life after his protracted stay in the civilian worlds of Detroit, Kentucky, and Arkansas. Known as "The Castle", the Fort Totten Officers' Club looked the part, a brick structure with an impressive roofline and flanking towers, all crenelated like a real fortified castle. The family enlivened Sunday dinners at the club while Sibert, who knew good food, delighted in its consumption.

Mamie enjoyed the family's new quarters where only a short trip separated her from the attractions of New York City. The urbane spell of New York City, after the long Arkansas assignment, brought significant cultural and educational changes for Mamie and the Sibert boys. Their mother, and likely the captain, too, continued to pray for a little sister to join their male quintet of Army brats. Ever the outdoorsman, the captain's opportunities to stalk deer and chase fox on the northwest corner of Long Island were nonexistent, but entertaining the three older sons more than took up the slack. Ranging in age from 6 (Harold Ward) to 8 (Franklin Cummings) to 9 (William Olin), they joined in their father's outdoor activities, at times to his detriment. On December 28, 1898, Sibert fell and sprained his right knee while teaching the trio to ice skate—the same knee he had injured at West Point.

Sibert received his next order in the spring of 1899, sending him TAD (temporary additional duty) back to Arkansas. Issued at the direction of President McKinley, Special Order No. 13 appointed Captain Sibert to a special board of three officers "to assemble at Little Rock, Ark., at as early a date as practicable ... to examine the Arkansas River and report plan for the permanent improvement of said river." Inwardly grumbling at the interruption of his teaching, Sibert knew he was a logical choice for the job after recently devoting four years of his professional life to the Arkansas River. The captain possessed a broader knowledge of the river's current condition than any other engineer. [11]

Senior member of the board was Lieutenant Colonel Amos Stickney, the officer Sibert first reported to for duty on Kentucky rivers; 1st Lieutenant Robert McGregor was the third member. The order was clear: Meet in Little Rock and formulate plans for future development of the river. The lieutenant did most of the board's legwork, and Colonel Stickney reviewed the raw data and polished the report for which he was primarily responsible. In between, Sibert outlined a development plan based on his long and intimate relationship with the Arkansas River's watershed.

Spurred by Sibert's fresh experiences, the board completed its report in late May 1899, with recommendations for future river development. Sibert wrapped up loose ends and received permission to visit his parents before returning to Willet's Point. The Gadsden visitor found his parents in reasonably good health considering their advancing age; his mother was 57 and his father would be 66 on his next birthday. The elder Sibert did not complain about the lingering effects of wounds he had received at the hands of the U.S. Army while warmly welcoming his son, now a captain in that Army. Marietta Sibert, herself a veteran of ten live births in a rural environment, remained sprightly.

The captain thought the overdue visit to Gadsden was efficient use of his travel time, it being generally located between Little Rock and New York. And the week's delay visiting his parents left ample time to be home with Mamie, time to help in preparing for arrival of the couple's sixth child. Sibert looked forward to being on post and ready to greet the new arrival, hoping that No. 6 might possibly be a little sister for the boys. The baby was not expected until after August 1.

When Sibert returned to the family's quarters at Fort Totten, well before the impending birth, he began assisting his wife and readying the boys for the new baby. But for Sibert, his personal participation in the birth of another heir ended with the few preparations he completed. By the time Mary Elizabeth Sibert entered the world on August 18, 1899, her father was gone! The captain would be unavailable to proudly display the little sister to fellow officers and their wives because the War Department intervened.

Finally!

The Philippines!

The order from Washington confirmed that the U.S. Army kept the promise it implied in the pseudo-order dated June 20, 1898. It directed Captain William Luther Sibert to leave immediately for duty in the Philippines as commanding officer of Company B of the Corps of Engineers!

Mixed emotions permeated the Sibert household where Mamie and the boys were sad to see him go. However, the expectant mother's sadness was somewhat tempered by the knowledge that her husband, the father of her children and child yet unborn, was a professional soldier in every sense of the word. She knew his new duties as a troop commander in a far off land fulfilled a previously empty spot in the warrior's soul. For that she was thankful. Soon, she would also be thankful when the new baby arrived and broke the gender barrier.

Chapter Nine

TO WAR BY PULLMAN
AND HOBO STEAMER

The Spanish were gone from the Philippines following Commodore George Dewey's decisive victory over the Spanish fleet in the Battle of Manila Bay on May 1, 1898. Interrupted only by Japanese domination during World War II, the Spanish withdrawal ushered in 48 years of American Army occupation before the U.S. granted full independence to the Philippines on July 4, 1946.

That early Army included Captain Sibert, ordered to the Philippines in 1899, even though the Treaty of Paris officially terminated the war with Spain on December 10, 1898. Under terms of the treaty, the United States paid Spain $20,000,000 for the islands and the opportunity to establish an American presence in the Far Western Pacific. Initially, that presence consisted of the Army and Navy and little else. American business followed.

Even if the captain wasn't expecting to face Spanish guns, he knew foreign service enhanced any officer's personnel file at the War Department. Of even greater import, Sibert relished the opportunity to command Corps of Engineers troops in the field, with or without a war. But that changed, rather unexpectedly, when the American Army soon faced yet another war in the islands, a war close on the heels of the conflict with Spain and a direct result thereof. Much more obscure than the contest with Spain, historians encounter difficulty even agreeing on a name for the long and bitter struggle in the Philippine Islands, lately the property of Spain.

Soon after Commodore Dewey destroyed the Spanish naval squadron in Manila Bay, the American military forces in the Philippines were, in the eyes of many Filipinos, dramatically transformed from a generally favorable role as the good guys who had liberated the Philippine people from the oppressive yoke of Spanish rule. Almost overnight, those Filipinos who yearned for total—and immediate— freedom from foreign domination, whether Spanish or American, or English, or French, or German, came to regard the Americans as just another force of oppressive foreigners.

Many Filipinos perceived the U.S. Army—now cast in the role of occupier—as an immediate threat to their dreams of freedom. They brushed aside Washington's assurances that its military presence was temporary, meant to protect the islands against incursions of other colonial powers until the new Philippine government was strong enough to fend for itself. Bolos and bullets quickly escalated the debate into bloody conflict, a debate not entirely resolved until the Commonwealth of the Philippines became an independent nation in the aftermath of World War II. [1]

The origin of the conflict between the Filipinos and the Americans, and how it bloomed into a bloody and bitter struggle lasting far too long, is best left to a history of the islands. Suffice it to say that the conditions following the American victory over Spain initially spawned nothing but trouble for Uncle Sam's first real effort to play that long popular European game of *Snatch and Grab It*. The game's object was to dominate, one way or another, all of those potentially rich but largely undeveloped areas around the globe, with the home country being the principal beneficiary of the colonial treasures.

So, thousands of miles across the Pacific, the U.S. Army began fighting another war in 1899 and, from Captain Sibert's optimistic perspective as a warrior, it furnished a real opportunity to put his West Point training in the art of warfare into practice. However, there had been no guarantee that combat awaited the captain in the Philippines; his call to duty may have been in an entirely different and noncombatant direction.

Always a voracious reader of newspapers, while at Fort Totten the engineering instructor read news dispatches from the Far East with growing professional interest. All signs had pointed toward a rapid deterioration of the fragile Philippine peace. The Army was not doing well in its custodial role as keeper of the peace between various factions within the Filipino population, including a sizable contingent willing to take on the U.S. Army.

With the Spanish-American War concluded, Americans gazed across the vast Pacific to the Philippine Islands where action had resumed, or perhaps merely continued with some different actors, except for the Americans. Once again bullets flew in the exotic tropical archipelago, and the U.S. Army and its Volunteers left over from the war with Spain, feeling not at all exotic, were in the thick of it. Sibert, the newcomer, found waiting difficult.

Newly liberated from the classroom, almost immediately Professor Sibert was called upon to issue decisive commands based upon his quick-step exercise of sound judgment. Far away from the nearest battlefield, Sibert assumed the burden of command long before boarding the steamship awaiting him in San Francisco Bay. At Fort Totten, he was far from being alone when the journey to the Philippines began.

Sibert greeted his orders with enthusiasm, mainly because they focused on his primary objective, commanding troops in the field. The package included command of Company B of the Battalion of Engineers, the same unit in which he had served as a brand new 2nd lieutenant fresh from West Point in 1884. Sibert also commanded Company B when ordered from Arkansas to the Fort Totten teaching assignment. Personnel changed over the years and Sibert had not been on post long enough to become familiar with the new roster when ordered to the Philippines. Still, he had a snapshot of the unit's profile and its potential for service in the field.

The opportunity to close with a hostile foe on a tropical field of battle remained in the future when Company B's "CO" first issued decisive orders in a stateside battle—in Jersey City. Previously, the Quartermaster Department of the Army contracted with railroad officials to be supplied with a special intercontinental train of tourist sleeper cars to transport Sibert and Company B from Jersey City to San Francisco. Something went wrong.

At Jersey City, instead of the more austere version of the popular Pullman, railroad authorities produced only enough regular day coaches for the soldiers. The railroad official explained to the captain that tourist sleepers were currently unavailable at Jersey City, but arrangements were made to transfer the troops to tourist sleepers when the train reached Washington on the first leg of the trip. It may have been an honest mistake but not likely.

American railroads ruled at the turn of the 20th century and seldom erred. Instead, after contracting with the Army to provide tourist sleepers for the trip, they took the calculated risk of foisting off the more available day coaches on Company B. Surely, railroad managers figured, an obscure Army captain, in command of some undistinguished pick and shovel soldiers, would never question the change; he would merely order the soldiers to board the day coaches readied for the run to the nation's capital. That, thought the yardmaster charged with making up the train, would be the end of it.

The railroader had never encountered Captain Sibert.

William Luther Sibert, Captain of Engineers, U.S. Army, refused to embark the troops until the railroad produced the tourist sleeper rolling stock it had promised under the contract with the Army. Based on principle and the legal sanctity of the written agreement between rail authorities and the Army, Sibert assumed an immovable position. He stuck with that argument throughout the first confrontation of his Philippine campaign.

Sibert reserved a much more logistical and practical argument: If Company B disembarked from one train to board another in Washington, where no transfer had been scheduled or planned, nothing was foreseen except trouble and delay while unloading and reloading all of their baggage, supplies, and equipment.

Finally, just the thought of the extra work required to make the transfer irritated the troops. Like their CO, they were conditioned to follow orders, no matter how disagreeable they might be, so long as they were Army orders, proper chain of command and all that—but never the whims of a mere civilian railroad employee! While maintaining the reserve expected of an officer and a gentleman, their company commander let the railroader know that he never enjoyed being pushed around, that he never ducked a fight, and that his irritation surpassed that of his men.

Company B's confrontation with the railroad ended abruptly when the railroad surrendered after recognizing the mettle of their opponent, not to mention the righteousness of his cause. Next, the railroaders faced a problem of large proportions. Having banked on the Army benignly accepting day coaches for the trip to Washington, and regardless of the contract requirement, the railroad had no tourist sleepers available in Jersey City. That left them with no choice.

Behind a southbound engine, the chastened railroaders hastily assembled a train of strictly first class sleepers—all Pullmans—the most luxurious of passenger cars and the only sleepers readily available in

Jersey City! Of its own making, that night the railroad's bed was both thorny and costly. Meanwhile, the entire Army contingent—Sibert, his officers and top sergeants, and including the newest buck privates—began their journey to the Philippines, dozing in luxury while traveling first class. It all boiled down to sound leadership with a touch of verve.

The soldiers knew about the railroad's ruse and witnessed their CO turn adversity into luxurious travel, all of which proved to be a great morale booster. After the experience, the troops never doubted that their welfare was uppermost in Sibert's thinking. Smiles broke out around the Washington headquarters of the Corps of Engineers when Sibert's travel arrangements came to light, and some of the engineering staff even developed a modest swagger usually reserved for the cavalry. This new spirit arose as the railroad episode unfolded westward toward San Francisco.

Trying to regain the upper hand and preserve the Pullmans for more affluent clientele, a top railroad official telegraphed Sibert an ultimatum as the train sped westward: Prepare to exchange the Pullmans for the originally promised tourist sleepers at Cincinnati. There was no hesitation before the answering telegram flatly rejected the order. The captain cited the delay and confusion associated with the transfer of men and equipment from one train to another as reasons enough for sticking with the Pullman.

Again exercising the leadership that would soon be tested in the Philippines, Sibert had a plan when he rejected the railroad's latest order. The officer knew that Company B was only entitled to tourist sleepers for the remaining trip, not the pricey Pullmans he captured in Jersey City due to their owner's high-handed tactics. As the troops extracted their final fun and at least some restful sleep from the affair, Sibert positioned himself to negotiate one additional measure of tribute from the railroad before acceding to an armistice.

In addition to providing the tourist sleepers required by the Army's contract, the railroad company also agreed to Sibert's suggestions that only top quality tourist sleepers be provided for enlisted personnel, that an extra car be added to serve as a kitchen, and that a private car be furnished for the company's officers. Once again, the troops laughed long and loud over their CO's handling of their westward travel.

The next skirmish occurred in St. Louis where travel switched to a different railroad line. The new railroad insisted that Company B's baggage be transferred to their own boxcar, a ploy to increase their revenue at the expense of the original baggage car's owners. It looked like more trouble, delay, and stevedore-type work for the troops until their mild-mannered captain ordered "fixed bayonets" when railroad officials appeared intent on forcing the change.

Sibert never raised his voice in ordering four sentries on duty in each car, baggage car included, their rifles firmly crowned by naked bayonets and with orders to match: Keep out unauthorized personnel, which freely translates "railroad workers." Unaware of the rest of Sibert's order—that part specifically instructing sentries *not* to actually bayonet anybody—the railroaders backed off, concluding that any attempt to transfer Company B's baggage against the wishes of its commander might actually be detrimental to their health.

To a close observer, many little things Sibert did on that cross country train trip to San Francisco added up in the leadership column. And some things he didn't do also scored leadership points with his men. Company B's recruiting station on rails is a good example: While waiting to be switched from one track to another in the rail yards of New York City (before transferring to the Pullmans in New Jersey), two men made their way trainside and struck up a conversation with the soldiers. All it seems the pair wanted, both of them being ex-soldiers, was to re-enlist for another hitch.

Being well aware that Company B was fully manned, with no room on the roster for additional soldiers, the company's first sergeant quickly conferred with Sibert, explaining that Company A of Engineers, already on duty in the Philippines, was shorthanded and in need of recruits. The sergeant said the two former regulars had good reputations as soldiers and could be enlisted in Company A if Sibert could only get them to San Francisco.

Sibert inquired how the trip might be accomplished in view of the travel orders specifying a precise number of soldiers. The first soldier explained that requisitioning various parts of the uniform from members of the command would soon make the recruits look like soldiers even if they were not. As for the periodic head count of the troops (to ascertain the proper number for record keeping), the conductors faced insurmountable obstacles. When a count began, it signaled members of the company to feign nervousness or boredom and be constantly on the move; this milling about swirled back and forth around the conductor who could never be quite certain whom he had counted and whom he had not.

The captain kept faith with his top sergeant; he looked the other way and sympathized with conductors when passenger counts never agreed, always yielding different sums. When pressed by a conductor's request for the number of men in his command, he merely smiled and did nothing, pointing out that he had transportation authority for a certain number of men, and it was up to the conductor to do his own checking. As a result, two worthy recruits for Company A arrived safely in San Francisco.

With the train ride complete, some of which had been in the lap of luxury, Company B and its CO first saw the ship chartered for their trip to the Philippines. The *City of Parma* was not a salty version of a luxurious Pullman, far from it! Spartan accommodations distinguished the old cattle boat that had been converted to carry troops. There were no bunks and only limited space within the ship's interior for hanging hammocks.

At the time, *Jim Crow* was alive and well in the Army; in addition to Company B and a dismounted squadron of cavalry, there was a company of black infantry aboard. Like traditional sailors on their last night in port, Army personnel celebrated their last night in San Francisco in boisterous fashion, particularly the infantrymen who consumed more than their share of alcohol in its various forms—easy to do in a wide open city where celebrating was easy. As a result, an epidemic of hangovers and morning after ill feelings dogged the troops returning to the ship.

Once the *City of Parma* was underway and challenging those impressive Pacific rollers, it was impossible for the old cattle boat to maintain anything close to horizontal decks. Motion was constant, not only from a rising and plunging bow to a fantail always gyrating in the opposite direction, but also on the roll of the starboard and port axis. All of this three-dimensional motion put the most sober of passengers to the test. As for the hangover epidemic, it worsened to monumental proportions and produced a potent plague of *mal de mer*.

With the ocean relentlessly churning stomachs, lately filled with San Francisco's finest food and drink, the troops could hold nothing down. When the seemingly endless dry heaves set in, victims agreed that the pre-heaving vomiting was the easy part. And after escaping the initial onset of seasickness, many troopers fell victim of the stench created by the voluminous gastric gurgitations.

As a result of the misfortune of the infantrymen, Company B was assigned the upper deck for its hammocks. The landlubbers among them, which included practically everyone—a fair number of whom were also feeling the first symptoms of seasickness—were at first skeptical. That was before they realized how lucky they were not to be within the ship's hold, prisoners of the persistent and sickening odor that would not abate. The abundant fresh air offered by the open deck was no panacea for those soldiers prone to motion sickness, but for others, it proved to be an effective prophylactic.

Sibert's role in moving Company B's quarters from the ship's interior began with opposite intentions: a request made to Colonel Jacob Augur, the ranking officer on board, that the infantrymen be confined to their own hammocks in order to make room for his engineers in the hold. (The infantrymen had arrived first and boarded before Company B embarked and, in the process, spread out in the hold, far beyond their assigned area.) The colonel deemed the request reasonable as did the officers commanding the infantry unit, who immediately went below to organize their charges and liberate space enough for the engineers.

Too late!

By the time the officers in charge of the infantrymen had descended the ladders, those abused and volatile stomachs had erupted in full force—the stench being too much for the officers to overcome. It was not a life-or-death battlefield scene, and they saw no need to endure the wretched below deck atmosphere for the sole purpose of issuing a mundane command to their troops to move over. Upon their hasty return to the open deck, the infantry officers were freshened by the constant sea breeze and quickly regained their equilibrium. The lesson was not lost on Sibert.

The captain of engineers made a strategic withdrawal, canceling his request for space in the hold and graciously agreeing that Company B would do its part to alleviate the crowded conditions below deck by stringing hammocks on the open deck. It proved to be a master stroke, helping keep most of the engineers reasonably healthy throughout the long passage. When the *City of Parma* steamed into tropical waters, the heat actually made the open deck the only place to be. Nevertheless, Sibert kept a close watch on the company, always fearing the loss of a man overboard. On his periodic rounds, the officer found his men genuinely enjoying the open deck living arrangement. He acknowledged their greetings, managed a small smile, and barked a hearty "Carry on."

It is unlikely that the *City of Parma* could have passed tests of seaworthiness recommended by the U.S. Coast Guard in the latter half of the 20th century. It was a rust bucket of the first order, its chartering by the War Department reflecting the budget problems which always haunt the U.S. military in peacetime. Korea was 50 years in the future, and the term "police action" had yet to force its way into the American lexicon.

The adventure underway in the Philippines was not very well understood by Americans, many of whom vehemently opposed the entry of the country into anything resembling European-style colonialism. But the budget-strapped military welcomed the opportunity to write a postscript to the defeat of Spain. Action in the Philippines aided in the Congressional budget battles and, harking back to the Royal Navy toast, there was the distant but bloody little war carrying with it the promise of fast promotion. And war it was, small and exceedingly brutal.

As carefree as well-heeled civilians on a grand tour cruise to Europe, the nasty nature of war in the Philippines held no immediate concern for the deck dwellers of Company B. They shared only one unnerving thought: The *City of Parma*, a ship that had seen better days, was on a downhill slide and could not be trusted. Kitchen facilities were practically non-existent, and sea water had to be distilled for drinking, the thirsty troops welcoming the lukewarm liquid and learning to like it. Fortunately, while stopped in Honolulu to take on coal, workers installed better kitchen facilities and increased the fresh water storage capacity.

Whether the ship would technically qualify as a tramp steamer, its long list of deficiencies and, particularly, its generally ill-maintained and unkempt appearance, strongly suggested it was a true hobo of the sea. It surprised and delighted the passengers by failing to sink and arriving safely at Manila, just in time for plenty of action, combat against a hostile and highly motivated force of Filipinos who were determined not to trade a Spanish yoke for one of American manufacture. [2]

Chapter Ten
PHILIPPINE COMBAT AND RAILROADING

The farm boy developed the habit of early rising as a child because that is what you did on a farm in the *post bellum* South. With an early start, the young farmer completed numerous chores before the heat built up on a typical cloudless summer day in Alabama. For much the same reasons, the reveille bugler on the plains of West Point awakened the Corps of Cadets much earlier than their peers in civilian colleges across the land.

While some grumbled, Cadet Sibert enjoyed sleeping in those extra minutes before the bugle sounded—a luxury for a lad conditioned to rising before dawn to work on his father's Etowah County farm. As a Corps of Engineers officer, stationed for years among civilians in Kentucky, Arkansas, and Michigan, Sibert kept to his early rising schedule, continuing the habit in the Philippines.

Sibert arrived in the Philippines as commanding officer of Company B of the Engineer Battalion; another officer directed Company A. In the unusual table of organization adapted for the mixed Army of regulars and volunteers, Charles L. Potter, a regular lieutenant of engineers, held the temporary rank of lieutenant colonel of volunteers, making him the senior engineer officer in the Philippines—Captain Sibert's superior in the odd administrative setup. As senior engineer, Potter also served as a member of the commanding general's staff.

It didn't take Major General Elwell S. Otis, commanding the 8th Army Corps, Department of the Pacific, long to learn of the spirit and talents quickly displayed by Sibert on his arrival in the islands. An after action report filed by Captain Millard F. Waltz, a regular infantry officer commanding the 2nd Battalion of the 12th Infantry Regiment, first attracted the general's attention.

Dated September 1, 1899, the report was a no-nonsense account by Walz of his unit's latest encounter with hostile forces not far from Manila. His engineers being attached to the 2nd Battalion during the engagement, Sibert directed Company B in successfully clearing jungle trails, turning them into crude but important roads over which the battalion's artillery train and supply wagons moved with dispatch. Engineers trained for such work and, except for its exceptional speed and efficiency, the company performed routinely. General Otis, however, sensed something beyond the routine and expected while reviewing Captain Walz's report. It was short and to the point:

"During the engagement Captain Sibert asked if he might deploy his engineers on the firing line, and as the men had never been under fire and were eager to embrace the opportunity, permission was given, and they promptly dropped tools and used their rifles. They comported themselves very well." [1]

Although it would be awhile before the letter arrived in Manila, on September 3, 1899, Marietta Sibert—the captain's mother—penned to her eldest son the kind of letter that countless desperately concerned mothers had written into various and sundry zones of war. Composed on a Sunday afternoon in Gadsden, the letter is to "My dear son" and first warns Sibert to exercise extreme caution while in the Philippines.

The concerned mother recounted a story she had read from a Honolulu newspaper concerning another Army captain who left camp alone to go fishing, only to be ambushed by insurgents, "much mutilated and thrown in the river." Then followed a patriotic mother's wise counsel: "I hope you will take warning and understand you are in enemy country. ... Of course I would not ask a son of mine to shirk his duty. I only hope you will be on guard in an enemy country."

Taking the pragmatic Sibert approach, Marietta Sibert tried to cover all the bases: "If you are wounded insist on the surgeons instruments being clean and the work being done well." His mother's unrealistic view of what a wounded soldier—even a captain—might insist upon likely produced a chuckle along with the captain's appreciation of his mother's concerns.

As for the home front, the doting grandmother was on the job, reporting that she was having "some suitable and rather handsome clothes made for Frank (Franklin Cummings Sibert, age 10 at the time). I don't want Mamie to feel ashamed of his appearance among her friends at the post (Fort Totten)." Mrs. Sibert closed the letter "with greatest love and anxiety about your health and welfare I remain your loving Mother." The captain saved the letter. [2]

Back in the Philippines, any officer welcomed the finding of an exceptional warrior within the ranks, and General Otis was no exception. From all indications, Sibert's combat engineering practices were sound, his leadership capable, and best of all, he was eager to mix it up with the enemy. The general recognized the leadership required to simply move Company B from Fort Totten on the East Coast, by rail and steamer, to the Philippines during the summer of 1899, just in time to join Captain Waltz's expedition and engage in a genuine shooting war before the end of August. To the general, it all looked like initiative with a capital "I", which, of course, described the captain of engineers.

Less than two weeks later, Special Order No. 251, dated September 13, 1899, issued from General Otis' headquarters in Manila, appointed William Luther Sibert chief engineer officer for both the 8th Army Corps and the Army's Department of the Pacific. This elevation—in duties if not rank—was made possible, much to the delight of General Otis, when Potter was mustered out as a lieutenant colonel of volunteers and returned to his regular rank as a 1st lieutenant of engineers, leaving the captain from Gadsden as the ranking Corps of Engineers officer in the Philippines.

Captain Sibert found himself with additional duties as a member of General Otis' staff while continuing to exercise command over Company B. More responsibility fell on his shoulders when Company A, unofficially at first, came under his command. Notice of his performance while leading troops in the field also earned Sibert some microscopic scrutiny from high-ranking officers, a natural consequence of assuming a staff position. He did as well at headquarters as he had on the jungle firing line.

Sibert's staff duties consisted of many things although his major responsibility continued to be the performance of the engineers. Some of the work was routine, ranging from dealing with personnel problems when they arose to arranging for the shipment of tools and appliances to the engineering troops serving with the various units in the field. As the staff engineer officer, he was also responsible for the Army's survey and mapmaking capability in support of combat operations.

Early one morning General Otis arrived at his office at sunup, prepared to work an hour or so before his staff appeared. Although the privileges of rank allowed the general to sleep late, Otis continued to be an early riser, believing he could accomplish much before the interruptions of normal office activity interfered. He was unaware that one member of his staff was also a morning person when, on this particular morning, he sent an orderly to the engineer office to find a certain campaign map. The orderly found that Sibert, too, was already on the job and was able to quickly produce the map the general desired.

Once the general learned of the kindred early bird on his staff, it became his practice to send the orderly not only for the maps which required his daily study, but to also summon Captain Sibert himself. These morning sessions, which occurred on almost a daily basis when Sibert was at headquarters, gave him an exceptional view of the 8th Army Corps' campaign against the insurgency and with it came a deep understanding of the task to be accomplished. The morning sessions with Otis afforded the Corps of Engineers officer, never bashful and always willing to express his opinions, a rare opportunity for input into the Army's tactics and strategy that was well beyond his pay grade.

The relationship between general and captain matured, the junior officer becoming familiar with his superior's pattern of thinking and planning for future movements of troops under his command. This led to Sibert's seemingly uncanny ability to anticipate the general's next move and to have the required maps and supporting information immediately available when requested by Otis. The manner in which he provided this small service impressed the general, underscoring the general efficiency of his chief engineer whose knowledge seemed to go far beyond engineering.

As for Sibert, he recognized an opportunity and took advantage of it. He never missed being at his desk at sunrise and, along with his maps, readily available to General Otis. Moving up in the U.S. Army in 1899 was little different from making progress in politics and life in general: pleasing and impressing superiors with your talent and personality could smooth the path to promotions, choice duty assignments, and general career enhancement. It really didn't matter in Sibert's case that there was no quick promotion, and since he was finally in a combat zone—a real war—exactly where he wanted to be, he did not desire reassignment.

Captain Sibert was delighted when, after he provided maps and helped at staff level to plan an expedition into Cavite Province, the officer commanding the venture requested that Sibert be temporarily assigned to his staff. Brigadier General Theodore Schwan, a volunteer officer, wanted Sibert's expertise during the major foray into the heart of insurgent territory. The object of the expedition was indeed ambitious: Oust the insurgent army from control of not only Cavite, but Batangas, Laguna, and Tayabas provinces as well. The thrust targeted the heartland of the insurrection, the area where the belligerency began, its population vehemently opposed to the United States. The expedition's difficulties and dangers multiplied in the absence of a rudimentary road system, capable of handling wagon traffic. Progress always slowed as Sibert's engineers hacked out a wagon track through the tangle, while existing jungle trails provided insurgents with myriad ambush opportunities. Around the clock dangers permeated the march.

In such an atmosphere, Schwan wanted a reliable officer on the expedition staff, and not just any officer. Although not an early riser like Otis, General Schwan knew all about Captain Sibert's work at Eighth Army Corps headquarters. The captain's appetite for work impressed the volunteer general and, beyond that, he welcomed the engineer's unexpectedly broad knowledge of tactics. But, primarily, Schwan wanted a competent engineer at his side, fully recognizing that any path to glory in Cavite province, if there was one, had to be ripped and torn from the jungle by engineers.

The route Schwan had in mind was not at all practicable without a contingent of reliable and resourceful engineers to clear the trails in an effort to avoid ambushes and ease the passage of troops and the necessary baggage of war. In Manila and on paper, it looked like Schwan had obtained the best possible engineering support when the expedition pushed off in early October 1899. Captain Francis Shunk, a highly competent engineer, took charge of the engineers assigned to the expedition, and Schwan expected to rely upon Captain Sibert's additional input when problems arose. However, early in the campaign Captain Shunk fell victim to fever and was returned to Manila.

With Schwan's blessing, Sibert stepped in and assumed direct command of the engineers' company while continuing his duties as a member of Schwan's staff. The transition went smoothly, and the resulting command structure worked well, due in part to Sibert's confidence in Lieutenant Horton W. Stickle, a younger Corps of Engineers officer, later described in Schwan's reports as "energetic and capable." Sibert had already measured the lieutenant and found him adequate to the task and endowed with a full quota of common sense. Thus, the captain confidently placed the junior officer in charge of the bulk of engineering personnel accompanying the main body of troops on the daily advances.

In turn, this freed Sibert to try, with Schwan's blessing, an innovative approach to combat engineering—the object being to speed up penetration of the insurgents' territory by avoiding delays resulting from unfavorable terrain, river barriers, and the absence of roads. It was up to the engineers to clear a foot trail and transform it into a crude road capable of handling troops, artillery, and supply wagons as promptly as possible. Sibert meant to do it even quicker.

Because the captain preferred working from the best possible vantage point, a place where he could look ahead and anticipate the next obstacle to the advance, Schwan permitted the engineer to leave his customary place with other staff officers in the line of march. Sibert moved well forward of the main column to join the advance guard, searching the jungle for possible ambush sites and scouting ahead to locate hostile forces. Sibert led a detail of 30 engineers with a single wagon loaded with tools—axes, picks, shovels, and the like. Their rifles were used as often as the other tools of the combat engineering trade. On the expedition's second day, the engineers were actively engaged with insurgents throughout the day.

It cannot be said that Sibert preferred the increased dangers prevalent when operating at the sharp end of the spear, as opposed to the relative safety enjoyed by the other staff officers surrounded by the main body of troops. The point, the advance guard, was simply the ideal location to learn firsthand—and quickly—what needed to be done to keep the troops moving forward. And with 30 engineers readily available, it was often possible to make short work of an obstacle that, if not disposed of, would temporarily halt the main body of troops trailing a short distance behind.

While operating with the advance guard, Sibert charted tiny deviations into the route, actually avoiding some of the more formidable obstacles, while keeping the march on the correct compass bearing.

The engineers cleared obstacles from the path of the advance—usually mats of vines and undergrowth supported by palisades of trees that required chopping with axes and bolos. Lieutenant Stickle and the main body of engineers further improved and widened the portal through which cannon, caissons, and supply wagons flowed.

On the Cavite expedition, Sibert's engineers were flexible, versatile, and attuned to adaptation, working with available materials in a climate and surroundings opposed to their every move. As in every military maneuver, surprise and timing were crucial and could be either allies or enemies. One word—*deadly*—succinctly describes the surprise of a well-executed jungle ambush, an assault designed to upset the expedition's timetable. The hostiles knew the American movement gained advantage with speed, which left little time for insurgents to prepare for battle. With sound leadership and ingenuity, Captain Sibert helped the expedition maintain momentum and, on numerous occasions, succeeded in tipping the balance in favor of the U.S. Army. The crossing of the Tibagan River displayed Sibert's engineers at their best.

When the advance guard reached the banks of the Tibagan on the first day of the march, they found the stream to be a formidable barrier to the advance. The river could not be chopped and sawed out of the way, its waters swift and too deep to ford. General Schwan halted the column and looked to Sibert for a solution he hoped would minimize delay.

The captain of engineers quickly sized up the problem and offered a solution: build a ferry! Easier said than done, there being no proper material easily available for boat building and constructing the corduroy approaches essential for efficient ferry operations—if there were one. Sibert, however, readily recalled the numerous homemade ferries stitching communities and commerce together across the Green and Barren rivers in the late 1880s. Strictly utilitarian and never objects of beauty, the flat-bottomed boats were constructed of whatever material was available and, best of all, they worked very well.

Halfway around the world and a decade later, the captain took a few minutes to sketch a design vaguely patterned after the simply built Kentucky craft. He knew there were no oak trees in the Philippines, but plenty of strong bamboo and even mahogany was scattered in the jungle. He then mustered his sergeants and explained what needed to be done; the actual work began at 3 p.m. when work parties from the ranks dispersed on the double—loggers, carpenters, joiners, teamsters, and the pick and shovel gang to smooth out the approaches to the proposed ferry crossing.

Under Sibert's direction, work continued after dark, the ungainly craft slowly taking shape as carpenters sawed, shaped, and spiked it together in the pale light of kerosene lanterns. From the captain on down to the greenest privates, no engineer slept that night, at least not until the job was completed at 2 o'clock the next morning—a short 11 hours from the time work began. General Schwan welcomed construction of a ferry in such short order and was delighted with its capacity—able to support cannon, wagons, and draft animals, as well as troops. The general became firmly convinced that Sibert's engineers could build practically anything the expedition might need. With only a couple of hours rest, the engineers were up early, a clear reflection of their commanding officer, ready to join in the advance at 8:30 a.m. The ferry, manned by engineers, worked efficiently, allowing the expedition to proceed with only minimal delay.

A certain rhythm developed as the Americans pushed farther into hostile territory, the route step cadence marked by the ring of engineers' axes clearing the way. Engineers forged a rude path through the reluctant landscape for the iron wheeled cannon and caisson, pulled by ever reliable mules. Supply wagons followed, often pulled by water buffalos, harnessed like oxen, and remarkably adept at heavy labor in the tropics.

At times, the unwelcome zing of hostile bullets, fired from one or more Filipinos concealed in the jungle and dedicated to killing the invaders, brought the axmen to a halt. Dropping tools, they hastily grabbed rifles, always loaded and stacked within easy reach, taking up defensive positions along with the advance guard. In spite of the dangers from hostile fire and the psychologically threatening bolos, the sweating troopers welcomed such breaks from their laborious struggle to turn impossible trails into passable roads.

The Americans were equipped with far better weapons than the Filipinos, notably the Krag-Jorgensen, a repeating bolt-action rifle adopted by the U.S. Army in 1893. Perfect for the hit-and-run guerrilla warfare practiced by the insurgents, the jungle tended to balance the scales of battle as deadly fire fights continually punctuated the Army's progress. Many skirmishes occurred, but no big battles. [3]

At least there were no major battles until the main body of troops, after having occupied Rosario, moved against insurgents entrenched at San Francisco de Malabon. General Schwan expected the strong force of Filipinos to give battle, and he was not disappointed. Once again, Captain Sibert's request that he and his engineers be assigned a place on the firing line was granted and, once again, the engineers stacked their tools and shouldered their Krag-Jorgensens in the finest traditions of the infantry—the Queen of Battle.

And battle they did. General Schwan's report of the expedition particularly cited the performance of the rifle-toting engineers on the Buena Vista Road during a hot firefight with hostiles on the afternoon of October 10, 1899. Disregarding the deadly hail of bullets, the engineers fired as they advanced, not only clearing the road to San Francisco de Malabon of natural obstacles—but insurgents as well.

In the official account of the incursion into Cavite Province, Schwan expressed his satisfaction with the performance of Sibert's engineers. The general's language amounted to rather lavish praise when measured against the Army's generally conservative 1899 reporting standards. After making a final mention of the engineers' extraordinary 11-hour construction of the Tibagan River ferry, the general noted:

"The services thereafter rendered by this company (of engineers) was constant and invaluable. In fact, but for its work numerous obstacles of various kinds would have indefinitely delayed or barred the passage of artillery and train."

In summary, Schwan concluded that "Captain Sibert, not only in his capacity as Engineer, but also on the firing line … contributed in a marked degree by his efforts to the success of operations."

The Cavite chronicles would be incomplete without mention of General Schwan's chief of staff, a key position in the military hierarchy, the officer usually entrusted to assist the commanding officer by coordinating activities while maintaining equilibrium and generally holding everything together at the staff level. Although the expedition's official table of organization did not list a chief of staff, the general lost no sleep over the oversight. He had only to look to his staff engineer—the same officer who also doubled as CO of the company of engineers, and did triple duty by personally leading the detachment of engineers accompanying the column's advance guard—to enlist an unofficial chief of staff. Sibert merely chewed on his cigar and unofficially accepted the new duties with a smile. Always outspoken and never bashful about expressing his engineering theories and practices, the captain remained the consummate team player.

When Sibert found himself in the thick of things, in jungles where careless sentries were often bloody bolo victims, and where his engineers routinely alternated rifles with axes, good things followed. By October 14, 1899, the Cavite Expedition was completed and regarded as a success even though the struggle with militant natives was destined to continue for years. Sibert, now relieved of his temporary assignment with General Schwan's fighters, looked forward to resuming his duties as official chief of staff for General Otis in Manila. There was more to come.

In Special Order No. 294, dated October 26, 1899, General Otis tapped his chief of staff to also command the Battalion of Engineers, composed of both Companies A and B, the appointment retroactive to September 15, 1899. It made Sibert's command of Company A official, a suzerainty he had unofficially exercised since mid-September, thereby bringing Eighth Corps records in line with on-the-ground reality.

This growing array of duties greatly increased the officer's responsibilities although his rank remained the same. While serving in his dual capacity as General Otis' chief of staff and as the Army's chief engineer, Sibert met numerous challenges, including the constant juggling of engineering personnel, always in short supply. Based on his personal experiences on the Cavite Expedition, Sibert knew that competent engineers were an essential attachment to the various Army units that continued to energetically chase insurgents through the jungles and rice paddies of the Philippines. Without the engineers, most punitive expeditions bogged down, unable to move effectively in the inhospitable natural environment. [4]

The campaign against the insurgency continued, limited only by the resources made available to the Army to accomplish the mission. Troops continued to meet with some considerable success, as in the Cavite Expedition, and also when carrying out smaller scale enterprises. This prompted General Otis to mount the most ambitious offensive operations yet undertaken in the war, a plan he hoped would break the back of the insurgency. Sibert's engineers, always eager to grab their Krag-Jorgensens, plunge into the jungle, and close with the elusive Filipinos, were once again destined to play prominent roles. This time there was a difference—a big difference.

The ink was hardly dry on Order No. 294 when Sibert again vacated Manila, ready to direct engineering activity in support of General Otis' triple threat thrust into central Luzon. This time, the Army struck north from Manila with three widely separated commands and with a much larger overall objective than merely pacifying the countryside. Otis aimed the campaign at a single goal—destruction of the only remaining group of insurgents regarded as an army, the only hostile force retaining an effective command structure and the capacity to engage in large scale warfare.

At the risk of oversimplification, the offensive looked like this: General Otis ordered General Arthur MacArthur's (father of General Douglas MacArthur) 2nd Division to strike north along the Manila Dagupan Railroad toward the port town of Dagupan on Lingayen Gulf while General Henry W. Lawton's 1st Division moved forward along the Pampanga River toward San Isidro. A smaller third force, consisting of the 1st Brigade which had been detached from the 2nd Division, under the command of General Loyd Wheaton, landed at San Fabian on the Lingayen Gulf.

Sibert committed the main body of his engineers to the reopening of the Manila and Dagupan Railroad in direct support of MacArthur's column. The retreating insurgents heavily damaged the rail line in an effort to deny its use to the Americans. As the Army advanced, Sibert planned incremental reopenings of newly secured track just as soon as engineers made it passable. The short-handed engineers faced difficult problems facilitating three forward movements of troops at once. As the Americans advanced, engineers kept open the lengthening supply routes that provided ammunition and supplies vital to the offensive. And Sibert had drawn what proved to be a wild card—the Manila and Dagupan Railroad.

Before the insurgency, the Manila and Dagupan Railroad was the only railroad in the Spanish Philippines. The narrow gauge line, typical of its colonial setting, commenced service in November 1892, between Manila and Dagupan on the Lingayen Gulf, a distance of around 120 miles. Sibert immediately appreciated the strategic importance of a functioning railroad linking the capital with Dagupan, a key objective of the offensive.

Sadly, the retreating insurgents practically destroyed long stretches of track, leaving behind a largely dysfunctional rail line. Sibert was no stranger to the woes of the railroad: Soon after his arrival in the Philippines, the Army had ordered him to inspect early railroad reconstruction work carried out by the Quartermasters Department. His report, no doubt written from the practical engineering perspective, resulted in the Army transferring responsibility for rebuilding the rail line to the Corps of Engineers. After completing his report, Sibert turned his attention to staff work, followed by the Cavite expedition where there was a complete absence of railroads, not even dysfunctional ones.

Even though engineers had made progress, much remained to be done in view of the widespread damages. Only the rapid advance of American troops saved portions of the railroad from total destruction. As it was, the retreating Filipinos still managed to wreak havoc all along the vital artery of supply. In the absence of a functioning railroad, the quartermasters were forced to rely on carts pulled by water buffalos moving over the poorest of roads. The powerful animals tolerated the climate—so long as they were periodically cooled down—but were agonizingly slow.

Quartermasters did their best, but the advancing Americans required more than the buffalo carts could haul. When the campaign began, railroad repairs extended service from Manila only as far as the town of Angeles. There, ammunition, food, and all other gear required by the Army was unloaded from rail cars and packed into the carts to continue the long trip toward the action at a much slower pace. The captain of engineers greeted the bleak transportation picture with determination.

Between Angeles and Bamban, Sibert found that fully seven miles of rails had been removed by the insurgents and, in addition, the wooden ties had been piled at intervals and burned. Although this segment of reconstruction involved only routine engineering problems, the scarcity of material and personnel turned it into an enormous task.

There were always engineering problems to be solved along the way, and Sibert was confident they could be worked out by applying sound engineering practices, tempered with imagination and common sense. As for the personnel dilemma, it seemed to defy solution because there were not enough engineers to go around. Detachments seconded to the three advancing Army units left Sibert with precious few troops to rebuild the railroad. Then the officer remembered Company B's train trip across America and how and by whom the railroad had been built.

From the large colony of Chinese residing in Manila, Sibert hired construction gangs to do the vast majority of heavy labor required to relay the rails. The Orientals worked under direct supervision of Corps of Engineers personnel with approximately 300 coolies on the Army payroll at any one time. By tapping this reservoir of manpower, railroad rebuilding accelerated, also spurred by arrival of a shipment of new ties, which had been purchased in Japan. Although few stretches of the railroad lacked problems, most were routine and could be efficiently solved by Sibert's well-trained sergeants, supported by the coolie laborers.

The bridge over the Paranao River presented an entirely different set of problems, none of which fit into the routine category. Retreating insurgents dynamited and wrecked the bridge—blocking the rail line and creating a highly effective chokehold on the American supply route. The bridge had to be fixed and the railroad reopened as soon as possible.

Prior to hostilities, the bridge had been a serviceable structure consisting of four spans, each measuring 71 feet in length and resting on piers approximately 30 feet above the river's surface. The piers consisted of cast iron cylinders filled with concrete, a pair at either end of the bridge and at each junction of spans.

Beginning at the south end of the bridge, gone were the southernmost piers, the tracks, the adjacent abutment, and 125 feet of embankment approaching the structure—the effects of robust dynamite blasts after which the Paranao's powerful flood waters took over. Dynamite also blasted one of the piers next in line that supported the second span. Although the demolition should have dumped the second span into the river, the damaged pier did not completely collapse. Instead, after the explosion blew away a portion of the column, the remaining upper portion descended like a pile driver until it stopped directly on top of the lower column, which had remained unmoved and firmly anchored in the streambed. A big break for the Americans, except the blown out section had shortened the damaged pier by two and one-half feet—tilting the span at a precarious angle. Blasting also heavily damaged another pier supporting the third span of the structure. If that were not enough, there was additional and highly creative damage.

Before setting the dynamite charges, Filipinos jacked up the bridge's superstructure, and then lowered it onto greased metal plates in its original position before steaming a locomotive, at full speed, against the north end of the bridge. Thanks to the greased plates, the impact from the collision slid the entire superstructure forward a full 10 inches, resulting in distortion of every angle and measurement vital to the bridge's load-bearing capacity. The maneuver changed the relationship between piers and spans, scrambling basically sound physics and rendering the structure totally unsafe.

When dynamite charges failed to fully accomplish the task, the insurgents exercised one final ploy in an effort to topple the entire structure into the river. First, they removed the rails from the center of the bridge and realigned them so that the path of an approaching locomotive lined up dead center with an important bridge girder. Next, the insurgents opened the throttle on a locomotive and sent it crashing into the bridge's superstructure, hoping to unseat one or more of the spans for a plunge into the river below.

The superstructure somehow absorbed the impact of the locomotive without losing purchase on the piers, moving laterally only a few inches before coming to rest. Despite failing to totally destroy the bridge as they retreated northward, the Filipinos left the U.S. Army—Sibert and his engineers—with more than enough problems. He had no material needed for reconstruction, no cast iron piers to replace the damaged supports, and even if he had the hollow piers, he had no concrete to fill them.

Perhaps the biggest impediment to the project was the absence of steam-driven heavy equipment—such as cranes—the normally indispensable tools of the bridge building trade, the machines designed to give engineers a mechanical advantage when lifting heavy bridging components to the required heights. Other equipment especially designed for railroad repairs was also absent. It seemed that Sibert must start from scratch and re-invent the wheel insofar as bridge building and rail installation were concerned, regardless of insufficient resources. In order to send supply trains safely across the Paranao, the captain compiled a catalog of must do tasks, none of which seemed achievable with the dispatch required to keep pace with the army's thrust northward. Enumerating some of the big ones:

1. A sturdy trestle 125 feet in length must be built to replace the earth embankment, which washed away following the insurgents' demolition efforts. The abutment at the south end of the bridge was a dynamite victim and had to be replaced and linked to the new trestle.

2. The southernmost pair of piers (one having lost two and one-half feet of height due to dynamiting), must be repaired and realigned to restore the bridge's badly listing second span to the horizontal and provide perch for the southernmost span of the four-span structure.

3. The southernmost of the bridge's four spans, which Filipino dynamite had sent crashing to the ground, must be salvaged, lifted, and reseated.

4. The damaged pier supporting the third span must be strengthened, restoring its capacity to support the bridge and the rail traffic vital to the American Army.

5. The superstructure at the north end of the bridge, damaged by the locomotive collision, must be repaired.

6. Once the bridge was soundly supported, the meandering rails, intentionally misdirected by insurgents, must be realigned and reunited with existing rails leading north off the bridge.

All supply trains stopped and unloaded and Army units north of the river continued to rely on buffalo carts for resupply so long as the bridge was out of commission. With much to be done before it re-opened, two important questions required answers: How might the bridge be repaired—actually more of a rebuilding job—and how long would it take? Sibert must find a way and be quick about it.

The details of just how the engineers first located those magnificent mahogany logs remain obscure, although the procurement procedures practiced by Sibert are self evident. With a critical shortage of conventional bridge building material and supplies, Sibert proceeded to list substitutes for the most desperately needed materials, and then edited the list, striking items he thought would be impossible to quickly obtain. After thinning the list, the captain huddled with his most experienced sergeants, all of whom immediately grasped the problem. Dispatched in all directions, they scavenged the countryside for anything on the list, or anything else, which might aid in building a bridge.

A sergeant's sharp eyes fell upon mahogany logs, already cut and awaiting export when fighting broke out, stored at Murcia, another station on the rail line just north of Bamban. Recognizing that the logs provided many answers to the captain's want list, the sergeant immediately appropriated the logs for use by the U.S. Army Corps of Engineers. *Finders keepers* was a game in which Sibert's sergeants excelled.

With no source of railway supplies in the Philippines, Sibert was hard pressed to secure replacements for the burned ties and the rails that had been removed and either hidden in the jungle or damaged into uselessness. The situation eased somewhat when another sergeant discovered a large quantity of undamaged rails the retreating insurgents had abandoned at Tarlac, another station north of the bridge. Being an original part of the rail system, it was unnecessary to play the requisition game.

In the ongoing search for replacement rails, the Corps of Engineers cannibalized the ribbons of steel from railroad yards and sidings. Every inch of precious rail was preempted and spiked into the railroad's main line, always pushing forward—the goal being a solid, unbroken link between Manila and the advancing Americans.

Moving the cache of rails from Tarlac south required intra-service cooperation. To keep the Army supplied, replacement personnel, ammunition, and supplies were ferried by rail as far north as possible. The supply trains stopped only when they ran out of track, the end of the line moving slowly northward as engineers completed repairs. When unrepaired damage barred progress, cargo was off-loaded and reloaded on buffalo carts. The same time consuming task had continued as the usable rail line inched north from Angeles. (Sibert had adroitly avoided the same dilemma by his Pullman ploy in New Jersey.) The supply-laden buffalo carts continued the trip north at a sacrifice of both speed and safety from ambush.

Quartermaster Lieutenant Michael Lennehan, the officer in charge of the fleet of caraboa carts, numbering 200 or so, bore heavy responsibility and pushed the bull train to its limits to deliver the supplies needed to keep the offensive going. Even with the carts under Lennehan's command in almost constant service, with time out only to rest, feed, water, and cool the buffalos, he knew that the slow moving beasts hindered Army operations. When presented with a plan by the engineer, the commander of the bull train welcomed the opportunity to cooperate with Captain Sibert.

Pointing out that once cargo was unloaded, the bull carts were essentially empty on the return trip south, Sibert suggested that each cart pick up one rail from the Tarlac stockpile on the return trip to the railhead where it could be used to extend the system farther and farther north. Sibert observed that the narrow gauge rails were lightweight, and Lennehan agreed that the load would be no problem for the southbound carts.

The Army realized immediate benefits from the cooperative venture between quartermaster and engineer as the bull train route grew short- er, and the railhead edged closer to the Army. Unless there was an ad- ditional obstacle on the rail line, such as a heavily damaged bridge, the rails carted south by the bull train added usable yards to the rail line on a daily basis, and those yards soon added up to miles. Conversely, the route of the caraboa carts continued to shrink in all-important time, as well as distance. The joint effort shortened the time required to move supplies from Manila to the Army's frontlines where troops got what they needed on an accelerated basis. [5]

Once Sibert was armed with the legion of mahogany logs, recon- struction of the bridge over the Paranoa River picked up speed with the logs heavily relied upon for construction of the trestle and the abutment at the bridge's south end. The trestle towered 30 feet above the flood plain, the same elevation as the bridge, in order to tie in at the south abutment.

With no material to replace the heavily damaged metal pier, the one that had lost two and one-half feet of its height, the logs were again em- ployed. After first smoothing the log faces, the timber was stacked in a rectangle—log cabin style without the chinking—one upon another to form a crib. Sibert knew all about cribs used to construct dams on Green River and was confident the tower of logs on the Paranoa was an eminently sturdy structure that would not fail.

Once the crib was installed, it was necessary to remove the top seg- ment of the fractured metal cylinder, the uppermost part of the pier. The sizable remnant of the dynamited pier was not only unstable, but leaning dangerously toward the crib which was now doing a vital job— supporting a heavy truss, the heart of the bridge, on which the super- structure rested.

The damaged part had to be removed without knocking down or damaging its replacement—the log crib. Pressured to reopen the bridge as soon as possible and handicapped by a lack of bridge build- ing equipment, Sibert relied on West Point book learning and prac- tical mechanics to attack the problem. First, he secured a quadruple block and tackle apparatus from Manila, likely providing his engineers with the greatest mechanical advantage they would ever enjoy on their

Philippine adventure. It was hard enough to find the block and tackle and almost impossible to fill his next requisition—eight of the Army's highly valued mules. A discerning eye revealed the diplomatic machinations of his trusted sergeants in the borrowing of eight sturdy mules. Mules were a scarce and valuable commodity.

Just how valuable in the Philippines? For example, mules were indispensable when an artillery battery deployed and trained cannon on insurgent targets. Mules pulled all of the field pieces, caissons, ammunition, and other gear necessary to mount an effective bombardment from a forward firebase. Always dependable, mules worked steadily at their strenuous tasks, and the Army was well aware of their value. More valuable than men, according to the dark humor of artillerymen, explaining that once cannon and caisson were unlimbered, Army muleskinners hastily turned the mules, quickly withdrawing to a place of safety well behind the front lines.

Only prospects of the great advantage the repaired bridge offered to the offensive's supply line convinced the Army to temporarily assign some mules to Sibert's command. Even at that, it took some wheeling and dealing by the sergeants to actually muster all eight mules, hoping they would furnish sufficient mule power to do the job. Once delivered to the bridge site, engineers quickly deployed the mules.

Sibert planned to dynamite the upper segment of the damaged pier, dislodging it from its precarious perch on top of the lower pier. If the blast succeeded, the upper part would be free falling unless somehow controlled, and that is where the mules came into play. Muleskinners harnessed the eight-mule team to prevent additional damage to the bridge by pulling and guiding the falling piece of pier—now blasted free—away from the log crib supporting the bridge. (The Army furnished the mule handlers, not quite trusting engineers to do the job properly.)

Engineers attached the block and tackle to the top of the damaged pier, a strong line leading from the apparatus to the pulling harness of the south facing and patiently waiting mules. After the explosive charge was set, the fuse attached but unlit, the powerful animals received the command to move forward, exerting their full strength, as multiplied by the block and tackle, on the upper end of the pier. Under insistent and continuous urging from their handlers, the mules pulled forward and continued to pull as the explosion shook the marshy ground.

The heavy concrete filled steel pier crashed down in accordance with Sibert's plan. Mule pressure succeeded in partially controlling descent of the blasted pier, which came to rest on the ground after missing the crib by a matter of inches. Once the pier was blasted free, resistance immediately dissolved while the obedient beasts continued to strain mightily. Despite efforts by the muleskinners, the mules were immediately knocked off their feet, ending up on the ground in a jumble of beasts, lines, and harness. Fortunately, the sturdy animals were uninjured and soon back on their feet, and Sibert breathed a sigh of relief. He had successfully removed the dangerous pier without damaging the crib and had done so without losing even one of the Army's valuable mules. As for the mules, they had earned their oats at the Paranao bridge.

With departure of the mules, Sibert returned to relying on his small band of engineers, the indispensable sergeants, and the large contingent of Chinese. The coolies furnished manpower—the day-to-day labor needed to rebuild the railroad—which became more important daily as the Americans advanced in spurts and starts. The Chinese seated ties, and then carried and spiked rails into place under the close supervision of the engineers. Now supported on its south end by Sibert's mahogany crib, the bridge was almost ready.

The major unfinished task involved realignment of rails which insurgents had unseated and twisted from their proper course crossing the bridge. In their damaged state, had a train attempted to cross the bridge, the rails would have shunted it off course and over the side into the Paranao River 30 feet below. The repair job did not require a watchmaker's precision; nor could unskilled coolies complete the task. And it could not be done without innovation *a la Sibert* and the patience and skill of his engineers.

The lack of standard construction equipment continually hampered reconstruction of the Manila Dagupan Railroad in support of the American offensive. Bridging the Paranao is a classic case of a difficult problem being solved by ingenuity rather than proper equipment.

Thanks to Sibert's crib—that high-end edifice of expensive mahogany logs—the track across the bridge returned to the correct height above the river. There was another problem: Although at proper elevation, the track remained a full four feet out of lateral alignment, aimed at pitching a train over the side as a result of the destructive efforts of the hostiles.

In other words, the ends of the twisted rails did not squarely meet the ends of the undamaged rails in the next section of track. With proper equipment, the rails could be routinely relocated to their original position in line with the undamaged section of track. But routine had been lost somewhere along the rail line, and now every problem seemed to be unique, even extraordinary, usually made that way by lack of the proper tools and equipment to fix the problem. Sibert came up with a plan.

The only appliances available at the bridge and capable of moving the track were a quartet of jacks, nothing more. After a few minutes of intense concentration, the captain, for the first time in his career, called his most trusted sergeants together and asked them to be careless, just a little bit—careless *on purpose*. The non-commissioned officers, all true believers in the ability of their commander, carried out his orders.

The plan: With two jacks, the ends of the damaged rails were raised a specified number of inches above the road bed, as computed by the former Alabama farm boy. In order to do a routine lifting job, jacks must rest on a flat, stable, and secure base so they will not tip over. The bases of Sibert's jacks were not placed flat and secure but, by design, engineers slightly tilted both jacks—a most unusual feature for any jacking operation. One side of each jack rested temporarily on a wood chock as the soldiers began to turn the screws, slowly raising the jacks and their burdens—the rails.

Sibert calculated the precise angle of tilt; chocks removed, the contraption looked more unstable than ever—precarious and destined to fail at any moment. It did!

According to plan, as the engineers jacked the rails a bit higher, the jacks finally lost their purchase—much like a person slipping on ice and going head over heels—popping out of the way as the rails fell back to the road bed. Also according to plan, the rails were in new locations—a substantial number of inches closer to the desired union with the undamaged rails. There were no injuries from the deliberately induced collapse, the soldiers having been warned by Sibert to stay clear of the falling rails and catapulting jacks.

By repeating the cleverly engineered collapse again and again, the four-foot gap was closed inch by inch until realignment was achieved. The final act of restoring the bridge to service succeeded through use of a couple of jacks, some rough sketches, and very precise calculations made by Sibert in his field notes. Later that day, the captain telegraphed a report of the successful realignment to headquarters in Manila. He also instructed his sergeants that the next day would be devoted to a careful inspection of their handiwork. Never afraid to try something new in the field when the conventional approach was impossible, Sibert always seemed to go by the book when safety was the chief concern. The next morning found him inspecting the undergirding of the bridge prior to reopening it to traffic; the engineer wanted to be sure the repaired structure was adequate to carry supply trains northward.

At river level, Sibert was not disappointed with what he saw and was concluding the inspection when he heard the piercing wail of a locomotive whistle. The unmistakable signal announced the rapid approach of a troop train from the south. The train's arrival surprised the captain, and the inspection party could do nothing but watch from river level. Other engineers scrambled off the bridge when the locomotive showed no sign of slowing, much less stopping short of the bridge. Instead, it steamed smartly across the Paranao while Sibert, from 30 feet below, witnessed the newly repaired structure taking the full weight of the passing train with no signs of weakness or collapse. The bridge passed the ultimate test of its restoration with flying colors. The train, carrying its precious cargo of badly needed replacement soldiers, transversed the river and steamed a little closer to the frontline action. [6]

More than just the approach of the train, its whistle also signaled the Army's faith in Sibert, not only to complete assignments in a workman-like manner, but to finish *on time*. To the brass in Manila, the telegram reporting successful joining of the rails was tantamount to announcing completion of the bridge repair. Headquarters wasted no time thinking about safety inspections, immediately dispatching a supply train north with orders to cross the Paranao on Sibert's bridge and steam as close as possible to the American spearhead. Once rails were lined up, the headquarters staff found it easy to conclude that their prize engineering officer would have the bridge ready, and he did.

Reopening the only railroad in the Philippines consisted of one adventure after another for the captain, his companies of engineers, and the contingent of coolies. More often than not, completion of a difficult job led to an even more bothersome obstacle down the line, and so it was after the troop train crossed the Paranao. There was little rest for weary engineers because there always seemed to be another river to cross, the Tarlac River being next in line.

This time no bridge was involved, only the Tarlac River on a particularly nasty rampage orchestrated by Mother Nature. The waters of the Tarlac River flow into the Lingayen Gulf well north of Manila, at least they did before a storm carrying an inordinate amount of rain, even for the tropics, soaked the watercourse. The intense deluge came so quickly that the banks of the river were overwhelmed, leaving an overabundance of storm powered water looking for some place to go.

A short distance north of the town of Tarlac, the powerfully swollen river found an escape route—a lengthy embankment, composed of a dirt fill, and evidently constructed by the colonial government to contain the river. The railroad right-of-way ran parallel to the river with the levee in between. Built at an elevation well below the river, the railroad relied on the levee for flood protection. With the river abnormally high in the fall of 1899, however, and with the increased pressure induced by flood waters, the earthen levee was finally breached, just a small break at first.

The surging waters expanded the breakthrough, swept away a major portion of the levee, and flooded the exposed rail line—washing away approximately three-quarters of a mile of track. The unstoppable water aimed in an entirely different direction, away from Lingayen Gulf. The flood joined the Ohico River, which flowed into the Rio Grande Pampanga River, and eventually into Manila Bay before the Tarlac finally retreated within its original banks. With the Army pressing toward Dagapan, the missing link of track must be quickly restored, another major undertaking by the engineers.

An initial reconnaissance, followed by an up close visual inspection, revealed that the powerful flood had separated rails at the northern end of the washout. After the breach, the water pressure literally peeled back the slender steel rails south of the break, the cross ties still attached, in an almost graceful curve pointing away from the eroded embankment and the normal course of the Tarlac. Except for being dislocated, the track was in good condition!

Conversely, the condition of the old right-of-way, now the bed of the wandering river, was terrible. Even with receding floodwaters and the restoration of the levee by the coolies, geologically speaking, the roadbed was a disaster. The flood surge scoured it of topsoil all along the path of the rails, some of it soon to be alluvium as far away as Manila Bay. In place of the reasonably stable topsoil, on which the rail line had originally rested, was a layer of pure trouble—lots of quicksand!

The soupy mixture, with seemingly no bottom, extended almost the entire length of the displaced rail line and was incapable of supporting the return of the track to its former roadbed. The simple answer would have involved employment of steam-driven pile drivers to hammer piers through the quicksand to the bedrock beneath. Only one problem: the Army had no pile drivers. But they did have the captain of engineers.

Early in his career, Sibert encountered the effects of scouring and erosion along river banks in Kentucky, and later, on a much larger scale, along the Arkansas River. As a result, he became a leading expert on scouring. With Corps of Engineers approval, the engineer conducted extensive experiments along 20 miles of the Arkansas River, just upstream from Little Rock, exploring ways to control scouring and erosion. Knowledge gained from the study and from installing spur dikes of woven materials on the Arkansas River helped Sibert cross the quicksand without a paddle—or a pile driver.

Once again, Sibert improvised, adding a new dimension to what at the time must have been the unofficial motto of his engineers: *It's what you do with what you've got that counts!* They solved the problem at the Tarlac by improvising and using, of all things, bamboo matting!

A scouting party led by a sharp-eyed sergeant located suitable material for what Sibert had in mind in the town of Tarlac. Woven from bamboo slats an inch or more wide, the matting ordinarily served as walls and partitions in the cabanas Filipinos called home. The plentiful supply of mats was immediately requisitioned by the U.S. Army for railroad duty even as the captain's most experienced engineers wondered how the CO was going to support a railroad with the flexible but flimsy mats. Maybe, some thought, the overbearing heat had finally gotten to their leader.

Sibert quickly applied the lessons he had learned in Arkansas, directing coolies to sink the matting at intervals along the rail line's original route across the shallow water, which then varied from two to six feet deep. At each site, mats were joined to form one big mat measuring 50 feet square and securely pegged to the treacherous riverbed. A corncrib style pier of railroad ties rose from the center of each mat,

SIBERT'S MOTHER, *Marietta Ward, sometimes referred to as Mary E. Ward, was "going on 15" when she married the General's father, William Joshua Sibert, age 22, on September 28, 1856. The Siberts' first child was born in 1859, a daughter. William Luther Sibert was born October 12, 1860. The couple reared six more sons and two daughters—a total of ten children. Photo courtesy of Sibert family.*

SIBERT'S FATHER, *William Joshua Sibert, survived serious Civil War wounds while fighting for the South. When hostilities ended, the farmer mounted his horse (the faithful animal minus an eye and part of an ear shot away by Union ordnance) and rode home to Alabama. Unable to continue farming fulltime because of the lingering effect of his war wounds, the elder Sibert became a successful Gadsden, Alabama merchant. Photo courtesy of Sibert family.*

OFFICIAL PORTRAIT – Major General William Luther Sibert looks every inch the officer and gentleman that he was. Sibert wears the Distinguished Service Medal, the Army's highest non-combatant award, which he earned by creating the Army's first Chemical Warfare Service. Photo courtesy of Sibert family.

THE BELLE OF BROWNSVILLE – *The Lieutenant's Lady, the vivacious Mamie Cummings Sibert, was the toast of her Texas hometown when she wed William Luther Sibert in September 1887. After the wedding, the couple set up housekeeping in Cincinnati and 2nd Lieutenant Sibert began working on the locks and dams on the Kentucky River. Photo courtesy of Sibert family.*

THREE FUTURE AMERICAN GENERALS – *Just prior to President Theodore Roosevelt ordering him to Panama, engineer Major William Luther Sibert sits for a family portrait in Pittsburgh. Like their father, sons Franklin Cummings Sibert (back row, far left) and Edwin Luther Sibert (front row, to left of Major Sibert) attained the rank of major general during exemplary service in World War II. Circa 1907. Photo courtesy of Sibert family.*

SIBERT BRAINPOWER was not restricted to William Luther Sibert. His younger brother, Martin David Sibert, earned degrees in mechanical engineering, civil engineering, and law from Lehigh University and the University of Alabama where he taught mathematics and engineering drawing. However, the Alabama lawyer probably made his most significant contribution to his hometown as owner and editor of the Gadsden Tribune newspaper. Photo courtesy of Sibert family.

THE SIBERT CHILDREN pose with their mother, Mamie, and grandmother (left) in Pittsburgh. Photo courtesy of Sibert family.

TIGHT SQUEEZE – The packet Bowling Green, a sternwheeler, was bound downstream when it negotiated Lock No. 4 at Woodbury with little room to spare. Sibert restored the Green and Barren rivers slack water navigation system after finding it dilapidated when he took command in 1888. Photo from author collection.

STUDENTS AND FRIENDS CROWD CHAPERONE'S rails as the packet prepares to leave the Bowling Green boat landing for an excursion on the Barren and Green rivers—perhaps to Mammoth Cave. Thanks to the locks and dams at Glenmore and Brownsville—that were surveyed and planned by Sibert—navigation was extended to upper Green River so that steamboats could dock, just a short walk away from the natural entrance to Mammoth Cave. Photo courtesy of Kentucky Library, Western Kentucky University.

ORIGINAL 1839 CAPSTAN at Woodbury was powered by lock workers pushing on three staves that were inserted in the capstan (see square receptacle, one of three in the top of the capstan). When turned, the capstan engaged teeth on a wand connected to the lock gate. Depending on the direction the capstan was turned, the wand either opened or closed the gate. Although the approach to the upper lock is now filled in with soil and overgrown, the toothed wand can be seen extending from the capstan to the lock gate. The capstans served for 126 years until the locks were closed in 1965. Photo courtesy of Ray B. Buckberry, Jr.

WASHED OUT – Only a small part of Woodbury Dam No. 4 remains (left) after it was breached by a devastating flood in 1965. To right of photo, Lock No. 4 remains. Photo by author.

WOODBURY'S ADMIRAL Claude C. Bloch won the Navy Cross for heroism in World War I, commanded American battleships between the wars, and survived the Pearl Harbor attack on December 7, 1941. He was the product of a river village that prospered during the heyday of commercial river traffic on the Green and Barren rivers at the site of Green River Locks and Dam No. 4. (Historic Marker at Woodbury, Kentucky)

Heidenkamp Mirror Company,
Manufacturers of
Polished Plate Glass,
and
French Mirror Plates.

Springdale, Pa., Jan. 26th., 1907.

Engineer Department, U.S.A.

Washington, D. C.

Gentlemen:-

We desire to express our appreciation of the prompt and strenuous measures used by your department to prevent damage to property by the recent washout around Dam No. 3 in the Allegheny River at Springdale, Pa. The river had washed out around the north end of the dam and for two days it continued to carve out a new channel, the force of the water steadily growing in power until it seemed as if all property below the dam, between the river and the railroad, for the distance of a mile, must be swept into the river. It also seemed as if the railroad communication between here and the city would be effectually cut off.

We cannot too strongly commend the energy and zeal of Major William L. Sibert during this crisis. His recommendation that the top of the dam be blown off with dynamite in order to divert the current, was most wise and resulted in saving a large amount of valuable property. Our factory seemed to be right in the river's path, and while we have lost considerable land and several of our smaller buildings, yet our main buildings are intact and our factory has continued in operation.

We feel that words of highest commendation are due to those men who have labored so earnestly and so wisely to keep the river within its proper bounds.

Very respectfully,

Heidenkamp Mirror Company

Jos. Heidenkamp, Pres.

A GRATEFUL MANUFACTURER'S LETTER enthusiastically commends Major Sibert (letter dated January 26, 1907) for dynamiting Allegheny River Dam No. 3 in mid-January 1907, thereby saving a valuable industrial plant from certain destruction by flood waters. It may be the only recorded event in which a Corps of Engineers officer was commended for destroying government property—Allegheny River Dam No. 3. Courtesy of National Archives.

CAPTAIN OF ENGINEERS William Luther Sibert sits astride his horse during Philippine Insurrection. Note the "castle" logo on the saddle blanket, the insignia of the U.S. Army Corps of Engineers. Legend has it that the insignia is modeled after the officers' club edifice at Fort Totten on Long Island, New York. The Army's Engineering School of Application—postgraduate engineering studies following West Point—was located at Fort Totten. Circa 1899-1900. Photo courtesy of Sibert family.

DEATH WAITS IN PANAMA – Cartoon on the cover of the magazine, Puck (June 22, 1904), reflected the prevailing conventional wisdom—predicting that only death and failure awaited America's attempt to build a canal across the Isthmus of Panama—a feat the French failed to accomplish in two decades and at the cost of thousands of lives. Photo courtesy of Library of Congress.

ENFORCING "GUNBOAT DIPLOMACY" in a peaceable fashion, some U.S. Marines relax in a plaza while others seem to be standing guard duty at the nearby belvedere, probably in Panama City. Marine and Naval presence from the Nashville and the Dixie midwifed the birth of the Republic of Panama on November 3, 1903. The insurgents were quickly recognized by American Secretary of State John Hay as the de facto government of the former Colombian province on November 6, 1903. Photo from author collection.

UNDER CONSTRUCTION – Men and machines look tiny within the excavations required to construct the Panama Canal. Postcard courtesy of Ray B. Buckberry, Jr.

A BIG STEAM SHOVEL IS DWARFED by magnitude of a rock cut along the Panama Canal route—probably in Culebra Cut. This photo appeared on a postcard issued during the construction period. Postcard courtesy of Ray B. Buckberry, Jr.

WORKERS TAKE A BREAK in torrid Panama while relocating a rail line along the canal route. Steam-powered drills loom in the background. Railroad track was continually relocated as the canal path deepened and pushed forward across the isthmus. The rail system's capacity to haul bulky material—supplies "in" and excavated rock and dirt "out"—played an indispensable part in the canal success story. Postcard courtesy of Ray B. Buckberry, Jr.

DIGGING AND BLASTING a path for Gatun Dam's spillway, a steam-powered drill (foreground) sinks dynamite holes in rock while (background) a steam shovel loads rail cars with spoil from previous blasting. Photo courtesy of Library of Congress.

HUGE PENSTOCKS being installed by workmen will eventually channel Gatun Lake water into the hydroelectric plant. The water will power the turbines that create electricity for use in operation of Gatun Locks and Dam. Part of the Gatun Dam spillway structure is seen in right background. Photo from author collection.

TWO GATUN CONCRETE MIXERS *discharge wet concrete into buckets aboard railway cars (foreground) for transport to the Gatun Locks construction site. Two adjacent giant mixers blend the next batch in a non-stop cycle of concrete production. The railway cars shuttle the concrete buckets to the locks where each bucket will be separately hoisted by an aerial tramway for the final leg of its journey to the concrete pour site. Photo courtesy of Library of Congress.*

AERIAL TRAMS HOIST AND DELIVER *buckets of wet concrete to the Gatun Locks construction site. The steel cables, from which the trams are suspended, carry the heavy loads of concrete and are faintly visible in this photo. One of the steel towers supporting the cables is at left of photo. The tower is mobile and moves on tracks to keep up with the concrete pour sites. Photo courtesy of Library of Congress.*

IMMENSE AND MOBILE STEEL FORMS were installed on tracks to move after each segment of a lock wall was completed. Each form molded tier after tier of wet concrete into a solid section of wall before a locomotive moved the form a precise number of feet to the spot from which the next section of lock wall would arise. Photo courtesy of Library of Congress.

THE FLOOR OF GATUN LOCKS is generously spread with concrete supplied by the aerial tram system. The towers supporting the tram's cable system are faintly visible in the background. Photo Courtesy of Library of Congress.

GATUN LOCKS TAKE SHAPE under the watchful eyes of Army engineers. Filled with varied building activities—all going on at once—the embryonic locks seem clogged with all manner of material, equipment, and debris. However, the apparent confusion was, in reality, acutely planned and finely tuned for efficient operation by Sibert's team of engineers. To the left of the photo is the mouth of a huge conduit that will fill and empty the lock chambers of water when operations begin. Photo courtesy of Library of Congress.

A CONCRETE CANYON designed to link ocean-going ships plying the Atlantic Ocean with manmade Gatun Lake and, eventually, the Pacific Ocean (and vice versa), nears completion— the world's largest poured concrete monolith. Central to the photo is a mobile tower that supported the aerial tramway by which immense amounts of concrete were consistently delivered to feed the enormous record-breaking concrete pour. Photo from author collection.

THE GATES OF GATUN LOCKS appear slightly ajar as workers scramble to complete construction well before schedule. Thousands of rivets were used to fabricate four pairs of leviathan gates to control the depth of water in Gatun's sea, middle, and lake locks. The finished gates were painted battleship grey. Photo courtesy of Library of Congress.

GATUN DAM SPILLWAY is open to the stops in this photo, discharging thousands of gallons of water per minute. During construction, the spillway remained open to accommodate the natural flow of the Chagres River. When the Gatun Locks and Dam were finished, the spillway was closed, effectively damming the Chagres and impounding its waters to form Gatun Lake. The spillway continues to function and control the lake level. Photo from author collection.

TRIUMPHANT ENTRY – The tugboat Gatun, with Sibert aboard, enters the wide open sea gate from sea level on September 26, 1913. Once closed, the sea gate will shut out Atlantic waters and the tug will be lifted upward by the triple-tiered locks almost 65 feet (precisely 64.70 feet). When the lake gate opens, the Gatun proudly steamed into Lake Gatun to complete the first full transit of Gatun Locks. Photo from author collection.

SIBERT'S NAVY consisted of dredges and barges, all searching for solid bedrock on which to base the approaches to the sea gate at Gatun Locks. The dredges succeeded in sucking out the soft overburden to expose the much sought after bedrock. Although not always a pretty sight, it was a deftly orchestrated water ballet—tactics imaginatively applied by Sibert to solve the last big problem and finally complete Gatun Locks. Photo from author collection.

THE STEAMER ANCON enters the sea lock at Gatun to begin the first full transit of the entire Panama Canal—all the way from the Atlantic to the Pacific—on August 15, 1914. Photo courtesy of Library of Congress

TR ON THE JOB – President Theodore Roosevelt (white suit, back to camera) interviews the operator of a huge steam shovel on the floor of the future canal. TR's First Lady, Edith Roosevelt, later visited the Canal Zone while the former president explored the Amazon jungle, an expedition that almost cost him his life. After a tour of Gatun, Mrs. Roosevelt shared a memorable lunch in then-Lieutenant Colonel Sibert's quarters. Photo courtesy of Library of Congress.

ROCK AND DIRT "SPOIL" EXCAVATED by David DuBose Gaillard from the Central Division canal route was shipped out by rail. In the Atlantic Division, Sibert recycled much of the debris into Gatun Dam. Railroad tracks and rolling stock moved practically everything that needed to be moved during construction of the Panama Canal. Photo from author collection.

LANDSLIDES IN CULEBRA CUT remained a constant foe of Lieutenant Colonel David Gaillard, commander of the Central Division during canal construction. The great Cucaracha Slide on February 2, 1913, involved in excess of 2,900,000 cubic yards of rock and dirt (dark mass near center of photo). Because of the unstable nature of the land in Culebra Cut, crews were kept busy removing avalanches from parts of the canal previously excavated. This problem has continued over the years. Photo from author collection.

ON THE PACIFIC SIDE of the Panama Canal, the approach to Pedro Miguel Locks (in background) nears completion. Contrary to Sibert's suggestion that a single dam, paired with multiple locks (like Gatun's design), be installed on the Pacific side, Goethals insisted on separate installations—Pedro Miguel and Mira Flores. The two Pacific sets of locks subsequently proved more complicated and costly to administer and operate for obvious reasons. Postcard courtesy of Ray B. Buckberry, Jr.

NAVAL SHORT CUT – With room to spare, the U.S Navy's pre-dreadnought battleship, the U.S.S. Kentucky, dominates the middle chamber of Gatun Locks while steaming from the Atlantic to the Pacific. The length of each Gatun lock chamber was expanded from 900 to 1,000 feet (and boosted in width from 95 to 110 feet) to accommodate the larger ships envisioned by the Navy in the future. Shortening the Navy's route between America's coasts was a key reason for President Roosevelt's push for an isthmian canal. Photo from author collection.

CANAL STAR William Luther Sibert displays the single star of a brigadier general on his overseas cap after Congress promoted him to flag rank—a reward for outstanding leadership and engineering excellence he displayed during construction of the Panama Canal. The elevation in rank was a welcome honor even though it created a serious "pedigree" problem for the engineer's Army career. Circa 1915. Photo courtesy of Sibert family.

SIGNATURE CIGAR – The unlit cigar was a Sibert trademark. Tightly clamped and jutting aggressively forward, the stogy meant that the Army engineer (pictured here on a Red Cross mission in China) was thinking—hard at work on the next problem demanding attention and a solution. Circa 1914. Photo courtesy of Sibert family.

WEST POINT ROOMMATES and dedicated U.S. Army Corps of Engineers officers were honored on Canal Zone postage stamps for their leading roles in the building of the Panama Canal. David Dubose Gaillard's portrait appears on the 12-cent stamp and William Luther "Goliath" Sibert's portrait graces the 14-cent stamp. Photo from author collection.

WORLD WAR I VINTAGE campaign hat graces portrait of Major General William Luther Sibert. Circa 1918. Photo courtesy of Sibert family.

SIBERT'S BIG RED 1 INFANTRY DIVISION maneuvers in France before an all-star audience. Sibert (in helmet) stands next to AEF commander John J. Pershing (in campaign hat). To General Pershing's left are French President Poincare (visored cap) and French Premier Painleve. With upraised hand, France's Marshal Petain looks away from camera. Pershing criticized the division's performance but his real target was the engineer (Sibert); he did not want an engineer officer commanding his only available infantry division. Photo courtesy of Sibert family.

BETWEEN THE WARS, a young Army officer and future general, Edwin Luther Sibert, visited his father's river farm in Bowling Green, Kentucky, on numerous occasions. The Sibert home offered the General's children and grandchildren a pleasant retreat. The welcome mat was always out at the river farm. Photo courtesy of Sibert family.

GENERAL SIBERT'S HOME still stands on the old Sibert farm (now the Hill farm) near Bowling Green, Kentucky. Located at the end of old McFarland's Beach Road (now McFarland's Lane), the farm looks down on Barren River from high bluffs on the front end, with lowland and islands on the backside. It was a perfect location for the General's fox hounds and the quarry they chased. Photo by author.

THE SURRENDER OF PARIS
25 August 1944

The background and salient features of the surrender of Paris are set forth in IS PARIS BURNING by Collins and Lapierre 1965 and in Vol. I of the official publication: FIRST UNITED STATES ARMY - REPORT OF OPERATIONS.

Below are the points as regards the surrender itself that I personally witnessed.

Early on 25 August 1944, accompanied by Major Paul Sapieha of the G-2 Section of the Headquarters of Gen. Omar Bradley's 12th Army Group, I drove to Porte Orleans on the southern edge of Paris and followed the command vehicle of General Leclerc's French 2nd Armored Division into the city arriving at the Gare Montparnasse shortly before noon. After some delay caused by a very trigger-happy group of French and American units, I reported to Major General Leonard T. Gerow, commanding the U. S. V Corps, in the railroad station itself.

In an improvised office, Gen. Gerow was in the act of accepting the oral, unconditional surrender of the city from German General of Infantry von Choltitz the commander of the city's garrison. Gerow told the German general to send out surrender orders to his various subordinate units in the city requiring an immediate cease fire and to that end asked if anyone present could type in German from dictation. Major (later Lt. Col.) Sapieha volunteered, seated himself at a typewriter and pursuant to von Choltitz's dictation typed an original and five carbon copies which when split up made about thirty copies of an order slip to his appropriate subordinates requiring that they cease resistance.

Sapieha gave some 28 copies to Gen. Gerow, gave me a copy (herewith) and may have kept a copy himself.

Twenty-five courier parties were dispatched, each consisting of a jeep with a U. S. driver, an American officer, a French officer and a German officer with the mission of delivering the order to the various German strong point commanders.

When these vehicles started out into the crowded Place Montparnasse they were able to proceed only with great difficulty due to the hatred evinced by the French civilian population toward the German officers in the different groups. They were cursed, struck and spat upon and were only saved from lynchings by the allied members of the parties. All parties got through and with one exception were effective. The exception was near Vincennes where a group of die-hards shot the French and German officers and held out until 27 August.

Edwin L. Sibert
Major General U.S.A. retired
formerly G-2, 12th Army Group

SAVING PARIS IN 1944 is the subject of Major General Edwin Luther Sibert's monograph containing details of his personal involvement in arranging for the German surrender. Although ordered by Hitler to defend Paris to the last man, and in the process, destroy the city, the German commander met Sibert and other Allied officers under a flag of truce and surrendered the German garrison guarding the French capital on August 25, 1944. Photo courtesy of Sibert family.

Native Of Bowling Green Leads Attack On Samar

10-29-44

MACARTHUR'S HEADQUARTERS, Philippines, (Sunday), Oct. 29—P—(Via Army Radio)—Destruction of 16 Japanese warships, including two battleships, by American planes and warships in the Leyte Gulf Oct. 25, was confirmed by Gen. Douglas MacArthur today.

The entire Japanese task force that came through Surigao Strait was wiped out.

MacArthur said two battleships, one heavy and one light cruiser and six destroyers were sunk in the immediate action.

The remaining two cruisers and four destroyers were severely damaged in this action and fled only to be sunk by subsequent air attacks.

The general said many survivors from the sunken enemy warships have been captured, including a captain of one of the destroyers.

The battleships were the Yamashiro and Fuso.

North and south, ground forces fighting toward a juncture reported successes as MacArthur's Leyte campaign proceeded swiftly. Troops moved forward all along the line in pursuit of the demoralized troops of the Japanese 16th division.

Aerial action on the island saw 20 Japanese planes shot down, 18 by American fighters and two by ack-ack.

Schools in the liberated areas of Leyte now are being reopened and enemy air raids while continuing are light and ineffectual.

Elements of the Seventh Division, driving up from the south moved to within one mile of Dagami, a gain of a mile since yesterday's

(Continued on page 13, column 2)

...e Of This City ...Attack

(Continued from page 1)

communique. Dagami is the main supply and troop junction of the Japanese 16th.

MacArthur's men were bent on destroying the Japanese 16th to avenge the death march on Bataan.

There was no further word on the action on Samar where yesterday most of the island was under American-Filipino domination. Troops of Maj. Gen. Franklin C. Sibert's 10th Corps are operating on the island which reaches to within 15 miles of Luzon, main island of the Philippines.

Gen. Sibert, who was born in Bowling Green, Jan. 3, 1891, is a son of the late Maj. Gen. William L. Sibert, member of the Panama Canal Commission from 1907 to 1914.

The elder Gen. Sibert commanded and trained the First Division which was the first division to reach France in World War 1. Gen. Sibert was recalled to the United States in 1918 to become director of Chemical Warfare.

The younger Gen. Sibert was awarded the Legion of Merit in January, 1944, for superior training in offensive warfare.

(John B. Hughes, of CBS, broadcasting from Gen. MacArthur's headquarters, said that Samar now is completely in American hands.)

Appearance of the army fighter planes brought cheers from troops as they swooped to landings on newly completed airfields on Leyte. In their arrival soldiers foresaw a possible end to enemy daylight raids.

MacArthur's communique disclosed today that more than 14,000 Japanese casualties had been counted.

ATTACK ON SAMAR – Major General Franklin Cummings Sibert led the American invasion and subsequent recapture of Samar Island in the Philippines in World War II. The Samar victory came 43 years after the commander's father, Captain William Luther Sibert, led fighting engineers during the Philippine Insurrection. Park City Daily News, October 29, 1944. Courtesy of Kentucky Library, Western Kentucky University.

GENERAL SIBERT'S DEATH commanded a six-column headline in Park City Daily News, Bowling Green, Kentucky, October 16, 1935. Courtesy of Kentucky Library, Western Kentucky University

with heavy wooden beams linking the piers and supporting the cross ties and rails installed on top.

The mats did their intended job—distributing the weight of the rail line across large sections of the unstable sand, as they floated, more or less serenely, on top of the soup. Then followed the Arkansas Effect: As river current scoured sand from around the mats' perimeters, the mats drooped around their edges, creating a shroud capable of protecting the mound of sand supporting the pier long after scouring ceased. Bridging the short stretch of deep water at the north end of the washout was routine, as was placement of the timbers joining the piers.

As for reseating the track on the new set of piers, Sibert did it the Army way with overwhelming muscle and manpower. Because the rails had remained securely spiked to the cross ties and attached to each other when floodwaters wrenched them askew, many hours could be saved reseating them if they remained in one piece. This time the job was too big for his sergeants, and it took the persuasive powers of the captain of engineers to borrow an entire regiment for the task.

Under Sibert's directions, hundreds of soldiers bent and strained in unison to pick up the entire section of washed out rails at one time. Then they began to patiently walk it back across the unstable sand toward the newly installed piers. At the piers, the soldiers executed one final, extremely difficult maneuver. Requiring coordination as well as strength, the troops hoisted the rails and ties atop the wooden beams, placing them exactly where they belonged—still in one piece. The rails were reseated without major injuries, just a few mashed fingers, and not a single man was lost to the treacherous quicksand.

The captain of engineers actually had minimal difficulty obtaining the manpower needed to reinstall the washed out track. His superiors were aware that closing the gap created by the washout was a key to the final push aimed at breaking the back of the insurgents' army and dislodging them from Dagupan.

It is, however, fortunate that another troop train did not surprise the engineers once the track had been reseated because, to the consternation of Sibert, the rails did not fit! In relocating the track, engineers had slightly shortened the route to the breakpoint by a grand sum of five inches. That made the rails five inches too long and impossible to rejoin to provide the unbroken ribbon of steel required by the northbound supply trains.

While Sibert puzzled over the problem, one of his engineers, an experienced track foreman before joining the Army, came up with the answer: "Captain, just let me throw a few kinks in that line; that will take up the extra length. ..." By adding kinks, he meant to pry several rails slightly out of alignment where they abutted each other, correctly figuring that the deviations would soak up those extra five inches from the straight line approach. Minus the extra inches, the rails were brought in line to correctly abut the undisturbed track.

The very temporary solution allowed engineers to push cars of rations across by hand during the night, using pinch bars to keep the cars on track as they crossed the kinks, the angles they had deliberately created. The following day, the ever-resourceful sergeants procured track chisels, cutting the rails to the correct length before mating them to the next rails running north. A good example of Yankee ingenuity! [7]

Nothing came easy, but once the Tarlac break was closed and successfully splinted across the piers, surprisingly stable on the bamboo mats, the engineers found fewer challenges along much of the remaining railroad leading to the town of Dagupan. There was a reason.

The rapidly advancing American troops, well supplied by the ever-lengthening rail line snaking along close behind them, routed many hostiles before they exercised opportunities for sabotage, thereby reducing the magnitude of damage to the railroad. However, from a point three and one-half miles from Dagupan, the American objective on the Lingayen Gulf, insurgents succeeded in removing the rails and burning most of the ties, but left the grade work undamaged. For Sibert's men, it was much like building a brand new railroad, three and one-half miles long, after someone else had completed the grading. Considered routine work, coolies were efficiently employed to do the heavy lifting under Army supervision.

While Sibert had pushed railroad repairs, fighting had been widespread with some large engagements, including the battle of San Jacinto during which General Wheaton's brigade soundly thrashed enemy forces on November 11, 1899. Still, it remained a war of countless small unit skirmishes, a deadly kind of infighting which required Americans to adopt many of the guerrilla style tactics favored by their jungle-bred opponents. For the most part, front lines were altogether fluid, and that had a sobering effect on Sibert's railroaders. They often found themselves targets for hostile rifles as they worked to repair the rail line. Firing from deep cover in surrounding jungle, careful snipers were difficult to spot while engineers working along the completely open railroad right-of-way resembled sitting ducks in a carnival shooting gallery.

The snipers, desperate to interrupt the American supply line, greeted engineers with daily doses of rifle fire, the engineers answering with their Krag-Jorgensen rifles.

Always kept stacked near their work, the Krag was highly accurate, if and when a target could be located. Its bolt action permitted engineers to pour a lot of lead into any tiny square of jungle where they observed smoke from a hostile muzzle.

On some occasions, more drastic measures were needed, a good example being the very first major project engineers encountered on the push north—repair of the bridge over the Abacan River. Retreating insurgents left a locomotive and rail cars parked on the bridge and then burned the wooden approaches. Rebuilding the approaches and removing the rolling stock from the bridge would have been difficult, but routine, except for the curtain of hostile rifle fire barring the way.

A trench dug across the right-of-way several hundred yards north of the bridge gave insurgent riflemen a protected and uninterrupted field of fire down the line, exactly where engineers needed to be working. Even though judged largely ineffective (except by a hapless engineer who happened to catch a round in his leg), the fusillade succeeded in disturbing the work in progress, prompting a highly irritated Sibert to call for assistance.

Overnight, a battery of three-inch guns was surreptitiously installed alongside engineers by Lieutenant W.L. Kenley. The field artillery officer and his gunners were waiting when the insurgents opened fire on the engineers' work parties the next morning. What a salute the hostiles received in return! It took only a few rounds of well-placed cannon fire to clear the trench, the riflemen withdrawing to the north. Engineers completed work on the bridge without further interruption.

Although loose ends remained, Captain Sibert completed the major portion of his mission on December 21, 1899, with uninterrupted rail service established between Manila and Dagupan, the port now being securely in American hands.

At headquarters of the Eighth Army Corps in Manila, the staff fully appreciated the work of Sibert and his engineers. From General Otis on down, they knew that any army, especially one engaged in combat on foreign soil while transitioning into the modern era of warfare, could go nowhere and accomplish nothing without timely delivery of ammunition, supplies, and personnel.

In his official report of the ambitious and successful campaign north of Manila, General Otis, Sibert's early rising superior, outlined in some detail the problems Sibert had faced and overcome at the Paranao Bridge and at the washout on the Tarlac River, as well as the difficulties replacing long stretches of right-of-way where rails had been removed and ties burned. The general noted the importance of restoring the Manila and Dagupan Railroad in support of the offensive: "The work of repair requiring a high order of engineering ability and great celerity, that the advancing troops might receive supplies, was performed by Captain Sibert, of the Engineer Corps, with two engineer companies and 300 Chinese laborers. ..." [8]

There is no indication that the captain of engineers found railroad engineering in any way disagreeable, certainly no more repugnant than any other activity an Army officer might undertake during combat operations. The job he accomplished reflects a high degree of engineering expertise and some astute handling of personnel, including relationships with quartermasters and artillery officers that helped the engineers fix the railroad. Above all else, Sibert's ability to accomplish assigned tasks with available resources, at times using unique or highly unconventional methods, set him apart.

So it was that the Army recognized that one of its own really did know how to run a railroad! So why not let him? By battling and building his way up the line to Dagupan, Sibert locked himself into the railroad business for so long as he was in the Philippines. He had not heard his last railroad whistle when the first Army supply train steamed all the way to Dagupan.

General Order No. 23, dated February 10, 1900, appointed Captain Sibert Chief Engineer and General Manager of the Manila and Dagupan Railway. In addition, the officer continued serving as chief engineer for the Eighth Army Corps and as commanding officer of the battalion of engineers (Companies A and B). As the name implies, general manager (not exactly a military title) encompassed more than just supplying the Army in the field where it remained engaged in chasing scattered bands of insurgents.

The railroad reopened for public use, providing both passenger and freight service between the capital and Dagupan, as conditions permitted. Not much new: Sibert's job involved another fix up assignment, this time spiced with a new set of problems. On the plus side of the ledger, the Americans aimed to reopen the rail line to civilians in an effort to boost the Philippine economy and restore a sense of normalcy to that portion of Luzon it served. In its quest for a successfully operating civilian railroad, the Army went all out, providing the new general manager with an impressive organization.

With small bands of hostiles still roaming free as the insurgency continued, the railroad manager addressed security concerns with two companies of infantry under his command. Sibert stationed one company in Manila, the other in Dagupan, with soldiers riding shotgun on the trains running between the two cities. His staff included:

Treasurer and Disbursing Officer – 1st Lieutenant Charles F. Parker, 2nd U.S. Artillery. (Lieutenant Parker was the son of Professor Parker, Sibert's tenacious tutor at Tuscaloosa, who, through Sibert, saw the educational opportunities offered at West Point.)

General Freight Agent – 1st Lieutenant John J. Haisch, 36th Infantry, U.S. Volunteers.

General Passenger Agent – 1st Lieutenant Robert W. Mearns, 20th U.S. Infantry.

Members of the Engineer Battalion, not attached to and supporting the 1st and 2nd Divisions in their continuing struggle with insurgents, drew railroad duty. Sibert utilized them and at least some of his sergeants to operate and maintain the railroad. He also hired civilians and selected additional enlisted men from the soldiers assigned to his command to perform administrative duties for the rail line. Although the railroad was far from the New York Central, or even the Louisville & Nashville, it was of equal importance to the Philippines as those lines were to their respective regions in the United States.

Sibert immediately conceded four absolutes when he assumed the throttle of the Manila and Dagupan Railroad (M & D): First, because the Army still had a hot war going with the insurgents, shipments of military equipment, ammunition, supplies, and personnel held top priority for space aboard the railroad cars; second, unless subjected to additional sabotage, the narrow gauge rails, although rickety in spots, were serviceable all the way from Manila to Dagupan; and third, the rail line had very little rolling stock available to carry either freight or passengers, the retreating Filipinos having destroyed or heavily damaged most of it.

Sibert tagged the fourth absolute as the most important, evidence of which piled high at each station along the route: rice, sugar, timber (especially mahogany logs) and other agricultural commodities sorely needing to reach markets. In that portion of Luzon served by the M & D, fighting had virtually destroyed an economy strongly dependent on agricultural products, the inability to transport produce to market being a major stumbling block to recovery. The vast majority of transportation woes flowed directly from damages inflicted by insurgents, putting the rail line out of business, at least until Sibert came along.

His military mission remained unchanged, keeping Army supplies moving while at the same time allocating civilians some freight space on the railway cars. With products moving again, the Dagupan and Manila markets reopened to the farmers and merchants along the route. The slender pair of rails furnished the key to economic revival. [9]

With the area under American control, more or less, all except the insurgents benefited from the economic revival and restoration of some normalcy to the Filipino population. The army believed that a return to the routine of everyday living and working served the cause of peace and stability. At least that was a good bet, even though some diehard local leaders were destined to continue guerrilla warfare against both their rivals and the American Army for several years to come.

Many ex-soldiers, choosing to stay in the islands when enlistments expired, joined the ranks of the railroad's operating personnel. Of these, a large number counted railroad experience in the United States on their resumes and, all else being equal, furnished experienced and reliable hands. The lot was, however, a mixed bag with many of the men having been blacklisted, for one reason or another, by their stateside employers. Some worked out extremely well while Sibert's troops caught others attempting scams for their individual profit and to the detriment of the company. Still, they were not the biggest problem by far.

To a limited degree, the Manila and Dagupan Railroad reopened to civilian traffic on February 20, even though Sibert initially faced an acute shortage of locomotives, boxcars, flat cars, and passenger coaches. Until replacement and repair of cars destroyed or damaged by insurgents, not enough rolling stock existed to handle all of the freight farmers and merchants had waiting for market. With demand far outstripping supply, freight space was at a premium—a vexing problem which created more problems.

In an effort to equitably distribute available shipping space (after Army needs were met), General Otis directed that local governments be organized at each village along the line. With creation of a local administration, those in charge compiled a list of shippers requiring rail transportation together with the size, weight, etc., of articles to be shipped. From such lists, the railroad planned to allocate available space among shippers with some semblance of equity. It didn't work that way.

Instead, graft and thievery mushroomed overnight with blatant bribery quickly savaging the orderly plan for allocating space on the few rail cars available. A rice merchant, for example, bribed the village president, paying $25 just to get his name on the freight list; otherwise, there was no chance his goods would be shipped. Then, the broker, an American entrepreneur with no regard for honest dealings, contacted the merchant (who had bribed his way onto the list), telling him his rice could be shipped—but quoting a price double the rate charged by the railroad.

Many rice and sugar merchants, desperate for the vital transportation services, actually paid twice the amount of the legitimate freight rate, to ensure their goods were shipped. The broker paid the railroad the regular rate while pocketing the rest, some of which he shared with unscrupulous conductors. Shippers, the honest ones or even those with limited means of bribery, didn't stand a chance until the railroad manager got wind of the schemes.

The corruption came to light when a shipper from one of the stations deep in the country happened to be in Manila on business and contacted Sibert at his office. He had a question: Since he was in Manila, and as a matter of convenience, could he just pay Sibert (the railroad manager) the $25 to get his name on the approved list, rather then paying the village chief back home? The captain of engineers was infuriated, not at the shipper, but at the corruption spawned by the system. From that day forward, things began to change.

Sibert's soldiers eventually nailed the American who had been passing himself off as a freight agent. One evening there was a knock on the door and an Army patrol took the broker into custody, depositing him in Bilibid Prison. Sibert and the provost marshal knew the American had procured three railway cars for a Chinese merchant at double the regular rate for shipping freight. Anxious to make an example of the suspect and seeking a reputable witness for the prosecution, Sibert met with the merchant and requested his cooperation.

The Army promised reimbursement of the shady half of the money paid for the cars as an inducement for the merchant to testify. A win-win situation if the victim agreed to testify: The perpetrator of the fraud would be convicted and the merchant would be refunded the overpayment. The Chinaman said "no", then pointing out that he had contracted with the swindler at the inflated price and, regardless of the fraud it was his duty to abide by the contract terms. Without the key witness, the government's case faced collapse if brought to trial. Given no choice, the Army backed off. When interviewed years later, Sibert said he was unaware of the fate of the fraudulent freight agent who was last heard of in Bilibid Prison.

Smarting from lessons learned from the corrupt payoff system of booking freight passage, the Army devised a new system in which the army provost marshal in each community took charge of the lists of shippers and their cargoes. Based on the lists, Sibert's Manila offices assigned freight cars, counting on the available space being fairly allocated among shippers at each location. Indeed a major improvement, but in seeking a competitive advantage over rivals for the freight space, some shippers thought to play their trump card, indeed a wild card.

Rather than sending a foreman or some equally innocuous employee to request the number and type railway cars needed, the more astute shippers assigned their most voluptuous daughters to the task of meeting with Army personnel to discuss father's shipping requirements. The soldiers proved easy targets for the sultry senoritas. A slight adjustment in the system was needed.

Besides being a superb engineer, Sibert was a close observer of the human condition, fully appreciative of the natural advantages the ladies had when dealing with young, impressionable, and usually romantically inclined soldiers. For that, he found a ready solution in the person of a crotchety old bachelor, a government-issue curmudgeon. Not only was he cantankerous, he also harbored a life-long aversion to any woman bold enough to enter the masculine world of business—an attitude not likely to change. *Perfect*, thought Sibert, as he issued an order placing the crusty gentleman in full charge of allocating freight space. The bevy of beauties failed to turn his head, and from then on the allocation of freight cars was even-handed, based strictly on business and the gruff administrator's innate sense of fairness.

After a few months under Sibert's management, the M & D continued to meet the Army's transportation needs while fulfilling most commercial shipping requests. Although not in great comfort, passengers could also ride the M & D. After paying its operational expenses, the railroad was soon clearing approximately $15,000 monthly from fees charged for the freight and passenger service. Sibert's sound management paid off, and the surplus money was turned over to the Philippine treasury. [10]

Sibert continued his farm boy habit of rising early. How else could he successfully manage a Third (or Fourth) World railroad—now turning a profit—while serving as the Army's chief engineer in the Pacific and as CO of the battalion of engineers? Each time Sibert received an order, the preamble read something like this: "Captain W.L. Sibert, Corps of Engineers, while performing the duties already imposed on him. ..."

Never was he relieved of duties when other tasks, always with increasing responsibilities, were added. In a matter of weeks after arriving in the Philippines as CO of Engineer Company B, he unofficially took over command of Company A. The additional duties were officially recognized when Special Order No. 294 dated October 26, 1899, placed the entire Battalion of Engineers under his command, with this post script: "... this in addition to his duties as Chief Engineer Officer of the Department and Corps." Some of his contributions were never officially mentioned, his service, for example, as General Otis' map consultant during those early dawn hours before headquarters offices opened. [11]

In January 1900, among his other responsibilities, the captain continued to serve as the chief engineer officer in the Philippines, thereby retaining a seat on the staff of General Otis, his map-reading companion. Beyond staff duties, there was, as a rule, always more for Sibert to do. He and his engineers had joined General Schwan's second Cavite expedition, which jumped off in January and concluded on February 8, just in time for Sibert to take over management of the Manila and Dagupan Railroad on February 10, 1900.

Recalling with delight how Captain Sibert and his fighting engineers operated with style at the sharp end of the spear during his first venture into Cavite Province, Schwan again chose Sibert for the second expedition. This time, the American meant to establish a resident military occupation force in the provinces of Cavite, Batangas, Laguna, and Tayabas. On his first incursion, General Schwan routed and expelled the more organized elements of the insurgency from the provinces. Still, highly effective guerrilla units continued to make a bloody contest of the American occupation. In his official report following the second expedition, the volunteer general again recognized Sibert's contributions to its success:

"Capt. William L. Sibert, Corps of Engineers, the senior engineer officer with the command, was utilized principally in making the investigations concerning lines of communication and supply, and roads over which movements of troops could be made. I cannot commend too highly the work of this officer. His constancy, his tact, his professional skill, are worthy of special recognition."

General Schwan strongly felt that Captain Sibert had the right stuff! Working through the proper chain of command, by first forwarding to the Army's Chief of Engineers a letter ultimately meant for the eyes of the Adjutant General of the U.S. Army, the brigadier general of volunteers recommended that Sibert be appointed a colonel of volunteers.

Read in the 21st century, the letter seems a little stilted, likely due to its use of the late 19th century idiom and the cultivated manner of expression through the written word at that particular time. Although it summarizes the military importance of the second Cavite expedition, the epistle goes far from a military report. In fact, after briefly noting the military background, it reads more like a personal letter. It is, for example, the kind of letter one friend might write to another friend for the purpose of recommending a third person for a job, some position of trust. It is shot through with personal opinion based on first hand knowledge. Referring to the second expedition, Schwan wrote:

"I know of no individual officer who contributed more to the success of the movement than did Capt. William L. Sibert, Corps of Engineers."

That succinctly summed up the volunteer brigadier's opinion of the performance of the regular captain of engineers. Not quite enough, thought Schwan, as the letter went on to outline just how Sibert had helped and what he had done to merit the general's praise:

"Not only as an Engineer Officer, in the surmounting, removal and avoidance of road obstacles, were his services brought into requisition. His good work extended to and had the effect of facilitating and expediting, every operation that was undertaken in the course of the campaign."

Like icing on a cake, the applause continued with the general commenting on Sibert's consistently superior military performances on not one, but two perilous thrusts into the incubator of the insurrection. An abbreviated personality profile followed:

"To me he proved, as he did on a former expedition, a safe and a most valuable prop. I cannot sufficiently emphasize my appreciation of the services of this accomplished, discreet, and withal modest officer."

Finally, General Schwan makes his pitch, beseeching Army brass to immediately recognize Sibert's potential by appointing him a colonel of volunteers:

"... I know of none who possess the qualities requisite in the command of a volunteer regiment in a higher degree than Captain Sibert..."

All in all, the Schwan letter, based on the general's observance of "the excellent work he [Sibert] has rendered in the field and with troops," is an outstanding character reference, both martial and personal. Although the letter's purpose was never served, it was not because the recommendation came from some obscure or inexperienced officer.

General Schwan was at the opposite pole. A native of Hanover, Germany, he migrated to America in 1857, the same year he joined the U.S. Army at age 16 as an infantry private. He was awarded the Medal of Honor for gallantry in the Civil War, engaged in the Indian conflicts, and served as military attaché to the U.S. Embassy in Berlin where his report on the German Army's General Staff became a classic in such literature. In the Spanish American War, Schwan commanded a brigade of regulars who swept Spanish opposition from the west coast of Puerto Rico and marched on San Juan. A proven leader of troops in all styles of combat, General Schwan was not a military lightweight, but an experienced veteran who instinctively recognized a real warrior when he saw one.

Schwan's recommendation was not ignored by Washington brass, only put on the back burner because the Eighth Army Corps needed Sibert's engineering skills more than his marksmanship with a Krag.

Nonetheless, Schwan's observations of Sibert's performance—under combat conditions in an inhospitable environment—reveal much about the captain. Professionally, Schwan viewed Sibert as a brave, dependable soldier and innovative engineer. On the personal side of the ledger, Schwan employed readily understood adjectives—discreet and modest—which, even in the rough and tumble U.S. Army of 1900—constituted unmistakable marks of distinction. Indeed high praise from the brigadier.

With the second Cavite campaign ending on a high note, Captain Sibert took up railroad management and, in a matter of months, had the Manila and Dagupan Railroad in full operation and making money under, arguably, the most efficient operational structure in its history. The railroad was fixed—a general tribute to the Army way of accomplishing a task and a monument to William Luther Sibert's capable management.

On April 20, 1900, it was time for the Army to get out of the railroad business. With the countryside along its route basically pacified, the Manila and Dagupan Railroad returned to its civilian management in the person of an Englishman, a Mr. Higgins. This left Sibert time to devote to looking after his battalion of engineers when not engaged in mapping and other duties as a key member of General Otis' staff, but not for long. [12]

Leaving his beloved battalion of engineers to continue supporting the Army's campaign to end the insurrection, Captain Sibert boarded a steamer in May for a cruise across the Pacific, this time in an easterly direction. He was going home. [13]

Arriving in San Francisco on May 31, 1900, the officer checked into the Occidental Hotel and telegraphed the Adjutant General in Washington: "Report for instructions as ordered request temporary duty at Willets Point answer OCCIDENTAL HOTEL. /s/ Sibert, Engineers." And the answering telegram: "Secretary War directs you proceed to Fort Totten, Willets Point, New York for temporary duty."

With the order he was hoping for in hand, Sibert wasted no time booking a one-way railway ticket to New York and then settled in for the long journey—by Pullman, of course. The exact date of his arrival at Willets Point is unknown, but after almost a year's absence, there was an emotional reunion with Mamie, and the boys were overjoyed to once again have a father. And then there was the daughter, brand new to her father, and the object of great delight.

Soon after arriving at Fort Totten, Captain Sibert learned that General Otis had a long reach, all the way across the Pacific and the North American continent, even unto Long Island. The revelation came in the form of the general's request for some very specific mapping information, the kind of tactical data, he believed, that only Sibert was capable of getting right.

In response to the general's cabled request for assistance, Sibert forwarded a hand-written letter to Brigadier General John M. Wilson, the Chief of Engineers in Washington, outlining the problem: General Otis requested certain maps to accompany reports which required the assistance of a draughtsman to prepare and, in addition, certain essential information available only in Washington. In Special Order No. 144, issued by the Adjutant General's Office and dated June 20, 1900, the captain of engineers was temporarily dispatched to Washington in order to prepare the requested maps. In another document, General Wilson assigned Sibert the services of a draftsman to complete the project. [14]

With the mapping chore completed, the Philippine chapter of Sibert's military career officially closed. Beginning in the spring of 1899 with his on-site contribution to the Arkansas River development plans, followed by the Philippine adventure, the captain had spent little time by the Sibert fireside in more than a year. The long absence from Mamie and the boys, now reinforced by the appearance of his baby daughter, Mary Elizabeth, left the officer altogether content and yearning for an extended tour of stateside duty.

So far as Mamie was concerned, the redeeming feature of her husband's long absence was the family's comfortable location at Fort Totten. It was close to ideal insofar as stateside garrison duty was concerned. The well-established post had good officer housing with all of the conveniences and, even when Mary Elizabeth arrived during her husband's absence, Mamie had plenty of help around the house. In addition to her friends on the post, the 1900 Census identified two female servants in the Sibert household, Lizzie K. Burns from Ireland and Frances Phappert from Germany, ages 26 and 21, respectively. [15]

While awaiting a permanent assignment, Sibert's temporary duty at Fort Totten was just that, a convenient spot to temporarily locate the captain and utilize his Philippine engineering experiences at the Army's Engineering School of Application. His duties at Fort Totten also left ample off-duty time for his on-post family. It may have lacked excitement, but was a good life while it lasted. Barely a year had passed before Mamie got word to begin packing. The Siberts were heading west, their destination familiar—the Ohio Valley.

Chapter Eleven
DEEP THINKING AND DAM BUSTING

Fireworks along the Louisville riverfront marked Independence Day on July 4, 1901—the same day Captain Sibert took command of the Louisville District for the Army Corps of Engineers. The pyrotechnical display was mere coincidence, concluded the strictly scientific engineer. Still, he counted the fireworks and the celebrating Kentuckians as extremely good omens, telling Mamie and the boys, with a wink, that he had arranged the festivities for the family's homecoming.

The new district engineer's plans for Ohio River development remained locked within his cranial vault—silent and not as dramatic as the fireworks display—mere ideas Sibert expected to ultimately produce an economic independence day for the Ohio Valley by nurturing industrial development along its rivers.

Only a few feet, mused Sibert, only a matter of precisely three feet, to dramatically transform the Ohio River from just another river into a catalyst for valley-wide economic development. Sibert knew the difference three additional feet of water made when placed under the keel of a riverboat! And with those three feet, Sibert abandoned his normal pragmatic stance for that of a visionary.

The engineer envisioned one additional yard of H_2O relieving masters of powerful towboats pushing strings of barges along the Ohio River of many worries about change, chance, and unscheduled surprises. With a deepened channel clearing shoals, gravel bars, and other underwater hazards from its length, the Ohio's union with the mighty Mississippi would be a marriage made in rivermen's heaven.

Things seemed headed in the wrong direction (or simply standing still) when William Luther Sibert returned to the Ohio River Valley where the same slack water navigation system—with a six-foot channel—remained in place as it had been since he first saw the valley in

1887. He believed that the big river, along with its impressive supporting cast of tributaries, deserved better and vowed to do something
about it.

Sibert knew the Ohio River contributed approximately 60 per cent
of the water to its wedding with the Mississippi (the Father of Waters
making up the remaining 40 per cent), just downstream from Cairo,
Illinois. A fair-minded geographer might well have extended the Ohio
southward past Memphis to flow by New Orleans levees into the Gulf
of Mexico. Regardless of labels, joining the two rivers with common
nine-foot channels—capable of floating big barges and the modern
towboats pushing them—held promise of a powerful and efficient
economic engine. The Mississippi had its extra yard of water, sorely
needed by the Ohio. [1]

In addition to daily duties as a workhorse carrier of goods, commodities, and people, the Ohio River served the Corps of Engineers
as a continuing living laboratory dedicated to finding the best ways to
develop America's inland waterways. Looking backward from the 21st
century, with its vast network of highways and an equally pervasive
web of airline routes, comprehending the importance of river avenues
not so long ago is difficult. Water offered a comparatively easy way to
travel when only birds flew, and there were no highways worthy of the
name. Like most useful devices, the rivers were not without problems
and, to be truly and significantly useful, those problems begged for
solutions.

That is why the Army Corps of Engineers became a major player
after being placed in charge of the nation's navigable inland waters in
the early 19th century. And with the Ohio River collecting the run-
off from the western slopes of the Appalachian Mountains, along with
the Allegheny and Monongahela rivers and the lesser streams flowing
westward, it became a useful and very important river. Experiments
along the big river chased various methods of harnessing its potential
as a gateway stream. The Army engineers' goal: Improve and develop
the waterways to be efficient carriers of commerce and people and, for
such laboratory work, the Ohio was pointed in the right direction—
westward. Ideas that worked immediately became useful in the movement west into the nation's heartland.

It wasn't all pretty from the engineering point of view, mainly because engineers tried solving unique river problems with new ap-

proaches, some of which did not come close to working. The trial and error approach was often the only way to go, with numerous errors along the way to a solution. However, the most pronounced smudges on river development came not from flawed engineering, but from anti-river development rhetoric voiced by the powerful railroad lobby in combination with Washington's infamous pork barrel politics. This played against a dismal backdrop of economic fluctuations and World War I.

As a result, an open and clear nine-foot channel throughout the length of the Ohio River existed only in dreams at the dawn of the 20th century. Only river visionaries such as Sibert recognized it as the best way to take full advantage of the river's slack water navigation system by enticing the commercial traffic such a river was capable of handling.

When Sibert returned to the valley, the six-foot channel proudly maintained on the Ohio by the Corps of Engineers left much to be desired among those with economic interests tightly bound to commercial river traffic. This group included packet boat owners and captains, towboat and barge operators, and dredge boat masters down to deckhands and those stevedores working the wharfs up and down the Ohio. Joining that colorful entourage were Pittsburgh industrialists and coal barons in Pennsylvania, West Virginia, and Kentucky, all of them seeking cheap transportation for bulk movement of coal and other raw materials, and for bulk shipment of finished products to market. With its existing six-foot channel, the Ohio managed competitive rates but a nine-foot channel was needed to capture the river's share of bulk shipping.

Despite the fact that the number *nine* never claimed mystical powers, so far as the 20th century Ohio River flowed, nine was indeed the magic number! The nine-foot channel was the holy grail of Ohio River development as the calendar kicked over into the turbulent 1900s. Rivermen chased the channel for one simple reason: Nine feet of water beneath the keel of the biggest boats and barges meant they would not scrape bottom and could forever travel the Ohio, even during seasons of low water. All they had to do was stick within the channel, the nine-foot channel.

Captain Sibert's experience with river transportation systems came full circle in Louisville on the waters of the Ohio River. Based upon vast practical experiences and his educational background, from the very first the returning officer became an advocate, indeed a zealot, for the nine-foot channel. His experience and studies convinced him that a nine-foot channel along the entire length of the Ohio (Pittsburgh to Cairo, Illinois), held the key to the valley's economic development and practically everything else.

Upon his return to the precincts of the Ohio River in 1901, as chief engineer of the Louisville District, it is doubtful that Sibert ever paused to wonder exactly what a mere captain in the Army Corps of Engineers might do to influence critical policy decisions affecting future river development. He simply took up his new duties with enthusiasm while never failing to speak out in favor of the deeper navigation channel.

A prime example of Sibert's ceaseless and usually discrete promotion of the nine-foot channel occurred in early 1903 after the officer had been transferred and placed in charge of the Pittsburgh District of the Corps of Engineers. As a result of Washington politics, six lock and dam systems under construction on the upper Ohio (just downstream from Pittsburgh) entered Sibert's jurisdiction. All were designed to yield a six-foot channel, the mere thought of which irritated Sibert. He deemed the unfinished structures already obsolete, inadequate for the assigned task because the barges then being towed up and down the waterway routinely drew more than eight feet of water.

Leland R. Johnson, with degrees from Murray State University, St. Louis University, and a doctorate from Vanderbilt University in history, was discovered by the Corps of Engineers and commissioned to research and write a series of authoritative histories of river development by Army engineers. Johnson excelled in his assignment and succeeded in capturing Sibert's zeal for the Ohio's nine-foot channel in his book, *The Headwaters District*. When a young and eager Corps of Engineers lieutenant reported for the first time to his new commanding officer at Pittsburgh, it did not take Major Sibert long to get down to some serious river business currently pending:

"Have you ever been down the Ohio?" Sibert asked George R. Spalding.

"No, sir," was the reply.

"Ever been assigned to dam construction? Know anything about dams?"

"No, sir."

At that point, the major picked up Spalding's records from his desk, leaned back in his swivel chair, and carefully thumbed through the papers, confirming that the lieutenant had just returned from combat engineering in the Philippines. That was enough for Sibert, who knew all about that subject.

"Spalding," he said, "you have a good record and I'm going to put you in charge of construction of Dam No. 3 on the Ohio. You will have some fine assistants who know their business and will handle the details, but I don't want you to finish the dam."

To say the lieutenant was surprised by the order would be an understatement. "Don't finish the dam?" he asked. And Sibert explained:

"That's right. You finish the lock and dam foundation, but not the wickets. I think Congress will soon approve nine-foot instead of six-foot pools and it would make us look silly to build dams for six-foot navigation, then turn right around and tear them out to install wickets for nine-foot slackwater."

Recognizing the young officer's bewilderment, Sibert took time to explain what Congress had previously done regarding Ohio River improvements and what it might be expected to do in the near future. Rivermen needed the nine-foot channel to improve the speed and maneuverability of the tows, with attendant savings in transportation costs. He also pointed out that Congress had approved nine-foot channeling of the lower Mississippi River and seemed determined to push an American canal across the Isthmus of Panama.

"If a similar nine-foot depth were made in the Ohio (River), from Pittsburgh to Cairo," Sibert reasoned, "by the time the Isthmian Canal is completed, Pittsburgh will be in a position to place her products at tidewater at a cost that would enable her products to compete favorably in the world's markets."

Once Lieutenant Spalding fully understood how his duties might impact his commander's long range quest for a deeper Ohio River channel, he left the office of the district engineer for the downstream construction site, fully prepared to supervise the work, but equally determined not to finish construction of Lock and Dam No. 3. It took a while, and the lieutenant must have tired of dragging his feet, when new orders were issued. By then, Spalding knew the facts and no longer regarded Sibert as a minor prophet. Instead, he realized that his commanding officer worked as diligently at promoting what he believed to be sound engineering goals as he did at the actual engineering. [2]

By the time the order was issued to actually finish Lock and Dam No. 3, plans were altered so that it was capable of pooling sufficient water for a nine-foot channel. It was the first positive fruit of a study Congress authorized in 1902, a study which opened the door for a more extensive investigation aimed at projecting future economic growth and the engineering problems associated with Sibert's vision of a nine-foot on the Ohio River from Pittsburgh to Cairo, Illinois. (The Corps of Engineers always considered a project's costs-benefits ratio, always a major concern in Congress.) A second highly experienced study board included the irrepressible Sibert, representing the Pittsburgh District, who willingly did much of the committee's heavy lifting. The group's final report predicted increased industrialization in the Pittsburgh area and generally throughout the Ohio Valley. The engineers pointed out that iron, steel, coal, and other area products could be economically shipped to far flung markets *if* a nine-foot channel was available.

The committee easily cranked in the obvious benefits to be gained by tying the deepened Ohio channel into a channel of like depth on the lower Mississippi. They labeled the anticipated opening of the Panama Canal as a further extension of the inland water network—including the proposed nine-foot channel on the Ohio River. The Panama Canal required quite a stretch, but the exhaustive report was impressively heavy with facts and reasonably solid projections. In more modern parlance: Spiced to some degree by Sibert's spin, the report concluded with a simple and understandable statement: "The greater the draft, the cheaper the transportation by water."

Although the study group was chaired by Colonel Daniel Lockwood, the Lockwood Board's report, in essence, was the Sibert Report! Much of its content and the board's conclusions were firmly based on data Sibert had collected during his long association with the Ohio River, its numerous tributaries, and the people along its banks.

Besides his foot-dragging order to Spalding, Sibert logged countless other nuances in favor of the deeper channel, most of them more subtle than Spalding's unwritten command. His efforts did not go unrewarded although results came slowly, given the railroad opposition and Washington politics. The final push from President William Howard Taft came in 1910 when Congress extended the nine-foot channel throughout the length of the Ohio River—from Pittsburgh to Cairo. And, yes, it's true: President Taft was elected from Ohio! Target date for completing the project was 1922, but that deadline skipped by due to World War I and political battles over budgets. Meanwhile, progress continued with planning, engineering, and construction underway along the banks of the Ohio, and some successful political infighting along the Potomac.

(Skipping ahead to October 29, 1929: Retired Major General William Luther Sibert stepped forward and snipped the ceremonial satin ribbon at Lock and Dam No. 53—just upstream from Cairo, Illinois—marking completion of the nine-foot channel. After locking through, the festive packets steamed the last few miles and tied up at the Cairo wharf under a golden sunset. There the celebration continued until 10 p.m., ending when the band played "Til We Meet Again" as the *Cincinnati* and the *Greater Pittsburgh*, with bells ringing, backed away from the wharf, now bound upstream for the return trip. River historian Johnson noted that the plaintive bugle call "Taps" may have been a more appropriate selection to play because of the stock market crash on October 25—Black Tuesday—sounding the death knell for the historic steamboat packet era. Nevertheless, the opening of the Ohio River to modern commercial river traffic was a personal and significant triumph for its enduring champion, William Luther Sibert. He was an Olympic-caliber hero, all the way from Cairo to Pittsburgh.) [3]

It had not always been that way. Shortly after his appointment as Pittsburgh District Engineer on December 11, 1901, an upstream move on the Ohio from his Louisville post, Sibert's plain talk got him into big trouble.

A survivor of innumerable firefights of the hot lead variety in the Philippines, Captain Sibert experienced an altogether different kind of battle while commanding the Corps of Engineers' Pittsburgh District. He arrived in Pittsburgh just when a very old and irritating problem came to a head. It was all about bridges! But, unfortunately, it was unlike the puzzle of patching together the heavily damaged Paranao River bridge in order to keep MacArthur's advancing army supplied. In fact, engineering was not the problem.

Briefly, the bridge problem was a mix of competing interests, each with its own merits and champions, and each hell bent to prevail by foul means or fair. Making for the most toxic stew Sibert had yet encountered, the combatants transformed debate over the bridges into a contentious political issue destined to spill into the very halls of Congress. First, a mixture of geography and history:

The Allegheny and Monongahela rivers, both being important water-borne trade routes since colonial days, meet at Pittsburgh to form the mighty Ohio River, which not only extended the trade routes, but also furnished pioneers a comparatively easy water route west. The confluence of waters draining from the colonies to the east was the original reason for 18th century Fort Pitt and the town that followed.

The westward migration generated much river traffic while at the same time trails were turned into roads, which had to cross the rivers. In addition, as the 19th century progressed, railroad construction followed with a similar need for bridges. At the same time, river traffic had evolved from pioneer flatboats to the barges and steamers with towering smokestacks. Rivermen competed with the railroads for freight and passenger business and, as a result, intense and often rough competition developed over the nature and primacy of those interconnected cardiovascular-like systems.

It was serious business when supporters of land transportation—wagon roads and railroads—butted heads with advocates of the river roads and the diverse fleet of boats that used them. The contest directly affected practically everybody, including merchants and consumers all along the river system. And, as for head-on collisions, bridges were made to order.

Because existing bridges, linking both rail and wagon routes across rivers, were not built with steamboats in mind, serious problems developed. All the ingredients of a collision were there, literally as well as figuratively. Ever increasing in size and topped off with their towering trademark smokestacks, packets did not have enough vertical clearance to pass safely beneath the bridges. In some instances, it was a *Catch 22* situation: If the water in the river was low, it was too shallow for the packets to safely navigate, and if the water was too high, there was insufficient clearance for steamers to safely slip under bridges hanging low over the stream.

As early as 1849, the bridge versus boat controversy erupted on the Allegheny, with nothing ever resolved. Years passed before Congress made a fateful move in approving the Rivers and Harbors Act of 1899. Among other more or less routine matters, Congress gave the Corps of Engineers jurisdiction over all bridges traversing navigable waterways. Because the engineers were responsible for improving the inland waterways and keeping them open for all sorts of river traffic, ranging from flatboats and barges to steamboats, something had to give.

Following his appointment as district engineer, Sibert moved his family into a comfortable home in Pittsburgh and made his usual first impression on local leaders. He came across as confident and competent in his profession, *and* also easy to talk to if you had a problem. Too, that first impression revealed a man who did not beat around the bush, choosing to talk straight even about disagreeable subjects. The Pittsburghers liked that and welcomed Sibert into their society, at least until some of his straight talk zeroed in on a sore spot.

Even before the 1902 dinner meeting concluded, by merely reading the expressions on the faces of a substantial portion of his audience, Sibert concluded that he had made a mistake, one he could not correct. It was an honest mistake to be sure because the district engineer had not set out to ruffle feathers when he addressed the Engineers' Society of which he was a member. The subject of his talk was "Full Use of the Rivers at Pittsburgh", and the captain proceeded to outline how that could be done. He focused on what he regarded as a major impediment to taking full advantage of river opportunities. The vast majority of his audience already knew about the concrete examples the well-prepared engineer cited.

He mentioned the area's only builder of steel boats, located upstream on the banks of the Allegheny, where new boat hulls were launched and floated under the Union Bridge. Only after clearing the low bridge and safely mooring the vessel on the downstream side, where river passage was no longer obstructed by low bridges, could the vessel's superstructure be added.

The officer cited manufacturing plants on the Allegheny that routinely contracted for their products to be hauled by wagon from plants to downstream terminals on the Monongahela or Ohio rivers. Once downstream, where channels were unobstructed by low bridges, the products were loaded aboard tall-stacked steamers which were effectively barred from reaching the plant sites by the low-hanging bridges. Sibert pointed out that it cost the manufacturer half as much for the short wagon trip as it cost to transport his product the remaining 2,000 miles to market—as far south as New Orleans—by water.

The bridges must be raised in the interests of unimpeded river commerce, Sibert declared. While removal of an obstacle to river commerce was the goal, the additional elevation would also spare bridges from flood damage. Sibert put the encroaching bridges in the same category as snags and gravel bars, which had to be removed to keep navigation channels open. All of this, in both theory and fact, was true, and Sibert ended up deeply wounded by the truth he had spoken. Editorial cartoons in the Pittsburgh papers lampooned the engineer and his vision of unimpeded river commerce, which the cartoonists little understood.

Currently, Sibert's office had the Union Bridge case under study, the question being whether or not the bridge should be raised to a sufficient height to allow steamers safe passage. Procedure required Sibert to conduct impartial hearings on the question and, based on the hearings' findings, make a recommendation to the Corps of Engineers.

To that end, in 1902 and 1903, Captain Sibert conducted a series of hearings regarding low bridges on the Allegheny. Widespread interest in the controversy drew large crowds of partisans and spectators, causing Sibert to adjourn the hearings and seek a larger venue. This he found in nearby courtrooms, an appropriate setting when Sibert found himself acting more like a judge than an engineer. Practically every party with an interest in the bridge question obtained the best legal counsel available because the stakes were high. The captain found himself constantly acting to prevent clever legal maneuvering from obscuring the facts bearing on the true merits of the controversy.

Had there been an impartial observer, it is likely that he would have given Sibert high marks for the manner in which the hearings were conducted. Sibert literally went by the book because that's the only way he knew to go. Some of the attorneys involved even suspected that the captain had studied law. Although that was incorrect, the district engineer had served under Chief of Engineers Henry M. Roberts, author of *Robert's Rules of Order*, some of which must have rubbed off. One lawyer registered grudging respect for the officer: By choosing the military profession, the lawyer opined that the soldier had missed his true calling, remarking that Sibert could earn five times his Army pay in the practice of law.

Pressure approached the unbearable during the lengthy hearings, including charges, based upon his 1902 speech to the engineering fraternity, that Captain Sibert was unduly prejudiced and had prejudged the case long before the hearings began. The determined engineer simply gritted his teeth and carried on. Attorneys for the owners of the Union Bridge referred to the hearings as a mock trial in which Sibert admitted testimony from "the ignorant class of people that generally compose the body of rivermen in the United States". That was as big a mistake as Sibert's revelations in the 1902 speech. It was sometime thereafter before attorneys could safely promenade along Pittsburgh wharves without risking their lives.

The leader in the campaign to have the bridges raised was Captain William B. Rodgers, his title originating not in the military but on the rivers. He owned a dredging firm and headed the rivermen's lobby in the long quest for relief from low bridges. Somewhat of a visionary who should never be accused of being ignorant, Captain Rodgers had a twofold agenda: first to raise the Allegheny bridges and free up the river for steamboats and, second, to establish slack water navigation from Oil City, Pennsylvania, on the upper Allegheny, to Cairo, Illinois, where the Ohio River joins the Mississippi.

The bridge interests carried their campaign into the halls of Congress, approaching members of the local congressional delegation with demands that Sibert be removed from Pittsburgh. That is when Captain Rogers passed the word to those same congressmen that if Sibert were transferred, they would answer for it at the next election. This blunt message was not lost on the legislators, and Sibert remained at Pittsburgh until he got the summons to Panama.

Captain Rodgers and his numerous colleagues, all of whom had serious economic interests—their success depending on maintaining thriving commercial trade along the rivers—presented facts, opinions, and arguments to justify raising the bridges. In the opposite corner were the local governments who owned the bridges, the railroad companies and other private companies, each of which had its own reasons for opposing any efforts to raise the bridges. The testimony was often caustic and rancorous.

Sibert shepherded the hearings to a conclusion after volumes of testimony and seemingly endless arguments by counsel for the respective interests. While trying to be as fair as his allegiance to engineering disciplines allowed, the captain carefully protected those parts of the record which could not be negated by even the most persuasive arguments. For example, the record took due note of the fact that the pack-ets could not steam safely under the bridges for an average of 52 days each year, also the fact that even smaller towboats were barred from passing under the structures an average of more than 17 days each year. This, in Sibert's opinion, constituted significant interference with commercial river traffic. [4]

Although the final decision was not Sibert's to make, based upon ev-idence gathered at the hearings, Sibert's final report in 1904 contained a recommendation that the Corps of Engineers require the bridges to be raised. However, the bridge controversy did not go quietly, but continued into the 1920s as succeeding administrations took opposite views. Finally, Sibert's view prevailed through strong Corps of Engi-neers leadership in 1923, with the last bridge obstacles removed by 1929, just in time for the demise of the packet trade and disappearance of the tall stacks that caused the problem. Tall stacks were not of daily concern when engineers were forever attempting to tame wild rivers. The powerful rivers themselves caused uncounted problems, especial-ly when propelled by destructive floodwaters. With danger riding the flood crests, locks and dams were not immune to damages and, on one rare occasion, prompted extraordinary action.

Dam busting—a rare occurrence—is always dangerous, especially when a major flood is involved in the Pittsburgh District. From co-lonial days, the British were drawn to the area by its strategic loca-tion—at the confluence of the Allegheny and Monongahela rivers, where they joined to form the westbound Ohio. Virginia frontiersmen recognized the importance of the junction to westward expansion and occupied the area, only to be expelled in 1754 during the French and Indian War. After routing a small British colonial expeditionary force led by George Washington, French troops built Fort Duquesne at the headwaters of the Ohio—the origin of Pittsburgh.

It requires a long historic stretch to connect King George II's ef-forts to thwart French expansion at Pittsburgh with King George VI's defense of England 200 years later. And liberal application of poetic li-cense is required to tie Major Sibert's engineering exploits in the Pitts-burgh District in 1907 to the George kings. Perhaps confusing, but maybe not if the student of history is patient:

Hurricanes and Spitfires became icons of the Battle of Britain dur-ing World War II, but King George VI's Royal Air Force engaged in many other equally heroic although less glamorous adventures during the long war. *Dam Busters* is a prime example of such service. After short, intensive training, highly secret Squadron X officially became No. 617 Squadron of the RAF, tasked with a single dangerous mission: destroy Ruhr River dams vital to German war industries.

The British devised a plan to skip bomb oversized canisters of high explosives into the center walls of the Mohne and Eder dams. Each especially modified Lancaster bomber carried only one of the huge bombs which, from a distance, resembled oversized gasoline drums or beer barrels. However, the bombs were highly engineered, designed to spin counterclockwise as they skipped across the water before colliding with the dams. The backspin forced the canisters to hug the dam walls where their subsequent detonation would do the most damage, rather than allow the missile to bounce away from its target and explode ineffectually.

Against long odds, the sophisticated bombs and the intricate plan for their delivery worked well on a full-moon night, May16-17, 1943— resulting in destruction of the Mohne and Eder dams. Thirty-six years earlier, Major William Luther Sibert didn't have any of the highly volatile explosives available to No. 617 Squadron, just dynamite and the determination to get a dicey job done at Lock and Dam No. 3 on the Allegheny River on a wet, cold, and bleak day in early 1907. [5]

Unlike the RAF lads, who were dedicated to the destruction of the Nazi war machine, the Corps of Engineers officer was ordinarily in the business of building locks and dams, not destroying them. Sibert knew that conviction of damaging or destroying the property of the U.S. Government carried heavy penalties—possibly prison. So what was going on in Pennsylvania in 1907 to send seemingly seditious thoughts coursing through Sibert's normally patriotic and rational brain?

A big flood washed through the Allegheny watershed beginning in early January 1907, the excess water interrupting the normal rhythm along the river, making travel by packet a bit more hazardous. There seemed to be no end to the upstream rains while normal procedures, such as locking through at Allegheny Dam No. 3, were followed with safety the paramount goal. Routine operations continued throughout the Corps of Engineers' Pittsburgh District and the district engineer, Major William Luther Sibert, hoped to be on time for supper with Mamie and their children. Not that particular night!

With the Allegheny at flood stage, an acutely serious problem developed, being first noticed early on the afternoon on January 15, 1907: The dam abutment failed at Dam No. 3 near Springdale, Pennsylvania, causing a breach through which flood waters poured from the upstream pool. The unimpeded water picked up speed like a runner on a downhill course as the gap continued to widen. The upstream pool elevation—more than eight feet above the downstream pool—added additional velocity to the floodwaters. Unfortunately, the escaping waters were not aimed into the downstream pool and channel where they belonged, even when at flood stage.

Instead, the failed abutment directed the torrent away from the river bed and onto the bank where a destructive path crossed previously dry land, carrying everything of consequence before it. Almost immediately, the flood embraced a nearby house and outbuildings, sweeping them away. At his Pittsburgh office, Sibert received the first telephoned report of the abutment's collapse. After instructing the lockkeeper to stay out of harm's way and promising to immediately visit Dam No. 3, he rang off and, without replacing the phone's ear-piece, requested the operator to ring up the offices of the Pennsylvania Railroad.

The Pennsylvania Railroad had a main track in close proximity to the damaged lock and dam, so close that the flood-induced erosion placed the main line in jeopardy. Major Sibert requested that the railroad immediately install an emergency track closer to the endangered river bank from which railway cars could dump stone, slag, and other heavy materials into the breach. Often at loggerheads with railroad officials over the height of their bridges, in this situation Sibert knew the railroad was his ally because of the danger to its main line.

The railroad laid about 600 feet of track to a point some 220 feet from the original top of the bank and succeeded in dumping some stone and slag on January 16, before recognizing in mid-afternoon that the break could not be closed before flood waters gobbled up the emergency rail siding itself. After abandoning the trackage to flood waters, railroaders retreated 80 feet to an existing siding next to the main track. Dumping continued, both large and small stone, along with slag, there being no shortage of the heavy, vitreous byproduct of the Pittsburgh steel mills.

Meanwhile, Sibert and members of his staff rushed to Dam No. 3, which was only a few miles from his office. The major wanted a firsthand appraisal of the break and what might be done to solve the problem. The quick survey yielded a dismal picture: The break and its consequences far exceeded their worst speculations. The engineers saw only disaster for numerous downstream properties—not only homes and outbuildings, but also a large industrial plant—unless they turned the tide.

Not surprised at the missing abutment, the engineers got mild encouragement from the dam itself, still holding and reasonably stable even without the support of the missing part. Still, water poured through the gap in ever-increasing volume, rapidly cutting into the sandy bank. By late afternoon the first houses and outbuildings dropped into the deluge, victims of the erosion's breakneck speed. The army officer ordered a tactical retreat, knowing of only one way to solve the dilemma: Think!

The rain never ceased. Sibert and two members of his staff, John Arras and Thomas Roberts, returned to the Corps of Engineers' offices well after dark, shucked their slickers, and put on the coffee pot. Once around the table and as relaxed as they could be in face of the crisis, discussions began—a council of war against those as yet uncontrollable waters. The major valued the input of the other men, particularly Arras, a gifted engineer who will accompany Sibert to Panama. Their thinking helped before the major shouldered responsibility, his alone, for decisions he hoped would avert a total disaster.

The engineers consumed several pots of coffee as the discussion continued well into the night. Thinking things through, while sticking with sound engineering principles and common sense, the trio reached what at first seemed a remarkably bizarre consensus. Initially proud that the dam remained stable despite the pressure of flood waters, the engineers analyzed its role in the crisis they faced: As long as the dam provided a formidable barrier to the river, the gap created by the abutment collapse gave flood waters a path of least resistance—the route water continued to follow through the ever expanding breach. Upstream river gauges left no doubt that the flooding was far from over and would continue to feed the cascade as it broadened the break.

In the face of the powerful floodwaters, engineers desperately needed to reduce the pressure at the breach. Reduction of the water's velocity promised to slow the rate of erosion, which, engineers believed, was the key to the puzzle. The question was: *How?*

Physics and common sense provided the answer. Liquids, such as water, tend to accelerate when their passageway is compressed or re-

duced and, conversely, liquids tend to slow when their travel channel widens. With no chance to overtake the fast-moving erosion by
merely dumping heavy materials in its path, the alternative became
clear: Widen the river's route downstream, turning a footpath, so to
speak, into a wide, unobstructed highway—easier said than done on
the Allegheny in 1907.

In order to curtail the flood that threatened scores of houses and
the Heidenkamp Mirror Company plant, a manufacturer of polished
plate glass mirror plates, Sibert faced an extremely difficult task. The
Heidenkamp plant was an important economic player and the source
of many jobs in the Springdale area—a facility worth saving. After a
long, uncomfortable night and with the coffee pot dry, he drained his
coffee cup to the dregs, chewed on his cigar, and made up his mind.
With no hesitation, he decided to attack the malady with radical surgery.

Major William Luther Sibert ran the decision by his subordinates.
The two men, having contributed to the process during the intermi-
nable roundtable discussion, and having no better solution in mind,
readily concurred with the theory behind the radical surgery the major
was planning.

Sibert's plan: *Blow up* Dam No. 3 with all the dynamite engineers
could muster!

At least in theory, blasting away the dam proper would widen the
water's gateway downstream. The narrow footpath, previously funnel-
ing the flood through the breach at erosion producing velocity would
no longer be the path of least resistance, superseded by a veritable highway, the blown dam furnishing a wide expanse—an avenue for water
to more easily escape downstream. Sibert counted on this new path of
least resistance directing most of the water into the downstream riverbed instead of into the breach and onto the calamitous cross-country
path it now pursued.

Blasting began the following day with odds weighted heavily against
success of the planned assault on Dam No. 3. Things looked dismal
as rain continued to fall all along the Allegheny as the breach widened and the rate of erosion accelerated. After deciding to blast, the
engineers determined the most effective way to employ the explosives,
ruling out haphazard detonations as both ineffective and unsafe. The
plan called for carefully positioned charges along the upstream wall of

the dam where the blasts were most likely to inflict the required heavy damage—the kind of destruction that would literally open the gates for the floodwaters to pass.

With the river running swiftly at flood stage, planting dynamite or, for that matter, anything else on the upstream face of the dam was indeed hazardous. If the actors didn't get blown up by a premature detonation, they could just as easily fall casualty to drowning. The plan was also fraught with danger to Sibert's career as a trusted officer in the Army Corps of Engineers. It was unheard of to blow up a practically new dam that had cost thousands of dollars to build three years earlier. And Sibert had no place to pass the buck. He telegraphed Washington, outlined his plans to dynamite Dam No. 3, and requested permission to do so. The major did not have the luxury of awaiting a reply from the Nation's Capital. He was out of time and it was full speed ahead.

Sibert decided a few good men and a venerable rowboat stood a fair chance of getting the job done. Recognizing the overriding importance of experience in the handling of explosives, Sibert recruited the best available powdermen and teamed them with equally experienced rivermen for the assault on the dam. A fairly simple plan of attack came from the previous night's conference.

First, the skiff was heavily loaded with dynamite, fuses, matches in a watertight container, and other gear required for the voyage to the dam and the placement and detonation of the explosives. With the blasters aboard, the rivermen launched the boat well upstream from the dam and, with an experienced riverman at the helm, allowed the craft to drift downstream at the speed of the current.

Next, the boat dropped anchor in mid-river, possibly 50 yards or less upstream from the dam. After setting the anchor to securely hold the boat against the current, the boat crew slowly and carefully played out a long rope attached to the anchor cable, easing the boat closer and closer to the crest of the dam until contact was made. The anchor held and the current secured the skiff tight up against the dam. After that, assisted by the boat crew, the powdermen went to work.

They placed the first of numerous 500-pound dynamite bundles, with fuse attached, on the dam face, after which the men paddled and heaved on the rope tether, slowly distancing the boat from the first explosion site. Once anchored a safe distance away, fuses ignited the dynamite, blowing away a large chunk of Dam No. 3. The crew carefully repeated this process time and again until the blasting party, in the space of three days, succeeded in removing 560 feet of the midstream crest of the dam to a depth of a dozen feet. The gate was open!

The performance of the boat crew and powdermen on that first day encouraged Sibert; they seemed perfectly suited for carrying out the dangerous and highly unorthodox errand of destruction. "Now we have a fighting chance to save the Heidenkamp plant. We are placing stone on the bank as fast as we can unload it," the major reported to Washington.

After the initial loss of the spur track to the crumbling riverbank, the railroad rendered yeoman service, making mammoth deliveries of stone and slag while operating from other spurs installed a safer distance from marauding waters. For four days (January 17-20), while Sibert's men blasted the dam, the railroad committed two wrecking cranes, a derrick car, and 275 laborers to the task of placing stone and slag where it would best serve to blunt the erosion, shore up the remaining riverbank, and close off the channel created by the abutment failure. Working on the spur tracks were another 150 men.

The two-pronged attack on the problem—blasting off the dam crest to relieve water pressure at the breach, and using rock and slag to slow the erosion and close the abutment gap—succeeded in stopping the misplaced flood. The Heidenkamp Mirror Company's plant was spared (thereby preserving the jobs of its employees), as well as numerous homes and outbuildings located within the direct path of the damaging waters.

Following the successful bombing and the efforts of the railroad to dump stone and slag along the newly defined riverbank, the work force gradually receded. By then, Sibert's riprap of both large and small stones protected the bank—the recent target of rampant erosion. Work ceased on February 15.

The good guys won in the final act of the drama played out at Dam and Lock No. 3, although not without a price. For example, it took more than 23,000 tons of rock and slag to stabilize the riverbank, all of which had to be hauled by rail before it could be dumped with the aid of hundreds of workers. Hundreds of pounds of costly dynamite were detonated under adverse weather and river conditions, remarkably, without the loss of a man. Ever the meticulous accountants, the Corps of Engineers allotted $80,000 for out of pocket expenses required to reestablish control of the Allegheny at Dam No. 3.

Geographically speaking, the water unleashed by the failed abutment washed away more than five acres, a big piece of riverbank shaped like a generous slice of pie, including nine houses and other buildings. The flood swept away a portion of the Heidenkamp property, but not the main buildings—indeed a close call. The factory faced destruction had Sibert allowed the slightest delay in confronting the problem.

Dam No. 3, which had been put into service in 1904, measured more than 900 feet in length. Sibert's demolition left the lock and 175 feet of the dam undamaged. In line with standard dam construction techniques still employed on the nation's inland waterways in the early 1900s, the dam was of timber crib design, a relatively inexpensive way to impound water. Likewise, the costs of restoring Dam No. 3 to service would not be onerous.

Sibert's radical surgery at Dam No. 3, a traumatic solution laced with dynamite blasts, briefly took on a life of its own and was prominently mentioned on the editorial page of the *New York Sun*. In the *Sun's* edition of January 30, 1907, the writer expressed the paper's displeasure with what the editor perceived to be the government's extremely slow progress in developing the nation's waterways.

The editorial championed accelerated and decisive action to improve American rivers, making its point by citing the swift response made by Major Sibert to the Allegheny emergency. The editorial writer concluded, with approval, that: "… no charges of dilatoriness can be brought against the officer (Sibert) who a few weeks ago saved a million dollars worth of property by assuming the responsibility of blowing up $80,000 worth of dam." [6]

Whether the incident on the Allegheny obtained the requisite dignity of legend is an unanswered question, but be assured it became the chief topic of conversation at the headquarters of the Corps of Engineers in Washington, around the bar at the Fort Totten Officers' Club, and at any other gathering of Corps of Engineers' officers. Beyond doubt, however, Major William Luther Sibert is numbered among the few—and probably the only Corps of Engineers' officer—ever commended by the Chief Engineer for destroying government property!

In response to the several accolades coming his way, Major Sibert quickly pointed out that the real heroes were the men who rowed boatloads of dynamite down a rain-swollen river and then calmly blew the top off of Dam No. 3. The officer was ready to put the incident behind him and rebuild Dam No. 3 as soon as practicable, a task he was destined to leave undone. And for good reason.

It was about that time that he received an order that had originated with President Theodore Roosevelt. The president required the services of Major William Luther Sibert down south. *Way* down south!

Chapter Twelve
AMERICA'S CANAL IN PANAMA

Teddy Roosevelt, ex-Rough Rider and hero of San Juan Hill, was at the helm as America began to get serious about its international role in the 20th Century. The States, yet to number 48, swaggered after dispatching the Spanish so quickly in 1898. Those well informed about international affairs, however, recognized Spain as an undernourished facsimile of its former self, and not a true test of America's prowess.

President Roosevelt never shared that view, never doubted America's destiny as a major player on the world stage and wanted to boost it along by any means at hand. Looking south, beyond his Cuban heroics and into the Caribbean, the president dreamed of demonstrating to Europe's old guard America's capacity for leadership and derring-do in the modern world.

Locked within the old dream of an isthmian canal joining the Atlantic and Pacific, Roosevelt saw a marvelous opportunity for the nation to flex its industrial and technological muscle and succeed where the Old World failed. Mounted from France by Ferdinand de Lesseps, already famed for building the Suez Canal, the French canal effort failed. Consuming the better part of 20 years, the effort not only fell short, but did so under a cloud of scandal and death.

Was it now the American turn at bat? If so, it was well overdue.

With no guarantee of success, popular and professional opinion was decidedly pessimistic in the wake of the colossal French failure. Still, it seemed to be a voyage—or trek—across the Central American isthmus the United States was compelled to embark. Once the Republic stretched "from sea to shining sea," a shorter and safer water route from the East Coast to the West Coast, and vice versa (without rounding Cape Horn at the Antarctic end of South America) became a commercial and military imperative. Many American leaders wanted a Central American canal for a long time, but as the French persisted in Panama, Washington concentrated on an alternative route through Nicaragua. The Nicaraguan route retained significant interest among lawmakers even as Congress approved legislation commencing the American effort in Panama. [1]

Actually, American interest in spanning the isthmus in some commercially useful form dated from earlier in the 19th Century, boosted by 49ers trekking through the Panamanian jungle to catch a ship bound for the California gold fields. The Panama Railroad soon followed, underscoring the short cheap route between oceans even if there was no water to float a boat. However, Americans directed most of their attention slightly north of Panama—to Nicaragua and its lake, which seemed to invite canalization.

Although it led nowhere, no lesser entrepreneur than Cornelius Vanderbilt once obtained an 85-year concession to exclusively navigate the country's lakes while establishing a water and road route across Nicaragua. Colonel Orville Childs surveyed Nicaragua in 1852 for the purpose of establishing an ocean-to-ocean canal route. Had the United States elected to build a Nicaraguan canal, it would have followed Childs' route except for a very few miles. The colonel reported his findings to President Fillmore, but the plans failed to generate any enthusiasm for the venture.

American interest in an inter-ocean canal once again flared up following the Civil War, attracting attention from the White House. Highly successful as a military commander, Ulysses S. Grant is not generally credited with much positive presidential acumen. Yet, he got some things right, including a genuine interest in a Central American canal. Regardless of location, any American canal spanning the isthmus owes President Grant a debt of gratitude. He selected Navy Commander Thomas O. Selfridge to lead the Darien Expedition of 1870 to Panama in search of a feasible canal route; a similar expedition again targeted Nicaragua. While Selfridge's meticulous survey failed to map a satisfactory passage across Panama, positive results came from the Nicaraguan expedition.

In all, President Grant ordered seven expeditions to Central America to map and study possible canal routes, all of this producing a mound of useful information on the subject, but nothing more. That is not to imply that Americans lost interest in the dream of an isthmian canal. One man, in particular, would not let the dream of an American canal die.

John Tyler Morgan gained fame in the United States Senate as a Southern Nationalist from Alabama and that body's foremost proponent of an American canal across Central America. The Alabama lawmaker also championed American territorial expansion and favored an aggressive military stance while serving as an influential member of the Senate's Foreign Relations Committee.

So far as the isthmian canal question was concerned, Senator Morgan held an even more important committee assignment as a long-standing member of the Senate's Committee on Inter-Oceanic Canals. He richly deserved his senatorial nickname—"Canal Morgan"—while passionately pursuing an American canal across Central America. Even as the French continued to labor in Panama, Morgan pushed for an American canal in Nicaragua, and has been called the ideological father of the Panama Canal.

It is not the purpose of this chronicle to tell the entire epic tale of the Panama Canal, already the subject of volumes. Nevertheless, in order to fully understand the role Sibert played in creation of the Panama Canal, some historical background is necessary.

In 1978, U.S. Senator Samuel I. Hayakawa vehemently opposed the return of the Canal Zone to the Republic of Panama and, at the time, was famously quoted: "We should keep the Panama Canal. After all, we stole it fair and square." An English professor by trade, and a noted semanticist and linguist, the Californian knew how to turn a phrase and, in doing so, captured the buccaneer spirit surrounding America's involvement in Panama. Like most momentous happenings, however, it was never that simple.

Becoming acquainted with President Theodore Roosevelt explains a lot. He was a man of principle, but when the stakes were high in the extreme, always remained flexible enough to allow the ends to justify the means. Putting it another way, Teddy may have seriously doubted that the Ten Commandments applied to nation-states when America's welfare was on the line.

Intrigue was the name of the game when the fate of an American canal across the Isthmus of Panama hung in the balance. Setting the Panamanian scene is important, it being the place where William Luther Sibert reached the pinnacle of his career as an engineer. However, by its very nature, the cloak and dagger aspect of the interoceanic canal controversy defies reduction to a meaningful, straightforward account. There are too many unanswered questions with intrigue around every corner. The subject remains ripe for all manner of speculation.

Much simplified for whatever clarity may be possible 100 years later, this account begins when the French give up and, for all practical purposes, shut down their efforts to build a canal in Panama. The company, hanging by a thread, hopes to cut losses by selling the project to Uncle Sam. Meanwhile, the Nicaraguan government welcomed Americans interested in building a second canal—this one in Nicaragua where, by utilizing the lakes and following Colonel Childs' 1852 survey, prospects looked promising. However, between coffee cup and Nicaraguan lips, a series of generally unexpected events occurred.

The commission appointed by President Roosevelt to study isthmian canal feasibility concluded, as expected, that Nicaragua was the preferred canal location. Then—in a totally unexpected finding—the commission unequivocally declared that the Panama route finished a close second. The commissioners liked the Panama location due to certain engineering and geographical advantages offered by the defunct French site and enumerated in the report. That said, the commissioners placed Panama second because they considered the price tag exorbitant—way too much for the French concession and the company's assets in Panama—tipping the scales in favor of Nicaragua. Then, at the eleventh hour, the French company surprised American leaders by reducing the sale price to $40,000,000, less than half of the earlier French evaluation and, more importantly, in line with American estimates of value. The pendulum rapidly reversed course, swinging toward Panama due to the unexpected price reduction, which prompted President Roosevelt to shift his support to Panama and request a new report from the commission based on the diminished cost factor.

Canal Morgan continued fighting for his Nicaraguan dream, making it a tough battle. But with Senator Spooner leading, the Senate authorized the president to buy out the French and build the canal in Panama in June 1902. Known as the Spooner Bill, the legislation quickly won House approval. Even at that, Canal Morgan had one final long shot: The influential senator succeeded in adding a contingency provision to the Spooner Bill, keeping the door ajar for the Nicaragua route. If the Republic of Columbia (the owner of the Province of Panama) should refuse to allow the United States to take over the French concession, the Spooner Bill decreed that the American canal must then be built in Nicaragua. No one expected Columbia to balk. [2]

In Washington, diplomats negotiated and signed the Hay-Herran Treaty between Colombia and the United States, the latter agreeing to pay Colombia $10,000,000 in cash and $250,000 annually during the life of the Panama concession. Colombia had only to allow the French company to sell its interests to the United States. After ratification by the U.S. Senate in March 1903, the treaty ran into trouble in Bogota when the Colombian president changed his position and mounted opposition to the pact. The Colombian Congress rejected the treaty in August, another totally unexpected event.

Without a treaty with Colombia, the Spooner Bill's alternative direction to build the American canal in Nicaragua became viable to the delight of Canal Morgan. At this stage, the game, match and set, seemed to go to Nicaragua.

As the last act of the protracted Panama drama neared conclusion, a richly diverse set of actors peopled the scene—rivaling those in a John le Carre Cold War spy novel. They ranged from Senator Morgan, honest, hardheaded, and by far the most knowledgeable U.S. Senator on all aspects of the canal question, to a powerful rainmaking New York lawyer. Key roles were filled by an opportunistic Frenchman, who survived the crash of the ill-fated French canal effort, and a genuine patriot dedicated to the cause of an independent Panama. And, most important of all, there was the trump card—President Roosevelt—reinforced by his lieutenants in the State Department, Army and Navy.

Even today, it is difficult to sort out the truth of certain events and whether or not they actually occurred. However, based upon undisputed facts, the final scenes of the canal struggle are difficult to top for excitement and intrigue. In September and October of 1903, secret agents, coded cables, cash for guns, a carbon-copy constitution, diplomatic doubletalk, and a brand new flag, were part of the scene in Washington and New York.

While his wife stitched together a flag for the yet to be proclaimed Republic of Panama, Dr. Manuel Amador Guerrero, prepared to leave New York for Panama, armed with a boiler plate constitution and instructions from the Frenchman, Philippe Bunau-Varilla, on just how to launch a Panamanian revolution. The New York lawyer and political heavyweight, William Nelson Cromwell, counsel for the Panama Railroad Company, is generally credited with supporting the rebellion through lobbying and other activities, for a fee, of course.

As a result of these machinations, many of which took place under the Frenchman's directions at the Waldorf-Astoria Hotel, an American cruiser (or gunboat), the U.S.S. *Nashville*, was standing off the Atlantic coast of Panama on November 3, 1903. On that date, a small, rag-tag group of revolutionaries declared their independence from Colombia at the provincial capital, Panama City, some 50 miles away on the Pacific side of the isthmus. Although the *Nashville* seemed to be on the wrong side of the isthmus to support the revolution, it was actually in the perfect position to ensure its success.

Gunboat diplomacy was put to the test and came through with flying colors even though things did not go according to Washington's plans. When it sailed for Panama from Kingston, Jamaica, under the command of Commander Hubbard, the *Nashville's* ostensible goal was to protect American citizens and properties during the unrest. The cruiser arrived in time to witness the landing of a battalion of Colombian soldiers dispatched from Cartagena by the Bogota government to deal with the unruly Panamanians. In all likelihood, this military force, organized and well-armed, would have experienced little difficulty in overcoming the insurgents in Panama City.

But they had to get there!

At this point, by guile and guts, a 72-year-old American railroader— backed by the guns of the *Nashville*—tipped the scales in favor of the insurgents with a simple but effective tactic. Having previously moved all of the Panama Railroad Company's rolling stock to Panama City— except for a single engine and passenger car—Colonel James Shaler, general manager of the American owned railroad, made his pitch.

Shaler warmly greeted Colombian General Tobar and his staff, explaining that he did not have the necessary cars available in Colon to transport the troops to Panama City. However, Shaler said he had a special train available to immediately transport the general and his staff to Panama City and that there would be ample cars available the next day for the battalion to follow. General Tobar fell for the ruse, only to be captured by the rebels upon his arrival in Panama City. It was a quiet surrender.

With 500 Colombian troops ashore, Colon captured more excitement than Panama City. When he learned of General Tobar's capture,

Colonel Eliseo Torres, the officer left in charge of the Columbian soldiers, threatened to kill the Americans in Colon and burn the town if the general was not released. After putting the women and children aboard ships, Commander Hubbard ordered the American men into the railroad company's warehouse and prepared to defend it with a landing party of 42 Marines and sailors—outnumbered almost 10-to-1 by the Colombians. Helping balance the odds, the *Nashville* moved closer to shore, bringing the warehouse under the umbrella of her guns. Sweetened with a well-spent bribe, the show of force convinced Colonel Torres that his best option was to return to Cartagena with his troops, safely away from the guns of the U.S. Navy.

As Colombian troops departed, a second American ship, the *Dixie*, arrived and landed 400 U.S. Marines. Under the command of Captain John Lejeune (a future commandant of the Marine Corps), the Leathernecks filled the military vacuum in Colon and made secure the Panamanian revolution. When, in an effort to save its sovereignty over Panama, a Colombian overture promised new life to the Hay-Herran pact, TR sanctimoniously declared: "I will not for one moment discuss the possibility of the United States committing an act of such baseness as to abandon the new Republic of Panama." America stood firm, very firm.

American Secretary of State John Hay recognized the insurgents as the *de facto* government of the new Republic of Panama on November 6, 1903. Twelve days later the new country's foreign minister concluded a treaty with the United States containing the same basic terms as the treaty rejected by Columbia, with one vital exception: the $10,000,000 payment (as well as all future payments) flowed into the Republic of Panama's treasury, enough to finance the uprising and launch the new government. [3]

Those segments of the press and the American political body who either opposed what they regarded as American imperialism, or the leadership of President Roosevelt, or both since they were difficult to separate, roundly criticized the entire affair. Meanwhile, under entirely new management, the herculean construction project got ready to resume work.

In light of the colossal French failure, could it be that the canal bisecting Panama could be built by those blustery Americans, led by their rambunctious president who favored speaking softly while carrying a big stick? The U.S.S. *Nashville*, which bore no resemblance to a stick, proved entirely adequate for the job.

—⚍—

From the beginning, unlike the French, the Americans invested much time and money in preparations for actual construction and one other thing: Concern for public health produced an ambitious program aimed at the eradication or drastic reduction of yellow fever and malaria, maladies which claimed thousands of lives during the French era. William C. Gorgas, hero of the Army's successful effort to wipe out yellow fever in Havana, Cuba, by attacking the mosquitoes which spread it, directed the public health program in Panama. By all accounts he did an outstanding job, sometimes working under stiflingly adverse conditions. His objective: Make it much safer to work, not only within what became known as the Canal Zone, but also including Colon and Panama City and numerous towns and villages crowding the canal's route.

The first American chief engineer in Panama, John Findley Wallace, though competent and well-regarded, lacked the right temperament to simultaneously cope with the oppressive climate, the dangers from disease, the frustrations born of Washington red tape, and his own difficulty in grasping the magnitude and importance of the canal project. Although he managed to salvage and renovate much valuable equipment abandoned by the French, things did not go well for Wallace. Confounded by what he perceived as the engineer's somewhat indifferent attitude and lack of dedication to the canal construction, Secretary of War William Howard Taft requested his resignation which was subsequently accepted by President Roosevelt on June 28, 1905.

When the second chief engineer, John Stevens—who took the job with the president's blessings—arrived in Panama on July 25, 1905, things changed. Rather than plunging headlong into moving dirt, he chose to first prepare a workable system for doing it efficiently. Equally important, he threw his full support behind Gorgas who, for the first time, received the resources needed to vanquish the mosquitoes.

Also for the first time, the chief engineer received a free hand, thereby freeing the work from being nitpicked and slowed by the Washington bureaucracy. Stevens made much progress in preparation for future construction, including railroad facilities designed to serve the huge excavation of Culebra Cut, a key ingredient in success of the project. Then, problems developed: Perhaps it was another case of apparent lack of enthusiasm for the job and the strain that went with the territory, or maybe it was a simple breakdown in communications between strong personalities, each accustomed to doing things his own way. Anyhow, Stevens wrote a highly undiplomatic letter to the president—the tone of the letter prompting the chief executive to regard it as Stevens' resignation. As a result, President Roosevelt accepted the resignation in February 1907—the unintended consequences of some ill-considered language.

Based on Army Secretary Taft's recommendation, the president immediately appointed Major George Washington Goethals to be the third—and last—chief engineer charged with building the Panama Canal. Appointment of the Corps of Engineers officer came before the end of February, coinciding with Major Sibert's early planning for reconstruction of Dam No. 3 on the Allegheny.

A new organization accompanied the new chief engineer: President Roosevelt installed a new Isthmian Canal Commission, replacing commissioners who had tried to oversee the project from the comfort of Washington offices. Major Goethals served as chairman—the new commission clearly designed and populated to be an on-site, hands-on board of directors.

The new commission (ICC) sported a decidedly military bearing with five of its members on active service in the armed forces of the United States. The two civilian members indicate that the ex-volunteer colonel of the Rough Riders and his chief lieutenant, Taft, tried to cover all the bases. Jackson Smith, who came to Panama with Stevens, was chosen due to his years of experience building railroads in Latin America. The sprawling project needed efficient rail transportation. The president and the war secretary demonstrated their sensitivity to the canal's host, the newly created Republic of Panama, through appointment of Joseph C.S. Blackburn, a former U.S. Senator from Kentucky. Experienced in negotiations, levelheaded, courteous, and diplomatic, Blackburn became the perfect emissary to treat directly with the government of Panama.

The military nature of the new commission involved far more than mere flavor. President Roosevelt wanted a chief engineer who would not under any circumstances flinch from the job to be done, or consider resigning, unless it was the president's idea. Actually a simple solution, the president appointed a military officer to the post. As commander in chief, Roosevelt was the engineer's boss and could veto any effort to quit the post. This same approach spilled into selection of members of the commission as well, giving the military and, consequently, the president, a 5-2 advantage.

The commission chairman and chief engineer, Major Goethals, came up through the ranks in the Corps of Engineers after graduating from West Point in 1880. Widely experienced, Goethals had served throughout the country and preceded Sibert working on the Ohio River system. He served as assistant to the chief engineer before being chosen a member of the Army's first general staff. His most notable achievement involved the design and construction of a dam and lock on the Tennessee River at Muscle Shoals, Alabama—the lock capable of lifting a ship a record 26 feet from the dam's lower to upper pools. Goethals had also taught engineering at West Point and, by any measure, was an excellent choice to head the canal project.

An obvious choice for the commission was William C. Gorgas, an Army officer to the core, who preferred to be addressed as Dr. Gorgas. He arrived early in Panama but got little support for his sanitation and mosquito eradication program until Stevens showed up. Conventional wisdom acknowledged the Gorgas approach had worked well in a small area such as Havana, while considering it useless within the wide expanse of canal construction. When appointed to the new commission, thanks to Stevens and Roosevelt (both of whom believed in his methods), Gorgas' program was already fully operational. It succeeded in protecting both Americans and Panamanians from yellow fever— the dreaded "Yellow Jack"—and made everything else possible. [4]

Captain Harry Harwood Rousseau, an accomplished engineer, represented the U.S. Navy on the commission. The naval officer stayed busy designing and constructing all nautical-related structures ranging from wharves and dry docks to coaling stations.

Further breaking down the military's presence on the commission, two additional officers of the U.S. Army Corps of Engineers joined Goethals on the directorate—making three Corps of Engineers officers, three dedicated West Pointers. Not by chance, under the command of Goethals, David and Goliath were reunited in Panama. For the first time, Sibert and Gaillard were assigned to the same project. The pair had spent more than 20 years accumulating valuable engineering experience in Cuba and the Philippines, and from the Great Lakes and Arkansas to Florida. Like Goethals, both David Du Bose Gaillard and William Luther "Goliath" Sibert counted extensive waterways construction experience in their Army records jackets.

Perhaps more important, like Goethals, they were veteran officers, ingrained with durable dedication and discipline dating from their days as cadets on the Hudson. Of all possible appointees, they were the most unlikely to abandon their posts in Panama. It mattered not how hot the climate, how adverse the politics, how daunting the engineering problems, and how frustrating the day-to-day strain when working in close concert with other independent thinking engineers on the world's most challenging construction project. They would never quit! Army officers did not normally quit in the face of perceived slights or injured feelings, but rode out any personal storms and, in the end, did what they were trained to do: Follow orders. President Roosevelt counted on such taut military discipline to win through in Panama. The ex-Rough Rider knew just exactly whom he wanted to build the American canal—the U.S. Army Corps of Engineers. And no time was to be wasted.

That is why Major Sibert sailed for Panama on March 10, 1907, although his and David Gaillard's appointments to the commission were not signed until March 16, 1907. The ex-roommates were destined to be key members of the second Isthmian Canal Commission, but with the president's full support, Goethals was definitely in charge. The details of how the mission should be accomplished were left up to the commissioners with the last word exclusively reserved for Goethals.

All of this was unknown to Major Sibert when the telegram arrived in Pittsburgh with travel instructions. It had to be unnerving, even for the stoic Sibert, this urgent and mysterious summons to Washington—without prior warning. He immediately suspected a professional crisis, perhaps resulting from the recent and highly publicized dynamiting of the dam on the Allegheny. A personal invitation to meet with President Roosevelt at the White House could not have been more upsetting—and that is exactly what it was. It deeply impressed the major, an invitation to the White House for a private conference with TR concerning Sibert's appointment to the commission and his orders to Panama.

Beginning with Goethals, the president met individually with each of the new appointees, part pep talk and part making certain that each man knew that Goethals was—without challenge—to be the president's man in Panama. Roosevelt, who was experienced at accepting resignations, candidly explained that he would immediately approve the resignation of any commissioner who found it impossible to abide by the chairman's decisions. He left no doubt about the rake-style command structure in Panama with Goethals alone perched at the top of the handle. Conditioned by years of active service in the Army, Sibert knew about the chain of command.

The urgency of the mission required Major Sibert to leave Pittsburgh in haste, sailing from New York for Panama on March 10, 1907. Owned by the Panama Railroad Company, the ship sailed some 31 degrees south, give or take a few minutes, where he assumed new duties. The Sibert family followed; a fellow engineer stationed at Pittsburgh, by letter dated May 23, 1907, requested instructions for shipping the family's household goods to Panama. A telegram from Washington, dated June 7, 1907, contained directions for shipping the furnishings to New York in time to be loaded aboard another of the railroad company's steamers for the final leg of the journey. [5]

Sibert previously experienced tropical weather, including oppressive heat, stifling humidity, and more than an abundance of rain, during his service in the Philippines, none of which adversely affected him and all of which awaited him in Panama. He knew a species of deer inhabited the isthmian jungles and wondered how it compared with deer in the Mammoth Cave region of Kentucky. Ready to roll up his sleeves and meet the new challenge, the dedicated hunter seriously wondered if there would be sufficient slack time in Panama to hunt and explore the jungle environ. No longer concerned with navigation on a stateside river, he sensed that Panama was a very special game.

The private audience with President Roosevelt convinced the mathematical farm boy that he was now in the big leagues, involved in America's first and by far its most ambitious engineering effort with international implications. With the eyes of the nations on the American engineers in Panama, hunting parties might have to wait.

Although the first airplanes, the first autos, and dozens of other contemporaneous innovations provided stiff competition, the mere size of the Panama Canal made it by far the most promising, the very best herald of achievements yet ahead in the 20th Century. Its technology was equally impressive although more difficult to understand.

Serious thinkers, ranging from engineers to philosophers, even as they ignored all the Yankee braggadocio, and looked only at its merits, had no trouble declaring the Panama Canal the engineering achievement of the age.

The story of William Luther Sibert cannot be told without a plunge into that 50-mile-long waterway which has joined the Atlantic and Pacific oceans since 1914. A contemporary view of just how the Panama Canal appeared to the Americans who built it, and to their countrymen in those last years of comparative peace before World War I, is revealing. Consider the following:

In 1913, the Canal Zone, under lease from the Republic of Panama, is described as extending out five miles on either side of the center line of the canal. The zone ran from deep water in the Caribbean Sea, a hefty arm of the Atlantic Ocean, to deep water in the Pacific Ocean on the opposite side of the isthmus. The trip from deep water to deep water would be slightly more than 50 miles in length when the canal officially opened for business in January 1915.

The Canal Zone contained approximately 436 square miles over which the Isthmian Canal Commission exercised total control for all practical purposes, if not downright sovereignty. Much of the acreage within the zone would end up under water that was directly devoted to making the canal's slack water navigation system work. Lake Gatun, created by damming the waters of the Chagres River and the lesser streams, contained approximately 164 square miles, some of which spilled over into the Republic of Panama.

Surprisingly, to steam from the Atlantic (Caribbean) waters east of Panama and Central America, a ship had to steer roughly southeast through the canal to reach the Pacific Ocean. Balboa discovered the world's largest ocean in 1513, calling it the South Sea. Generally, the Pacific lies to the west and washes the western shores of the isthmus, a coast that could just as easily be called the south coast of Panama.

The width of the actual channel, capable of handling ocean-going traffic, varied from 1,000 feet along the unimpeded route across Gatun Lake to a more restricted 300-foot wide course through Culebra Cut in crossing the continental divide. As it crossed the lake, the depth of the channel varied from 85 feet to a minimum of 45 feet. Minimum depth through Culebra Cut was a uniform 45 feet. Generally speaking, canal statistics tend to overwhelm.

The French excavated more than 78,000,000 cubic yards of Panamanian landscape, of which 30,000,000 cubic yards of rock and soil ultimately proved useful in construction of the canal. The Americans excavated more than 200,000,000 additional cubic yards of material before completing the canal.

By the spring of 1912, the relocation and upgrading of the Panama Railroad was complete and serving canal construction in the short term; it provided a more efficient land link between Panama's coasts over the long haul. Slightly more than 47 miles long, it was the busiest short line railway in the world during canal construction. The railroad work alone cost Uncle Sam almost $9,000,000.

In addition to the Panama Railroad's relocated main line and its rolling stock, track engineers laid down miles of additional track within the Canal Zone to support construction. In 1913, the Isthmian Canal Commission counted more than 300 locomotives and more than 4,500 railway cars dedicated to moving materials vital to the construction. Cargoes ranged from rock and soil continually excavated from Culebra Cut and tons and tons of cement and steel used in lock construction, to food and other supplies required to keep 40,000 workers on the go. Additional tons of coal required to keep machinery humming and the railroad functioning also required hauling. On average, the locomotives, steam shovels, drills, dredges, and other steam driven equipment consumed 35,000 tons of coal each month. [6]

The list of statistics, most of them in the superlative category, seems endless. The unimaginable size of the undertaking boggled the minds of ordinary mortals. Routine functions of management, altogether simple in the abstract, or when applied to much smaller construction projects, became large and complicated exercises in logistics along the canal route. Take, for example, administering the payroll.

Soon after the United States assumed control of the canal properties and construction activities, the workforce reached its nadir in September 1904 when some 500 workers were counted on the job. Within 14 months, by November 1905, the Americans recruited an army of workers numbering 17,000 as they settled in and cranked up to build a canal. Almost 32,000 were on the job in October 1907, and even more in the years that followed as the Army cracked the whip on the behemoth construction project. More than 40,000 workers graced the November 1912 payroll. By March 1913, 44,733 were on the list when payday arrived.

More accurately, each month had not one, but several paydays included in a program designed to pay every employee on time while minimizing the loss of man-hours required for the transactions. The ICC operated from two permanent offices, one located at commission headquarters on the Pacific side, the second at Cristobal on the Caribbean coast. However, the bulk of employees laboring along the rough-cut canal route received pay near their work sites from a unique rolling bank. The ICC paymasters dispatched the mobile pay car, with its own locomotive, to every corner of the elongated construction site served by rail. By delivering their earnings to workers at or near their workstations, the ICC lost minimal man hours to the payment process.

As for the pay, it was the real thing: gold and silver coins, none of that paper stuff. Americans got the gold and, generally speaking, all other ICC employees were paid in silver. The system worked well after earlier variations were tried and, as the project neared completion, the Americans were paid in bills. During the fiscal year ending June 30, 1913, the last full year of record employment, ICC tellers disbursed $20,524,705.75 in salaries and wages, of which $9,228,633.99 was of the gold variety, the remainder in silver. Think of the weight of the specie: for each monthly pay period the ICC paid out approximately 1,600 pounds of gold for the Americans and an astounding 24 tons of silver for other employees, ranging from the huge army of West Indians to the smaller European contingent. If for no other reason, the weight of the coins made a railroad car the transport of choice. [7]

—∿∿—

The handling of payroll followed the ICC's streamlined management style, based on the Army way of getting things done. Because Goethals was virtual czar of the Canal Zone, his word amounted to law, allowing rapid implementation of innovations, whether they were of the engineering or administrative variety, in order to improve the overall efficiency of the enterprise.

With the new commission in place and solidly behind him, Goethals made a fundamental change by shaking up the engineering table of organization. Previously, duties were divided along the lines of particular tasks to be performed. For example, the engineer in charge of excavations was responsible for all digging. This included not only Culebra Cut across the Continental Divide, but also moving the rock and soil necessary to build facilities—locks and dams—on both the Atlantic and Pacific ends of the project. And if another officer's assignment was lock construction, it was another case of work sites located at opposite ends of the canal, creating conditions that defied efficient coordination. Too much geography was the problem.

There was no way to carry out these widely separated tasks efficiently and avoid constant and wasteful collisions between both machinery and personnel. Goethals installed a simple solution: Effective July 1, 1908, engineering responsibilities, regardless of their nature, were divided geographically—three ways.

Major Sibert took charge of the Atlantic Division, with Major Gaillard being assigned responsibility for the Central Division, which included Culebra Cut. The Pacific Division chief was S.B. Williamson, the only civilian to head a construction division. The Pacific and Atlantic divisions contained all of the locks and dams. By appointing an Army engineer (Sibert) on the Atlantic side and a civilian on the Pacific end, the chairman envisioned friendly competition, as another spur for the construction projects.

Goethals made a few exceptions for some highly specialized and very important duties which were not directly associated with engineering and construction, and which, by their very nature, cut across divisional boundaries. The foremost exception involved retention of Colonel Gorgas in overall charge of health, sanitation, and his offensive against mosquitoes and the yellow fever and malaria they carried. His responsibilities covered the entire Canal Zone and then some. Nor did law enforcement have divisional restraints, the constabulary organized by George R. Shanton, an ex-Rough Rider, enjoying zone-wide jurisdiction. By 1912, approximately 270 police officers, most of them ex-U.S. Army personnel, were on duty. The commissary was another zone-wide task with responsibility for feeding and housing personnel by the thousands. Through the commissary, the ICC even entered the hotel business.

The nature of Goethals' reorganization left his staff of engineers free to concentrate on what they did best: engineer! And that is what they did, and they did it very well. The plan produced a largely efficient organization with the capability of constructing a highly workable canal. The best evidence of the plan's wisdom and efficacy: *It worked!* [8]

Given that Goethals was a Corps of Engineers officer, who, along with Sibert and Gaillard, accounted for three of the seven slots on the

Isthmian Canal Commission (eight if the secretary is counted), it remains remarkable that a pair of ex-West Point roommates, David and Goliath, ran the bulk of the construction show after 1908 and until the canal was practically finished. Only construction activity within the Pacific Division (headed by the civilian) was beyond day-to-day control by the former academy roommates. Even at that, as members of the commission (the civilian, Williamson, was not a commissioner), Gaillard and Sibert had considerable voice in the Pacific project, even as Goethals sometimes ignored Sibert's sound suggestions while fulfilling TR's desire for a strong executive. Colonel Goethals was the final arbiter on controversial questions and Gaillard and Sibert obeyed their commanding officer.

Although each division had its own problems, those faced by Gaillard in the Central Division almost exclusively concerned management of the unprecedented excavations within Culebra Cut, a nine-mile stretch of canal route crossing the Continental Divide. The mountainous continental spine had to be breached in a big way, opening a yawning canyon with dynamite and steam shovels. Once removed from the future canal channel, the spoil relocation had to mesh with other work and, where possible, be put to good use. Of equal import—which with time became the overriding problem—were the steep banks of the gigantic trench across the Continental Divide that had to be stabilized to form miles and miles of canal walls.

Now renamed Gaillard Cut in his honor, the officer presided over steam shovels, drills, railway cars, battalions of pick and shovel laborers, and those daring powder men, the dynamiting experts, with all efforts bent on carving, blasting, and scooping out a stupendous waterway capable of handling vessels of a size yet to be designed. The Army engineer coordinated men and machines masterfully to clear the cut and haul off the spoil. Efforts to stabilize the banks of the manmade gorge were another story with landslides destined to hamper construction and continue to cause problems thereafter.

Well away from the problems besieging Culebra Cut, the Atlantic and Pacific divisions involved construction of locks and dams and a different set of riddles ripe for solving. In both divisions, plans demanded safe methods for connecting with the deep waters of the Atlantic and the Pacific, the oceanic connection being the object of the entire exercise. Although each had huge helpings of dredging, digging, and blasting, the two oceanic divisions were very much on the constructive side of the ledger. While Gaillard's goal was to achieve open space, the blasting and excavating in the oceanic divisions opened the way for construction of locks and dams on a gargantuan scale.

The ever-practical Sibert viewed the entire canal project as a king-sized version of those slack water navigation systems he had bossed in Kentucky and Arkansas. Identical engineering principles applied in Panama where locks and dams remained indispensable. Commissioner Sibert drew the task of constructing a single integral dam and locks structure. But what a dam and locks it would be!

—✦—

The challenging assignment required much preparation, and Sibert was an apostle of thorough preparation. A good example of the important work done on the front end of the Gatun Dam and Locks construction sounds mundane: Engineers searched for an adequate supply of sand and rock for making concrete to eventually build dam spillways and the Gatun locks. They soon located high quality rock, capable of producing crushed stone suitable for the concrete mixers. After testing beach sand, engineers found it lacking, probably due to its constant exposure to salt, and the search for quality sand broadened. Sibert's geologic scouts finally discovered a convenient and suitable sand deposit away from the beaches and fairly close to Gatun. He planned to excavate the sand and barge it to the construction site, once arrangements were made to purchase the common mineral from its owners.

The Kuna Indians owned the inland sand deposits although they lived on the San Blas Islands, an archipelago of approximately 360 tiny coral islands lying off the coast of Panama in the Caribbean Sea. Because none of the islands had a fresh water source, only about 70—located opposite the mouth of a mainland river—were inhabited, close enough to canoe fresh water to the islands. The islanders fished and, in addition, farmed jungle gardens and attended coconut plantations on the mainland where the high quality sand deposits were located.

With no State Department officials handy, the pursuit of sand required Sibert to don his diplomatic hat, meet with the Kuna, and negotiate a contract for purchasing thousands of tons of sand needed for Gatun concrete. The dependable, steam-powered *Gatun* transported the diplomatic mission to the San Blas island where the most powerful and influential Kuna chief resided. *The Construction of the Panama Canal*, the book he co-authored with John Frank Stevens, the chief engineer replaced by Goethals, tells of Sibert's encounter with the Kuna.

The squat *Gatun* must have been a strange sight to the Indians as it approached the chief's island under a full head of steam. Through binoculars, women were seen seeking hiding places, which seemed to be the standard drill when strangers approached. And at the sight of the boatload of American engineers, a naked Indian boy, frightened by the apparition, turned about and frantically paddled his dugout for the safety of the shore. Sibert found the boy's efforts so appealing that he ordered the boat to slow, allowing the youngster ample time to reach the beach. "These Indians are efficient sailors and learn to handle a boat when very young," noted Sibert.

Upon landing, the Americans learned that the chief was away but expected to return later in the day. Told to return in the afternoon, at that time they would learn if the island prince would receive them. Under those instructions, the boat returned to the mainland for additional inspections of the sand deposits; the visit reaffirmed the initial engineering opinion that the sand was of the desired quality for concrete production.

Returning to the island, it became apparent that the hoped for parley with the chief was big news, attracting many Indians from the outlying islands to observe ceremonies. Sibert smiled, rightly concluding that the crowd would not have gathered if there was to be no parley. Again, all of the women hid as the landing party made its way through a labyrinth of native dwellings to the chief's quarters.

Inside was the throne—a block of wood—on which the islands' king sat with great dignity as he motioned the visitors to be seated on the sandy floor. Sibert noted that "an air of solemnity surrounded the whole proceeding." Through an interpreter, "Ambassador" Sibert began at the beginning: He explained that he and his countrymen were going to build a canal for boats to travel between the two oceans, thereby opening new avenues of trade for the Indians. With the canal in place, the engineer predicted that the Kuna could more easily market coconuts and other farm produce at appreciably higher prices. The canal, said Sibert, promised to stimulate the Kuna economy, an economic surge, so to speak.

The old chief (estimated by Sibert to be approximately 70 years of age) listened politely and seemed deep in thought before responding to the tall visitor through an interpreter. Like Sibert, he also began at the beginning, an even more remote starting point than the American decision to build the canal. God, the chief said with royal authority, gave the Kuna their mainland property, including "the land and the water, and the sand that was under the water." That which God had given the Kuna, the chief explained, "they would neither sell nor give to the white man." The chief greeted a second attempt to justify the concession with a wave of his hand—and an unmistakably negative response: "There is no need to talk further."

Still, Sibert did not immediately give up, beseeching the chief to reconsider, discretely pointing out that the Americans could simply take the sand by obtaining permission from the Republic of Panama. The engineer told the chief, however, that his kindly and considerate visitors much preferred to pay the Kuna for the sand if suitable arrangements could be negotiated directly with the chief—more money for the Kuna than the chief could imagine.

In an even more emphatic statement, the chief declared that the people of the islands owed no allegiance to the Republic of Panama and would never permit the United States to take the sand! End of the negotiations, for sure, although Sibert had one additional and entirely different request. Because darkness had descended on the islands while the talks were in progress, he requested permission to remain anchored at the island for the night, rather than attempt a return to the mainland in the dark.

The chief granted the request, but not without a condition: Leave early next morning and never return. They left as instructed, not, however, before the Kuna and their chief made a lasting impression on the American diplomats: "The discipline of these people, the power of the Chief, and the respect of the tribe for him, as shown during this visit, is remarkable," wrote Sibert.

The only way to procure sand from the Kuna involved bloodshed, Sibert concluded, and he was having none of that, and there were other considerations: "In addition," the officer penned, "it seemed a pity to disturb a life that was so unique and strong, in an Indian way at least."

The ICC left the Kuna undisturbed, while a most persistent missionary lady, Miss Annie Coope, had better luck. After being turned away several times, the Kunas allowed the missionary to establish a mission school near the mouth of the Rio Diablo in early 1913. The tribe finally warmed to her efforts, glad they had allowed her to stay and establish the school. She was far more successful in dealing with the Kuna than Sibert had been. Part of her success, without doubt, came about because she had no wish to appropriate Indian sand. And part of the blame for Sibert's lack of success fell squarely on his refusal to employ gunboat diplomacy (not even the peashooter variety), for which the United States became, rightly or wrongly, infamous among Latin Americans.

For doing the right thing, the Americans literally paid a higher price for the sand they later obtained in the vicinity of Nombre de Dios. Sibert caught criticism for the higher costs of both sand and the crushed stone obtained at Porto Bello; both materials were less costly on the Pacific side of the isthmus, with the railroad available to get them to Gatun. The additional costs, according to Sibert, were offset by relieving the railroad of another huge hauling chore—daily moving 3,000 cubic yards of crushed stone and 1,500 cubic yards of sand across the isthmus to feed the Gatun concrete mixers. Already overtaxed moving other canal materials, along with general freight and passenger services, Sibert's argument was sound. When viewed from afar, however, control of uninterrupted access to the materials essential for concrete production was likely the major factor in Sibert's planning. Both the Porto Bello quarry and rock crushers, and the sand deposits at Nombre de Dios were within his Atlantic Division bailiwick, a convenient arrangement when anything needed fixing. This represented foresight and preparations if Major Sibert was to have a fighting chance of beating the deadline for completion of the locks and dam at Gatun. [9]

—◊◊◊—

If a Goliath existed among engineers, Gatun needed him. There Sibert found a most worthy opponent, one capable of taxing to the limits his enthusiasm and unbridled confidence in himself and his fellow officers in the Army Corps of Engineers. It helped that Major David DuBose Gaillard—the David to his Goliath at West Point—shared duties in the Canal Zone,

When the ICC met at Ancon, its headquarters on the Pacific side of the Canal Zone, a glance around the room reassured the academy roommates who occupied two seats on the seven-member commission. They also commanded two of the three construction divisions in the Canal Zone—Sibert directing the Atlantic Division and Gaillard in charge of the Central Division. Both were destined to serve with distinction in Panama although Gaillard became seriously ill while taming Culebra Cut. With the end of the project in sight, he was relieved of duty and returned stateside for medical treatment. Afflicted with a brain tumor, the officer died on December 5, 1913, while under treatment at Johns Hopkins Hospital in Baltimore. His death constitutes one of the more poignant episodes in Sibert's life.

Unlike the Biblical account, Goliath survived this time while sadly, his David perished. More than just surviving, William Luther Sibert thrived on the Gatun challenge. Thanks to the restructured canal command, Sibert assumed command of the Atlantic Division—a fiefdom short on mileage, but heavily weighted with engineering problems begging for solution.

And, as it developed, the Gatun dam also attracted major controversies, congressional questions, and a full-blown investigation. Regardless of outcome—either success or failure—the ICC's brutally simple table of organization placed responsibility squarely on the broad shoulders of Sibert. His job: oversee the design and construction of a dam and locks, each of monumental proportions, which had to be engineered and built exactly right to make the American canal work.

None of the work was easy and all of the parts to the Panama puzzle had to be finished and in good working order if the Americans ever hoped to float ocean-going vessels across the isthmus from the Atlantic to the Pacific and vice versa. If completed it would truly outweigh the sum of its vital parts. Although the entire system had to be capable of handling all manner of vessels from the world's maritime nations, one piece of the puzzle is nothing less than the key to operation of the entire canal system.

Gatun Dam.

Gatun Dam, plus the waters it impounds, makes everything else work. It was Sibert's job to build it with the capability of safely storing adequate water to operate the adjacent locks as well as those on the Pacific side. Locks and dams are naturally paired, the Gatun locks also being Sibert's child, and his responsibility to rear, or erect, in the language of construction.

Once an observer fully comprehends Gatun Dam's immense size, both length and girth, and goes one step farther to fathom its overriding importance to the smooth and safe operation of the Panama Canal, there comes an understanding of just why it attracted more than its share of broadsides from opponents of the canal in Panama. They probed for a weak spot in the Panama project's armor, a vital area where the canal in progress might be fatally wounded before it could be finished, thereby reopening prospects for a Nicaraguan canal. At Gatun Dam, they thought they had found it.

While learning the dam building trade on the rivers of Kentucky, the dams were uniformly small when compared with the dam planned for Gatun. The Kentucky dams worked even though crudely constructed by modern standards. The typical dam (such as Green River No. 4 at Woodbury) consisted of log-cabin style timber cribs filled with stone, gravel, clay, and sand, and faced with wood or stone cut from a nearby quarry. The Kentucky dams counted only one feature in common with Gatun Dam: All were meant to contain water. On the Monongahela, Allegheny, and Ohio rivers, Sibert was exposed to larger facilities and different dam designs—ranging from ancient to experimental. He had even destroyed one dam with high explosives. Before leaving Pittsburgh for Panama in 1907, and as a result of continuing study and practical experience, the officer probably knew more about dam construction and the operation of locks in a slack water navigation system than any other engineer.

The question of locks and dams in Panama bubbles over with irony. When the Americans took control of the old French properties in 1904, there were no plans in Washington to construct Gatun Dam, or, for that matter, any other dam in Panama. Except for the bundles of blueprints inherited from the French, the United States had no specific plan detailing how to build and operate the American canal. At that point, Panama looked much like an overpriced and costly undertaking—some said a reckless gamble—for several reasons, including unsolved engineering problems, adverse diplomatic effects, and a price too high.

Roosevelt's political opponents singled out his Panama initiative and tagged him as an imperialist. With business as usual continuing in Washington, other pressures and issues arose, all capable of causing trouble in the Canal Zone. True to form, it was first things first and full speed ahead for Roosevelt, who decided his pet project, needed a plan.

On June 24, 1905, in order to obtain the best expert guidance available, the president named 13 members to the International Board of Consulting Engineers. The board pursued the best method to connect the two oceans—by either a sea level route with no need for locks and dams, or by creation of the world's largest slack water navigation system, totally dependent on locks and dams.

On January 10, 1906, the consultants delivered two separate reports to the ICC, a majority of eight members signing off on an impressive report favoring a sea level canal. The five-member minority aggressively favored locks and dams and said so in strong language. But for one member, the ICC also favored locks and dams, as did John F. Stevens, then serving as chief engineer before Roosevelt's *junta* took reins in the Canal Zone. The ICC reported its opinion to Secretary of War Taft (another locks and dams supporter), and he delivered the message to Roosevelt, who felt the same way.

Even as his own blue ribbon panel of international experts delivered a majority report contrary to what the president wanted—citing doubts about the stability of a dam large enough to impound the Chagres River—the president endorsed the minority report. He counted on strong support for his own position among the highly competent engineers composing the panel's minority, as well as those on the ICC. Recognizing that he and Taft were not alone in supporting the locks and dams plan, the president did what both his supporters and detractors would have expected the ex-Rough Rider to do.

Roosevelt delivered the various reports to Congress on February 19, 1906, along with a statement from Stevens and a letter from Taft supporting the locks and dams approach. Topping off the documents was his own letter reciting the facts behind the controversy and declaring his unequivocal support for locks and dams and a slack water navigation system to carry the world's ship-borne commerce through this great American canal. On June 29, 1906, Congress responded to the president's message by approving a locks and dams canal, its waters to be confined 85 feet above sea level. Sibert needed plans.

Even more irony surrounds the now official American plan for construction of the canal in Panama—utilizing locks and dams to create a slack water navigation system. A French engineer, Adolphe Godin de Lepinay, envisioned the same basic concept in 1879. At the time,

Ferdinand de Lesseps—not an engineer but a promoter—rejected the idea in pursuit of the ill-fated sea level version.

Locks, dams, and the slack water system they would create, comprised the core of the canal plan when Sibert reported for duty in the Canal Zone in 1907, and remained virtually unchanged until construction was complete. In November 1908, by which time Sibert was well established as chief engineer for the Atlantic Division, opponents mounted, arguably, the most serious threat to the accepted design. After extremely heavy annual rains, a portion of the unfinished dam's toe on the upstream (lake) side sank into soft silt and mud deposited at the bottom of the old French canal route. This subsidence was no surprise and had been anticipated by engineers.

Nevertheless, sensational press reports of the incident, spun and magnified out of proportion, caused quite a stir stateside where opposition to the Panama project (including proponents of the Nicaragua route and anyone else opposed to the Roosevelt administration) persisted. The anti-Panama elements remained alert and on the lookout for any opportunity to ambush the American efforts in Panama.

For canal opponents, the dam at Gatun presented a big target, one they couldn't miss if only they succeeded in convincing enough people that the dam was ill conceived because, in their opinion, it was just too big and, well, highly dangerous. If opponents failed to gain support from a congressional majority, the marshaling of public opinion against the dam offered another option. They argued that the dam was likely to fail with catastrophic results under the pressure generated from holding back an artificial lake covering more than 163 square miles. Opponents, none of them engineers, attacked both the method of construction and the materials used.

The same line of attack had continued—and failed—for several years, and included charges that the dam's foundation was poor and its superstructure not watertight. While the majority of consultants appointed by Roosevelt in 1905 registered doubt in the stability of so large a dam, there were sound engineering opinions to the contrary.

Recognizing a possible public relations disaster in the making, and acutely aware of the political consequences which might follow, Roosevelt took the offensive. He named another blue ribbon engineering board and sent them to Panama, accompanied by President-elect Taft, to examine the works in progress—including an onsite inspection of

Gatun Dam. After the Panama visit, the board's positive analysis, delivered February 16, 1909, delighted Roosevelt. Concerning the sufficiency of Gatun Dam, the report stated: "The design upon which work on the dam is now being prosecuted abundantly fulfills the required degree of stability and goes far beyond the limits of what would be regarded as sufficient and safe in any less important structure."

In addition, the panel recommended that engineers could safely reduce the original height proposed for the dam by a full 20 feet. This suggestion illustrates the tendency of canal planners to overbuild; if the canal engineers erred, it would be on the side of extra caution and safety. After the project received the 1909 engineering and political stamp of approval, Sibert breathed a sigh of relief and redoubled efforts to build the biggest and best dam the world had ever seen.

And just exactly what kind of dam would it be? Certainly not one of the Kentucky variety composed of timber cribs filled with all manner of debris and capped with cut limestone. The answer to the question must necessarily begin with a close look at the Gatun area. A second factor: By superimposing a super dam on the existing landscape, what exactly did the Americans hope to accomplish? Obviously, dams are built to contain water, but there is more to the dam at Gatun than being a glorified bucket. Other factors to consider involve the geography, geology, and topography of the region. There is overlap for sure, but all three have something to offer. [10]

Starting with geography, the broad mission of Gatun Dam can actually be seen and understood in a foldout bird's-eye view of the Panama Canal, which appeared in 1913 in the magazine of the National Geographic Society. For purposes of the aerial view of the Canal Zone, the Gatun Dam, Culebra Cut, and other locations of lesser importance, are depicted in full flower, as completed. Ships are sketched crossing Gatun Lake while other vessels await transit at each end of the canal.

The *National Geographic* painting offers instructive perspective looking northeast across the isthmus. It is oriented with the Caribbean, Colon, and Gatun to the left and Culebra Cut, the Mira Flores locks and dam, Ancon, and the Pacific to the right. The remainder of the canal, including its route through Gatun Lake, crosses the center of the picture.

By deft use of shadow and shading, the artist succeeded in revealing the contours of hills, ridges, and mountains, making the painting a skillful blend of geography and topography. The painting illustrates how Gatun Dam takes full advantage of the natural mountains, hills, and ridges by filling a large gap between the highlands to create a huge basin for collecting water.

The illustration deserves another look toward the northeast end of Gatun Dam to see the second reason for its construction: The dam serves as an immovable anchor to the southwest abutment of the triple-decked Gatun locks. By storing the water required to float ships between the oceans, and by safely securing the locks in place so that shipping can be lifted to and lowered from the canal proper, Gatun Dam qualifies as the truly indispensable party to success of the canal. [11]

The highlands, whether called small mountains or big hills, and their connecting ridgelines run roughly parallel to Panama's Caribbean coast and help form a bowl, a natural shoreline for the planned artificial lake. There was only one problem—a wide crack in the bowl where the region's most prominent river had cut a path through the mountainous barrier on its way to the Caribbean. To form the lake and make the canal work, that crack, the low gap in the highlands chain, had to be sealed by a very big dam—Gatun Dam—closing the Chagres River's path to the sea.

Based on the magnitude and difficulty of the various tasks to be completed, an early analysis predicted the Gatun segment would be the last segment of the canal completed. Sibert seriously doubted the projected timetable, regarding it as a goal worth surpassing.

Sound engineering design required the dam to be built in the form of an arc, a segment of a huge circle. In other words, the structure would be bow-shaped, projecting out into the artificial lake, its lines a long graceful curve. From its junction with the locks, the dam bowed out ever so gently one and one-half miles (7,920 feet) to its bonding with the highlands, thus closing the Chagres River Valley gap. The captured water would have no way out except by those paths engineered by Sibert.

Engineers originally planned the crest of the dam at 135 feet above sea level, this elevation, according to studies, more than sufficient to contain the waters of the new lake even when the Chagres River was well beyond flood stage. They designed the enormous structure to reduce leakage to a minimal level and spared not a cubic yard of material in pursuit of an impenetrability.

The base of Gatun Dam, the distance from the lake or upstream side to the downstream or ocean side, was a full half mile—2,625 feet of thickness. From this broad base, and all along its one and one-half mile length, the dam rose gradually with induction of an estimated 22,000,000 cubic yards of assorted building materials.

Considering the enormous size of the canal project, relatively little waste occurred in the construction operations. For example, much of the spoil, the rock and soil excavated from Culebra Cut, rode the Panama Railroad north and became a part of Gatun Dam. In this way, both projects superintended by the ex-West Point roommates benefited from the closely coordinated planning.

At one spot, however, Culebra spoil was unnecessary in fabricating the dam's course across the Chagres River Valley. Had Sibert carefully surveyed and meticulously blueprinted the location of the geologic formation rising above the valley floor near the dam's midpoint, it could not have been better located for integration into construction plans. Happily, the engineer used the perfectly positioned monolith of almost solid rock as a natural anchor for the spillways' facilities. Sibert designed the concrete spillways' complex to receive and control the Chagres' waters while providing the river's only outlet to the Caribbean. The spillways' massive gates remained open until the dam topped out, after which they closed, trapping the water and turning the river into Gatun Lake.

The lake eventually inundated approximately 164 square miles of the isthmus, an expanse of water easily able to accommodate two-way traffic by the largest of ships. Steaming out of Gatun Locks and bound for the Pacific, the first 16 miles of channel are 1,000 feet wide, narrowing to 800 feet over the next four miles, before tightening to 500 feet for the remaining four miles to Bas Obispo where lake waters enter Culebra Cut. The generous widths provide ample maneuvering room for east and westbound steamers (actually moving north and south within the canal) to safely pass. Lake waters reach into the infamous cut where Gaillard's army of workers and equipment succeeded in carving a 300-foot wide channel through the Continental Divide. Although narrower than the lake portion of the channel, 300 feet provide plenty of elbow room for passing ships.

Then, after the shotgun expanse of Gatun Lake and the rifle caliber dimensions of Culebra Cut's channel, lake waters can go no farther west (south within the canal) except for those which escape when the Pedro Miguel Locks operate to lower a Pacific-bound steamer to Mira Flores Lake, a small lake backed up by Mira Flores Dam. The lock at Mira Flores completes the process—lowering departing ships to Pacific Ocean level—the waters captured in Gatun Lake once again making the system work.

The canal's slack water navigation system depends on waters from the Chagres River and its tributaries to operate the locks and maintain Gatun Lake's normal pool at an elevation of 85 feet above sea level. During the rainy season (May to December), the lake easily rises to the 87-foot mark, with the extra water welcomed and stored for use during the dry season (January through April).

Because the Chagres drains a watershed of more than 1,300 square miles—much of it located near Panama's Caribbean coast where annual rainfall far exceeds 100 inches—it sometimes delivers too much water into the lake. It is then the gargantuan spillways serve as a giant safety valve, capable of discharging water at a tremendous rate should heavy rains threaten the dam's integrity. With all of Gatun Dam's spillways wide open, each second more than 140,000 cubic feet of water cascade downstream, returning to the Chagres' original streambed for the remaining journey to the Caribbean.

The dam's huge spillways are housed in a crescent-shaped concrete structure and firmly anchored to the natural stone buttress. The concrete structure rests on the narrow valley floor, blocking the Chagres River's natural channel. An integral part of the dam, it provides a stable base on which an impressive rank of concrete piers serve as mounts for 14 electrically operated spillway gates. By opening and closing the gates, the outfall of water from Gatun Lake is regulated with precision. In all, including dam, piers, and gates, the structure's total height is 115.5 feet, exceeding the normal lake level (85 feet) by 30.5 feet.

With its imposing height and all that concrete reflecting the tropical sun—especially when the sluice gates are open and gushing Gatun waters—that portion of Gatun Dam closing the old Chagres River channel and housing the spillways looks like a modern dam. It resembles a model or smaller version of yet to be built Boulder Dam, another project in which Sibert played a prominent role. The concrete spillways and the electricity-generating powerhouse, occupying 800 or so feet at the center of Gatun Dam, are prominent, highly visible structures. But what of the remainder—more than 7,000 additional feet of dam built across the Chagres River Valley to complete the bowl and form Gatun Lake? [12]

With the exception of the spillways' structure, inconspicuous best describes Gatun Dam. After completion, native tropical plants quickly encased the remainder of the structure—a canopy which would never grow on concrete—flourishing on the composite dam, a thoughtful product of a variety of material, all of it close to nature. The construction materials join with the dam's design to produce a modest blending with the surrounding landscape—looking every bit like the adjacent hills, only a bit more regular and exceptionally flat on top. Call it a gradual dam, certainly not an engineering term, but highly descriptive of Gatun Dam. The dam's design and the materials and methods of construction deserve a lucid explanation in terms a layman could comfortably grasp. If queried on the subject, Sibert might have explained:

"Forget for a moment that Gatun Dam contains 22,000,000 cubic yards of material which, if loaded into ordinary two-horse dirt wagons, would form a procession 80,000 miles long. Like most large construction projects undertaken by men, it had a very conventional beginning although I must point out that in the planning and in the execution of routine tasks, the most obscure and mundane features of the plan drew extra attention. This is because, not only as engineers, but as Americans, we wanted to get it right and not fail at the task entrusted to us by the President of the United States.

"Gatun Dam's footprint is a big one. The base is a half-mile wide and covers approximately 288 acres of land. Prior to moving the first shovel full of material, we carefully surveyed and core drilled the area, and otherwise put it under the microscope to ascertain the quality of the terrain. With the exception of the area where the old French canal route crossed our dam site, we found the land stable and capable of adhering to and supporting the dam's structure which eventually contained almost 30,000,000 tons of material.

"With a half-mile wide base, there was ample room for the dam to gradually slope upward from both its upstream or lake side and the downstream side. Workers deposited load after load of dry material— mostly soil, pebbles, and small rock removed from Culebra Cut—in a long line, outlining the base's perimeters from one end of the dam to the other. Immediately adjacent to the perimeter material, we used high quality rock blasted out of Culebra Cut to build up a formidable toe, the structure's first line of defense against future lake waters. Like all such material, railway dirt cars hauled it from Culebra to a huge dump at Gatun and from there to the dam. A high quality rock toe also defined the downstream, or ocean side of the dam. Beyond the toe, ordinary rubble extended seaward, feathering into the existing terrain. Within the downstream toe, workers placed a wide expanse of additional dry fill, about 400 feet of it.

"The tightly packed rock toes created between them a crude but workable basin capable of containing slurry—a gooey syrupy mixture of sand and clay we removed from the Chagres River bed and pumped into the tub between the toes of the dam with big steam-driven centrifugal pumps. In the pond which was formed, heavier particles settled to the bottom where, layer upon layer, they formed the core of the dam. We skimmed the water and the lighter particles off the surface of the mix and piped them away. Once dry and self-compacted, the residual mixture proved impervious to water.

"This hydraulic mix solidified and climbed upward, to an elevation higher than the projected surface of the lake. A final layer of dry material capped the structure, adding more elevation until reaching the summit where more rock protected the dam's crest. On the lakeside, rock riprap covered and protected that portion of the dam's face exposed to the lake's waves.

"At about 85 feet above sea level, the dam's gradually sloping sides tapered down from the half-mile thick base to a girth of 300 feet at the lake's waterline. The dam's crest measured 100 feet wide, with a final elevation of 105 feet above sea level.

"Original plans required Gatun Dam to be built to an elevation of 135 feet above sea level, 50 feet above the expected elevation of the lake it created, but a funny thing happened only a short time after we Army engineers arrived in Panama. I had not been in charge of the Atlantic Division for long when a portion of the toe on the upstream side of the dam sank into a bed of silt and very soft mud which had been deposited along the route of the old French canal effort. We expected the subsidence and were prepared to stabilize the ground where the defunct canal's path crossed the dam site. Although sound engineering promised a timely solution to the problem, the press reacted in sensational fashion. Already tightly focused on American activity in

Panama, newspapers printed wild speculation and, before it was over, the stateside journals even created an underground river which, journalists accused, threatened to undermine the entire dam.

"Well, that is when we got investigated, the entire canal project, but with the emphasis on Gatun Dam. Fortunately, the consulting engineers appointed by President Roosevelt to conduct an investigation were first-rate and knew a thing or two about geology and construction. The seven-member board wasted no time, immediately journeying to Panama for an on-site investigation. On February 16, 1909, they reported that the dam design, and the ground on which the ponderous structure rested, met all requirements for stability. Investigators found no evidence of any underground river and, I suppose, concluded that only the press did the undermining and that truth was the victim.

"Reading between the lines of the report, the rank-and-file of knowledgeable American engineers probably got a good laugh out of it all because our canal plans did indeed deserve criticism based on recognized engineering standards—Gatun Dam being a good example. Because we did not intend the dam to ever fail, there was no question about the approach we took: We chose to overbuild the structure, not just a little bit, but by a wide margin, and for good reasons. Much of this involved efforts to quiet the very vocal opposition to the Panama route which continued even as we successfully prosecuted the work. A second reason was grounded in an effort to allay fears in the general public that an earthquake or other calamity might destroy the dam and other parts of the canal. Last but not least, we represented the United States and wanted the American effort to connect the oceans with a canal across Panama to be crowned with success. So we engineered extra strong. Any errors fell on the side of caution.

"Our plan to placate doubters by hammering interlocking sheet pilings in the ground across Chagres Valley is a prime example of our cautious approach. This drew a snide question from the investigators: 'What's the use trying to stop a river (of the underground variety) that does not exist?' We eliminated the pilings.

"The inquiry actually shortened the time for completion of Gatun Dam, again in recognition of the ICC's tendency to overbuild, never doing anything by half measures. In their report, the consultants recommended lowering the dam height a full 20 feet below the planned elevation of 135 feet above sea level after concluding that the additional height was unnecessary to safely control lake waters. We revised plans accordingly and, before completion, another revision lopped an additional 10 feet from the dam's height, settling its final elevation 105 feet above sea level. Still, the apex of the dam rose a full 20 feet above the normal lake level.

"I remain forever grateful to my West Point roommate, David Gaillard, for providing a wealth of excellent building material for the dam—the spoil he removed from Culebra Cut. Excavating across the Continental Divide was demanding and coping with the landslides was indeed frustrating—chores my talented roommate handled with great professional competence. It is sad that illness required David's return stateside and indeed tragic that he succumbed to the illness on the eve of the canal's completion before enjoying the accolades he richly deserved as the conqueror of Culebra Cut." [13]

That is close to the way William Luther Sibert might describe the construction of Gatun Dam and his sadness over Gaillard's death. Like the dam itself, the description carries no pointless frills. Designed to last a long time, the solidly built structure speaks for itself and needs no rhetorical embellishments, much like the engineer in charge of its construction. The dam and other construction within the Atlantic Division kept Sibert busy for more than six years.

In addition to engineers, the ICC's table of organization included many competent managers responsible for feeding and housing thousands of workers, for protecting them against mosquitoes, and for dispensing justice and maintaining public order within the work force. They relieved the division engineers of all of these collateral, but necessary responsibilities, freeing them, Sibert, Gaillard, and Williamson, to engineer and do what they did best—build.

Still, with construction simultaneously underway all across the isthmus, and even beyond into Limon Bay and the Caribbean Sea on the Atlantic side, and involving off shore islands in the Pacific Ocean, the engineering chiefs kept on the run, always stretched thin. The juggling act with personnel, equipment, supplies, construction materials, and schedules never ended. In addition to engineering savvy, the roommates, Sibert and Gaillard, and S.B. Williamson, the civilian running the Pacific Division, needed an unusual amount of administrative genius just to keep all of the separate parts of their jobs moving.

In the Atlantic Division alone, as Gatun Dam rose from the floor of the Chagres Valley, Sibert's engineers harvested construction materials from two remote sites for barging to Gatun. At the same time, Gatun Locks began taking shape, the sea-going channel to the locks site opened, and Sibert installed a breakwater to protect Limon Bay.

—⟨⟩—

If ever there was a monumental array of concentrated tasks, the locks of Gatun qualify. The finished product—a gleaming expanse of concrete—reminds imaginative romantics of a giant, elongated three-tiered wedding cake. During construction, it even had decorations: Lots of steel towers, cableways, girders, buckets, and locomotives—all animated—perhaps Salvador Dali's impression of filigreed confectionary sugar—if you didn't look too close.

You would never think of William Luther Sibert as a confectioner, possibly because of some innate fear that all or a substantial part of his trademark cigar might fall into the cake mix. He was masculine to the core, a big man who towered over many of his contemporaries, hams for hands, and, of course, the cigar. But when it came to engineering, you might say he had the delicate touch—at least with locks and dams.

If nothing else, the Atlantic Division covered two grand enterprises. First, build a workhorse dam to capture the waters of the Chagres River and create Lake Gatun. Next, erect the largest, most finely engineered and spectacular set of locks the world had ever seen to take full advantage of the waters of Lake Gatun. The Gatun package, dam and locks functioning together, dominated the American canal in Panama. Also part of the package, the Limon Bay anchorage required breakwater protection from the ocean and needed a connecting channel cut to the sea gates of the locks.

Dams and spillways, locks and their approaches, all came within Sibert's territory, a familiar cup of tea. When the subject was locks and dams, Goethals recognized that Sibert had no peer. He owned a solid reputation within the Corps of Engineers, respected as a knowledgeable engineer who got things done, although his record revealed nothing spectacular unless dynamiting the dam on the Allegheny counts.

Except for its array of spillways and a hydroelectric plant, Gatun Dam appeared bland and altogether unobtrusive, all except its top 20 feet to be covered on one side by the lake it contained. Removal of railroad tracks, cars, and locomotives, and the heavy equipment used in the dam's construction opened its oceanside and crest to quick camou-flage by fast-growing tropical foliage. Soon the dam looked as if it had been strung across the Chagres River Valley by Mother Nature with-out any engineering assistance whatsoever. At the Gatun Locks, Sibert painted an entirely different picture—a visual tribute to contemporary engineering at its best.

Any discussions of the Panama Canal encourage offloading reams of statistics, impressive numbers when Europe's guns began to thunder in 1914, which remain cogent today. While too many numbers risk deadening the senses, a few help observers to more fully appreciate the marvelous structure the Gatun Locks turned out to be.

Gaillard was not the only digger in Panama: Sibert directed exca-vation of almost 5,000,000 cubic yards of overburden—just to expose the underlying bedrock at the site of Gatun Locks. Once the spoil was hauled to the dam, workers drilled holes in the bedrock for insertion of steel rails left behind by the French. The rails projected vertically from the rock; they pierced the first courses of engulfing concrete to securely bind the locks to the bedrock. Sibert directed installation of a concrete apron, poured outward from the bedrock into the lake's path, to pre-vent lake water seeping between the bedrock and the locks structure.

The Gatun Locks underwent some design changes between the original blueprints and the finished product, the most apparent and significant being enlargement. The dual series of three-tiered locks, de-signed to simultaneously handle traffic going in both directions, plus the guide walls leading to the outer gates at either end, extend approxi-mately two miles. Of that distance, the locks proper account for almost 7,000 feet. At the request of the U.S. Navy, engineers lengthened each lock chamber from the originally planned 900 feet to 1,000 feet and increased the width from 95 to 110 feet. These dimensions not only accommodated the largest existing battleships but also allowed leeway for larger future men-of-war. Canal gates were painted battleship gray with the best quality lead-based paint available, either to match the color scheme of American battlewagons or because it was available at a bargain price. Maybe both. [14]

To reach Gatun's lower lock gate, a ship approaching from the Ca-ribbean (Atlantic) first rounded a breakwater, a two-mile projection terminating at Toro Point, which protects the harbor at Colon from storms. Breakwater construction began by driving a parallel row of pilings into the seabed, then stabilizing them with stone. Railway cars bore stone blasted from the locks site to dump among pilings and form the barrier. Barges also delivered stone. As additional protection from Caribbean storms, a parade of larger stones, each weighing eight to 10 tons, topped the breakwater.

Once inside and across the bay, a navigation channel covered the remaining seven miles to the sea gates of Gatun Locks. Dredge boats cleared most of the 53,167,000 cubic yards of material removed to create the 40-foot-deep channel. Where the channel route penetrated the existing shoreline, steam shovels were also employed to cut through two small hills. Except for the sea-going suction dredges, the other dredge boats, although more modern and efficient, worked, in principle, the same as those dredges Sibert first used in Kentucky, Michigan, and Arkansas. [15]

With Gatun Dam essentially finished in 1912, Sibert concentrated on the locks' construction. Completion of the locks at Gatun officially became Sibert's fulltime obsession, as if it had not already contributed significant exercise to his analytical thinking process. In his view, he needed to build the dam for one purpose and one purpose only: to make the locks and the canal work! While indispensable, he regarded the dam as only a preliminary step toward building and activating the locks. And with the dam's completion, all of Sibert's energy and expertise focused on the locks. This attention was sorely needed to overcome horrendous engineering problems encountered near the end of construction.

In any given engineering assignment, even dating from his shavetail days on the Kentucky River, a high degree of preparation on the front end marked Sibert's work. This approach to engineering, deeply ingrained in the officer, paid dividends over the years as measured in projects completed on time and under budget. He maintained an almost reverential regard for thorough preparation and, shortly before the completion of Gatun Locks, he explained why:

"The most important stage in any great undertaking is the preparatory stage. During this stage a proper conception must be formed as to relation of plant (the equipment and organization to be employed) to work to be done, and as to the relation of plant to those appurtenances necessary in keeping it working at maximum efficiency. Any failure during this period as to design of appliance commensurate with the size of the undertaking is a basic mistake and can never be fully corrected." [16]

Gatun locks received a lion's share of the engineer's attention early, much thought devoted to devising a transportation system for raw materials, plus a sophisticated system for delivery of ready-mixed concrete—the locks' primary ingredient—directly to the pour sites. The systems were up and running long before completion of Gatun Dam. By 1912, with the initial bugs eliminated, the intricate system capably transported massive quantities of a variety of supplies and raw materials to the right places for incorporation into the locks. The system not only delivered tons and tons of materials where needed, but performed within strict timing parameters. In fact, the system required much elaborate engineering to cope with the vital time element.

Builders unanimously agree: Mixed and wet concrete waits for no man, but insists on being poured and formed at a certain stage of elasticity if, that is, there is an expectancy that it will dry and cure rock-hard and capable of lasting 100 years or more. Sibert expected no less in Panama at the dawn of the 20th century. So, he needed some finesse—as much as mere brute force harnessed from steam and electricity to move impressive amounts of tonnage—to transform the largest poured concrete structure the world had ever seen into an enduring monument to Yankee engineering.

A stopwatch, Sibert rightly figured—the perfect catalyst for the Gatun Locks job. It was a huge building project with myriad and complicated moving parts, all of which had to be orchestrated with the precision of a Swiss movement. Once wet, impatient concrete demanded pouring before it was too late. Before mixing, however, concrete is not wet, its components not in so much of a hurry. Ships delivered literally millions of barrels of dry cement to Panama. Sibert's men harvested sand and crushed stone, the remaining ingredients (other than water) for making concrete, at separate sites on the Panamanian coast and barged the materials to stockpiles at Gatun. The quarry operation at Porto Bello, 20 miles to the east, and the sand mining at Nombre de Dios, another 20 miles down the coast, ran smoothly without stopwatches. Once the raw materials were stockpiled, the game abruptly changed, and the concrete delivery system began operating with precision. Minutes counted and failure awaited a plan or system unable to keep pace with Gatun's voracious appetite for concrete.

Under Sibert's directions, engineers devised an electric-powered railway with four stops on its closed circuit track. Without motormen, each year the 42-car system handled more than a million tons of material and, unless stopped by an emergency switch, the cars ran continuously. Each car, capable of hauling enough material to produce a two-cubic-yard batch of concrete, first motored under the cement hopper where it stopped long enough to receive a charge of cement. The 24-inch gauge track next ran the car beneath a shed from which sand dropped into another compartment. At its third stop, the car's remaining compartment filled with crushed stone, gravity having powered each of the loading operations. Once loaded with the recipe for Gatun concrete—six parts gravel, two parts sand, and one part cement—the car rolled on at a steady four miles per hour to its fourth and final stop, the concrete mixing plant.

Specifically designed to deliver a high level of performance, Gatun's efficient concrete mixers kept the concrete pours going. After entering Gatun's main mixing plant through an underground tunnel, each electric car dumped its contents into a mixer where water was added. Once emptied, the electric cars obediently followed the rails back to the cement hopper where another roundtrip to the mixers began.

At four miles per hour, the 42-car rail system furnished the materials for mixing concrete with unprecedented regularity, becoming, according to Sibert, "one of the most insistent accelerators on the job," always pushing the mixing crews and motormen to stay a step ahead.

Once thoroughly mixed in one of the eight mixers in the plant, the mixer dumped the wet concrete into a bucket large enough to hold two cubic yards of wet concrete and carried on a flatcar. Meanwhile the mixer, which had never ceased turning, received a new supply of gravel, sand, cement and water, and began churning out two more cubic yards of concrete. The concrete production system worked well, all a matter of timing, according to the engineer.

You might say the concrete moved up in class, each bucket of the wet stuff now securely ensconced on its own flatcar, part of a separate electric railway system. This time, the cars did not operate automatically; instead, a motorman controlled each mine-type electric locomotive pulling its own two-car train of flatcars. Without ceremony, the train delivered concrete, two buckets at a time, following a north-south route from the mixers to the locks. The train always stopped at the terminal of the aerial cable system currently in use. Then, Gatun's towers and cables—a complicated erector set for giants—turned the mundane ground-hugging delivery system into an aerial circus—nothing short of the spectacular.

Two cableways spanned the construction area, each supported by a pair of towers, one tower on each side of the locks' site. Each portable tower rested on a railway carriage that moved along almost a mile of parallel tracks installed along each side of the locks. The tracks allowed positioning of the cableways exactly where needed to facilitate the concrete pours.

Once the motorman stopped under the cable system, two empty buckets suspended from pulleys were returned by cable, lowered, and deposited on the flatcars just behind the buckets loaded with concrete. In turn, the pulley system lifted the loaded buckets onto the cableway for the final ride to the pour site for dumping. While workers moved swiftly to spread the wet concrete, the cableway returned the empty buckets to make another exchange for full ones.

On and on they went—concrete mixers, two tracks of railway cars, cableways, and buckets—always moving at a measured rate. This allowed the various parts of the concrete pour to work in harmony—not requiring a stopwatch, but keeping within an established time frame where seconds counted. The mere size of the job required the system to operate continually and efficiently in order to supply sufficient concrete to keep the pouring crews busy.

Although impressively delivering concrete where and when needed, the cableways didn't quite reach the extreme southern end of the locks' construction. For that reason, Sibert installed a second concrete mixing plant near the south end of the locks. It contained two mixers with the same capacity as those at the main plant; large overhead storage bins housed crushed stone and sand, which arrived by regular railroad. Once mixed, workers loaded concrete on dumping cars bound for the pour site on a narrow gauge steam railroad.

Originally intended to furnish concrete for building the locks' south guide and flare walls, all well beyond the reach of the cableways, the auxiliary mixing plant did that and much more. By furnishing most of the concrete for the floor of the locks, the smaller plant made it possible to complete pouring the locks' floor in ample time for the floor to support the giant track-mounted forms used to pour and shape the locks' walls.

Construction of the Gatun Locks began with thorough preparation, followed by the launching of numerous tightly monitored building tasks, all progressing at a measured pace. When things went according to plan—and kept within Sibert's timetable—completion of one phase of construction opened the way for the next step.

Over an extremely long haul, the engineer's goal remained the same: Keep things constantly moving on a day-to-day basis. Much of Sibert's daily concern centered on coordination, making sure activities carried out by one work crew did not materially interfere with the work of another. He constantly searched for and attempted to avoid bottlenecks likely to impede the project. Sibert's decision to use concrete from the auxiliary mixing plant to speed pouring of the locks' floor is a good example of sound planning. As a result, the finished floor speeded construction by providing a ready-made base for wall forms.

Despite the best efforts of Sibert and one of the most competent staffs of engineers ever assembled to work on a single project, things did not always go according to plans as Gatun Locks slowly took shape. It did not always look like the Crown Jewel of Panama it was destined to be. [17]

—⁓—

While explaining the step-by-step process engineers had to follow, and how each task within the locks construction could vitally affect other construction activity, Sibert's construction philosophy came through in succinct terms:

"The success of a great construction job like the Gatun Locks depends upon an orderly procedure of the various parts. No part must be allowed to delay another part if it be practical to avoid such delay." [18]

All good engineers shoot for that lofty standard, an especially difficult target to hit when a construction project contains as many opportunities to go wrong as did the building of the Gatun Locks and its outlying structures meant to safeguard approaching ships and the locks themselves. In as much a tribute to his organizational ability as to his engineering expertise, Sibert kept excavation work within the locks a step ahead of the concrete crews throughout the grueling project, but for one mighty big exception.

As steam shovels scooped out enormous bites of spoil at the upstream (lake) end of the locks' site, as expected, they exposed the underlying bedrock. Of great importance as the foundation of the future locks, the bedrock appeared to be grossly uneven. While tracking forward a mere 50 feet, a digging machine often faced a 30-foot drop in the bedrock's elevation. Or the elevation change might increase as much. Despite the cuspate nature of the bedrock, the steam shovels did their jobs, each shovel moving, on average, in excess of 1,100 cubic yards of spoil, consisting of loose rock and soil, on a daily basis.

The highly-irregular anatomy of the bedrock precipitated earth and rock slides into the valleys between its erratic contours, making it difficult for shovels to work. And when excavations approached the north end of the lowest lock—the sea lock—conditions worsened. When engineers thought the end of excavations for the locks was truly in sight, the picture darkened, with cramped working space making it difficult to maneuver the steam shovels. And because the machines were then working 45 feet below sea level, removal of excavated material posed problems; lifting the spoil to sea level, where it could be moved from the locks site by rail, was a task. The steam shovel crews still managed to inch forward ahead of the concrete pours so long as there was support for the machines, remarking that it couldn't get much worse—but it did!

From the geological perspective, a dramatic change occurred in the composition of the overburden—the rock and soil covering the bedrock. The overburden turned soft in the extreme, much too soft to support a steam shovel traveling on rails. The problem was widespread. More pronounced on the east side of the lock where bedrock dipped rapidly to the northeast, the bedrock also plunged northward on the west side of the lock, causing, according to Sibert, "many difficulties in making the excavation for the flare and guide walls" leading into the locks.

Despite these difficulties, steam shovels completed the excavations required for the sealock proper—reaching a depth of 66 feet below sea level along the last 400 feet of the lock's east wall. A succession of landslides tipped over steam shovels and, on more than one occasion, covered up workmen. Only the fact that the bedrock dipped both north and east enabled engineers to keep the shovel and loading track on a stable base. The experience left a bad taste and convinced Sibert that excavation plans had to be altered to cope with the subterranean conditions, if the guide walls and flares were to rest on a stable foundation of bedrock.

The area to be occupied by the flares and guide walls coincided with more extremely soft overburden covering extremely deep bedrock. Tests determined the overburden too soft to safely support the tracks required to move the steam shovels and spoil trains. Sibert chomped down on the omnipresent cigar and executed a strategic withdrawal—retreating from the expected—to plan his attack. The new problems required a brand new approach and Sibert's rewritten plans were replete with imaginative use of nature, personnel, and equipment. If not a radical procedure, a glance at the equipment inventory at least suggested something on the whimsical side. For Sibert's part, he saw nothing capricious or amusing about the new plans—just a dangerous problem begging for solution.

There was only one true test of its efficacy: Would it work? At the risk of oversimplification, this was Sibert's new plan of attack:

First, the lock walls were completed. With lock gates yet to be hung, Sibert ordered a strong, steel reinforced temporary dam to be installed across the mouth of the locks, joining the new lock walls to protect the lock chamber from seawater while installation of the lock gates and machinery proceeded without delay.

Originally, excavation of the seven-mile channel from Limon Bay to Gatun Locks commenced in the bay and temporarily terminated 1,000 feet short of the unfinished locks it was meant to serve. Leaving the channel unfinished protected the construction site from flooding by seawater. Sibert originally planned to complete the channel once the locks were finished with gates in place.

But things changed.

When subsurface conditions prevented completion of the work by conventional use of land-based steam shovels, Sibert ordered an amphibious attack on the problem. The Atlantic Division's chief engineer directed dredges to cut a narrow opening through the remaining 1,000-foot barrier to admit Limon Bay seawater into and over the flares and guide walls construction site. Once admitted, the seawater formed an artificial lake, lapping harmlessly against the temporary dam, which held firm and protected the locks.

In the deep pool of seawater at the base of the locks, Sibert deployed seagoing dredges from Limon Bay and began excavations in search of a firm bedrock foundation for the flares and guide walls. Huge suction pumps aboard the dredges pulled the soft overburden from below—to a depth of 41 feet, the effective limits of the pumps' reach. (The pumps discharged the spoil through pipes into a nearby swamp.) Another 30 feet of material remained, still covering the elusive bedrock lying a full 70 feet below the water's surface. With dredges stymied, unable to excavate deeper, Sibert initiated the next phase of his plan.

Meanwhile, engineers had carried out additional soundings outside the blueprinted locations of the flares and guide walls and, much to their delight, located bedrock much closer to the surface, only 40 feet down, making it possible for the suction dredges to expose the rock. Once the bedrock was accessible, workers drove pilings to establish a rail trestle above the bedrock and rail cars followed, dumping vast quantities of rock fill on top of the bedrock to establish a crude but effective retaining wall. The wall kept mudslides from the work site after engineers lowered the water level. And, yes, Sibert planned to dramatically lower the water level over the work site.

Remember the narrow channel opened to admit the dredges through the final 1,000-foot sea barrier before the locks? Sibert ordered an earthen dam constructed across the channel, shutting off additional ocean water and confining the water covering the construction site within a small lake. Now cut off from the sea, the dredges floated on the artificial lake, and that is just what Sibert wanted.

The suction dredges immediately went to work removing water from the lake at a rate six or more times as fast as they could suction solid material. As the lake level fell, the dredges naturally floated down with it, dropping them close to suction out the remaining overburden—exposing the underlying bedrock. When needed, a water supply was pumped into dredged space while the crude rockfill dam protected most of the work site from mudslides.

One problem remained: Like an itch that cannot quite be reached to scratch, Sibert's irritant was a stratum of bedrock, much deeper than the rest and underlying the north guide wall site. Its extreme depth made it unmanageable from a suction dredge, even when operating in water at its lowest level. Numerous slides at the guide wall site were a recurring problem. In response to these problems, Sibert decided to drain the relatively small pond left after lake waters were siphoned off.

The ironic first step toward draining the pond required unblocking the channel to Limon Bay to readmit seawater, returning the pond to lake size and sea level. Through the small breach in the temporary dam, the dredges exited the lake—all but one. The breach was then reclosed, and the single dredge left behind began pumping. Finally, the pump cleared most of the water from the excavation. Accomplishing its task required the craft to deliberately run aground about 55 feet below sea level. Even as it remained in dry dock, so to speak, the dredge continued to pump water and debris from the excavation until installation of another pumping plant completed the job. Sibert heaped praise on the marooned dredge, while not losing sight of its humorous side.

Indeed an odd sight, one probably never seen before—a 20-inch suction dredge firmly planted on the ground 55 feet below sea level and busily engaged in doing useful excavation. Actual construction of the flares and guide walls rapidly followed. Only after construction was completed, and the sea gates were in place, workers removed the dam protecting the locks. Beginning the final act, dredges pumped seawater into the mainly dry lake, refloating the dredge left behind. When the lake water returned to sea level, the refloated dredge cut through the temporary dam, reopening the channel to the bay. All of the dredges were next employed to widen and deepen the last 1,000 feet of channel approaching the locks—deep enough and wide enough to accommodate the largest of ships then afloat or reasonably planned for the future.

With the job complete, and with the steamships of the world locking through Gatun Locks in transit between the two oceans, Sibert never hesitated to identify his most trying experience in Panama:

"The excavation for the flare and guide walls of the Gatun Locks was the most difficult task in connection with the building of the Gatun Locks, if not the entire Canal. An open cut over 70 feet below sea level in soft mud is most difficult to make and even more difficult to maintain. Had the rock foundation for these walls been at a suitable elevation and the banks reasonably stable, the masonry of the locks could have been completed about 10 months sooner."

In his evaluation of the difficulty, Sibert may have been right, even when comparing the problem on the north end of Gatun Locks with Gaillard's storied struggle through Culebra Cut. At least the Culebra engineering problems were straightforward: keep blasting, digging, loading, and hauling spoil away until you open a channel wide enough to accommodate ocean-going ships. At the same time, the slopes of the cut had to be slanted to a degree that would, if not eliminate, greatly reduce the danger of slides. Culebra was a war of attrition, with Gaillard leading frontal assault after frontal assault, pushing men and steam shovels to their limits. It was excavations and more excavations, a great endurance contest nearing its end when Gaillard was stricken with what proved to be a fatal illness. When ordered home for treatment, Gaillard had clearly beaten Culebra.

Gatun was entirely different, a war of maneuver in which conditions forced Sibert to change in order to subdue a subterranean foe—a problem undiscovered until the locks neared completion. That is when the engineer departed from the ordinary, employing imagination and innovations to substitute sea-going dredges for steam shovels when the land-based shovels were unable to safely dig. Sibert created a lake, then drained it and filled it again to get the job done—the avant-garde activity symbolized by the lonely dredge pumping away and doing useful work while sitting low and dry on the erstwhile lake bottom 70 feet below the level of the Atlantic.

Workers enjoyed an unbelievable view from the top of the locks where they were installing lock gates and the machinery required to operate them. Down below, well below sea level, the sea-going dredge sat beached on dry land while suctioning the last spoil to expose the bedrock. Concrete flares and guide walls rose before the dredge was refloated and allowed to escape seaward.

Once dredges completed the channel from Limon Bay, the waters of the bay finally washed against the sea gates of Gatun Locks, completing an unimpeded highway of water from the Atlantic through the locks to Gatun Lake. When, on September 26, 1913, the *Gatun* steamed from sea level through the locks to Gatun Lake 85 feet above, Lieutenant Colonel William Luther Sibert's greatest engineering triumph was safely in the book. [19]

Chapter Thirteen
FRICTION AND FUN IN PANAMA

A crimony is never pleasant and, when practiced among reasonably cultured, highly competitive American professionals, it can get downright nasty, always seeming to thrive where pressure is greatest. So far as pressure is concerned, the previous French failure, the national and world political interests, its somewhat experimental nature, and above all, the colossal dimensions of the Panama Canal project, combined dangerously to produce a boiling caldron. There were more witches than Macbeth could ever imagine. They stretched all the way from Washington to the Canal Zone, each jousting to add a favored element to the brew. Under the right conditions (actually wrong conditions, altogether detrimental to success of the canal construction), the stew might easily evolve into a toxic mix.

Sometimes sweetness and light deserted the canal construction project, a phenomenon psychologists—even physiologists—easily understood: Spending seven years working under adverse conditions in a hot and humid environment far from home wears thin, even before the canal applied its own special brand of excruciating pressure. President Roosevelt bet heavily on the ability of military officers to overcome normally expected personality clashes, professional abrasions, and petty annoyances and see the canal through to completion. The president expected Army discipline and respect for the chain of command to turn the trick. He got that part right.

If, however, the president sought harmony by relying on a preponderance of Army-flavored senior leadership, he missed the mark. There were bound to be collisions between the chosen engineers, mostly trivial and soon forgiven if not forgotten, and, of course, there were exceptions. Viewed honestly and objectively, with the human factor in mind, there is no surprise when the simmering caldron sometimes boiled over. Perhaps the builders needed to let off steam—a lot of it—before the cream of American engineering expertise came to the top and won the day in Panama. And the pot never ceased to simmer.

William Luther Sibert was not immune to the infighting, nor was David Gaillard. Even Dr. Gorgas, the victor over Yellow Fever, and arguably the team's most valuable player, was not vaccinated against the ICC's internal friction. Sibert's personality—straightforward with few, if any, hidden agendas—made him especially vulnerable to internally launched slings and arrows. Believing in himself, he seldom sidestepped sensitive subjects and, as a result, managed to ruffle superior feathers on several occasions. One incident, which evolved beyond a mere personality collision, quickly escalated into an attack on Sibert's engineering competence. After that, it indeed got serious.

Roosevelt's international board of engineers set the stage for Sibert's travail when the majority report recommended a sea level canal, citing the dam planned for Gatun as a major reason for avoiding dams and locks with a sea level approach. The majority minced no words, concluding that "no such vast and doubtful experiment (referring to the Gatun Dam) should be indulged in." If built, some highly competent engineers predicted its collapse under the weight and pressure of the deep artificial lake it was designed to contain.

President Roosevelt, of course, rejected the report and ramrodded through Congress a slack water navigation plan—a system born of dams and operated by locks, as recommended by the panel's minority. After appointment to the ICC, Sibert studied the alternatives in detail and found himself in full agreement with the locks and dams concept. He welcomed the opportunity to participate in building the world's greatest slack water navigating system. He knew it would work as it had worked on the Green and Barren Rivers back in Kentucky, only exponentially bigger and more complicated.

Washington inspired adventures, those which cost money (and all of them do), nearly always come under close scrutiny by Congressional committees controlling the purse strings, the isthmian canal being no exception. Numerous hearings were held, most concerned with how much money Congress planned to wager on what many viewed as a longshot gamble, always citing the French debacle. The Panama project required a defense and none was better qualified to explain and defend the impending locks and dams of Panama than Major Sibert, an unrepentant zealot for the impressive but mute structures. That explains why the officer sat before the congressional committee with a microscope already focused on a dam described by its detractors as too big for its own good.

Obviously concerned about the majority report's conclusion, labeling Gatun Dam as sheer folly, congressmen quizzed Sibert concerning the proposed dam's durability. The officer answered all of their questions directly and unequivocally asserted: The dam's concept and design were sound and, in his professional opinion, it would not fail under the stresses to which it was likely to be subjected. A very professional approach Sibert knew he could successfully defend. So far, so good.

Then a questioner asked a hypothetical question: Either a legitimate quest for insight into the controversy spawned by the majority report's dim view of the dam, or a deliberately loaded question inspired by forces still favoring the Nicaragua route. The question: "*If* the Gatun Dam should fail, *how* will it fail?"

Sibert kept his temper well in check, measured the question, and sized up the situation: Hadn't he just told the panel, under oath, that the proposed dam at Gatun, in his professional opinion, was not going to fail? Nothing hypothetical blemished his answer—an unmodified *yes*—an opinion on which he willingly risked his professional reputation. Briefly, he wondered if the congressman understood plain English or was, perhaps, a wee bit retarded?

But, the major concluded, the congressman posed a question, and Sibert believed he deserved an honest answer, even if it was a "what if" kind of question. In addition, because the questioner had both a vote and influence bearing directly on the question of appropriations vital to the canal project, diplomacy concerned Sibert. Above all, the inquiry deserved a courteous and truthful response that was unlikely to antagonize the legislator.

Sibert chose to play it straight, not a difficult call since he usually relied on that approach when dealing with life's problems and congressional questioners. He refused to hedge or evade or deflect the question. Sibert's answer did not come out of left field, as if he were responding to an entirely different question, one which had not even been asked. Instead, the major answered the question directly, truthfully stating his considered opinion on the subject.

If the proposed dam at Gatun were ever to fail, the major was of the opinion that the cause of the hypothetical failure would be the inability of the underlying material (the terrain upon which the dam would rest) to support the immense weight of the barrier. And, *if* incapable of providing the firm foundation required by the dam, the underlying material would slide from beneath the weighty structure, the end result being a lowering of the dam's crest. All of this was hypothetical because, as he had stated under oath, Sibert did *not* expect the dam to fail.

It was strictly hypothetical, both question and answer, and followed close on the heels of Sibert's earlier testimony extolling the virtues of the Gatun Dam and the plans for its construction as a bar to the Chagres River's natural channel to the sea. Actually, he rendered a very down to earth explanation of problems recognized early in Panama, none of which was insolvable in light of sound engineering practices.

Even though the question was hypothetical, Sibert did not guess in order to come up with a hypothetical answer. Well versed in Panamanian geology, he knew the ground was unstable in numerous locales, most notably in Culebra Cut. He also knew that tests revealed extremely soft and unstable soil along the ancient channels of the Chagres River as it meandered delta-like toward the Caribbean—the precise location of Gatun Dam. Sibert based his answer to the hypothetical question on facts, including tests and actual experience coping with Panama's underpinnings.

Unfortunately, Goethals, the ICC chairman, saw Sibert's testimony before the congressional committee in an entirely different light. The chief engineer was highly critical of his fellow commissioner, interpreting Sibert's "what if" answer as reflecting the major's lack of faith in success of the canal project. Going a step farther, the chief engineer likely regarded the answer as a betrayal, an episode reflecting personal disloyalty on the part of Sibert and, therefore, an affront to Goethals' leadership. Objectively, Goethals' characterization of Sibert's testimony borders on the absurd.

Even under the most intense and objective analysis, nothing in Sibert's response remotely suggests any lack of confidence in the canal project as a whole or, explicitly, the Gatun Dam, or by extension, the leadership of Colonel Goethals. Because all parties were grown men, competent engineers, and experienced Army officers, the tempest should have blown its course and never been allowed to escape from the teapot. (As a hindsight solution, the theory supporting West Point's behind-the-barracks fistfights comes to mind.) Goethals was, of course, the commanding officer; had Goethals' temper cooled, all would have smoothed out so long as Sibert did not disobey the orders of the man in charge of the canal. Although Sibert had not disobeyed any orders, his clash with Goethals over the congressional testimony never died. In fact, things got worse.

Over the years, political infighting has changed little in Washington. There were leaks in 1908, and one of those leaks illustrates what a dangerous position Sibert found himself in, due, at least in part, to the honest answer he gave to the hypothetical question. The incident left Goethals with ill feelings over the perceived breach of faith, and with Sibert likely brooding over his superior's failure to understand his testimony within the context of its delivery. Next came a head-on collision—a clash of diametrically opposed engineering opinions centered on Gatun Dam and Locks for which Sibert was primarily responsible. Personal animosity magnified serious engineering questions into an ugly professional confrontation.

The first engineering conflict surfaced when, as dam·construction progressed, a significant subsidence or slide of underlying material occurred. It involved approximately 1,000 feet of the dam's course between Gatun Locks and the dam's spillways' structure. The slide was not unexpected, and Sibert stood prepared to cope with it. He attributed the problem to unstable soil along the old river route, the slide having taken place just exactly as he said it would in testimony before the congressional committee. The engineer knew what caused the problem and also knew how to fix it. Sibert said lateral pressure within the dam's hydraulic fill had nothing to do with the slide. Goethals disagreed and discussions were sharp.

A second rift between the two engineers developed when Sibert insisted that, according to his calculations, the existing specifications— for concrete floors in the upper pair of locks at Gatun and along the spillways' channel below the dam—were inadequate to withstand water pressures beneath the structures. Goethals took the opposite view.

The difference of opinions between the chief engineer and the engineer he had placed in charge of building Gatun Dam and Locks, two competent and strong-willed professionals, resulted in a major crisis of direct concern to Sibert. It seems that a senior authority, maneuvering behind the scenes, buttonholed Secretary of War Taft, requesting the secretary to funnel the senior authority's request to the chief engineer of the Corps of Engineers that Sibert be reassigned to other duties, thereby removing him from Panama and the canal project.

The source of the leak, a person of unquestioned integrity, reported that Taft followed through as requested, relaying the request for nothing less than sacking Major Sibert, to General Marshall, chief engineer of the Corps of Engineers. After being apprised of a controversy between the two officers, General Marshall remarked to Taft that if "the difference of opinion between Sibert and the Chief of the Panama construction was on a question of engineering, he felt that Sibert was right." Then, after Secretary Taft revealed that the differences did in fact arise over a question of engineering, General Marshall requested Taft's permission to look into the problems personally. Once he had studied the engineering questions in detail, the Chief Engineer advised Taft "that Major Sibert was right and that in his opinion the War Department was fortunate in having in Panama not only a good engineer but one who was not afraid to stand for his convictions."

Without fanfare, a panel of civilian engineers also quietly reviewed Sibert's recommended strengthening of the floors of the upper locks and the spillways channel, only to confirm his calculations and recommendations. In the end, Sibert remained chief engineer for the Atlantic Division and, in the long run, the Gatun construction greatly benefited from the crisis. Without interference from the top, Sibert altered the inadequate specifications and poured concrete floors according to his calculations. He knew his specs produced floors able to resist the upward pressure waters of the lake would eventually produce.

If the senior authority seeking Sibert's scalp was in fact Goethals (and it is difficult to imagine anyone else among the Panama crew with the necessary horsepower to enlist the Secretary of War as an errand boy), and if he later became aware of the chief engineer's reaction and the unfavorable engineering comparison made between himself and Sibert, he would have felt a stinging professional affront. And, although of his own making, Goethals would have blamed Sibert for the indignity, further worsening their strained relations.

Colonel Goethals' relations, not only with Sibert, but with other key members of the commission—including Gorgas and Gaillard—were "strained from the outset," made worse on Sibert's part by his frequent disagreements with Colonel Goethals' engineering decisions. The chief engineer characterized Sibert as "cantankerous and hard to hold." Nor did Goethals speak highly of the others, suggesting that they had all "developed corns," making it "difficult to step without treading upon one." There was little chance of Goethals verbally stepping on Sibert's corns because they spoke directly to each other only when necessary.

Above all else, Goethals shouldered enormous responsibility as chairman of the ICC and, without doubt, concentrated on one goal—completing the canal in exemplary fashion. At one point, Goethals actually defended Sibert's management decisions in a letter to a prominent engineering journal, which had published an article critical of Sibert's performance. Goethals' overriding passion for the Panama project obviously vetoed the animosity he reserved for Sibert. Yet, Panama's heat never thawed the frigid personal gulf between the two engineers.

Gorgas, Gaillard, and Sibert—all Southerners—shared a feeling that Goethals engaged in a "sectional bias against those from the South that made service under him almost unbearable." More than 40 years had passed since the Civil War, making such a mindset difficult to understand, particularly in the U.S. Army. Goethals' roots in Missouri—a border state that had been hotly divided during the conflict—may account for lingering animosity, if any.

Seeming to contradict the idea that Goethals continued the War Between the States in the Canal Zone, he reportedly got along well with another Southerner, Sydney B. Williamson, chief engineer for the Pacific Division. However, because Goethals had worked with Williamson before, and the fact that Williamson was a civilian—not a member of the highly competitive cliché of Army engineers—may have offset any southbound bias. [1]

One factor, however, seemed to have overriding importance on the strictly personal side of the canal leadership. And that peculiarly difficult aspect sprang directly from the rigorous training and academic backgrounds of the *Big Four*, Goethals, Sibert, Gaillard, and Gorgas. All of them were trained to believe in themselves and to be the best at whatever they did. To say that each was an expert in his field would be the grossest understatement.

It is difficult to imagine a member of this quartet taking a back seat to anybody, and it should not be forgotten that the advancement army officers yearned for in peacetime was usually accomplished as part of a free enterprise system. It was a free for all to outperform other officers engaged in the same line of work, to demonstrate that you were the best at commanding an infantry company, or setting up an artillery base, or even building the best ever locks and dams. After all, the Army is all about competition at the most serious level.

Each of the West Point roommates believed he was every bit as capable an engineer, administrator, and commanding officer as Goethals, and secretly wondered why he had not been chosen as ICC chairman and chief engineer instead of Goethals. Both Sibert and Gaillard were convinced that Goethals wanted to ship them back stateside. As for Gorgas, it was no contest: He *knew* he had the knowledge necessary to destroy the mosquito menace and protect the health of the Canal Zone, a mission Goethals sometimes made difficult.

At times, the ICC chairman barely spoke to Sibert, Gaillard, and Gorgas—nothing any of the four could be proud of, and uncharacteristically juvenile for the lot. In Sibert's case, it was a little different: Their disagreements over engineering problems—especially when Sibert always seemed to be right—added fuel to the highly combustible discord. Human nature being what it is, it would have been exceedingly difficult for Goethals to forgive and forget those clashes over engineering questions when his subordinate was always correct. Can it be doubted that Sibert somehow managed to rub it in without being insubordinate? Regardless, Sibert enjoyed the vindication of his engineering opinions—but at the lingering cost of Goethals' ill feelings. Civility among the Canal Zone's top brass remained in short supply.

Thanks to the iron discipline and respect for the chain of command which had, beginning with West Point days, been drilled into the top echelon of engineer officers, Sibert and Gaillard included, these abrasive and potentially destructive conflicts were kept within context as they soldiered on to not only build the canal, but to build it the Army way, as the ex-Rough Rider knew they would.

In no way should the intra-squad scrimmages between these talented and ambitious Army engineers detract from the magnificent job they did in constructing the American canal across Panama. From the strictly human relations viewpoint, it makes the canal success even more outstanding. [2]

—w—

The presence of their families, Army wives with sympathetic ears, and animated children capable of diverting attention, helped calm those magnificent minds and soothe nerves tense from the day's conflicts. Family presence worked the same magic on other American personnel—both military and civilian—at work on the canal. Families brought stability to the community of workers and probably made the work of the constabulary a little easier.

In January 1910, the family's monthly budget increased, at least a little bit, with Major Sibert's promotion to lieutenant colonel of the Corps of Engineers. As during their concluding years at West Point, David ran a little ahead of Goliath, his promotion to lieutenant colonel coming five months earlier. Clearly the roommates were doing something right in the Canal Zone. At least the Army thought so. They and their fellow engineering officers wearing khaki formed the nucleus of a brand new American colony in Panama, a Little America (not to be confused with the later American outpost established in Antarctica). [3]

This Little America on the isthmus—officially the Canal Zone— would have welcomed a wintry polar breeze although Panama's sultry climate failed to stop the Canal Zone from becoming the most Americanized community in the world at large, including the Lower 48 and the latter day arrivals, Alaska and Hawaii. In many respects, including jobs, schools, civil administration, public health, recreation, religion, and its law enforcement and court system, the Canal Zone encapsulated the American way. Even if there were a wart or two, the Canal Zone model benefited many—not only the Americans, but also the foreign workers.

It all began with the idea, not at all off the mark, that Panama in 1904 was a generally inhospitable place to live and work due to several factors. Its oppressive tropical climate, with equal parts of high temperatures, high humidity, and rainfall enough to prompt ark construction during the rainy season, failed to excite Americans. Major health concerns, yellow fever and malaria being at the forefront, made the isthmus even less appealing and downright dangerous, especially to North Americans.

Beginning early, one of the most important missions of the ICC involved war on the mosquito to bring malaria and yellow fever under

control. Dr. Gorgas pushed the long, arduous task to a successful conclusion, actually eliminating Yellow Jack for all practical purposes, and
reducing the threat of malaria to manageable proportions. That, more
than any other single factor, made possible the Americanization of the
Canal Zone. It became a choice place, not only for the more adventurous American men to work, but a place where they could safely establish their families.

In retrospect, the ICC simply followed Sibert's major tenet of construction: Complete adequate preparations if you wish a major enterprise to blossom. So far as creating an atmosphere familiar and welcoming to American families, the commission's efforts were rewarded
by the influx of talented American workers, many with their families.
The presence of their families exerted a positive influence on American
technicians and professionals, encouraging them to stick with canal
jobs much longer than originally anticipated. The collective experience
of these veteran canal workers was invaluable to the project.

It was a completely different story for Sibert and his fellow officers
from the Corps of Engineers. Under orders from their president, they
were on a mission and, regardless of working conditions, knew orders
must be followed. Nevertheless, the presence of the military families
was equally important to the engineers as to their civilian counterparts. And it gave military society an opportunity to flourish in the Canal Zone—a place where West Point roommates and their wives might
occasionally dine together. [4]

Compared with the unsettled lot of many soldiers' families, for almost seven years immediately before his assignment to Panama, Major Sibert's family enjoyed an exceptionally stable American home
life. (Frayed nerves were few and far between.) What could be more
American than to reside in the heartland of the Ohio Valley with the
mother cooking and minding the children and the working father usually home in time for supper? The cozy arrangement suited the officer
who bossed the Louisville District of the Corps of Engineers for almost
18 months before steaming up the Ohio River to command the Pittsburgh District from Christmas Eve 1901 to March 1907.

Sibert enjoyed home life and watching his children mature while
spending more than five eventful years in Pittsburgh where he built
locks and dams, championed unrestricted river navigation, and promoted a nine-foot channel. He also blew the top off of Dam No. 3 on

the Allegheny to avert a catastrophic flood. Still, in the Sibert tradition, he remained a family man. When appointed to the ICC, the engineer envisioned a long campaign in Panama and had no intention of leaving the family behind.

When Sibert embarked for Panama, his youngest child and only daughter, Mary Elizabeth, neared her eighth birthday. The next youngest, Martin David Sibert, celebrated his ninth birthday September 11, 1907, and Edwin Luther Sibert turned 10 on March 2, 1907. Then came Harold Ward Sibert, reaching 15 on May 9, 1907. Franklin Cummings Sibert turned 16 on January 3, 1907, and Sibert's oldest son, William Olin Sibert, celebrated his 18th birthday on October 23, 1907. Although stateside college enrollment loomed on the horizon for the teenagers, plenty of nurturing remained for the veteran military wife when she set up housekeeping in the Canal Zone.

The Siberts' Panama house, appropriate to his station as an ICC commissioner and chief engineer of the Atlantic division, looked good when appraised through the engineer's eyes. Thoroughly modern, the Siberts' home for the better part of seven years looked comfortable. Even if some stateside comforts were beyond duplication, the house design aimed for survival in the tropics. Screens kept mosquitoes out, shutters and veranda like overhangs produced cooling shade, and plenty of cross ventilation captured any breeze that stirred. Colorful tropical vegetation flourished in the neighborhood.

Like most women, Mamie Sibert loved flowers. She always appreciated the vital color her gardening efforts produced to ward off drabness at whatever location the Siberts currently called home—Little Rock, Detroit, Pittsburgh, or Bowling Green. She found, however, to her everlasting delight, a brand new game in Panama with brand new flowers. She liked the profusion of color found everywhere, particularly on her veranda where she fussed over numerous varieties of delicate and bright orchids.

In addition to presiding over the Sibert household, looking after the children and growing orchids, Mrs. Sibert participated in the Canal Zone's active American social scene. She conceded the ICC covered practically everything required for the complete care and comfort of all of the Americans who, along with her husband, were hard at work on the canal. She and other Army wives kept up with the social side of life in the Canal Zone by reading a unique publication called simply the *Canal Record*.

The weekly newspaper, an in-house journal published under the authority and supervision of the ICC, devoted barrels of ink to recording numbers reflecting progress on the canal: the cubic yards of material removed the previous week from Culebra Cut and the cubic yards of concrete poured into the walls of Gatun Locks. Like every other aspect of Canal Zone activity controlled by the ICC, the *Record* heavily supported canal construction activities. On balance, however, at least upon superficial examination, the ICC's control of the *Record* did not stifle its writers, thereby faintly echoing another American value: freedom of the press.

In addition to the ubiquitous government statistics documenting construction progress, the *Record's* standard fare, fortunately, contained more. Volume 6 of the *Record*—covering activity between August 28, 1912, and August 20, 1913—is typical of the publication's weekly newspaper flavor. In addition to laudatory accounts of positive accomplishments, basic All-American Freedom of the Press shines through. The ICC permitted publication of accounts of the disasters that, from time to time, struck the canal populace. It made news when three workers were killed in a premature dynamite blast, none of them from the States, but among countless workers imported from Trinidad, Barbados, and Montserrat. Others were injured in this particular blast, including "white American foreman Joe McNalley." [5]

Beyond its comprehensive coverage of the canal construction *per se*, the weekly published reams of notations covering American social life, including church notes, a broad schedule of YMCA activities, and the agendas of women's clubs, the Shriners, and the Elks Lodge. Countless personal items—who was visiting whom, the kind of information Mamie enjoyed in stateside newspapers back in Bowling Green, Pittsburgh and Little Rock, filled its pages, along with stories describing band concerts, parties, and baseball games. The July 2, 1913, edition announced Lieutenant Colonel Gaillard's scheduled arrival at Cristobal aboard the *Colon*, a steamer regularly plying between the Canal Zone and New York. (Gaillard soon returned to the States for treatment after being stricken with his fatal illness.)

Any mention of Sibert in the *Canal Record*, as might be expected, appeared in articles detailing construction activity in the Atlantic Division, not in the society columns devoted mainly to the distaff side, tea parties and such. Of course, the engineer officer engaged in at least one non-engineering episode. The event began with a visit to Gatun by several rather patrician ladies, Edith Roosevelt among them.

No longer the first lady, Mrs. Roosevelt and her entourage scheduled the visit to the Canal Zone while homeward bound after leaving her husband, ex-President Theodore Roosevelt, to his Amazon adventure that nearly cost him his life. Before TR ventured into Brazil's unexplored territory, the Roosevelts visited Chile where the former president spoke in passionate defense of America's canal enterprise. On the return trip to New York, Edith Roosevelt sailed from Valparaiso, north along South America's Pacific coast to Panama as the canal rapidly neared completion. Two months earlier, the *Gatun*, with Sibert aboard, ceremoniously rose from the Atlantic into its namesake lake.

At Gatun, Sibert greeted Mrs. Roosevelt's party, which included her favorite traveling companion, Margaret Roosevelt, the adventurous former president's 25-year-old cousin. The travelers received the colonel's personally conducted tour of the locks and the construction activity still underway. When distinguished guests visited Gatun, the officer customarily invited the visitors to lunch at the Sibert family's quarters, and he did so, Mrs. Roosevelt politely accepting on behalf of the ladies. He had only to telephone his home and inform the cook there would be guests for lunch. There shouldn't be any problem, Sibert thought to himself, even though Mrs. Sibert was away on a trip to New York. Although Mamie would not be present to preside over lunch, her husband knew she had thought of everything. The Sibert household was staffed, complete with a Jamaican cook and butler. The family found it easy to communicate with the servants, all of whom spoke excellent English. But to guard against calamities during her absence, the cautious Mamie prepared three different menus for lunch at the Sibert table. Each had a number (one through three), each being appropriate for an American luncheon. That ensured that the cook and her helpers knew exactly what was needed.

With great confidence in the simple foolproof procedure devised by his wife, the Corps of Engineers officer telephoned home, informed the cook that there would be five guests for lunch, and ordered Mamie's No. 1 menu. During the conversation he mentioned that Mrs. Roosevelt would be in the party. To the Jamaican cook, that was electrifying news, indeed a shock, but she quickly recovered her poise and informed the staff that the "Queen of America" would be having lunch "at our house today!" Her enthusiasm for the job to be done, a perfect luncheon for Mrs. Roosevelt, was understandable: The Jamaicans, all being subjects of the British Empire, had a healthy respect for royalty.

Even if Mrs. Roosevelt was not, technically speaking, the Queen of America, and never had been, she and her companions faced royal treatment in the Sibert household—Jamaican style! As the officer escorted the ladies into the living room of his home, the place where the Siberts received guests, he immediately noticed a striking change. It looked like a bad but exceptionally bright day for an interior decorator. The room glistened from the shiny display of, literally, every piece of silver and every dust catching piece of bric-a-brac to be found in the house. Regardless of its purpose, as long as it glittered, it now reposed in the living room—on parade before the Queen of America. Embarrassed by the display, Sibert said nothing.

When the host adjourned the party to the dining room, he noted with relief that everything appeared normal with no ostentatious frills added. He anticipated smooth sailing through a delicious, well-prepared lunch No. 1. A lover of good food, when possible, Sibert made sure that Mamie had the services of an excellent cook, and the portly Jamaican qualified. Only one description fit the queenly luncheon she served: Too much! In an all-out effort to do justice to the visiting royalty, not only did the cook prepare menu No. 1, but menus No. 2 and No. 3 as well.

Course followed course, enough food to satisfy the luncheon guests times three. Something had gone wrong, but remembering his clearly delivered instructions, a perplexed Sibert sat dumbfounded. He thought he detected a glint in Mrs. Roosevelt's eyes as she, like the others, finessed her way through the courses, until all that was left was the serving of coffee. It was done boldly, five tiny after-dinner cups of coffee, almost lost in the expanse of a big silver serving tray, fully three feet in length with a two-foot beam. That is when Sibert tried for a graceful exit before charging into the kitchen and demanding an explanation for the bizarre display of silver and the excessive offering of food. The parade ground tone of the officer in charge didn't at all intimidate the cook.

Summoning all of her plentiful Jamaican dignity, the cook did not back off, but stood toe-to-toe with her flustered employer and informed him that she knew how to entertain royalty! With that, Sibert surrendered, did an about face, and returned to his guests, now, at least, armed with a good punch line. In the wilds of Panama, he reported to Mrs. Roosevelt, being a resourceful army officer, he had succeeded in hiring a cook who knew how to entertain royalty! Then, Edith Roosevelt disclosed that she had sensed what was happening early, that she had avoided laughing only with the greatest of difficulty, and that she sympathized with Sibert's plight. So, chalk up a luncheon success for the major; the details, fortunately, never made headlines in the *Canal Record*. [6]

With canal construction came regular steamship service between Panama and New York and, as a rule, it did not cause luncheon problems at the Sibert quarters. The passenger service made life for the ladies within the upper echelon of Canal Zone society, Mrs. Sibert included, much more acceptable. As the wife of a member of the ICC, Mamie always stood within a comfortable steamship cruise to New York City—temporary escape from the oppressive Panamanian climate that no amount of ICC manipulations could ever change.

With Franklin already undergoing Beast Barracks at West Point, Mamie took the Sibert children, Mary, Martin, Edwin, and Harold north on the steamer *Esperanza*, arriving in New York on August 6, 1908. The stated purpose of the trip was to enroll Harold as a freshman at Cornell University where he would later star as a member of the university's fencing team. Mamie always reserved abundant time for shopping and for the younger children to see the sights in New York; as the years passed, with the older boys in school, the Siberts' daughter, Mary Elizabeth, generally accompanied her mother to New York. [7]

While Mamie delighted in her trips to New York City and the importation of a few fashionable hats and dresses suitable for tropical wear, her husband kept busy during his rare off duty hours. With the assistance of friends back in Kentucky, Sibert imported a pack of hunting dogs and prepared to hunt deer and other game in the jungles of Panama. If the ICC transplanted a little bit of America along the canal route—including afternoon teas for fashionably dressed ladies of the high command—Sibert felt duty bound to transport Southern backwoods hunting and hounds into the Panamanian jungle.

No record tells what Mamie Sibert thought of the huge boa constrictor, not your usual household pet, which her husband kept caged in the family's quarters, mainly as a curiosity to show visitors. At least she let him keep it, and no children were lost in the process. [8]

Now a lieutenant colonel, Sibert made the society section of Volume 7 of the *Canal Record* in a big way. In the March 18, 1914, issue of the weekly, this headline appeared: **Farewell Entertainment for Colonel Sibert**. The Washington Cotillion Club planned to host a dinner and dance in honor of Colonel and Mrs. Sibert at Hotel Washington in Colon on March 21, 1914. The Saturday evening dinner-dance preceded a farewell banquet for the Sibert family on the following Thursday. The program for the farewell banquet contains a generally routine agenda for farewell dinners. [9]

The menu, however, is elaborate, an accurate reflection of the efforts made by Americans to, well, just be Americans! The happy, celebratory occasion signaled success of the American canal effort in which Sibert played a major role—all well worthy of banquet treatment. If the bill of fare is any indication, Americans in Panama, at least when they were celebrating, ate well—and fancy, too.

The dinner began sensibly enough with olives and celery, followed by grapefruit cocktail. There followed *Potage* and *Tomates Roses* and then *Maquereau Espagnol Grille, Maitre D'll.* The main course, or at least one of them, featured *Filet Mignon au pate de foie gras*, accompanied by Punch Astoria. Perhaps the roast turkey with cranberry sauce could be counted as another entree. The menu included *Pointes D'Asperges* and *Haricots Verts*, as well as *Pomme De Terre* and *Tomates Farcies*. Not yet finished, the diners next faced *Crème Glacee* and *Patisseries* before concluding with *Fromage* and *Café.* [10]

By the 9 p.m. starting time, attendees from the other side of the isthmus had arrived by train, and it had cooled a bit. The *bon voyage* party, "hosted by their friends and associates in the Canal Zone", the program noted, honored the Sibert family, as well as the colonel. If the ICC chairman supped with the Siberts at the farewell dinner, he took no part in festivities, and the name of Colonel Goethals does not appear on the program.

Justice Thomas E. Brown, Jr., a member of the Canal Zone's Supreme Court, served as toastmaster, leading the well-fed congregation through a quartet of speakers and subjects:

The Rank and File was Charles E. Woods' subject, and probably concentrated on Sibert, as seen through the eyes of those ordinary American workers who had done an extraordinary job in Panama. The titles of Tom M. Cooke's subject, *Reminiscences*, and George A. Bates' subject, *From an Old-Timer*, need no explanation. Richard Lee Metcalfe, appointed to the ICC in 1913 to head the Canal Zone's civil administration, anchored the speeches with an intriguing subject, *Colonel Sibert – the Man*, most likely on the serious side. Any treatment of Sibert, however, required the application of some early 20th century humor.

A clear indication of Colonel Sibert's happiest hunting grounds followed the speeches: A sing-along of *My Old Kentucky Home*. The program concluded with *Auld Lang Syne*.

The end of William Luther Sibert's duties as Atlantic Division commander—the builder of Gatun Dam and Gatun Locks and all of their supporting structures and channels—appears unofficially marked in the personals column of the April 1, 1914, issue of the *Canal Record*. It noted that Lieutenant Colonel Sibert and his family would board the steamer, *Ancon*, at Colon on April 2, 1914, destination New York City. [11]

William Luther Sibert was on top of the world, a position he delighted in sharing with Mamie and their children.

Chapter Fourteen
CHINA SERVICE AND 'FRISCO FUNERAL

The seven-year Panama marathon successfully run, Lieutenant Colonel Sibert returned stateside, no longer on special presidential assignment as a member of the Isthmian Canal Commission, no longer chief engineer of the ICC's Atlantic Division, and no longer engaged in building Gatun Dam and Locks.

In such a position, what does one do for an encore? The U.S. Army Corps of Engineers readily supplied the answer: Return to the Ohio River Valley where Sibert had previously served as district engineer in Louisville and Pittsburgh. This time his domain included the entire Central Division, a big promotion. The engineer looked forward to resuming his crusade for a nine-foot Ohio channel and resettling the Sibert family where it all began—Cincinnati.

Sibert anticipated with relish his first order as the Central Division's chief engineer: Move the division's offices, currently located in Washington, back to the old location in Cincinnati, the city where Mamie first established the Sibert household. She always loved the Crescent City, and its location in the middle of the division fit perfectly into Sibert's management plans.

It all added up to another Sibert homecoming! Or it would have except that another rather unusual order issued from Washington, putting on hold Sibert's return to the slack water navigation system he knew so well. The Army temporarily deferred to a request from the American Red Cross for engineering assistance with serious river control problems in China, where the new republic was trying to survive. Flooding made life miserable for thousands of Chinese living and working on broad plains squarely within the path of the annual rampages of the Huai River and other streams and lakes within its watershed. China needed help formulating plans to control the Huai and utilize its waters to the best advantage of those thousands who were currently its victims.

Because the river management involved a complicated combination of flood control, agricultural irrigation, and navigation improvements, Major General George Whitefield Davis, retired chief engineer of the Army Corps of Engineers, then serving as chairman of the Red Cross' central committee, requested Army assistance.

Fortune smiled on the Red Cross: General Davis provided leadership and possessed the requisite horsepower to attract help from the Corps of Engineers. Also favoring the humanitarian organization's plans, completion of the Panama Canal freed up perhaps the world's foremost expert on the care and control of finicky rivers—William Luther Sibert, Lieutenant Colonel of Engineers. Well acquainted with Sibert's capabilities, the retired general never hesitated to request the Army's old boy network to make Sibert available for a Red Cross expedition to China.

So, fresh from Panama and seconded to the Red Cross, Sibert found himself leading an important engineering mission to study the Chinese flooding problems. For the duration of the investigation, Sibert and the other members of the engineering board, Daniel W. Mead and Arthur P. Davis, headed a team of 15 American engineers and their assistants. The engineering officer delayed command of the Central Division and immediately pitched in to help organize the expedition to study the Huai River Conservancy Project. The group sailed from Vancouver, British Colombia, on June 11, 1914, barely two months after the *Ancon* had steamed out of the harbor at Cristobal to return the Sibert family to the States.

On the voyage to China, the steamer stopped at Yokohama where Mamie Sibert and their 13-year-old daughter, Mary Elizabeth, left the engineers to their task in favor of a tour of Japan. Once the ship arrived at Shanghai on June 18, Sibert cracked the whip and had the investigators in the field by July 5. The expedition endeavored to determine how much land—then rendered useless as a practical matter because of annual flooding—could be reclaimed for agricultural, industrial, and other related uses if flooding were, at least to some extent, controlled through a sound engineering plan.

Ironically, the Chinese, who were technological leaders a thousand or more years in the past, were ill-equipped to cope with the river problems, mainly due to lack of trained engineers. Mrs. Mabel Boardman, then serving as chairwoman of the Red Cross' executive committee, first recognized the basic problem and dreamed of offering American engineering expertise to reduce the human misery.

The 1914 expedition came about only after numerous delays caused by the Chinese government. When Sibert arrived in China, however, the American engineers carried with them broad authority from the Chinese government to conduct a comprehensive engineering study of the flood-prone region. First, the engineers concentrated on determining exactly what caused the annual floods; once identified, the board's instructions called for formulation of a practical plan to alleviate or minimize the flooding.

From the very beginning, Sibert recognized one fundamental flaw with the expedition—not enough time for a detailed study of the entire region. The engineer knew that a complete picture required studying not only the hundreds of square miles of China's coastal provinces directly affected by the floods, but also the vast territory lying to the west where precipitation fed rambunctious rivers flowing eastward toward the Yellow Sea. All too soon, the board confronted a November 1, 1914, deadline for reporting its findings and recommendations. Chinese travel, whether aboard a houseboat, a railway coach, astride a horse, or on foot, proved difficult and slow throughout the provinces, draining valuable time from engineers. The Americans did, however, find earlier surveys by the Chinese Conservancy Bureau, including locations and elevations of streams and lakebeds, to be well done and extremely helpful, although only a beginning of a comprehensive study.

Trying to use the limited resources of time, men, and equipment to best advantage, Sibert divided his forces into mini-expeditions to search for basic data required to identify the source of the problem floodings and develop a remedy.

A partial listing of the expeditions included a party of engineers and surveyors inspecting the Grand Canal and adjacent lands between Chinkiang and the mouth of the Yi River at Yaowan by houseboat. From there, engineers and their instruments went horseback upstream along a branch of the Yi, which connects with Loma Lake (Luoma Hu). Another boating expedition inspected "the Loma Lake country and all important channels leading from the Grand Canal." A houseboat of engineers surveyed the Huai River from 12 miles upstream from Pengpu (Bengbu) downstream to its junction with Hungtse Lake (Hongze Hu), and its transit into the Grand Canal.

It was by steamer that another expedition traveled upstream on the Yangtse (Yangtze) as far as Hankow (Hanchuan) before switching to the railroad to cross the western edge of the Huai river basin to Kaifengfu (Kaifeng). From Kaifengfu, horses took engineers to the Yellow (Huang) River where a short boat ride allowed them to view the spot where, in 1853, the Yellow River abandoned its ancient course to follow an entirely new channel to its mouth in the Bo Hai. Back on land at Kaifengfu, Sibert's group crossed the old riverbed, abandoned since 1853, before boarding a train for Peking (Beijing). This longest of the mini-expeditions ended with a train ride on the Tientein-Pokow Railroad from Peking to Shanghai where the engineers and staff embarked for the trip home.

The language barrier interfered with obtaining firsthand information from both Chinese officials and the everyday citizens encountered on the various expeditions. A Chinese interpreter, assigned by the Chinese president to accompany Sibert, proved to be a bright spot in the communications picture. Although Yen Yeting had never ventured beyond the borders of China, he spoke perfect English and possessed broad general knowledge. Sibert warned his colleagues to brush up on English literature should Yen lead them into a discussion of the subject.

Ancient Chinese river records intrigued Sibert as he studied the capricious nature of the Yellow River. The meticulously maintained records indicated that the river followed its old course for more than 500 years—from 1324 to 1853—before abruptly changing directions and further complicating flood patterns along China's coastal plains. Until 1853, the river emptied into the Yellow Sea well to the south of the Shantung Peninsula (Shandong Bandao), the old channel clearly depicted by dotted lines on a map of China in *Crain's Atlas*, circa 1880s. And, by 1914, the river switched course again into Bo Hai north of the Shantung Peninsula, more than 250 miles from its 1853 mouth. A major concern of the Americans was the distinct possibility that the Yellow River would again change channels.

Other problems facing engineers, when attempting to devise flood control plans for such sprawling provinces as Honan (Henan), Kiangsu (Jiangsu), and Anhwei (Anhui), included the absence of records indicating the magnitude of water discharged when the rivers were at flood stage and the lack of accurate tabulations of upstream precipitation likely to find its way into the flood plain. Still, they carefully considered and framed numerous proposals, all of which were finally rejected except for one the board thought feasible.

For good reasons, the engineers established Hungtse Lake (Hongza Hu)—into which the flood-prone Huai River flowed—as the plan's centerpiece. It didn't take long for floodwaters pouring from the Huai and Sui rivers, and other smaller streams, to swamp the lake to overflowing. Then, once free of the lake and with no obstacles in its path, the high-powered waters quickly spread eastward, producing devastating floods all across the coastal plains.

Hungtse Lake, even absent the floodwaters, is of impressive size, stretching 65 miles along the borders of Anhui and Jiangsu provinces. Of varying widths, its waters cover 757 square miles. Sibert planned to dry it up! To make that happen, he proposed a dike from the mouth of the Huai River. Utilizing the lake's existing shoreline as one levee, a new channel would be excavated to divert the Huai River away from Hungtse and into Lake Paoying.

As for the Sui River and other waters collected from a large portion of flood prone territory, they would cross former Hungtse Lake, now dry, while safely confined between two high dikes dissecting the dry lakebed. After the crossing, these waters (much like the Huai) would be channeled away from Hungtse Lake directly into Lake Paoying. From Lake Paoying, where the floodtide would have been slowed, excess water would drain Lake Kaoyu before finally being discharged into the mighty Yangtse (Yangtze) River. The Yangtse was big enough to absorb the previously destructive water which, when regulated, could be dispersed with minimum damage to the surrounding country. In addition, the excess water conserved within Lake Paoying and Lake Kaoyu could be released during the dry season when it was needed to maintain and improve navigation on the Grand Canal. To conserve water for irrigation and navigation, the plan envisioned installing two sets of locks and dams on the Grand Canal.

In addition to the pure engineering aspect of the expedition—determining the problem and how best to fix it—there were important overtones of what, in the Corps of Engineers, might be labeled a costs vs. benefits ratio. Taking into consideration China's economic limitations and any help expected from the American Red Cross and other sources, those sums were compared with the value of benefits likely to accrue to the republic and its citizens through implementation of the proposed development plan.

For example, a price tag was put on approximately 350,000 acres of irrigated farmland to be reclaimed from Hungtse Lake, and another 36,000 acres of lakebed reclaimed but not irrigated. Surrounding the lake, a value was assigned to an additional 300,000 acres of land, previously subject to frequent flooding, which would be protected and provided with drainage channels. An additional 6,700,000 acres of the coastal plains would benefit from installation of main drainage channels and by regulating the waters of the Grand Canal.

There were also indirect benefits from the proposed Huai River Conservancy Project, including improved navigation on the Grand Canal and an increase in the Chinese tax base on the reclaimed lands. The engineering board concluded that the project could be completed within six years at a cost of $30,000,000, and that revenue from the increased tax receipts and Grand Canal tolls could support a bond issue to cover costs of the project. [1]

The board submitted its report to both the American Red Cross and the Chinese government before the November 1, 1914, deadline, only to have the project effectively shoved to the back burner by the opening stages of World War I.

Having toured Japan before taking a steamer to China, Mamie Sibert and Mary Elizabeth rejoined Colonel Sibert and his party at Shanghai for the return trip across the Pacific. The engineer looked forward to his new post in the Ohio River Valley. Just around the bend, however, a pair of surprises awaited Sibert—one an extraordinary and exciting tribute to the engineer's professional excellence—the other an unmitigated family tragedy.

It was still *Lieutenant Colonel* Sibert when he returned from the engineering expedition to China in October 1914. With the report on Chinese rivers delivered, and after taking a few days of overdue leave, Colonel Sibert, as expected, took command of the Central Division of the Corps of Engineers. He regarded his appointment as division engineer to be practically perfect, returning the division's centerpiece—the Ohio River navigation system—to his care.

Following assumption of duties as division engineer in December 1914, one of Sibert's first official acts involved relocating the division office from Washington back to its former location in Cincinnati. On the far bank of the Ohio River opposite North Kentucky, Cincinnati was near the center of river development activities anticipated by the new division engineer. For the second time, Mamie prepared to manage a Sibert home in Cincinnati. [2]

Sibert set up camp in the same space the division office had previously occupied in the Federal Customs House. When it opened for business, the division office's Spartan furnishings included a desk, a revolving chair, four file cabinets, and three map cases containing 192 tin tubes. In addition, there was one in-and-out tray to manage paper distribution from the desktop, a loose-leaf binder, and a Remington standard typewriter complete with stand.

With Sibert, securing the best personnel and organizing them for maximum efficiency carried the highest priorities in establishing his new command. Impressive office fixtures ran a poor third. As his principal engineer, he hired Lorenzo Cornish, a graduate of Syracuse University, who had assisted with the design of the Ohio's proposed nine-foot canalization while serving on Sibert's Pittsburgh staff. When the president ordered Sibert to Panama, the major made certain that Cornish followed. Working in Sibert's Atlantic Division, Cornish had general charge of lock design, gaining national recognition for the design of Gatun Locks. Sibert envisioned Cornish overseeing redesign of lock gates on the Ohio River.

Sibert centralized and streamlined existing river engineering agencies, moving more personnel to Cincinnati near the center of action. The Ohio River Board's design staff embarked from Wheeling, West Virginia, eight employees, their drafting equipment and files arriving in Cincinnati aboard the steamer, *City of Parkersburg*. This design force formed the nucleus of the staff Sibert recruited for the express purpose of planning the extension of the nine-foot channel.

In February 1915, as senior member of the Flood Board, Sibert initiated cooperation with the U.S. Geological Survey to establish 16 new stream gauges on Ohio River tributaries. The Flood Board office relocated from Pittsburgh to Cincinnati, completing the reorganization Sibert envisioned in an effort to better serve and continually improve the Ohio's slack water navigation system. [3]

More constants exist than death and taxes: Washington had its leaks in 1915. After the Panama Canal officially opened on January 1, 1915, rumors constantly circulated around impending rewards for the leaders of the highly successful construction project. Since the majority of the key players wore uniforms, promotions seemed in order and that is exactly what Congress did.

By a special act passed on March 4, 1915, Congress dropped stars on Panama! Or, more accurately, the lawmakers distributed stars among the engineers—and the doctor—considered instrumental in the successful canal construction project.

Lieutenant Colonel Sibert bypassed the rank of full colonel (bird colonel) to obtain flag rank—as symbolized by the single star of a brigadier general. It literally took a special act of Congress for Sibert to hurdle the colonelcy, and he was not the only one to benefit from the Congressional action. Goethals and Harry Foote Hodges, both full colonels during their service in Panama, skipped the single star rank, and were elevated to the two-star rank of major general. Once appointed to the ICC, Hodges served with distinction as Goethals' second in command and as acting chief engineer when Goethals was absent from Panama. The Army medical officer who still preferred to be addressed as Dr. Gorgas—the nemesis of the mosquito—also received a brigadier's commission.

Filed at 4:16 p.m., on March 11, 1915, a telegram from Cincinnati to the Adjutant General of the U.S. Army in Washington wasted no words:

"My commission as Brigadier General accepted.

/s/ Sibert, Engineers."

The promotions drew bipartisan support from a grateful Congress, especially grateful that American engineers succeeded in building the canal within budget. True, it cost much more than the original estimates, but the project never exceeded the annual congressional appropriations. Congress breathed a collective sigh of relief, the new American canal in Panama positive proof that millions of dollars had been wisely spent. And, at least for a short time, congressmen and senators of every stripe basked in the reflected red, white, and blue glory of the Panama Canal.

Only a few months earlier, Sibert opened the division office in Cincinnati and prepared to prosecute some serious river engineering. He intended pushing the nine-foot channel throughout the length of the Ohio River and launching many other river improvements.

And then things changed!

Overnight by Army standards, Sibert, a field grade officer in the Corps of Engineers, became a general officer in the U.S. Army with his own flag and everything that went with it. That created problems for both Sibert and the Army.

It was unheard of for a Corps of Engineers division to be commanded by a general, a billet usually occupied by a colonel or an officer of lesser rank. Thus, Army protocol denied General Sibert the opportunity to upgrade the Ohio River system with a nine-foot channel, a project which, in his mind, lagged seven years behind schedule because of his duty in Panama. Sibert wanted to use the experience and prestige earned in Panama to deepen the Ohio's channel so that, when the river joined the Mississippi at Cairo, Illinois, their channels would match. He envisioned a powerful economic aorta, flush with sufficient depth to accommodate cheap and reliable barge traffic, and hated to leave what he regarded as unfinished business. But leave he did, as ordered—the first sacrifice he made to the silver stars on his epaulets.

Also coming with promotion to brigadier general, Sibert became a line officer, an officer designated to lead troops in wartime, as opposed to an officer of the Corps of Engineers. Both within and outside Army circles, an engineer officer was often stereotypically portrayed as much more engineer than warrior. Fair or not, this mindset prevailed among many line officers and left the Army brass with a chronic question: Can engineers effectively lead troops in battle? Were they builders or destroyers? Or could they be both?

In its infinite wisdom, Washington military leaders reassigned one of its newest generals to command the coastal artillery on the nation's West Coast. The choice made some military sense: Installation of effective coast artillery batteries required sophisticated, hard-nosed engineering, imaginatively applied to existing geographical and topographical conditions. Never short on imagination, Sibert always scored high when tested by the Army on such topics as seacoast defense, fortifications, ordnance, and gunnery. [4]

The San Francisco posting smacks of irony, it being a modern American city, recently rebuilt and recovered from the devastating earthquake and fire which occurred on April 18, 1906. With reconstruction largely completed, very little visible damage remained in 1915. A festive atmosphere greeted the Siberts as San Francisco prepared to host the Panama-Pacific Exposition, a dual celebration of the city's rebirth from ashes and the opening of the Panama Canal. General optimism prevailed in San Francisco, now rebuilt after being 80% destroyed. Opening of the Panama Canal also contributed to the cheerful outlook, the city anticipating vast economic benefits from the shortened sea route between the American coasts. [5]

The canal connection bathed the new West Coast artillery commander in a favorable light, and he had no complaints about the food and the cosmopolitan atmosphere of the City by the Bay, but doubted the euphoria would last. Like most military leaders, Sibert anticipated the United States becoming embroiled in the European conflict. Meanwhile, he hoped to train West Coast artillerymen for future deployment, probably not in defense of the American coast but, more likely, in the European war.

Times were tense among professional military men who sensed that Congress was moving altogether too slowly with war preparations. Still, Sibert's new command qualified as a choice assignment for the new brigadier general as Mamie busied herself relocating the Sibert home to the Presidio, the Army's permanent base in San Francisco since its acquisition from Mexico. Beyond duty hours, the brigadier and his lady looked forward to an active social life in one of America's most colorful and romantic cities. It was not to be.

The story appeared in the *Brownsville News* on May 21, 1915. Two Brownsville ladies, Mrs. R.B. Rentfro and Mrs. E.F. Vivier, both identified as nieces of Mary Margaret Cummings Sibert, reported the death proclaimed by the headline: **Mrs. William L. Sibert is Dead in San Francisco.**

According to the nieces, their 52-year-old aunt died May 16, 1915, a victim of meningitis. Known familiarly as Mamie, the story identifies Mrs. Sibert as a native of Brownsville who left when she married William Luther Sibert in 1887. Thereafter, she accompanied the Corps of Engineers officer to his various postings, but always found time to visit her hometown, her last visit being in 1911, according to the paper. General Sibert is listed as a survivor along with the couple's children and Mamie's brother, C.E. Cummings, then working as superintendent of Mexican Cable in Mexico City. T.B. Russell of Brownsville was named as Mrs. Sibert's brother-in-law. [6]

Devastated by the death of his companion and confidante for more than 27 years, General Sibert erected a spartan but imposing monument at Mamie's gravesite in the San Francisco National Cemetery. The inscription is simple: *Mary Cummings, 1862-1915, wife of Brig Genl W.L. Sibert.*

Thanks to Dr. Gorgas, the scourge of yellow fever had been eliminated from Panama when Mrs. Sibert and the children took up residence, and the dangers from malaria had been greatly reduced. Still, although tropical Panama had more than its share of other fevers and maladies, Mamie and the children survived the canal adventure with no ill effects. This held true when Mamie and Mary Elizabeth visited Japan in 1914, followed by their brief appearance in China. With health and sanitation standards in Shanghai questionable and perhaps little better in Japan, neither mother nor daughter encountered health problems, making the unexpected death of Mamie Sibert in San Francisco indeed ironic.

The general grieved as much as his stoic disposition allowed and wondered how the vivacious Belle of Brownsville could possibly get sick and die. Always spirited and filled with contagious vitality, Mamie left a void in Sibert's life and uncertainty how well he would do without Mamie by his side. When ordered back east again as American preparations for war escalated, William Luther Sibert left more than Mamie, her casket, and the monument in the national cemetery. Also forever consigned to the Bay City was a big part of Goliath's heart.

Located just north of Bowling Green where it nestled within a sweeping bend of Barren River, his friends described the Warren County farm as the perfect place for their soldier buddy and his lady when retirement time arrived. By water, the farm lay slightly more than two miles downstream from the boatlanding.

Like her husband, Mamie Sibert became entranced with South Kentucky's lifestyle and climate, not nearly as brutal as that of her native Brownsville down on the Mexican border. But it really boiled down to people—the friends she and her husband had made and kept in touch with over the years—to settle the question of their retirement home. Now, ironically, a home never to be shared by the devoted couple, the general having left his dearly missed lady in San Francisco.

But did he really leave Mamie in the City by the Bay? Despite her interment in San Francisco, Sibert's most loyal confidant and the mother of his six children never strayed beyond his thoughts. That Warren County farm had been as much her dream as his, as both looked forward to establishing a permanent Sibert home for the first time following his long and mobile military career. For the first time, its attainment meant that the Siberts owned a genuine home to come home to.

Strange how a place and its people can grab a person and never let go. That happened to the lieutenant and his lively young bride in 1888. The gracious if not grand lifestyle suited the two Southerners with a young and growing family. Beyond that, William Luther Sibert formed a lifelong bond with, of all people, his foxhunting buddies, those men who preferred being in the woods in hot pursuit of fox and deer, rather than comfortably ensconced behind their desks of authority.

These friends of the hunting and outdoor variety served as scouts, keeping an eye out for the kind of real estate that might interest the lieutenant turned general. Because all hunted and enjoyed the challenge of a chase, and because some were members of the Courthouse crowd along with a prominent banker or two, the group knew a lot about Warren County real estate. They had hunted over most of the farms at one time or another and usually knew what was for sale. The expectations of their military friend made the search difficult.

While still a young officer, Sibert carefully described just exactly what he needed to gracefully evolve from a soldier to a country gentleman. If a farm had no frontage on Barren River, Sibert wasn't interested and, if it did, the more acreage the better. The officer dreamed of abundant woodlands and saw no problem with including rough land unsuited for cultivation. He did, however, insist that a fair percentage of the farm consist of tillable land because he planned to grow corn and hay, mainly to feed the horses he expected to have. The engineer wanted a serviceable house, not necessarily grand, along with a barn or two and a smokehouse.

Some requirements were non-negotiable, such as ample room for kennels to house his foxhounds and plenty of unoccupied land—the rougher land and undisturbed woodlands—perfect for attracting fox, both the red and gray varieties. There is no question that, in addition to his friends and the river, the love of his favorite sport, foxhunting, drew Sibert back to Kentucky. It was a very special kind of foxhunting: Engaging in the sport with friends who shared his enthusiasm made all the difference. While moving from lieutenant to general during a quarter century of soldiering, William Luther Sibert never altered the description of the dream farm he and Mamie hoped for when the uniforms were laid aside. [7]

Stuck with such precise instructions, the merchants, bankers, and lawyers, the sheriff and the judge, always kept Sibert's perfect farm in the back of their minds when farm families left the county for elusive greener pastures, when hard economic times resulted in farm foreclosures, and when death caught up with a successful farmer with too many heirs for an economically practicable division of the farm.

The death of J.W. Stephens, a respected farmer, finally opened the gate to the Sibert farm in 1915—a little late for Mamie. During the October term of Warren Circuit Court, an order issued directing the master commissioner to sell the Stephens farm at public auction to settle the farmer's estate. A dead-end country lane branched off Barren River Road and ran about two miles along the high north bluffs of Barren River to the farm's front gate. Except for mention as "the lane leading from Barren River Road to the Stephens farm", the road was unnamed in 1915. (Later, it was known as McFarland's Beach Road, now shortened to McFarland Lane.) After publication of the legal notice, the auction took place on December 27, 1915.

Court records indicate a purchase price of $18,225.00 with W.L. Sibert listed as purchaser. Judge McKenzie Moss confirmed the sale during the January 1916 term of court and ordered Master Commissioner Will R. Speck to execute a deed to the purchaser. Judge Moss approved the commissioner's deed conveying the farm to Sibert (now unmarried since Mamie's death eight months earlier) on January 10, and County Clerk E.C. Smith recorded the instrument on January 13, 1916.

A marginal note on the recorded deed in the clerk's office indicates: "Purchase money bond mentioned herein being paid in full & lien released. This June 28th 1916." Signed by O.A. Roup, deputy clerk of Warren Circuit Court, and attested by County Clerk Smith, the marginal release means that the auction price had been paid and that General Sibert thereafter owned the farm free and clear of debt, at least until the next tax bill came due.

The farm approached the ideal—just exactly what the lieutenant had in mind 25 years earlier. It contained 265 acres of an acceptable ratio between acreage dedicated to human uses as opposed to land reserved for the fox and other creatures of the wild. The greater percentage of his Warren County domain being devoted to wildlife—the woodlands and unfarmed fields polka dotted with limestone outcroppings—surprised none of his friends. Due to its size, the farm still managed ample room for the general's corn and hay crops, gardens, and the family compound.

In addition to 265 mainland acres, the Stephens property purchased by the general included two islands, Boat Island and Onion Island. The old deed descriptions assign nine acres to Boat Island and four acres to Onion, now called Sibert Island after somebody renamed it. The islands increased Sibert's total holdings to 278 acres. [8]

Now a bachelor, Sibert found the former Stephens home, a rambling, two-story frame farmhouse, perfectly adequate and comfortable. With the U.S. on the verge of entering the European conflict, however, Sibert initially spent little time at the farm. Nevertheless, the mere fact of his farm's existence, joined with his development plans, gave the general something to chew on besides the unlit cigar. The memory of Mamie insisted that the home be made hospitable to all of his family and friends. Although absent from the river farm, just thinking proved therapeutic. More than just a farm in fox country, it was a part of Mamie never to be surrendered.

Fortunately, the youngest two of the Sibert children neared college age in 1916, reducing the homemaking demands on their father. Although Mamie was sorely missed, somehow Martin David and Mary Elizabeth, ages 16 and 15, respectively, managed to muddle through with their father's help. Sibert hoped for the best while preparing himself and the family for an uncertain future. It helped when Mount Holyoke College in South Hadley, Massachusetts, accepted Mary Elizabeth as a student. Not that Sibert didn't worry about his only daughter, but the welfare of his sons resulted in heightened anxiety. No longer children, two of the Sibert boys chose the profession of arms and followed their father to West Point and Army careers. In addition, the remaining trio was ripe by age for any conflicts the United States chose to fight during the teens of the 20th century. Sibert sometimes wondered if, by himself, he could handle the potential loss of a son to the meat grinder in France. [9]

Sibert's warrior spirit never allowed such morose thoughts to linger long enough to be a problem. His stoic composure, which helped pull him through the loss of Mamie, blunted any thoughts of family casualties during the war in Europe. Even though the river farm furnished a certain balm to Sibert's sagging spirit, the action spawned by war preparation helped even more. That is how Brigadier General William Luther Sibert and his children managed to shake melancholy lingering from Mamie's loss as the general prepared for his role in the 20th century's first global conflict. For Sibert, the war years brewed a strange mix: Elation came first before deep, desolate professional disappointment. Then, ultimately, redemption!

Chapter Fifteen

PERSHING AND GAS: THE GREAT WAR

When the subject of World War I came up, the average mid-to-late 20th century American usually managed to nail three iconic personalities: Sergeant York, Eddie Rickenbacker, and General John J. Pershing. York's Tennessee marksmanship and courage, and Rickenbacker's duels with German aces while flying his cloth and wood Spad above the trenches are the grist of legend. While generating far less excitement, General Pershing is generally acknowledged to be America's preeminent military leader in World War I.

An acquaintance with General Pershing and a general understanding of American efforts—or lack thereof—to prepare for war on the European continent are essential to understanding what otherwise is an ironically puzzling role played by General Sibert in the Great War.

After the Civil War, like the general from Alabama, Pershing also grew up on a farm—the Pershing farm located in the border state of Missouri. After exhausting local educational opportunities and teaching school at a tender age, John Joseph Pershing thirsted for more education. He answered a newspaper notice and signed to take the examination to qualify for admission to the U.S. Military Academy. He won the appointment and, at age 21, was a few years older than his fellow plebes when he arrived at West Point. This additional maturity accrued to Cadet Pershing's benefit. When he graduated 30th among the 77 members of the Class of 1886, his resume included service as class president and senior captain of cadets—the captaincy considered to be the highest honor a cadet may receive.

Unlike Sibert and Gaillard, Pershing's commendable standing in the upper half of his class did not qualify him for a Corps of Engineers appointment which both had received in 1884. Instead, his notable record as a cadet earned him a mount in the most glamorous branch of the service—the U.S. Cavalry—then engaged in frontier service fighting Indians in the American West. Pershing won his first combat citation as a young cavalry officer and participated in the famous (or infamous, depending on the point of view) battle of Wounded Knee.

While Sibert tackled navigation problems in Kentucky, Arkansas, and along the Great Lakes, Pershing served as professor of military science at the University of Nebraska at Lincoln. After the academic interlude, Pershing was back in the saddle in 1895, this time as an officer in the 10th Cavalry Regiment. In the segregated American Army, the 10th was an all-Negro unit (with white officers) and, as a result, "Black Jack" became Pershing's nickname.

In June 1897, on the eve of the war with Spain, Pershing was back from the frontier, assigned to be an assistant instructor in tactics at West Point. He came into serious disagreement with the academy's superintendent over Pershing's push for more practical training in tactics. The superintendent vetoed the suggestions and added insult to injury by publicly ridiculing Pershing. War may have saved Pershing from further collisions with his superior at the academy.

When the Spanish-American War flared, every regular Army officer worth his salt scrambled for combat, Pershing calling in a favor to secure reassignment to the 10th Cavalry. While Sibert remained marooned on the Arkansas River (in spite of his best efforts to join the war), Pershing saw combat in Cuba. He witnessed ex-Confederate General Joseph Wheeler dodging Spanish bullets to save the initial landing in Cuba from disaster before pressing forward to win the first American victory at Las Guasimas.

Pershing's coolness under fire caught the attention of his superiors and also of Theodore Roosevelt, a volunteer with the "Rough Riders". After that, the lives of Sibert and Pershing shared some significant and sometimes tragic parallels.

Both officers served in the Philippines immediately after hostilities with Spain ceased, after which some much nastier conflicts broke out. While Sibert and his fighting engineers showed coolness scouting trails on punitive expeditions and repairing railroads under hostile fire in support of the Army's northward advance on Luzon, Pershing enjoyed success fighting the Moros on Luzon. His accomplishments, first in fighting the Moros, then in formulating a system of laws to govern the Moros (and other far distant and different peoples coming under

American rule), again attracted the attention of Roosevelt, now president. The president liked an officer who not only subdued a foe, but also devised a way to govern him.

In 1906, President Roosevelt promoted Pershing all the way from captain to brigadier general! Pershing bypassed three intervening ranks and, more importantly, he vaulted over 862 other officers who were his seniors. The meteoric elevation sparked widespread resentment among the officers' corps, including rumors of favoritism and political deals.

The year before, Pershing married Helen Frances Warren, daughter of U.S. Senator Francis E. Warren, an influential congressional leader holding a key post as chairman of the Senate's Military Affairs Committee in 1906. The president's interests coincided with keeping Senator Warren happy and, obviously, promoting his new son-in-law was a step in the right direction. Regardless of TR's motive, these personal relationships made Pershing's out of sync elevation to general an irresistible and naturally juicy subject of Washington gossip. For Pershing, the rapid elevation in rank resulted in problems of jealousy and protocol that never really ended. Nevertheless, Pershing continued to serve with distinction.

Much later, in April 1915, in recognition of his service in Panama, Lieutenant Colonel Sibert also skipped a rank to be commissioned a brigadier general. The canal promotions of the military officers who served on the ICC proved popular with the public, but for Sibert, the promotion carried with it an insolvable problem for the Army hierarchy. Happiness surrounded Mamie's ceremonial pinning of the single star on the epaulets of Sibert's tunic, the euphoria destined to tragically end with her death in San Francisco on May 16, 1915. Pershing's equally tragic loss came only three months later—the deaths on August 27, 1915, of his wife and three daughters (ages eight, seven and three) in a house fire in San Francisco.

Having deployed his command—the 8th Infantry Brigade—to El Paso, Texas, in response to unrest along the Mexican border, Pershing took leave from duty only long enough to arrange the burials and put his surviving son in the care of his sister at Lincoln, Nebraska. Returning to the border, Pershing pursued Pancho Villa into Mexico, but never succeeded in catching him. However, the Army's mere presence and its incursions into Mexico achieved a positive result—stopping Villa's brand of border terrorism. The border campaign earned Pershing his second star—promotion to major general. [1]

Meanwhile, the war in Europe raged on, and the United States took its first tentative steps toward entering the fray while Pershing's troops engaged in a series of small unit actions and skirmishes in Mexico. Congress responded to the struggle in Europe by passing the National Defense Act in May 1916 to begin the first real effort to modernize, as well as expand the size of the Army. The objective was to double the size of the country's peacetime Army of less than 130,000 officers and men over a five-year period. During that same time frame, the National Guard would be quadrupled, and the Reserve Officers Training Corps would be introduced into the nation's colleges.

When compared to the bloody trenches of France—and the enormous toll of men and equipment modern warfare had drained from the combatants since the guns first opened up in August 1914—the congressional action was a mere drop in the bucket. In the Battle of the Frontier in 1914, the French sustained a quarter-million casualties, and the first day of the 1916 Battle of the Somme claimed more than 19,000 British dead. In all, the Somme campaign cost Allied armies 794,000 men while German losses reached 538,888. Even five years down the road, the total strength of the American Army would not have covered any of these losses!

Nonetheless, when seen against the backdrop of America's pre-World War I isolationist viewpoint, the National Defense Act looks a bit more robust. The act began the building of an American Army that, by the end of the war, numbered well over four million men, of which two million saw duty in France.

Almost a year later, on April 6, 1917, with the Army less than a year into the five-year plan, the United States declared war on Germany. Washington abounded with more questions than answers. With America unprepared to fight in the large-scale modern war unfolding in Europe, England and France applied intense pressure, both countries seeking immediate relief for their war-weary armies in the form of American troops in the trenches. Also, the United States had not engaged in a big war since its own Civil War and, by 1917, Union and Confederate muskets were ancient history—replaced by machine guns, tanks, airplanes, and poison gas. No living American general had experience commanding armies in the field of the size engaged in Europe.

Only General Pershing had any recent experience handling a relatively large number of troops in a campaign, albeit the limited action against Pancho Villa. Recalled to Washington, he seemed an obvious candidate for an important command, just as soon as President Woodrow Wilson and the Army decided *how* and *when* the Americans were going to fight. None of the questions were easy, with perhaps the most disturbing one involving a delicate balancing act: How soon can the United States shore up the weary Allies with American troops, while at the same time training the American Army for 20th century combat? [2]

Time passed with Sibert fidgeting over his West Coast cannon pointed in the wrong direction, a long way from the Atlantic and the German U-boats scouting its shores for Britain bound freighters. Time did help ease the pain of Mamie's departure and, in 1917, Sibert prepared to take a new mate—a not unexpected turn of events for a healthy soldier.

Certainly love and affection were involved in Sibert's marriage to Juliette P. Roberts in Pittsburgh in June 1917 before his departure for France with the American Expeditionary Force. Realistically, however, the nuptials also suggest a father's concern for a daughter without feminine companionship in the family, and the garden variety loneliness experienced by a family man deprived of his mate. A likely lesser factor centers on a soldier's—any soldier's—yearning for familiar feminine affection and companionship before facing battlefield dangers in a foreign land.

The bride, believed to be a native of Chambersburg, Pennsylvania, was born in 1887, and may have met the Sibert family in Panama. The prevalent theory places Miss Roberts on the office staff of an American contractor in the Canal Zone. Crossing paths in Panama, although based purely on conjecture, provides a logical connection that may have led to the marriage—the union regrettably ending with her death.

For the second time, Sibert endured the termination of a marriage by premature death—Juliette Roberts Sibert counted among the thousands of victims of the Influenza Epidemic of 1918. As a practical matter, the multitude of war problems eclipsed and papered over the general's second marital loss. He had little time to grieve.

When in charge of all that coastal firepower, Sibert fumed because it was on the wrong coast! Even with opening of his beloved canal, San Francisco was a far piece from the Atlantic action and Sibert once again craved a combat command. Relatively trim, Goliath felt fit and still towered over his contemporaries, at the ready to engage the Huns. It was, however, well beyond Sibert's pay grade and, as it turned out, any other American general's station, to decide when and how the country would enter the shooting war in France. Things then began to happen in a hurry: Recalled to Washington, a major general's commission awaited him in the capital on May 15, 1917. [3]

Meanwhile, Lieutenant General Tom Bridges, leading an English military mission which arrived in Washington just 16 days after America's declaration of war, succinctly stated his thoughts in a letter to General Hugh Scott, the American Army's chief of staff:

"The sight of the Stars and Stripes on this continent (Europe) will make a great impression on both sides. ... To this end I would like to see one of your regular divisions sent to France at once."

On April 25, 1917, the French military delegation arrived in Washington and wholeheartedly agreed with the British appeal: The Allied trenches in France desperately needed American troops, sooner rather than later. While understandable, the Allied request brimmed over with problems. Explicitly aware of the urgency, the Army's best military thinkers feared the consequences of quickly introducing a largely untrained body of American soldiers to the hazards of total war. The absence of basic training for new recruits, and without more thorough planning and preparation at command levels, they argued, courted chaos on the battlefield and American lives unnecessarily lost.

The British proposed seconding American recruits directly to the British Army, shipping them to England for training under English officers, and eventually assigning them to British units already in France. The British promised release of the Americans to American commands once sizable American units arrived in France. The Army rejected the English proposal outright and established a fairly firm policy: Americans sent to France would be assigned exclusively to American outfits, led by American officers, and fighting as part of an American force under the American flag.

A vital question remained unsettled after talks with the British and French military leaders: *When* might the Allies expect to see this 100% American contingent, or any part of it, in the trenches opposing the Bosch? The Army insisted on adequate time to train thousands of raw recruits, to mold them into a bigger and better Army. The American

General Staff thought premature commitment of ill-trained soldiers to the trenches—simply to boost Allied morale—an unwise gesture which, in the longer view, they expected to impede efforts to bring the war to a successful conclusion.

For a time, it looked as if the advice from the Army's War College Division—not to neglect training for the sake of speed—had carried the day. Then, a 65-minute meeting at the White House between President Wilson and French Field Marshal Joffre on May 2, 1917, changed everything.

Apparently without consultation with either the Army General Staff or Secretary of War Newton Baker, Wilson promised Joffre an early commitment of American troops to France. On May 10, Baker directed Army leaders to prepare to land American troops in France. This was not a military decision on the part of the White House. Instead, it appears to be a long-range ploy by President Wilson to strengthen his hand at any future peace conferences, a political move with little regard for hard-nosed military realities.

The Wilson promise foretold the birth of the American Expeditionary Force—the soon famous AEF!

General John J. Pershing led the AEF from its founding, the recipient of vast, unprecedented power to direct the American war effort in France. Pershing and a party of 190 boarded the steamer *Baltic* and sailed from New York on May 28, 1917, a bare 18 days after Baker asked for plans for the AEF. Despite the interruptions of lifeboat drills—made necessary by the ever-present threat of U-boat attacks—the crossing gave Pershing and his staff precious additional days to plan the American Army's future in France.

Meanwhile, General Sibert took command of a large contingent of soldiers, practically all of them untrained, soon to be designated the 1st Infantry Division—the Big Red 1! These troops, 14,500 strong, landed at St. Nazaire in late June. Except for some scattered Army personnel and a Battalion of Marines among them, the vast majority were raw recruits. Many experienced officers and noncommissioned officers stayed behind to train the influx of additional recruits, this being the Army's response to the president's unanticipated commitment of troops to Joffre.

The experienced regulars, including Sibert and every other career officer commanding troops in France, from division down to regimental, battalion, company, and platoon levels, shared the same job: Prepare eager doughboys—fresh off the streets and farms of the USA—to fight a modern war. Compounding the difficulties, the AEF lacked an indispensable training tool that was missing from the table of organization. Where is the *cadre*?

A term not often used in the civilian world, *cadre* has a clear meaning in the Army—referring to the nucleus of experienced officers and noncommissioned officers around which raw recruits are trained to create ever-larger units of effective soldiers. The idea is simple and practical: The experienced personnel teach recruits all aspects of military life from peeling potatoes to wielding bayonets in hand-to-hand fighting. Of highest importance when preparing new soldiers for battle, the cadre administers basic training—its lifeblood consisting of experienced sergeants and corporals, motivated to teach the profession of arms. (This is, for example, the domain of those legendary Marine Corps drill instructors, highly competent and experienced noncommissioned officers.)

Unfortunately, most of these seasoned veterans of Army life remained on duty stateside to train the huge American Army then under construction for eventual duty in France. Inexperience prevailed at every level. Sibert, for example, never before commanded a full infantry division, his experience in troop command limited to bossing the Engineer Battalion in the Philippines. True, he served as chief engineer and leader of all Army engineers in the Pacific, an important assignment for which he drew commendations. The scope of his responsibility in the Pacific, however, did not compare with the multi-faceted job of a divisional commander. A rookie at the divisional command level, Sibert had much to learn during those first few months in France. Perfecting a command structure peopled by trustworthy officers proved difficult because practically all available officers, like Sibert, struggled with a steeply ascending learning curve. Sibert's problems repeated themselves in all other units shipped out in haste—with little or no training. Pershing's staff encountered similar problems, never having handled large armies and the equipment they require to survive on a modern battlefield. [4]

Wilson conjured these problems by his impetuous decision to prematurely commit American forces not fully trained for modern warfare. The dilemma arose just as the brains in the Army War College had feared from the beginning. The absence of adequate training and the lack of planning for a lengthy ground war on the European continent, far from its arsenal across the Atlantic, handicapped the AEF. And General Sibert carried an additional burden of a professional nature that ended up overshadowing all else. Much like distinguishing one of his prize foxhounds from another: Army pedigree matters.

Sibert believed in pedigree when it came to both hounds and people; his experiences with both taught him that bloodlines usually ran true. In addition to Sibert's abundance of self-confidence and a deserved reputation for fearlessly speaking his piece, he also qualified as a practicing pragmatist, never given over to self-delusion. That combination, for Sibert, produced a well-connected double worry, first about his Army pedigree and, second, concern about jumping rank to general. Although Pershing could ill afford to complain about bypassing rank, the AEF commander regarded Sibert's pedigree as a burr under the ex-cavalryman's saddle.

With two broad categories of officers—line officers and engineer officers—the vast majority of officers in the small peacetime Army qualified as line officers while a much smaller contingent of engineer officers wore the fort/castle insignia of the Corps of Engineers. When Sibert was a cadet (1880-1884) few disputed labeling West Point as the nation's premier school of engineering—not only military but civil as well. Corps of Engineers appointments went to the academy's leading engineering scholars in the 19th Century, allowing the Army to take advantage of their book learning. The remaining graduates drew duty in the more military-sounding branches such as infantry, artillery, and the colorful and glamorous cavalry. (It is altogether likely that the vast majority actually preferred the other more exciting, warlike branches rather than the engineers.)

Human nature being what it is, it is easy to see how some engineers might be accused of elitism, while at the same time some line officers of the infantry, artillery, and cavalry looked down on their engineering brethren as a lesser breed of warrior. That is why Lieutenant Colonel Sibert feared his promotion to brigadier general was a mistake! True: He voiced no moral or ethical objections to skipping over bird colonel to the single star status with increases in both pay and professional prestige. Indeed it was a big leap to flag rank, something officers—regulars in the peacetime army where promotion, if at all, was slow—usually only dreamed about.

The mistake, Sibert thought, concerned lineage—pedigree—no fault of either the Army or Sibert. When Congress promoted Sibert to brigadier general, no billet existed within the Corps of Engineers where the chief engineer was also a brigadier general, and there was no room within the organization for another. Left with no choice, the Army classified Sibert—and the other new Panama generals, Goethals and Hodges—as officers of the line. Sibert's 30 years of outstanding service as an engineer didn't count as he joined the Line of the Army— not the engineer's choice and contrary to his well-established military pedigree. That is how the three Corps of Engineers officers became generals of the line. Sibert related a story reflecting the attitude of line officers on the subject:

During a frank and friendly discussion of his promotion dilemma with another major general of the line (never identified by name, but probably a West Point cadet during Sibert's time at the academy), a line officer, offered a straightforward illustration of the typical line officer's view of generalships for engineering officers. "Congress," he said, "might as well have promoted a doctor—as it had the engineers—to be a General Officer of the Line." Elevating a specialist to such high rank as a line officer, he explained, undermined the whole training system aimed at preparing officers to command troops. His fellow general suggested to Sibert that commanding troops was in and of itself a military specialty and that those trained to do so were the logical choice to lead troops into combat. The general also thought promotions outside the natural Army order were detrimental to the Army.

Sibert, the pragmatist, did not disagree with his companion's analysis, but also recognized a strain of jealousy that was widespread among the Army's officers of the line. Some engineer officers shared the opinion that the jealousy and resentment dated from the Civil War when engineer officers, such as Robert E. Lee, proved to be highly successful commanders of troops in the field.

Goethals never faced Sibert's problem, retiring soon after his appointment as a major general of the line in order to become governor of the Canal Zone. When recalled to active service, he rendered splendid service by reorganizing the quartermaster system in support of the troops in France—a noncombatant job where his organizational skills paid huge dividends. The Army also took advantage of the administrative ability of Major General Harry Foote Hodges by placing him in command of Camp Devens, Massachusetts. There, Hodges trained the 76th Division and 40,000 other men for duty in France—another non-combatant command where a canal engineer excelled and established a model system of schools and training for the outbound troops.

As for Sibert, the Army chose him for a combat command in France. He followed orders and took command of the 1st Infantry Division, determined to do his best to train the extremely raw, inexperienced personnel to survive and give a good account of themselves in the trenches of France. Regardless, his path paved with pedigree put him on a collision course with John J. Pershing, a General of the Line.

Pershing stood at the head of the AEF, an extremely able officer of the line, carrying with him all of a line officer's prejudices against engineer officers which had been building since his Indian-fighting days as a cavalry officer. In Pershing's case, however, it is difficult to imagine his being jealous of the engineers and their reputations within the Army. Instead, he probably based his blanket aversion to engineer officers on an innate distrust of their capability to lead troops in combat situations. Strange as it may seem, Sibert found himself, at least in theory, in agreement with Pershing's position, notwithstanding his desire to lead troops in combat.

There was more: Pershing preferred not to have a 56-year-old general—Sibert being only a month younger than the AEF's commander—as an AEF divisional commander. He preferred subordinates to be younger than himself, on the slender side, and energetic. The early-rising Sibert exhibited remarkable energy throughout his career and, although trim considering age and mileage, there was nothing he could do about his superior's distaste for engineer officers. [5]

Sibert set to work organizing and implementing a comprehensive training program to provide all 1st Division recruits with rudimentary basic training—acquainting them with the proper end of the Springfield to point at the Germans. After three months in France, came an important exercise on October 3, 1917, field maneuvers, perhaps a practical test to determine how well the officers and men of the 1st Division were learning their lessons.

The division looked unimpressive when marching in review over muddy ground before dignitaries that included the president of France. A demonstration of tactics devised to attack an entrenched enemy—the Germans being well entrenched—seems to have succeeded under the direction of Major Theodore Roosevelt, Jr., son of the former president. But everything collapsed at the post-maneuvers critique, presided over by the AEF commander. Pershing turned the maneuvers into the worst of days for Sibert and the officers working hard to turn the 1st Infantry Division into an efficient fighting unit.

Sibert failed to answer Pershing's questions to his superior's satisfaction, and further attempts by members of Sibert's staff to explain the current state of the division's training fell on deaf ears. No constructive criticism here, only an angry explosion of temper came from the AEF commander. The performance of the officers and men of the first American division destined to fight as a unit in combat—Sibert's boys—were the ostensible object of Pershing's rage. The real target, however—Sibert personally—caught the brunt of the verbal assault. Without difficulty, Sibert recognized the tantrum as a thinly disguised attack on his pedigree—his status as an interloper—an officer of engineers instead of a born and bred line officer Pershing preferred.

The *post mortem* contained rich and varied factors contributing to the division's performance. Possible deficiencies in the training protocol, the inexperience of recruits, and the shortage of experienced noncoms and officers to teach the new soldiers played into the picture. A critically short training time and Sibert's failure to sense the best way to communicate with the AEF chief likely contributed to the bad scene.

The quality of the performance, good, bad, or middling, may have been difficult to judge since it was a first—a sizable American Army unit maneuvering in unfamiliar territory before a commander who sought perfection. Nevertheless, General Pershing leaped to the conclusion that the entire performance, particularly Sibert's part in the critique, was unacceptable. An old-fashioned Army ass-chewing followed, laid on vigorously by Pershing with Sibert on the receiving end.

This was not a drill instructor verbally taking apart a hapless recruit, but a general officer lambasting another general officer. Most surprising of all, the railing occurred in front of the troops! In no sense private, the scolding audience mainly consisted of the officers composing Sibert's divisional staff. Intended or not, such a performance by the AEF commander—in front of the very soldiers he expected Sibert to inspire—only served to undermine his authority and the efficacy of his leadership. As a rule, Pershing seldom acted precipitously, and there is no reason to believe he did so in this instance.

Aside from the verbal abuse, as commander of a division under intense criticism from the AEF commander, Sibert knew a very basic military rule (what a bespectacled AEF artillery officer, Harry S. Truman, would much later succinctly express): The buck stops here! The here, obviously, was General Sibert's plate. He alone stood responsible for any so-called divisional failures. When Pershing declared the division's performance below par, he placed blame squarely on Sibert's shoulders. [6]

General Peyton C. March, Army Chief of Staff in 1918—the officer credited with transporting a sizable American Army and its supplies to France in time to tip the balance in favor of the Allies—not only thought Pershing had a problem, but that he knew the source of the problem. Pershing, said March, lacked the ability "to function in teamwork" with his superiors and to work with other generals, including George W. Goethals, Leonard Wood, Tasker H. Bliss, and William L. Sibert. This shortcoming, as perceived by General March, resulted directly from Pershing's advancement from captain to brigadier general, which denied him the training and experience that progression through the grades affords. Due to skipping ranks, March believed that Pershing lost "the very foundation of a complete knowledge of the art of war and the command of men." [7]

Generals, even the good ones, don't always observe the rules, and, as AEF commander, with the broadest powers ever conferred on a field commander by an American president, Pershing expected to have his own way on all matters of import. Crass behavior even by Army standards, Pershing's treatment of Sibert drew an immediate rebuke. Surprisingly, it came from a very junior officer on Sibert's staff, his name destined to become an American household item in World War II.

After General Pershing ended his harangue, a response erupted, not from General Sibert, who controlled his temper and remained stoically silent, but from a lowly captain who had heard enough. Understandably upset at witnessing his commanding officer raked over the coals (unfairly in his eyes) before his own staff, Captain George C. Marshall, Jr., intervened. Catching General Pershing by the arm as he was leaving the meeting—a brash act to say the least—the captain hurriedly exclaimed that "there are some things to be said here, I think I should say them."

With that preamble, Marshall launched an angry monologue in General Pershing's direction, touching on factors which affected the division's performance, including inadequate supplies and transportation and the substandard condition of the new troops when they arrived in France.

A potential death knell for Captain Marshall's military career, the incident turned out just the opposite. Pershing subsequently transferred Marshall to AEF headquarters at Chaumont where he later became General Pershing's top aide. Pershing obviously admired the spunk displayed by Marshall in confronting the AEF commander, an occurrence of great rarity in the American Army—or in any army! In addition, Pershing, never accused of being a fool, may have realized that he had gone too far, that the public tongue-lashing of Sibert was ill-conceived and just plain wrong and that Marshall's criticism had been justified.

Regardless, a strong theory suggests that the division's performance, on a day devoted to maneuvers to impress the French president, placed Sibert's command in jeopardy. An even better theory suggests that Pershing preordained Sibert's fate long before the maneuvers for one reason alone: Pershing abhorred an engineer commanding his only division! And the 1st Infantry Division was the only division he had in October 1917. In retrospect, the maligned maneuvers were diaried— much as a modern human resources specialist builds a file to justify firing an office malcontent—because General Pershing refused to tolerate this officer (a refugee from the Corps of Engineers) commanding the 1st Infantry Division. With Sibert's rude treatment, Pershing fired the opening salvo—at least publicly—of his campaign to purge Sibert from the command structure of the AEF.

On another occasion, Sibert drew Pershing's ire by being away from his command for a short period of time, apparently without first seeking Pershing's approval. Captain Marshall explained that Sibert was on division business, but the incident only widened the gap of misunderstanding between the line officer and the engineer. In all likelihood, the chasm was insurmountable due to the pedigree problem.

Meanwhile, Sibert continued training and, as planned, gradually introduced 1st Division troops to trench warfare. Various units manned trenches for short periods of time—on-the-job training at its deadliest. Before dawn on November 3, 1917, a battalion of the 1st Division, occupying a comparatively quiet stretch of trenches in the French sector, caught the full weight of a German raid, in strength, into Allied lines.

Heavily supported by artillery, combat-toughened German troops poured into the American trenches, killing three Yanks and taking some prisoners before withdrawing. By all accounts, the 1st Division's doughboys—trained under Sibert's tutelage—stood their ground and slugged it out with the veteran enemy raiding party. Sibert believed they had performed well and told them so, but heard nothing from Pershing. The training entered its final phase as the division prepared to go into action as an American unit. [8]

In letters sent to several generals in December 1917—Sibert included—Pershing attacked what the AEF commander perceived to be a defeatist attitude among his divisional commanders. The letter suggested that several high-ranking officers, Sibert among them, may be failing to inspire their men while shrinking from the hardships they had encountered in France. The missive was blunt, even implying a lack of courage. [9]

Objectively speaking, can Sibert's dedication to his mission ever be doubted? He hadn't changed since dedicating seven years to the construction of the Panama Canal, where he often worked under difficult circumstances. And courage? He was the same officer who volunteered his engineers to join the infantry in a firefight with insurgents just days after arrival in the Philippines. He was the same captain of engineers who volunteered to take the point and clear the way for General Theodore Schwan's thrusts into the jungles of Cavite—the heart of the insurgency. An incredulous Sibert found it difficult to believe such a message—questioning dedication and courage—could be seriously directed at him. Then, he remembered Pershing's prejudice toward engineers. The letter may have been Pershing's final hint that his division commanders needed to seek other posts.

Regardless, Sibert did not take the hint. He continued training the 1st Infantry Division until AEF headquarters at Chaumont relieved him of command of the *Big Red 1* later in the month. Infuriated, Sibert hotly protested to Pershing, but it came to nothing. Although temporarily devastated by what he considered to be a grossly unfair decision, Sibert decided to forego any further protests and, instead, dutifully return to the United States. At least two cogent reasons prompted the decision, neither of which touched on his abilities to command the division. [10]

When Sibert departed France, the public view of Pershing was decisively positive and Pershing's image fit perfectly into the propaganda boat promoting the war effort—a propaganda boat not to be rocked. Within the Army, practically no one wanted to pick a fight with the AEF commander—a fight likely to be lost. In addition, being familiar with the facts of Army life, his indelible sense of duty to the Army and his country prompted the pragmatic Sibert—ever the good soldier—to accede to the relief order as graciously as possible.

After shepherding the men of the 1st Division through training and actually putting its first units into the trenches, the Great War became the second conflict in which Sibert missed most of the shooting. So, the general had no choice but to leave the troops of the Big Red 1—and his own sons—to face the Kaiser's cannons without him.

The Sibert family remained heavily engaged in World War I. In addition to General Sibert, Lieutenant Colonel Franklin C. Sibert, Major Harold W. Sibert, Major William O. Sibert, Lieutenant Edwin L. Sibert, and Corporal Martin D. Sibert helped fill the ranks. All of the general's sons were not professional soldiers, but all answered the call to the colors! [11]

Back stateside in January 1918, Sibert once again presented the Army with a dilemma—what to do with a quasi-general of the line who did not gain Pershing's ringing endorsement to lead troops into combat in France? A major general with a wide range of experience should be useful to the War Department, but where?

At least temporarily, the Army solved its Sibert problem by appointing him commanding general of the Southeastern Department of the United States with headquarters in Charleston, South Carolina. With no serious threat of invasion by the Central Powers, the posting appears of little importance to America's war effort except for the training camps located within the region. It was the kind of obscure post where an older general might be put out to pasture.

From Sibert's view, the best features of the posting were non-military, including exposure to low country cuisine and the opportunity to visit some original Sibert country in South Carolina. Abbeville, where his great grandfather farmed and preached on the other side of the state, fell within Sibert's jurisdiction. Sibert cousins still peopled the area, and the general welcomed an opportunity to visit them during his tour of duty in South Carolina.

From the Hamilton Hotel, where the general resided after being ordered back to Washington to attend to more serious matters, Sibert wrote to his brother Sam about his visits with South Carolina relatives while stationed in Charleston. After expressing some regrets at leaving South Carolina so soon, the officer related details of his visits with kinsmen in the letter dated May 21, 1918.

Sibert mentioned a particularly fruitful visit with a cousin, 79-year-old George M. Sibert, at McCormick, South Carolina. He also met members of the Cook family, pointing out in the letter that it had been almost a century—actually 99 years—since their grandfather and his bride, Elizabeth Cook, left Abbeville on the journey to their new home in Alabama. Sibert took an immediate liking not only to the Carolina Siberts, but to the Cooks as well. "I enjoyed the visit, (and) they came from far and near to see me. They all seemed to be good stock—the Cooks all big people," the general happily remarked. And the Cook contingent seemed equally pleased with the general, explaining that the Cook family emigrated from County Downs, Ireland.

"They say I may have the Sibert name, but I look like the Cooks," Sibert wrote. "They had Pa's picture at Cousin George's and the Cooks found a marked resemblance to their people." From it all, the general concluded: "The size and blue eyes of the Siberts came from the Cooks."

General Sibert also heard an alternative theory to the Hessian story of how their great grandfather got to South Carolina: It seems that another line of Siberts migrated from Alsace-Lorraine to England where they spent a generation or two before making the journey to America. The question remains unresolved. The general obviously hated to leave behind such stimulating discussions of family history. [12]

Until recalled to Washington, Sibert had conscientiously continued to carry out what duties there were for the commander in the Southeast, never quite understanding why fate had furnished him a safe billet in Charleston while his sons were locked in mortal combat on the Western Front. All of that, including Sibert's somber mood, changed on May 11, 1918, when he was called to Washington and handed his most important wartime assignment: Organize the Army's first Chemical Warfare Service (CWS) because the Doughboys needed lots of poison gas (and protection from such gas) in order to defeat the Germans. They needed it in a hurry! [13]

—ᘯ—

If a well-aimed shell fell into Allied trenches and if the barometric variables were just right—especially the wind—within minutes enough casualties resulted to overwhelm aid stations and sow panic in regimental headquarters positioned well behind the front.

English officers and their French counterparts always hoped they were far enough behind the trenches to escape an agonizing death. Never quite sure how far was far enough, even the Imperial German General Staff, responsible for unleashing their secret weapon along what they called their Western Front, worried about the consequences.

Poison gas!

Although the French first employed tear gas grenades against the Huns in 1914, it remained for German chemists and strategists to devote serious study to development of chemical weapons and to use poison gas on a large scale. In October 1914, the Germans captured Neuve Chapelle after firing shells containing a chemical irritant—which induced violent fits of sneezing—into French lines. In January 1915, the Germans hit Russian troops at Bolimov with howitzer shells containing liquid tear gas, but the gas failed to vaporize due to the freezing temperature. Undiscouraged, the Kaiser's chemists and ordnance experts made improvements and had better luck with tear gas against the French at Nieuport in March 1915. As things developed, tear gas was mere child's play.

As the second battle of Ypres began on April 22, 1915, French territorial and Algerian troops holding part of the line witnessed a yellow green cloud drifting from the German lines toward the Allied trenches in late afternoon.

Chlorine gas!

Physically, effects of the newly-deployed chemical weapon were severe: Within seconds of inhaling the toxic vapor, destruction of the victim's respiratory system began, bringing on choking attacks. Equally devastating, the gas attack caused panic among the French troops which fled in disorder, leaving a gap four miles wide in the Allied defense line. Fortunately for the Allies, success of the experiment even surprised the Germans—catching them unprepared to take advantage and turn the retreat into a major breakthrough. British and Canadian troops quickly responded and closed the gap after limited German gains.

After the Ypres Salient experience, both sides accelerated development of poison gas warfare for the remainder of the war. The Germans managed to stay ahead, with the Allies mainly copycatting their innovations, an exercise not always helpful to the Allies. After training special gas companies to direct canisters of chlorine gas at German lines, the British attacked German positions at Loos from 400 gas emplacements along the trenches. Hundreds of cylinders released the gas as the wind blew toward German lines, only to have the wind shift, spiriting much of the gas back into British lines where it caused as many casualties as suffered by the Germans. After that experience, the English relied on artillery shells to deliver gas to the enemy!

Phosgene, an insidious choking agent, caused more deaths than any other gas, mainly because it did not cause immediate violent choking symptoms, making it more easily inhaled by unsuspecting victims than chlorine. Soldiers often experienced phosgene poisoning 48 hours after exposure. During the protracted Somme campaign, the Allies mixed phosgene and chlorine into a witch's brew called "white star mix", the chlorine vapor serving to carry the phosgene to the enemy.

The Germans introduced mustard gas in 1917, an almost odorless chemical agent that caused blisters—both internally and externally—several hours after exposure. It was difficult to protect against mustard gas, which was quickly added to the Allied arsenal. By 1918, the use of poison gas by both combatants was widespread on the Western Front. Had the war continued into 1919, an estimated 30% to 50% of all artillery shells manufactured were destined to carry poison gas. By 1918, protective gas masks—filter respirators using charcoal or antidote chemicals to make air safe to breathe—were in universal use in the trenches.

The German chlorine gas attack at Ypres in 1915 should not have surprised the Allies because German prisoners warned of the development of poison gas weapons. The warnings, however, either got lost somewhere within the chain of command or, after receiving the warnings, Allied strategists chose to ignore them.

Gas procreated a psychological horror for the men in the trenches— the very idea that such an enemy existed, an agent of death against which trenches, sandbags, and steel helmets were powerless to protect them. Poison gas qualified as a true weapon of terror, never far from the minds of the men in the trenches even if a gas shell never fell within their sector of the front. The mere thought of lethal gas, which could be neither shot nor bayoneted, demoralized. Necessity invented countermeasures quickly—foremost among them the first crude gas masks—once the seriousness of the threat was recognized.

Meanwhile, safely across the Atlantic, the Army's bureaucracy slowly responded to the threat of chemical warfare despite the altogether terrifying reports from along the European trench lines. The American Army showed up late in the poison gas competition, again tardy as it had been in other preparations to fight a modern war 3,000 miles from home. Although effective use of poison gas had been demonstrated in the trenches, the American response remained anemic in early 1918, a time when all signs pointed to a long European war. Something had to be done—and quickly!

That summed up the Army's problem: They needed equipment and chemicals and troops trained not only to protect themselves against gas attacks, but to unleash poison gas on their adversaries. As early as 1917, the Department of the Interior, in an effort to help with war preparations, ordered its civilian Bureau of Mines scientists to study the problem with Army personnel. Although a civilian organization, Bureau of Mines personnel gained much practical experience while coping with various lethal gases generated within underground mines. The bureau's personnel knew more about poison gas than the military men. In addition, some very bright chemistry professors from major universities pitched in to research and try to understand this new method of warfare. Handicapped by the late start, these largely uncoordinated efforts failed to prepare the AEF for the realities of gas warfare. More was needed—and quickly! [14]

Maybe it was the need for immediate results—only possible through a rare combination of speed, efficiency, and know-how—that reminded War Department planners of their painfully dislocated major general who might be able to pull things together. With time rapidly running out and with American lives at stake by the thousands, absolutely no room existed for mistakes. And there might not be a second chance. The job must be done right the first time—and in a terrible hurry! That is when the War Department recalled Major General William Luther Sibert from Charleston.

Trained to be a warrior, Sibert wasn't the typical bricks and mortar man. However, he was, first and foremost, a builder—more like a steel reinforced concrete man. Think about the bridges, railroads, and rudimentary jungle trails carved in the Philippines, the forging of

America's first fighting division in France from a stockpile of raw recruits, and the mammoth undertaking in steamy Panama with a cast of thousands. Sibert's common denominator was consistently positive—always pushing forward with a program and a plan to accomplish a task—sometimes an almost impossible task of making something useful out of almost nothing, and to do it quickly.

That sums up Sibert's assignment when he took over the Army's poison gas program on May 11, 1918. Up until that time, the Army's approach to the problem lacked a central command structure to coordinate activities aimed at rapidly developing offensive chemical capability while protecting the Doughboys from German gas attacks.

For Sibert, his new role involved no trails to cut under enemy fire and no concrete to pour at Gatun. Instead, he assumed management of America's poison gas program. He mixed no chemicals to produce a brand new lethal gas, nor did he invent any revolutionary system for delivering it to the enemy. Instead, he served as the administrator and chief executive officer of the Army's infant poison gas business, quickly sizing up the situation, then organizing personnel and resources to meet the emergency.

In order to meet the Army's wartime needs, Sibert engineered a huge increase in the production of chemicals required for lethal gases and "smokes" (gases used to conceal movements of troops, etc.). The country's chlorine production quadrupled and the phosphorus supply approached a tenfold increase when the war ended. Sibert's managerial approach coaxed hefty increases in production from a chemical industry that was unprepared for the demands of war. When the Armistice was declared on November 11, 1918, the American chemical industry, coordinated and spurred by Sibert, produced war gases at a rate exceeding production by the other Allies and Germany combined. Also, the Germans abandoned their original method of manufacturing mustard gas in favor of the American recipe developed under Sibert's tutelage.

So far as protecting the Doughboys from gas attacks, Sibert presided over the manufacture of more than five million gas masks. By war's end, an American-made gas mask protected every American soldier, a quick turnaround from the AEF's early days when French and British gas masks were used because the Americans had none which worked. [15]

While extolling the virtues of science and American industry, and the initiative and individuality which characterized the nation, Sibert did not neglect some of his more basic ideas during a dedicatory speech at the University of Nebraska in 1919:

"We need something that will temper this individualism with an ever-present national spirit that will always have in mind the nation's advancement and safety. ... I know of nothing that will do it to the same extent as will universal military training ... coupled with a system of instruction extending from the kindergarten to the university, instilling into the youth of the land the precept that to do its part in maintaining fairness and justice among the peoples of the earth." [16]

Small wonder TR admired Sibert—an American patriot to the core—a red, white, and blue nationalist with a pragmatic view of the world. Reading between the lines of the Nebraska speech, Sibert obviously did not believe the Great War had ended all wars and, as a consequence, he admonished the nation to remain prepared to defend American values and interests when the next test arose. Preferably, with TR's big stick! But, he told the House of Representatives, greatly altered in form.

Based on experience derived from creating the Chemical Warfare Service and pushing its rapid development in 1918, General Sibert believed that research laboratories were destined to play a key role in the weaponry of the future. To develop chemical weapons—including defenses against poison gas and a means to efficiently deliver lethal chemicals into enemy ranks—Sibert favored retaining a strong Chemical Warfare Service as a separate branch of the Army. He didn't want the military caught short on chemical weapons and defenses as had been the case in 1917.

Through his testimony at congressional hearings, the general made no secret of his views that were quite the opposite of War Department plans to scale back the Chemical Warfare Service. Once again, as with his Gatun Dam testimony, Sibert exhibited candor before a Congressional committee on behalf of a cause in which he believed.

According to *The New York Times*, the deed and testimony did not go unpunished! A story in its April 7, 1920, edition revealed that "by his own application" Major General William L. Sibert retired on April 6, 1920, after almost 40 years in uniform. "By his own application" meant that the retirement was altogether voluntary and in accordance with Congress' 1915 directive. The terms of the Congressional act by which Sibert and the other canal stars had been awarded the stars of

Army generals was generous on the subject of retirement. In addition to advances in rank, each of the canal's military *junta* was at liberty to retire—with full honors and pension intact—anytime he might choose. (The War Department fully complied with Congress' flexible retirement directive, including Goethals' immediate retirement to govern the Canal Zone.)

Citing details obtained from friends of the general, *The Times* reported that Sibert had been detached from the Chemical Warfare Service and reassigned to command the Army's 5th Infantry Division at Camp Gordon (Georgia) just a short time after his testimony on Capitol Hill. Sibert believed the transfer was the War Department's way of degrading the Chemical Warfare Service by replacing a general with a mere lieutenant colonel. And he didn't like it.

This was indisputable proof, friends pointed out, that Sibert's testimony concerning the Chemical Warfare Service made a deep impression on the committee members, moving the congressmen away from the War Department's plans to reduce its stature. With its champion reassigned to other duties, the Army chiefs were in a much better position to do as they pleased with the Chemical Warfare Service. As for Sibert, the signal was clear and the Barren River farm need wait no longer for return of its master. [17]

In the 21st Century, the jury is still out on chemical and biological weapons. International attempts to outlaw poison gas have had limited effect, and it remains an issue on the world stage. Regardless, when William Luther Sibert retired from Army service in 1920—40 eventful years after enrolling as a West Point cadet—he counted a highly effective Chemical Warfare Service of the U.S. Army to go with his Panama Canal legacy. The Distinguished Service Medal was icing on the cake.

Chapter Sixteen

HOME AND HOUNDS

The newly-minted civilian made a beeline for the Big Barren following retirement as a major general in 1920. The trip by rail from Washington terminated at the Louisville and Nashville Railroad's Bowling Green passenger depot where automotive transportation awaited the retiree for the final leg of his journey. A small enthusiastic contingent of foxhunting friends greeted the soldier, prepared to escort their long-absent hunting and dinner companion on the final leg of his journey.

Model T type transportation—a three-car convoy loaded with the general, his baggage, and companions—left the depot and crossed the L & N tracks on Main Street. Turning on Clay Street, the caravan quickly raised Woodford Street, aligned in the general direction of Barren River Road and the river itself—Big Barren River. The river road crossed Jennings Creek and ascended a hill from the creek bottoms for less than a mile before the travelers turned right on the unnamed country lane skirting river bluffs to the front gate of the Sibert Farm.

The General knew he was *home*! The home label reminded him just how much he missed the Belle of Brownsville, but numerous tasks immediately diverted his thinking to more positive channels. Some involved construction on a much smaller scale than Sibert normally managed—barns, fences, and tenant houses needing attention and the smokehouse to be put in good order. The two-story frame farmhouse overlooked meadows reaching to the front gate, the river just out of sight behind a curtain of trees. He refurbished the residence, the kind of renovation that made it more comfortable than grand. Sibert envisioned his home as the perfect place to entertain his hunting friends and members of the XV Club, when and if a slot opened up and he was invited to rejoin.

Every major general, even a retired one, needs a staff. And if the retired general officer doesn't really intend to retire from the business of everyday life as a good citizen and enthusiastic hunter of the fox, he needs all the help he can get. Sibert hired a cook and a man he placed in charge of the hounds. Both were black folk and came highly recommended for their respective positions, the cook endorsed by XV wives, and the man described by foxhunters as young but promising in the ways of the hounds.

With the house and farm in good order, with a dependable cook and a skilled handler of dogs on the payroll, things looked good for the General except for the void where Mamie once stood by his side. To his delight, a vacancy occurred on the XV Club roster and Sibert, a former No. 3 in the club, returned, this time as No. 5. Contrary to the stereotyped reputation of engineers—tightly focused professionally, with little interest and even less knowledge of other subjects—Sibert possessed diverse interests and expertise in a number of areas. That diversity of interests and knowledge made him an especially attractive candidate for renewing his XV membership. The dinner club's programs usually consisted of reports and discussions of topics ranging from science to politics, literature, and world affairs. As each program ended, members freely questioned and commented on its contents, and Sibert loved it. Never bashful expressing his opinion, regardless of the subject, Sibert's candid and often incisive comments brightened XV gatherings.

The club's minutes record a good example of the ex-general's comments made during a meeting on February 15, 1923, the program's subject being the Great War's leaders, including President Wilson, Lloyd George, and Georges Clemenceau. In the near quotes and close paraphrasing contained in the minutes, Sibert fired a few volleys at the politicians and expressed his views on national preparedness:

"The Army was never able to understand why no preparations were made for War while it was apparent for a year or more that we were drifting into War. If proper preparations could have been made, we could have struck a tremendous blow, instead of almost being too late. We furnished men but no material although in a year longer we would have had a supply that would have engulfed the world."

Sibert vividly recalled his personal contact with Clemenceau, the French premier:

"During the War, Clemenceau came to headquarters of the First Division and spent Sunday with a battalion at field sports. He refused to drink wine but made a great hit with the soldiers. Clemenceau had a great knowledge of men and was willing to compromise to gain his point."

When the XV Club convened on February 16, 1928, the subject was Kentucky Governor Flem D. Sampson's message to the General Assembly. Sibert thought the proposal to place a severance tax on sand and gravel would yield much revenue. (The Kuna Indians taught Sibert all about the value of commercial grade sand.) Additionally, the ex-soldier pointed out that one man must be responsible for planning and building Kentucky's road system. He said large undertakings, like the Panama Canal construction, required a central command structure and cited inefficiency as the worst feature of public projects. Industrial development, Sibert suggested, would solve many Kentucky problems and that the salvation of the nation depends on industrial development.

The May 9, 1929, minutes of XV reflect that No. 5—that's the general—entertained club members "at his country home near Bowling Green on the banks of Barren River." The subject seemed appropriate to the host—The Proposed Nicaraguan Canal—with the program conducted by another club member. When No. 5 commented, he emphatically declared that President Roosevelt correctly chose Panama for the American canal effort. Nevertheless, Sibert expressed concern about exactly how long the Panama Canal would be adequate to handle the ever-increasing inter-ocean traffic.

Sibert took note of the American troops (Marines) in Nicaragua in 1929, their presence due to continued American interest in a second canal across Central America. He strongly suggested that the United States build a canal across Nicaragua—a slack water navigation system with locks and dams. The canal construction, according to Sibert, would bring stability to the government of Nicaragua, much the same as the Panama Canal had impacted the Republic of Panama.

"I think the United States should control all water canals south of us," Sibert declared, strongly inferring that he regarded any isthmian canals as the practical southern borders of the United States. That statement placed Sibert squarely in the company of American expansionists, beginning with Presidents Jefferson and Polk and continuing with

Theodore Roosevelt. Although he anticipated economic expansion, the ex-general never neglected the military aspects of canal politics.

"I prefer two canals to just one" he said, a second inter-ocean waterway being militarily priceless in the event hostile forces threatened closure of the Panama Canal. With foresight forged in 40 years of military experience, Sibert identified a possible Achilles heel in defense of the Canal Zone. "We must also maintain air superiority. The fortifications of the Panama Canal are at the ends. No nation would (be foolish enough) to attack it at the ends," Sibert noted. He feared, however, that the canal was highly vulnerable throughout its length to attack by hostile aircraft. Enemy bombers had nothing to fear from the big coastal cannons, all of which were pointed seaward and designed to target ships. "We ought to have a large air and navy force there," said No. 5, essential parts to canal security.

Sibert's other side spoke more softly: Despite years in uniform and control over weapons capable of inflicting massive casualties and inciting terror on the battlefield during the closing days of World War I, Sibert greatly respected the vital role constantly played by diplomacy. Also, he recognized the sensitive feelings of native peoples while locked in combat with the Filipino insurgents, and later had similar experiences with Panamanians and West Indians in the Canal Zone. "We should not offend South America," admonished No. 5, pointing out Latin America's growing importance.

Well versed in global affairs as a result of his travels and military experiences, General Sibert never neglected problems closer to home, as documented in the XV minutes covering the November 7, 1929, meeting when No. 5 entertained the club "at his home on Barren River." The program concerned a local issue—Sewage Disposal in Bowling Green—a major question in the growing town which had yet to install a municipal sewage disposal system.

Though the immediate issue may have been local, Sibert quickly mounted the soapbox, calling the club's attention to the nearby waters of Barren River which, he insisted, were in grave danger. With foresight, No. 5 declared that "this country must realize that the pollution of its streams must cease." He had, as usual, done his homework. The engineer cited problems encountered at a sewage disposal plant in Chicago as justification for Bowling Green employing qualified experts to design and construct a sanitary sewer system.

Both nationally and internationally, a lot was going on in 1931 when, Manchurio (sic) was discussed at XV's November 13 meeting. After tagging Russia as the weak sister in the Far East, Sibert opined that Japan was on the move, unalterably bent on a course of expansion, first industrially, followed by a quest for more territory. As early as 1931, other club members also saw Japan as a menace to the United States.

In a December 1931 meeting, discussions spotlighted the Eastern Problem, with No. 5 expressing concern for India, which was still under British rule. Speaking with the respect he had acquired for the peoples of the Far East while soldiering in the Philippines and surveying Chinese river systems, he characterized India's millions as an "intellectual people" who must be reckoned with. The people of India, said Sibert, "must be either freed or put in bondage."

"The club was royally entertained by No. 5 at his home on Barren River," reads the opening line of XV minutes for December 17, 1931, a meeting devoted to domestic issues on which the host had strong opinions. The retired general found himself in agreement with President Hoover on "balancing the budget." As one means of cutting expenditures, he suggested abolishing "about forty bureaus" within the Washington bureaucracy, pointing out that the proliferation of such organizations results in "expensive overlap and are not conducive to economy in governmental affairs." Not included on the Sibert hit list, and not a bureau but a part of the U.S. Army, the former engineer considered the Corps of Engineers' peacetime mission—flood control and development of the nation's waterways and harbors—important to peacetime economic growth and indispensable in wartime. Waterways development and flood control projects also cost money, but Sibert said the economic benefits justified the expenditures.

The exchange of ideas between club members stimulated Sibert who delighted in debate while maintaining a high regard for his XV friends; he awarded them equal station with his foxhunting companions, there being some crossover between the two groups. Still, at times during the 1920s, his attendance grew spotty, not at all due to disinterest, instead attributable to the engineer's active practice of his profession after retirement. [1]

His home remained ever open, ready and awaiting visitors on the river, as his youngest child, Mary Elizabeth, graduated from Mt. Holyoke College and left the nest. Transient in the past, the Sibert nest seemed firmly and permanently established in the big farmhouse on Barren River; after leaving in 1921, Mary Elizabeth listed it as home on her passport. The absence of children from the house increased the general's yearning for a conventional home place. Not only a place to live comfortably, he wanted a real home where his children would be free to visit, hopefully, with his grandchildren. The Siberts thought big families were the way to go, and they liked to get together.

The problems associated with creating a suitable and welcoming domestic scene for his grown-up children to visit and enjoy were shoved far in the background during Sibert's misadventure with Pershing in France and Juliette Sibert's untimely death. Nor was there room for wife hunting during his monumental effort to organize the Army Chemical Warfare Service while accelerating American poison gas production from zero to world leadership in those questionable military agents of death. Thus, upon Army retirement, it was the bachelor, Sibert, who took up permanent residence in the farmhouse meant for a family on the banks of the Big Barren.

Sibert enjoyed feminine company and his bachelor days in Bowling Green were not unhappy. Always a popular choice when the hostess needed a mature and urbane male to fill the vacant chair at a summer dinner party, he maintained an active social calendar. Currently unattached ladies scored high socially when escorted to a concert by the retired general. All well and good, thought Sibert, so long as such activities did not interfere with other engagements of considerable importance—foxhunting, XV meetings, and engineering assignments which continued to come his way despite retirement. Actually, the general never retired from anything he loved and that is why his appointment book remained full, always a source of great delight.

Still, things weren't quite right out there on the river without a woman to preside over his table and do all those little things that make for a smoothly running household. Sibert particularly missed Mamie's classy touch—even his Jamaican cook's misdirected efforts with silverware and menus in Panama—when it was his turn to host the XV Club's dinner meeting. Those numbered gentlemen liked to eat, but the food had to be better than good and graciously served. Something had to be done about it.

Just exactly how William Luther Sibert met the third—and final—Mrs. Sibert is just as unclear as his initial encounter with Juliette Roberts, although there are several possible avenues she could have followed to the banks of Barren River.

Evelyn Clyne Bairnfather was a native of Scotland who emigrated to America at some time prior to 1910 when the Census listed her as a 26-year-old nurse employed at a Gadsden, Alabama, hospital and boarding at the home of Dr. Arthur W. Ralls. Sibert may have met Miss Bairnfather on one of his infrequent visits to see family members in the Gadsden area. During World War I, she served in the Army Nurse Corps stateside where, from July 1918 to March 1919, her duties consisted of providing medical care for soldiers returning from France. Upon his less than triumphant return from France in December 1918, it is possible, but unlikely, that Sibert encountered Miss Bairnfather in New York.

The recently retired general may have met the Scot nurse socially while visiting his old Corps of Engineers offices in Cincinnati, the city Nurse Bairnfather chose for resumption of her civilian nursing profession after Army service ended in April 1919. According to the 1920 Census, Evelyn, age 38, and Elizabeth W. Bairnfather, age 40 (probably her sister), roomed in the home of Nora S. McCoy, a widow living at 2158 Sinton Avenue in Cincinnati. But by 1922, Miss Bairnfather returned south and was residing in Macon, Georgia.

Regardless of the circumstances of their meeting, courtship developed between the general and the nurse, culminating in marriage on the morning of June 8, 1922, at Christ Episcopal Church in Bowling Green where the general's two older sons had been baptized. Described by that day's edition of the *Park City Daily News* as a "quiet church wedding" with the Rev. A. Elliston Cole, rector, officiating, only members of General Sibert's family and some in-laws, the family of Dr. J.O. Carson, were present. (Elizabeth Collins Carson, Dr. Carson's daughter, was married to the general's eldest son, William Olin Sibert.) [2]

As one XV member, something of a wag, irreverently remarked, there was really nothing unusual about the Sibert wedding which he succinctly described as: "No. 5 (on the XV role) simply joined up with No. 3 (the third wife)."

The Siberts planned a short wedding trip to Louisville "and other points" according to the paper. Those unidentified other points very likely included Cincinnati and Pittsburgh, with a steamboat voyage along his old bailiwick—the mighty Ohio. Sibert remained critically interested in the Ohio's much delayed nine-foot channel and welcomed the opportunity for an up-close inspection of progress. Completion of the deepened channel remained several years shy of completion.

Now that the old farmhouse had a proper mistress, Sibert declared it a complete household—a genuine home. The XV's resident wag really meant it this time when he noted that there was a marked improvement in the river kitchen's cuisine after the club's No. 5 enlisted the services of (wife) No. 3.

Ida Ray, a black lady who was an outstanding cook in the Southern tradition, continued to do her share to make those XV dinners at the river house memorable culinary events. She had long been a master of the iron skillet and bacon drippings school of cooking when Evelyn Sibert expanded her horizons in the Sibert kitchen. Following the general's suggestions and Evelyn's directions, she became adept at preparing a wide variety of meals ranging from fancy French to earthy Filipino and Panamanian fare. Ms. Ray, a 55-year-old widow in 1930, lived in a tenant house on the farm with her unmarried daughter, Geneviene, age 21, who assisted in the kitchen and with housework. Ms. Ray's five-month-old grandson, William, completed the cook's household. [3]

With Evelyn's help, Sibert's unpretentious country home quickly evolved into a happy place for his scattered children and their progeny to visit, while also serving from time to time as a family refuge. His children and their children continued to hold the general's attention while, between foxhunts, he pursued a highly selective engineering practice—only the big ones.

Lively talk always circulated about the river house and the Sibert farm, with the general enduring much good-natured ribbing regarding his role as a farmer. His roots deeply planted in farming—having worked his father's farm as a teenager before enrolling at the University of Alabama—Sibert maintained a genuine interest in the soil. And, although Sibert actively directed agricultural activity on the Barren River farm, he and his friends knew that the farm mainly functioned for the benefit of the general's foxhounds and the object of their spirited chases—the fox—and also the general's horses. Often a visitor at the farm, another distinguished military officer, Major General Lytle Brown, knew all about Sibert's affinity for fox and hounds.

General Brown graduated from West Point (Class of 1898) just in time to see action in Cuba. Commissioned into the Corps of Engineers, the Nashville, Tennessee, native followed Sibert to the Philippines and later served as Louisville District Engineer. He adroitly selected Douglas MacArthur as his Adjutant while commanding a battalion of engineers in 1911. During World War I, Brown headed the War Plans Division of the Army's General Staff. His career as an Army engineer peaked when he was appointed Chief of Engineers in 1929. The officer's Army service concluded as commander of the Panama Canal Department (1935-1936), his appointment coming when the Army Chief of Staff, General Douglas MacArthur, graciously returned Brown's 1911 favor.

General Brown, however, is not mentioned because of his brilliant Army career, nor because he was Sibert's protégé, but because Sibert numbered him among his closest personal friends. In 1930, he wrote the foreword for Edward B. Clark's biography of their mutual friend. Brown extolled Sibert's virtues as "a leader of men, known as such by sterling qualities of mind, heart and soul"—a fine summation of Sibert's character. Then the chief engineer got to the good part. After acknowledging that General Sibert had retired from Army service and was fast approaching his 70th birthday, Brown wrote that Sibert had yet to retire "from the service to his fellow man." When retirement does occur, Brown explained:

"… a rest will have been well earned, and with a clear conscience, he can listen to the music of the hounds reverberating in starlit nights among the wooded hills of old Kentucky."

Almost poetic!

At least old-fashioned Kentucky foxhunters thought the barking of a pack of hounds pleasant to the ears. [4]

An appropriate way for the Army Chief of Engineers to end the short tribute, it revealed General Brown's intimate knowledge of his mentor's taste in sport. To this day, when General Sibert is mentioned in the Green River Valley, several subjects always come to mind: steamboats, locks and dams, Panama, poison gas, and foxhunting—following those hounds which made the music! Sibert loved his foxhounds and—as tightly bound to the quarry as those ancient hunters had been to theirs—he lavished almost as much affection on the fox they chased. He considered the fox a worthy adversary and would protect the animal—whether red or grey—from all enemies but his hounds. From time to time, such devotion resulted in confrontations, usually at the wildlife refuge known as the Sibert farm.

There were three of them, all boys in their teens—outdoor types having a grand time on Barren River on a bright, crisp late fall day. After it was all over, Charles Garvin and the Funk boys, Marshall and Jess, tried to explain the weekend adventure to an audience of contemporaries.

Armed with a pair of shotguns and a .22-caliber Winchester Model 1890 pump, the lads launched the johnboat from the boatlanding shortly after dawn. They had nothing scheduled on the Saturday but a good time along the river, plinking at cans and other targets of opportunity with the rifle while hoping to scare up more exciting prey. Young Garvin regularly trapped along the river and had mastered the art of curing hides for sale, usually raccoon or muskrat, sometimes fox or beaver, the latter two worth a lot more money. On a short paddle upstream to the Donaldson place, the boys checked empty traps, then reversed course downstream.

They knew exactly where they were when they eased the boat into the slough separating Boat Island from the mainland part of General Sibert's farm. The boys carefully and quietly pulled the boat on a mud bank at the rear of the farm, its northern boundary defined by the river and lots and lots of trees. More nature preserve than farm, the heavily wooded area masked the landing site—about as far from the farmhouse as one could get and still keep feet dry.

By design, they concealed their landing because, although they did not know the owner personally, they knew he did not allow hunting on his land, not even the legal in season kind. The friends also knew of one exception to the rule—when the general and his friends turned hounds loose in an effort to flush out a fox—a different kind of hunting altogether.

If they were careful, the boys saw nothing worrisome about the invasion, having decided that this general would never object to their exploring the river bottoms so long as they did not molest the fox population. Because of the hunting ban, they anticipated seeing a wealth of small game and birds, including ground hogs (woodchucks), rabbits, possibly a muskrat along the shore, but probably not the nocturnal raccoon. They might be lucky enough to scare up a dove or a covey of quail, always challenging targets even with the shotguns. They planned no mercy for crows, utterly useless pests in the eyes of farmers.

Because the Sibert sanctuary protected game, the intruders concluded with teenage logic that the owner would not begrudge them a rabbit or two that would never be missed. They considered a more important question: What if they did see a fox? They probably wouldn't, but if they did? Without further debate, the answer was unanimous: They would bring it down, then hightail it for the boat with their trophy!

It happened, just as each had not so secretly hoped—a grey was surprised by their stealthy downwind approach. It had been napping beneath a huge beech tree on a small patch of ground that managed to catch the sun's rays. Almost simultaneously, the rifle and shotguns blasted away at the hapless creature, the close range volley guaranteeing instant transit to fox heaven. And then it happened.

Suddenly and unexpectedly, a man they would never forget confronted the trio. He was large, sitting militarily erect on the biggest horse the boys had ever seen. Like an unworldly apparition, the equestrian seemingly materialized out of thin air. Recovering at least a portion of their wits, the boys realized the horse and rider had simply been hidden from view before topping the hill less than 50 yards to the west. Backlighted by a sun not yet beginning its afternoon descent over the Sibert farm, the horse and rider resembled an imposing statue—and forbidding.

"He scared hell out of us!" That summed up the trio's report to their spellbound buddies.

And there they stood, speechless and afraid, in spite of their shotguns and rifle. The tree and brush blocked the rider's view of the lifeless fox, and the immediate question arose: Should they stand their ground or run for the johnboat beached some hundred yards to the east? Still mounted, the apparition, after a long pause, finally broke the silence:

"What are you boys up to?"

"Just messing around on the river and taking shots at crows when we see them," responded Marshall Funk, the only one capable of speech during those first minutes with—they guessed correctly—the general himself staring down from the high ground. He was intimidating.

"And to whom am I speaking?" inquired Sibert, from his commanding position astride the horse. For the first time, the interlopers noticed the pistol, a standard Army service revolver, riding conspicuously in a G.I. holster on Sibert's right hip. They had no ranks, no serial numbers, but finally managed to state their names—names prompting the general to smile inwardly—while maintaining his stern outward visage.

"Ah, yes, I know your families," the general said, the short declaration fanning the smoldering fires of fear within the bewildered trio, as Sibert knew it would. Next question:

"Have you boys seen any fox?"

Now over their initial shock at being caught by the general, and well aware of his high regard for Reynard and his kin, they were of one mind, speaking as a chorus:

"No, sir!"

After another pregnant pause, the equestrian posed a final question:

"Was it a red or a grey?"

Stunned and speechless, the boys realized the game was over and they had lost. Not knowing what to do next, his friends glanced helplessly at Marshall, hoping the future Warren County attorney might dredge up a suitable response; he remained as mute as his companions. After shared glances confirmed surrender to the circumstances—recognition of their position at the general's mercy—the three raised beseeching eyes to the top of the hill and the tree line which was still in place. But gone, just as quickly and silently as they had appeared, the horse and rider vanished.

No longer paralyzed, the boys shared the same thought—turning as one and sprinting for the river and the safety of the escape boat! Halfway to the river bank, Garvin turned and raced back to retrieve the fox—always thinking a step ahead, not wanting to leave evidence behind—lending support to later courthouse opinions that he, too, should have pursued a legal career. Garvin also considered the value of the pelt, dropping the grey in the boat and pushing it away from the mud bank.

Now paddling furiously upstream, putting distance between them and the Sibert farm, the boys feared they had not heard the last of their hunting expedition. Because the general knew their families and had taken names, they expected the worst. They had little doubt their parents would hear his telephoned complaint before they reached their homes. They had even less doubt that justice awaited them for the fox slaying.

As it turned out, they were wrong. Perhaps remembering his youthful days in the mountains of northeast Alabama—where he first expe-

rienced the thrill of bringing down game with his own shooting skill—
Sibert made no calls and, consequently, no indictments were returned
that night. Days passed without repercussions, and the young hunters'
fears gradually dissolved into everlasting gratitude to the big man on
the horse whose silence signaled his understanding of them and why
they did what they did. [5]

For foxhunters, confrontations were rare, except with whatever fox
the hounds happened to be chasing at the moment. Most of their activity amounted to pure pleasure for men who loved dogs, horses, the
thrill of the chase, and the camaraderie of the campfire. In south Kentucky, however, it was all about the dogs and what they could do on
the trail of a fox. General Sibert was instrumental in briefly turning the
national spotlight on foxhunting—in Kentucky—and the colorful men
who engaged in the sport.

Although a rarity in south Kentucky in 1924, the Green River Valley's foxhunters claimed a genuine celebrity as one of their own: Since
Sibert's starring role in building the Panama Canal, he had been a figure on the national stage. His service in the Great War—including the
troubles with Pershing in France and his birthing of the Army's new
Chemical Warfare Service—made him no less prominent in the public
eye.

Trading upon the retired officer's reputation and prestige as an outstanding engineer, military leader, and a skilled foxhunter of at least
regional renown, Bowling Green foxhunters succeeded in attracting
the national field trials to Warren County in 1924. It was the Super
Bowl of the sport which enjoyed its greatest popularity in the South, a
region where men traditionally admired fine hunting dogs, paid small
fortunes to ride the best available horses, and participated in all forms
of hunting.

A true-to-form Southern sportsman, Sibert enjoyed and excelled at
field sports. While never losing his early love of the shooting sports,
the engaging sport of foxhunting—no shooting involved—became by
far his favorite. With total honesty, the general happily and engagingly
served as poster boy, first for the locals' efforts to secure the national
field trials, then to focus attention on this unique happening in South
Kentucky. General Sibert made a few telephone calls and wrote some
letters to influential leaders of the sport in the campaign to bring the
field trials to Bowling Green. After that he served as unofficial public-

ity chairman—dedicated to letting the world know about the national field trials taking place in Warren County the week of November 17-22, 1924. The best example of Sibert's work—spreading the word—appeared in *The New York Times.*

Sibert believed the national fox hunters' meeting, highlighted by field trials to determine the best foxhounds in the nation, a worthy cause—important enough to merit a visit to New York City for an interview with Silas Bent, a feature writer for *The New York Times.*

Sibert's natural style and grace, polished by West Point and a life filled with challenge, quickly established him as an editorial favorite; reporters loved him, an easy man to interview, well informed and articulate, but not a bit stuck up. The scribes found great juxtaposition—the skilled and urbane soldier-engineer being one and the same as the earthy handler of a pack of foxhounds. The general regaled them with stories on a variety of subjects, including the foxhounds destined for the spotlight when the national field trials opened in Bowling Green. The results of the interview with Silas Bent, complete with artwork, appeared in a five-column wide feature in *The New York Times'* rotogravure section on November 2, 1924. Never had foxhunters received so much national publicity—neither before nor after—Sibert's priceless contribution.

At the time, in all likelihood, no other Bowling Green personality commanded the attention Sibert routinely received—he being the only Warren Countian capable of dominating a feature page in the rotogravure section of the nationally prominent newspaper. Sibert wanted the world to know about the hounds and the hunters' meeting in Bowling Green to determine their champions. The reporter began the article routinely, asking why the general retired to Bowling Green. By stretching, New Yorkers knew of Louisville (the Kentucky Derby), even Lexington in the horse-producing Blue Grass region. But a Warren County farm—a sort of Timbuktu so far as Manhattan Islanders could tell? The celebrated engineer and military leader patiently explained:

"I've lived pretty much over the world. I've lived in the Far East, and I know Europe, and of course I've been all over the United States. But in Bowling Green there are more men than anywhere else who will stop whatever they're doing, no matter how busy they are, to go fishin' or foxhuntin' with me."

Had his friends back home been present at the interview, all heads would have nodded in unison, knowing their 64-year-old companion spoke the truth. Bowling Green, according to the article, had "ideal environment, where sport takes its proper place as the very spearhead of human activity"—at least a minor triumph of hyperbole. But it explained why Bowling Green suited Sibert and why the town beckoned in November as the "the Mecca of fox hunters from Canada and the United States." By recounting several stories about colorful local personalities, Sibert suggested that visiting hunters were in for a treat—by being exposed to the sport's resident characters—even if they never saw a fox.

There was the Negro child, Pete Strange, reared as a houseboy in the home of "old Major Covington", educated by the major (including Latin), who graduated to take charge of the fox hounds of the Bowling Green Kennel Club. He enjoyed legendary success with the hounds and earned the reputation of "knowing more prominent men than any other negro (sic) in Kentucky." That said a lot in 1924 and, according to *The New York Times*, also created a bit of a problem for Mr. Strange:

"Wherever he went, so he said, some white gentleman was shore to ask him to take a drink; and then the talk would turn to dogs, and that always called for more liquor. ... Pete's white friends found it rather a strain, paying his fine and getting him out of jail so they could go hunting. The hounds, it should be explained, 'wouldn't run for anybody but Pete.'" Mr. Strange cooked "cawn (corn) pones and cracklins" (cracklings) for the kennel club's hounds until he died.

The preparation of corn pones and cracklins figured prominently in a story from the other end of Kentucky's 1920s social spectrum. The tale told by Sibert involved his first foxhunting companion, Captain William S. Overstreet, master of the snagboat on the Green and Barren rivers during Lieutenant Sibert's early days in Kentucky. In the early 20th century, English sportsmen doubted their Kentucky cousins' ability to breed superior hounds for chasing red fox, said to be far more cunning and elusive than his brothers across the Atlantic. Such uncertainty brought numerous titled Englishmen to Bowling Green "just to go fox hunting," one of whom was being entertained at Captain Overstreet's home when Overstreet invited him to witness the preparation of supper for his pack of hounds.

It was dusk when the pair approached the roaring fire, over which big pones of water-ground corn meal and cracklins were cooking. Retrieving a pone, the captain proceeded to sample the concoction, his visitor looking on in disbelief.

"You don't tell me you eat that stuff?" said the shocked visitor.

"Sir," said the Cap'n—he told the story with great gusto, and Sibert expected it to be repeated during the trials—"Sir, no food is fit for a hound that isn't good enough for me."

"Whereupon, the Captain used to say, the visitor took a taste and smacked his lips; for this was water-ground meal, not the tasteless floury product sold over most counters; and then he squatted down on his haunches and made his own supper from the skillet," according to *The Times*. [6]

General Sibert got his message across, and the national meet tested not only the quality of the hounds, but also the ability of Bowling Green to handle the army of 500 visiting hunters. The town of 12,000 met the challenge by opening scores of homes to guests and utilizing the brand new Helm Hotel.

Surrounding the serious hunters and their prized hounds—the Trigg and Walker breeds being among the most popular—a carnival atmosphere offered entertainment for practically everyone. On opening night, General Sibert and his hunting companion, Robert Rodes, president of Citizens National Bank, spoke at a smoker attended by 500 visitors and locals, followed by the formal Fox Hunters Ball on Tuesday night. There was an afternoon bridge tournament on Thursday, a silver cup at stake, and H.H. Cherry, president of Western Kentucky State Teachers College (now Western Kentucky University), hosted a luncheon for hunters, prepared by the college's home economics department, on College Heights. [7]

Foxhunting falls on the quiet side of sporting events—except for the baying of the hounds slicing through a cool winter night. No cheerleaders inspire its participants and, never confined to a stadium, it plays out over rural landscapes—some open fields, but mostly wooded hills, brushy undergrowth, and small creek branches—perfect terrain for a clever fox to elude pursuit and find sanctuary. A typical hunt usually runs within two or three square miles and might last six hours or more. However, the range and time depended entirely upon the maneuvers of the fox and the countermeasures taken by the hounds.

It is impossible to actually observe a typical hunt carried out in the pitch black of a fall or winter night, unless you count the faint glow offered by moon and stars, and the greater candlepower of a welcoming campfire around which hunters gather. Lanterns help brighten the convivial scene and a coffee pot is not out of place, nor an occasional flask of bourbon to ward off the chill. Indeed, foxhunting is a quiet sport because the nocturnal woods is a quiet sort of place. And the hunters themselves, gathered around the fire, quietly and attentively listen for the only reliable news of the chase—the game being played in earnest between the hounds and the badly outnumbered fox.

Belying the quiet label, however, is the enthusiastic barking of the dog that first picks up the scent of Reynard, quickly followed by a chorus of excited yelps as running mates join the action—the complete antithesis of quiet! Notwithstanding the urgent cacophony conjured by the canine chorus, the gathering of hunters—much like the audience in a great symphony hall—remains respectfully quiet. Except to identify the bugling cries of individual dogs to estimate their location, silence prevails among the hunters even as excitement rises with a pack's determined pursuit. Veteran hunters are all good listeners, capable of estimating a pack's location with amazing accuracy. Regarding the barking of individual hounds, they never err as to the identity of the dog.

For the dedicated foxhunter, the pack's continual trumpeting is considered the finest of singing, the music of the chase—having the same effect on the hunter as bagpipes have on a Scotsman. For a quiet sport, a pack of hounds in full cry, tracking a fox through dark, silent woods, is contradiction enough, but it works.

A more astounding contradiction comes to light when considering the hunting aspect of the pastime: No blood! At least none unless a hound runs into a thorn bush in the dark—quite different from the blood sport as originally practiced but now banned in England and Scotland. Still, the competition is fierce between the pack and the fox. Hunters believe they've struck the right balance—the perfect match— in an imminently fair game, a contest involving endurance, athletic ability, and skill on the part of worthy contestants—both the fox and the hounds.

The ultimate reward for an owner-trainer is basking in the reflected glory of his foxhound's superior tracking ability, along with the animal's flair for narrating the contest in a voice which is musical—at least to the ears of the hunters.

And then there is the ultimate contradiction: Even after carefully training their hounds from puppyhood to be fearless trackers and hunters, after pampering the pack and bragging on its virtues, many a foxhunter grudgingly admits that once the chase is on, he often pulls for the fox! That is the essence of true sportsmanship, a hunt Grantland Rice might cite as a prime example of *how you play the game* meaning far more than the score, and foxhunting is like that. [8]

In addition to the actual field trials, a bench show—a sort of beauty contest for foxhounds—was held in Bowling Green's Fountain Square, and a fox horn-blowing contest took place in the Helm Hotel lobby. There was even an air circus scheduled late in the week, featuring seven Army planes from the 36th Division Squadron, with plans for the aircraft to track the first cast (contest) of the day.

All of the extra-curricular activity failed to detract from the performances of the hounds and hunters in the field. (Only the daylight hours separated the field trials from the sport's usual practice after dark.) All else was mere window dressing when the hounds were loosed each day at dawn or shortly thereafter. Monday's first cast drew 3,000 spectators (in addition to 300 hunters) as 78 hounds managed to flush a fox for an exciting chase near White Stone Quarry.

With 77 of the country's finest foxhounds involved, the newspaper described Tuesday's final cast at the Davenport Farm (next to the Sibert Farm) as the "most spectacular cast in the Chase Futurity" during the meet. The pack quickly jumped a fox that led them in a great circle before crossing his original path before spectators and escaping the hounds.

And so it went the entire week, hounds and hunters never tiring of the chase and Warren County's fox population seeming to relish it—a race they always won—through the final castings at the Davenport place on Friday (1,500 spectators) and Saturday. Winners received trophies and cash prizes, but it was the owners' bragging rights which counted most.

Capping the success of Sibert and his foxhunting cronies in attracting the national meet to Bowling Green, the hunters elected Robert Rodes, the congenial and respected banker, as their national president. Although Rodes was a master of the banking game, as well as a popular community leader, it was his skill with hounds, horses, and fellow foxhunters which decided the issue, just as General Sibert had predicted. [9]

Foxhunting ranked as William Luther Sibert's favorite sport by far—his passion. Thus, the elusive fox, along with Sibert's fellow hunters, his

XV friends, his memories of those earlier, happier days with Mamie in Kentucky, comprised the magnet which irrevocably drew the retired general back to the banks of Barren River. He loved it and all that made up the Green River Valley. Still, he did not withdraw from the outside world—far from it. After all, there were always more engineering projects to be pursued and, like a determined foxhound, he kept to the chase.

Chapter Seventeen
BOULDER DAM AND MOBILE DOCKS

The docks in Alabama's only port city are not the Panama Canal! That assertion is not a put down because there are really no comparables to America's successful engineering of the canal across the isthmus in the early days of the 20th century. Still, modernization and expansion of Mobile's waterfront in the 1920s was a notable undertaking which had a markedly positive and enduring influence on the venerable Alabama city and the state as a whole.

And it was altogether appropriate that one of Alabama's favorite sons made it happen.

William Luther Sibert was the living, breathing personification of the local boy who did in fact make good as a world-class engineer and—even more important to at least some of the wielders of power in capitals such as Montgomery and Washington—this engineering and construction genius was scrupulously honest. Nothing had altered his moral compass, set early by his Methodist forebears in northeast Alabama before being reinforced and protectively clad in the Honor Code iron of West Point. It endured.

General Sibert had been retired almost four years from Army service when the call came from the Alabama executive mansion in Montgomery. Governor William W. Brandon (1868-1934) had a problem, and he believed that Sibert was just the man to solve it. Standing only an inch above the five-foot mark, he had to stand on a ladder to be seen when addressing the Democrat Party's national convention in 1924. His booming voice, however, made a public address system unnecessary. [1]

Governor Brandon had Sibert's name alone on his *A list*, and there was no *B list* because Brandon did not think in those terms and seldom required one. Even though people generally found it hard to say "no" to the highly-successful politician with the over-developed vocal cords, he could foresee all sorts of difficulties in convincing the retired general to leave his hounds and hunting and fishing in Kentucky to tackle a public works project in Alabama which carried much promise, along with a heavy load of potential pitfalls. The governor did not need passionate oratory to lure Sibert back to Alabama, at least temporarily, but he did need to convince the ex-general that the ex-general would be fully in charge—and, consequently, fully responsible—for the success of the undertaking.

Actually, Sibert was chomping at the bit after a long layoff, more than ready to do some serious engineering. The contemplated construction of the Mobile docks struck a nerve, reigniting enthusiasm within the bosom of the builder of Gatun Dam and Locks. It sounded like a worthy project, and he was immediately interested if a bit reluctant.

The engineer was initially concerned about the role politics might play and if some practical ground rules, consistent with his rather lofty engineering and ethical standards, could be formulated to protect the project's integrity. These rules, he believed, must also protect his ability to command. He did not immediately jump through the Alabama hoop, but the discussions quickly got serious; Sibert was pleasantly surprised to learn that the governor's ethical views coincided with his own while experiencing an acute attack of skepticism when Brandon labeled the Mobile project an experiment with the use of public money in Alabama. The chief executive furnished background for the port crisis in Mobile as he explained the situation:

Business and civic leaders in Mobile had long recognized that Mobile Bay and the city's port facilities were major economic assets which, without extensive and costly improvements, were incapable of the full utilization required to establish Mobile in the world trade picture. Private financing had never been enough. [2]

When the Corps of Engineers inferred that work would cease on harbor improvements and the 35-mile channel to the gulf—unless there was local initiative aimed at waterfront improvements—the Alabama legislature passed legislation in 1915 to provide state funding for port improvements. The legislation was subsequently declared unconstitutional by the Alabama Supreme Court, and nothing happened in Mobile.

A proposed state constitutional amendment—which would have authorized the state to develop the seaport at Mobile—was defeated by Alabama voters in 1920.

In 1922, voters were once again asked to support Mobile port development by approving a constitutional amendment permitting Alabama to spend $10 million on port development. By that time, the voters were educated to the importance of the port to the state's economy and ratified the amendment. Still, the procedure, financing the project with bond money, was considered a political hot potato.

Enabling legislation followed in 1923 when the legislature created the Alabama State Docks Commission, the bill being signed into law by Governor Brandon. The stage was set for Alabama to issue bonds to cover costs of the improvements. The administrative framework and a means to pay were finally in place, and it had not been easy. Part of the problem centered on voters' distrust of any plans hatched in Montgomery to spend large sums of state funds—not only on the port project—but on any project in which sizable expenditures might fall within the grasp of greedy politicians.

Governor Brandon was acutely aware of the Alabama voters' mindset and was determined that this experimental use of funds obtained from issuing state bonds would be free of the scandals which often plagued public works, not only in Alabama, but throughout the country. The governor firmly believed he had a cure for the perennial problems of political influence and graft in the personage of the retired general and his reputation for honest, hard-headed business and construction management. Sibert wasn't quite sure it would be possible to insulate the Mobile project—putting it safely beyond the reach of manipulative politicians, regardless of stripe.

Governor Brandon appointed the first three-member Docks Commission in 1923, including George Gordon Crawford, a Birmingham industrialist, Frank G. Blair, a Tuscaloosa businessman, and Charles Henderson of Troy, a former Alabama governor. It was Crawford, the commission chairman, who immediately recognized the advantages of recruiting Sibert to ramrod the project and personally joined in the governor's efforts to bring the general aboard.

It would only work, Sibert made clear to the governor and Crawford, if he, Sibert, were given a completely free hand to manage the project from start to finish. The governor agreed, placing his entire trust in the former officer's professional competence and personal integrity. Crawford not only concurred but—in an unselfish and statesman-like act—he agreed to surrender his seat and the chairmanship of the commission, but only if Sibert would take it.

Sibert accepted the commission chairmanship and, coupled with his appointments as chief engineer and general manager of the Mobile docks project, he obtained the strong central control he deemed essential for success in a project of such magnitude. With political influence safely sidelined and the red tape factor destined to be minimized by the administrative structure envisioned by the chairman of the board, Sibert signed on with a firm commitment to see the project through to fruition.

Always a hands-on manager, regardless of the nature of the enterprise within his current responsibility, the general knew he could never manage the port design and construction from a command post at his Barren River farm. Just the opposite from a vacation home, Sibert decided he needed a second home in Mobile for the duration of the project. He would go to work from the house he leased at 1004 Government Street, not far from downtown Mobile.

Close to the old courthouse, at 59 St. Joseph Street, the Alabama State Docks Commission opened offices on the second floor of the State Office Building. This would be Sibert's command post until Mobile had a fully operational terminal system consisting of modern docks, warehouses, and a network of ground transportation.

It was an unbroken pattern, a thread running true through all of Sibert's activities, his long view of the enterprises in which he had engaged. Before the first shovel of dirt was turned, he had the ability to see the end result of all the effort expended. He was confident that the daily grind of his personal efforts—ranging from slide rule calculations at the drafting table to manning a level to confirm elevations at the job site—followed by the sweat of the pick and shovel gang, would produce an end product worthy of his signature.

Geographically, Mobile was not far from the Panama Canal by steamers plying the Gulf of Mexico and ports of call in the Caribbean although it was a world away culturally. Another distinct difference, of even more importance to the general, involved the prevailing climate on the Gulf shore where the work would be prosecuted—far better than the tropics of Panama. There was another huge difference between the canal construction and the installation of modern port facilities in Mobile: The Panama Canal had to be completely finished before it could render useful service whereas the Mobile port facilities could be activated as each segment was completed.

The Mobile docks, of course, were much more than docks. Even though the focus was squarely on the modern docking facilities, it is abundantly clear that the new waterfront would have been of limited use without the rest of the package. The equally modern terminal facilities—including an intricate net of railways and highways which, by extension, connected the docks with all 48 states—were located on the 500-acre docks site along the city's northern rim, some of which was reclaimed from swampland.

It was an ambitious and costly project for a state to undertake, requiring careful coordination of dock, rail, highway, and warehouse work, all of which would proceed simultaneously. Without tight management—the kind of control Sibert had exercised at Gatun—more likely than not, the project would have collapsed under its own weight, unfinished and with the State of Alabama deep in debt.

Once Sibert completed final planning, bids were accepted and contractors went to work. Appropriate for the state, the first unit of the terminal to be completed was a modern cotton warehouse with a high-density compress capable of handling 120 bales per hour. When linked with the first unit of the new docks, it efficiently fed Alabama cotton into the world's markets.

Other parts of the docks and their supporting infrastructure followed in an orderly fashion and were put to immediate commercial use transporting products and commodities of every description in and out of the United States. The sprawling terminal had been in operation long before formal dedication of the modern port facilities took place on June 25, 1928.

Even if no medals were involved, Sibert was once again cast in the role of hero, this time a champion of economic development in the Deep South. The modernized port saw a striking increase in shipping activity at a time when the South was experiencing a different kind of invasion from the North—an influx of industrial plants. This time, the fat payrolls and collateral commercial benefits were welcomed with open arms. In no small measure, the Alabama State Docks at Mobile were a major factor in the city and state getting their share of the Yankee dollars.

In the final analysis, the new docks and attendant facilities were a bargain—a big bargain—as a result of Sibert's frugal management style.

Always willing to pay fairly for services and materials, he also insisted that the Docks Commission receive full value for the dollars expended. Sibert's record of completing construction projects within the parameters of the prescribed budget was, more likely than not, just as important to Alabama authority as his honesty and engineering expertise.

Of great assistance to Sibert in keeping the project within the budget constraints was a small, efficient, and intensely loyal staff with little change in personnel during the four years of construction. Agnes G. Orton served as secretary-treasurer of the Docks Commission and, in addition, may have done double duty as Sibert's secretary. John L. Cummings was principal assistant engineer, A.C. Davis was designing engineer, and H.W. Bell was resident engineer. Rounding out the staff was F.G. Lawton, purchasing agent, and J.H. Bruce, auditor. (Late in the program, C.U. Irvine replaced Bell as resident engineer.) [3]

Reflecting the lingering distrust of politicians and the way they handle big money, the enabling act of 1923 placed in the governor's hands an effective device for monitoring the Docks Commission's expenditures as if the funds were being administered by an irresponsible ward heeler with larceny in his heart, rather than the general and Agnes Orton.

In addition to providing for the appointment of the Docks Commission, the law also provided that the governor may appoint a second body—a Board of Censor—to review the activities of the Docks Commission semi-annually, keeping an eye out for anything inconsistent with good management and wise expenditure of funds. The three-member Board of Censor was directed to report to the governor any criticisms and suggestions deemed appropriate.

The key word in the act was the permissive *may* rather than the mandatory *shall*. Having complete faith in Sibert's ability and integrity, Governor Brandon never felt it necessary to appoint a Board of Censor, and his successor was of like mind. However, with construction completed and the new port facilities in full operation—fueling the economic engines of Mobile and the State of Alabama—the governor appointed the Board of Censor only once, and then only because William Luther Sibert insisted upon the review before relinquishing control of the project.

General Sibert believed it prudent to have an impartial board review the work done, the manner in which $10 Million in bond funds had been spent, and the final product—the modern port facilities—before he retired from the scene and returned fulltime to his Barren River farm. The Board of Censor was duly appointed and, in accordance with the act, consisted of an engineer, an architect, and Alabama's examiner of public accounts. Nobody was surprised, least of all Sibert, when the Board of Censor added its stamp of approval to the completed project.

Although the entire project was not finished before Governor Brandon's term as governor ended, the state's construction of modern port and terminal facilities at Mobile is regarded as the most notable achievement of the Brandon administration, a highly successful construction project which wasted no public money and was accomplished without a hint of scandal or corruption. It exemplified William Luther Sibert at his very best. [4]

Even though operation began on the eve of the Great Depression, from the very first the new port facilities were an economic success and measured up to the task at hand. Today they continue to add economic muscle to Mobile. An independent evaluation made by the Federal Reserve Bank of Atlanta—an institution far beyond the influence of the Alabama authorities who hired Sibert to build the Mobile docks—provides a highly objective, unbiased opinion of Alabama's approach to the public works project, the man chosen to spearhead the project, and the quality of the resulting accomplishments.

Based upon exhaustive research by Earle L. Rauder, a senior economist, the bank published a lengthy, detailed analysis of the Mobile project, the object of the study being, according to W.S. McLarin, Jr., bank president, "to contribute to a better understanding of ways and means by which new industrial development can be stimulated." The Mobile docks did in fact foster industrial development in Alabama even in the face of a depressed economy. For example, the Southern Kraft Corporation, a subsidiary of the International Paper Company, installed a king-size paper mill on State Docks' property in 1928.

Regarding the contributions made by Sibert, the report by the bank wasted few words:

"To his (Sibert's) vision, engineering ability, and sense of economy is attributed the present technical excellence of much of the state's present layout of docks and terminals."

The high opinion of Sibert—particularly regarding his vision of the future—is afforded additional weight by its timing. The Federal Reserve Bank's report was published in 1945, a full 17 years after construction of the docks was completed—and still considered a model of waterfront efficiency. It is doubtful that a more impressive tribute could be found—a memorial to Sibert's innate ability to think ahead, visualize what demands would be made on the Mobile Docks by the fickle and fluid future, ever changing in directions yet to be charted—except in the fertile mind of Sibert. [5]

William Luther Sibert, an adopted Kentuckian, will no doubt forever remain a favorite son of Alabama. His major legacy—the modern port at Mobile—is much like the man himself. It just seems to roll up its sleeves, go to work, and get the job done on a daily basis—more than 80 years after the ribbon cutting. If he happened by today, the unsurprised chief engineer might suggest a few innovations.

—⟋⟍⟋—

Practically everyone in Kentucky with kinship to its rivers has an opinion of the Army Corps of Engineers. The connection may involve business and commerce (including coal shipments at bargain prices), or the attachment may be an alluvial rich bottomland farm. Riverside villages dramatically awash in uncontrolled floodtides meld with the engineers' interests. And whether you love undisturbed nature at its best, content to fish picturesque, naturally flowing streams, or whether you didn't want granddaddy's gravesite disturbed by impounded waters, opinions of the engineers are always strong and never neutral.

Adjectives describing their works and the officers peopling the ranks of the Corps of Engineers tell the story in concise and unmistakable terms. Engineers, such as Lieutenant Sibert, circa 1888, when being discussed in a complimentary fashion, qualify as dam engineers. Conversely, a Kentuckian—who has a bone to pick with the Army's finest—can't avoid calling them damned engineers! Dam is the operative word because, regardless of your view, Army engineers built dams—the Corps' most famous peacetime activity.

Adroit handling of dam construction and management was Sibert's thing, his trademark, much like the unlit cigar that often protruded from the engineer's countenance when he was working—and thinking. In the 1920s, the Sibert name remained synonymous with dams, along with his hard-earned reputation as a world-class engineer who always answered questions honestly. This landed his final appointment to serve the country by overseeing a dam problem—the biggest dam problem the world had yet witnessed—a different kind of big from Gatun's elongated mass blending with the Panamanian jungle.

At the heart of the matter: Engineers designed a huge concrete dam to impound the waters of the Colorado River, a project affecting water rights in California, Nevada, and Arizona, and expected to provide hydroelectric power for regional development. No stranger to political infighting, powerful forces jousted for years for shares in the waters of the turbulent and majestic Colorado. As the decade waned, Herbert Hoover, then secretary of commerce, assisted in settlement of the interstate dispute over water rights. With the water war resolved, gaining congressional approval and funding remained the biggest hurdle for such a large project. [6]

Because the nation rode the crest of Roarin' Twenties prosperity, it may have been a little easier to obtain congressional approval of spending on such a large scale. And the devastating Mississippi flood of 1927 ended up being a boon to plans for a dam across the Colorado River in Boulder Canyon. The Mississippi disaster changed the attitude of numerous congressmen across the South and Midwest as they recognized the need for federal dollars to finance expensive flood control projects. Opponents of the Colorado project, however, continued to point to the size and the design of the dam—a concrete arch-gravity configuration—arguing that it was unsafe. Once raised by the dam's vocal opponents, the safety question demanded answers for Congress and the public. [7]

Even after congressional trade-offs prompted by flood control concerns helped garner the necessary appropriations, there remained some final questions that necessitated a heaping measure of honest engineering to answer. Although a multi-faceted inquiry, the primary questions concerned safety and the feasibility of constructing the huge dam on the lower reaches of the Colorado River. House Resolution No. 5773 of the 70th Congress authorized appointment of a Board of Engineers and Geologists to study the problem and sort out the answers.

President Calvin Coolidge appointed the board consisting of three engineers: Robert Ridgeway of New York, Daniel W. Mead of Madison, Wisconsin, and General Sibert, and two geologists: Charles P. Berkey of New York and Warren J. Mead of Madison, Wisconsin. Invested with broad powers to examine the proposed dam site on the Colorado

River, review the proposed construction plans and cost estimates, and catalog any other conditions it might find related in any way to the project, the board's chairmanship went to Sibert.

The resolution set a December 1, 1928 deadline for the board to advise the Secretary of the Interior "as to matters affecting the safety, the economic and engineering feasibility, and the adequacy of the proposed structure and incidental works." For these services, each of the five board members earned $50 per day, plus travel expenses and *per diem* not to exceed $6 in lieu of subsistence. These amounts were payable only "for the time employed and actually engaged upon such work. ... "

The work of Sibert's engineers (and geologists) was essential to launching the Colorado project—truly a make or break proposition—because the resolution declared that "… the work of construction shall not be commenced until plans therefore are approved by said special board of engineers."

Not of the rubber stamp school, the board disregarded Congress' willingness to spend the money and President Coolidge's favorable view of the project—their collective views having no impact on the decision making process—and got down to business. When the board decided some of the dam's dimensions and specifications were anemic—considering the burden it was expected to carry—it warned that in the event of the dam's failure, the resulting torrent of water would sweep every town and village from the lower Colorado. "To avoid such possibilities," the board concluded, "the proposed dam should be constructed on conservative if not ultra-conservative lines."

The board disputed the original plans to prosecute—and complete—initial work on the dam's base during a single dry season, making it unnecessary to temporarily divert the river from the work site. An unrealistic view, insisted the board, citing insufficient time during a single dry season to build to an elevation safely above river level. In order to protect the work as it progressed from the lower elevations, the board said diversion was a necessity. To meet the board's objections, workers drilled conduits (50 feet in diameter) through adjoining cliffs to divert the river's waters during construction and later to be used for spillways.

In many respects a rerun of questions Sibert faced while successfully engineering Gatun Dam into an ageless wonder, the board adopted the general's conservative approach. After encountering problems in Panama, Sibert modified plans, broadening the base of Gatun Dam in order to cope with the pressures destined to be imposed upon it. Faced with the powerfully turbulent Colorado, the board applied Sibert's hard-won knowledge and insisted on a much wider base for Boulder Dam. Just as Sibert employed open Gatun spillways to keep the Chagres River out of Gatun Dam's lower elevations during early construction, the board backed the diversion tunnels to protect initial work on Boulder Dam's base from the flood-prone Colorado.

Much like an Arizona town marshal of an earlier era, the Colorado board's word was law, or almost so. Congress apparently meant what the resolution said: No work on the dam until the plans were approved by the board!

The board's report answered several concerns of Congress and the public and, at least to some extent, took the wind out of the sails of the dam's opponents. Whether built in Boulder Canyon or Black Canyon, the board declared it feasible to build the towering structure which, at the time, was among the largest manmade structures on the planet. (Black Canyon is the actual site of Boulder Dam. The Boulder name, however, persisted until 1947 when its renaming honored President Hoover.) [8]

From Sibert's family, as well as Kentucky friends of the Sibert family, there comes an interesting postscript to the story of the dam on the Colorado River, regardless of its name and precise location. When requested to serve as chairman of the investigation board, there was also a second request which, at least at first, he enthusiastically entertained. As the story goes, the second request came from the White House.

Assuming that the board approved construction of the Colorado dam, the president wanted Sibert to superintend the job, to serve as chief engineer and general project manager—from start to finish—just as he had recently done on the Mobile Docks. True, at age 67 Sibert regretted long separations from his farm and foxhounds. However, construction of the gigantic dam on the Colorado River presented an irresistible engineering challenge, an offer Sibert found difficult to refuse—at least he did until he found out just exactly what it would cost him.

How could that be? If he accepted the job, a handsome salary awaited the skilled engineer, no more $50 a day and $6 *per diem* as board members were paid for their investigation. Building Boulder Dam offered Sibert an opportunity to cash in on his priceless experience in the art of dam building. Even better, the challenge intrigued the engineer. Unfortunately, one huge fly spoiled the ointment.

If Sibert took the job as chief of dam construction, it meant returning to the federal payroll for the first time since retirement from the U.S. Army in 1920—probably as an employee of the Department of the Interior. No question about the excellent pay his record and experience justified, also no question that federal regulations of the day required a retired Army officer to forfeit his Army pension if he took another federal job. (Because Sibert carried out the assignment with the Colorado River board as a private contractor—not as an employee on the federal payroll—no forfeiture was required.)

Over the long haul, figured Sibert, if he was to maintain Evelyn in appropriate style, operate his farm, feed his horses and foxhounds and, occasionally, host members of the XV Club for dinner, the major general's pension was a dependable asset he did not wish to relinquish. And being fiscally conservative by nature, he also wondered how much life remained in the nation's long upward economic spiral. For the first and only time, the retired Army officer reluctantly said "no" to a President of the United States.

Even at that, as chairman of the Colorado River board, General Sibert contributed heavily to the success of the project. The board's technical contributions, in the form of modifications in design and specifications, enriched the project. And the board's reassurance of Congress and the public that the dam was feasible—and safe—falls in the priceless category.

Because he could ill afford to sacrifice his Army pension, Sibert left to others the difficult task of building Boulder Dam in Black Canyon on the Colorado River. It became another hugely successful product of All-American engineering—carrying the Sibert stamp of approval—capable of withstanding the test of time. [9]

When Sibert delivered the board's report before the December 1, 1928, deadline, its positive impact set off a chain reaction—at lightning speed when compared to the normal lethargic pace of the United States Congress. With only slight changes to the original proposal passed the previous summer by the House of Representatives, the Senate approved the Boulder Dam legislation on December 14, followed a few days later by House passage of the amended bill. President Coolidge wasted no time signing the landmark legislation into law.

As might be expected, the professional engineering periodical, *The Engineering News-Record*, crowed loudly, extolling the virtues of superior American engineering, particularly the Sibert group's careful study, which opened the way for actual construction of Boulder Dam to begin. Its December 13, 1928, issue trumpeted:

"Public service of unusually high type is reflected in the report of the Engineering Board of Review on the Boulder Dam Project. Responding fully, sanely and unequivocally to the queries placed before it, the report answers the major doubts with which Congress and the general citizen were disturbed last spring in the discussion of this contentious issue. It illuminates many points in which the main issue has been obscured. It accomplishes these things by means of broad and wise treatment of the subject—and herein the report is distinguished. All too often the work of a board or committee exhibits less wisdom than is possessed by its individual members; in the present instance the excellence of the results embodies the conjoined wisdom of the group."

In addition to the expected self-congratulatory rhetoric from an engineering publication, the detail and depth of the entire article reflects more basic concerns. The engineers were ecstatic—if ever that is possible for the slide rule boys—seeing Sibert's report as a triumph of common sense and careful engineering over the forces of political greed and ignorant opposition to progress.

As for Sibert, he happily retreated—or advanced in another direction, according to the legendary Marine, the late Chesty Puller—to his farm and sanctuary on Barren River, very near to the place where his enduring love affair with locks and dams began. Besides, he had much to do, farm chores postponed due to extended absences directing dock construction in Mobile and compiling the Colorado River study.

It had been awhile, but the older foxhounds instantly recognized their towering master who immediately turned to their care and training with the 1929 national field trials in mind. The National Fox Hunters' Association had scheduled its annual meeting and the featured field trials for Nashville in November 1929. It turned out to be an extremely bad time for the American economy, coinciding with the Wall Street collapse which plunged the nation into the Great Depression.

For the general, worry over economic chaos had to wait because the 1929 field trials promised excellent competition in hunt-conscious Nashville, just 60 miles south of Bowling Green. That was close enough for easy travel from the river farm and, best of all, Sibert thought he might have a winner within his pack.

"Sooky" was the general's favorite hound, a veteran in his 1929 kennel. The origin of the dog's name is lost, although it may be derived from the region—southern Kentucky. More likely, the name was simply a term of endearment for the talented tracker. Regardless of the name, Sooky was entered in the all-age competition, an open event as the name suggests, always hotly contested by the best of the dogs.

With 160 dogs competing, the all-age match included events on three days in the countryside surrounding the Tennessee capital. The courses followed by the hounds were judged unusually difficult with the scent trackers twice working across ground covered by an early snow. When it was all over, Sooky claimed the National Field Trials championship in the all-age chase, and the general beamed. [10]

At the next meeting of the XV Club, the question caused hot tongue-in-cheek debate: Which of the general's triumphs was most treasured—the construction of the Panama Canal or Sooky's impressive win in the field trials in Nashville? The question was never resolved, but the facts are undisputed: Sooky's preeminent postion in the pantheon of foxhounds is secure. As for Major General William Luther Sibert, U.S. Army Corps of Engineers—the family man and foxhunter, the railroader and warrior, the builder of monumental docks, locks, and dams—Goliath turned out to be a damned fine engineer!

EPILOGUE

On its October 16, 1935, front page, *The Park City Daily News*, one of Bowling Green's daily newspapers at the time, ran a banner headline eight columns wide concerning the war between Ethiopia and fascist Italy. Next, a six-column heading announced: **Gen. William L. Sibert Passes Away Today.** Ill for several months, some high blood pressure problems, complicated by the age factor, overwhelmed the general—after a full 75 years, plus two days, of living to the hilt. It was minutes after 3 a.m. on Wednesday, October 16, 1935, when the general quietly withdrew—never surrendering. He knew the ideal place to make his last stand—the farm house on the banks of Barren River. [1]

Edwin Sibert recalled some of the details of his grandfather's death and what followed. The general's body lay in state at the Bowling Green Armory that afternoon and remained there until shortly before funeral services beginning at 1 p.m., Thursday at Christ Episcopal Church, the church Mamie joined in 1891, and where two Sibert sons were christened. After the rector, Dr. Walter C. Whitaker, conducted services, the casket and accompanying family entrained for Washington. The Louisville *Courier-Journal* published an Associated Press photo taken as the caisson bearing General Sibert's body entered the gates of Arlington National Cemetery where burial took place on October 18. Visible in the photo was the Army escort and the riderless horse following the caisson, boots and side arms traditionally reversed. [2]

In Bowling Green, Sibert's death even upstaged politics! A rally by Democrats, scheduled originally for the armory, was moved to Fountain Square Park. That same day, another President Roosevelt, Franklin D., enjoyed himself aboard a cruiser, the U.S.S. *Houston*, in the Canal Zone. On tour, FDR planned to inspect the canal's fortifications and to entertain the president of the Republic of Panama. The return stateside included fishing and relaxation for FDR, once the *Houston* exited the canal through Gatun Locks, courtesy of the late William Luther Sibert. [3]

Although totally unnecessary, a heroic life-size equestrian statue in the town square might appropriately proclaim one of the general's most cherished commands: He reigned as the unchallenged field marshal, commander-in-chief, and chief engineer in charge of a most remarkable family which includes numerous overachievers within its ranks.

Prime examples of the engineer's genes running true, two sons chose Army careers and collected an equal number of stars as had their sire. Major General Franklin Cummings Sibert followed his father to West Point, served in World War I, and soldiered through the lean years between the wars. He commanded the 32nd Infantry Regiment on the eve of World War II. After serving on the staff of the 44th Infantry (1941-42), he joined General Joseph "Vinegar Joe" Stilwell's staff for a rugged tour of duty in Burma. Franklin Sibert next commanded the 6th Infantry Division during the New Guinea campaign before taking over command of the Army's X Corps. Sibert and his X Corps participated in the liberation of the Philippines where his father previously fought and built railroads. [4]

Edwin's father, Major General Edwin Luther Sibert, settled on Martha's Vineyard following Army retirement. Another West Pointer, and a younger brother of Franklin Sibert, General Edwin Sibert followed in his father's footsteps to France, thus accounting for a Sibert presence in the European Theater of Operations (ETO) during World War II. After directing the 99th Division's artillery, he headed Army intelligence (G-2) on the ETO staff and served in that same capacity with the 12th Army Group in Northwest Europe.

As the 12th Army Group's G-2, Sibert participated in the parley at Gare Montparnasse shortly before noon on August 25, 1944—resulting in surrender of the German garrison defending Paris. This spared the City of Lights from the damage and loss of life it faced if the German troops had conducted a determined defense of the French capital. When the German commander, General of Infantry Dietrich Von Choltitz, surrendered, his surrender order had to be prepared and delivered to German soldiers scattered about the city.

Fortunately, according to Sibert, with him at the white flag conference was a member of his G-2 staff, Major Paul Sapieha. The major understood the German commander's dictation and simultaneously typed out a surrender order in German—the only Allied officer capable of successfully completing the linguistic exercise. Once Sapieha typed the order, Von Choltitz signed it for distribution to about 25 German strongpoints in the city. All but one unit abided by the order and surrendered. Only the single pocket of resistance required force.

After the German surrender, the intelligence game changed. Sibert assumed the role of an American James Bond in the contest with the Soviet Union for the secrets and the ultimate mastery of those countries comprising the recent European battlefields. [5]

There is no end to the Sibert story, which reaches across generations to also include an aeronautical engineer, additional military officers, university academics, clergy, and numerous good citizens. The original General Sibert's great granddaughter (Edwin's daughter) is Anne Sibert, a Professor of Economics at Birbeck, University of London, where, until recently, she headed the School of Economics, Mathematics, and Statistics. In addition, Professor Sibert recently served as an external member of the Monetary Policy Committee of the Central Bank of Iceland, a sub-arctic version of the Federal Reserve, for lack of a better description. She currently serves on the Panel of Economic and Monetary Experts for the European Parliament's Committee for Economic and Monetary Affairs and also on the Council of Economic Advisors to the Opposition Front Bench in the United Kingdom. Her doctorate in economics is from Carnegie-Mellon University. The mathematical farm boy's genes ran true because the lady academician knows all about numbers and the impact they can have on practically everything. She even helped with this book.

My interest in the general came early during World War II when my grandmother, Blanche Overstreet Mitchell, managed her 200-acre farm alone after Uncle Dick volunteered for the Army. While my grandmother rattled around in her big farm house alone, our family lived in Bowling Green where my father worked, a few miles northeast of the Mitchell farm.

Because my mother never liked the idea of her mother living alone, it became one of my wartime duties to spend as much time as possible at the farm. On graveled Smallhouse Pike and within easy range of my bicycle, weekend visits sprinkled the school year and summer visits extended a week or more. Of limited value as a farm hand, some chores came within my capability: feeding the chickens, gathering eggs, helping feed the cows and pigs, and filling coal buckets for the big kitchen range. I also hunted arrowheads, picked blackberries, and helped Blanche hunt poke along fencerows, delighting in her aim when she killed a copperhead with the grubbing hoe she always carried. It amounted to fun for the grandson and very possibly extra trouble for the grandmother. That is how my tolerant grandmother, Blanche, became one of my very best friends.

She captured my imagination by introducing me to her memories of William Luther Sibert—a real Army general! As the reader may have guessed, my grandmother, Blanche, was the daughter of Captain Overstreet, Lieutenant Sibert's snagboat master and foxhunting mentor. Blanche grew up knowing the lieutenant, and the families remained close over the years.

Tangible evidence of the general's close association with the Overstreets and the Mitchells, General Sibert's World War I service revolver made an indelible impression on the pre-teen brain of a boy caught up in the drama of World War II. Sibert's six-shooter seemed to be the size of a cannon. Always loaded, it was off limits to me except on special occasions. After the death of my grandfather left Blanche with the farm, its tenants, and four stair-stepped children, the general raised concerns about the family's safety. Sibert's solution: the gift of the pistol, its regulation holster, and ammunition. This began a practice that continued for 30 years—Blanche never going to sleep in the lonely farmhouse without the pistol under her pillow. And she knew how to use it.

After dark on one balmy summer night, while listening to WSM on the radio, we heard a car turn off Smallhouse Pike into the lane leading to the house before abruptly stopping. With the house set far back from the road behind a screen of trees, the car rested in a fairly secluded spot—the stop being no more sinister than hugs and kisses although I didn't understand it at the time. I knew one thing for sure: Blanche didn't like the invasion and intended to do something about it. She asked me to bring General Sibert's pistol to her—just carrying the weapon being an honor usually reserved for times when I had been especially good.

I followed her to the front porch where, barely pausing, she fired off two rounds in quick succession, deliberately aiming overhead and toward the cornfield where no damage was possible. On an otherwise silent summer evening, the deafening report had the desired effect. In a matter of seconds, the car engine started, lights flashed on, and tires threw gravel as it reversed out of the lane before retreating full speed down the pike in the direction of town.

Unfortunately, the revolver disappeared at the time of my grandmother's death. But the poison gas shell (inactive of course), another gift from the general, is still around, an unusual conversation piece heavy enough to double as a doorstop. To me, as a child, everything about the General Sibert story seemed seriously heavy with importance, and the man himself loomed bigger than life. Maybe he was. The Panama Canal certainly was and remains so. [6]

Considering its 100 years on the job, the Panama Canal ages gracefully and continues to work as intended by the U.S. Army engineers who designed and built it. Of course, if one seeks the thrills of a rollercoaster ride, transiting the canal from ocean to ocean is not recommended. On the other hand, if one delights in colorful and exciting history, and appreciates the monumental engineering achievements accomplished against all odds, the leisurely pace of the canal transit is without rivals. A friend, however, warned against locking through on a big ship, explaining that the king-size canal's intricate, operational apparatus, as well as the overall feel and ambiance of the lockage procedure, is missed when seen from the deck of a steroidal cruise ship. That is why I coveted a spot on the bow rail of the *Pacific Queen*—a good place to be on Saturday, March 16, 2013, a sunny day near the end of the dry season in the Republic of Panama.

As a rule, the *Pacific Queen* makes a complete transit of the canal once each month, always on a Saturday, and is large enough to comfortably carry more than 100 passengers. It proved ideal for observing the locks in action, the huge container ships and delicate sailboats which shared the waterway, and the landmarks—Contractors Hill and Gold Hill flanking Gaillard (formerly Culebra) Cut, the Smithsonian Institution's research island, and even the old Canal Zone prison near Balboa where ex-Panamanian strongman Manuel Noriega puts in his time. He did not wave.

To the east of the canal are quick glimpses of the Panama Railroad, which, during canal construction, ferried material and personnel across the isthmus. As the ship approached Gatun, the dam that makes canal operations possible trails away to the west, looking for the most part like another inconspicuous jungle ridge except for its monolithic spillways structure. The three-stage descent orchestrated by the Gatun Locks proceeded routinely until the boat was in the third chamber—the sea lock—which would return us to sea level on the Atlantic's doorstep. Then something happened.

The *Pacific Queen* appeared suddenly out of control, unresponsive to rudder, and drifted to starboard where motion stopped only when its bow unceremoniously bumped the east wall of the lock chamber. Deckhands scurried about but were powerless to prevent the bump repeating before the captain restored control.

Damage to the ship, if any, was likely confined to scraped paint as we exited through Gatun's sea gate for the final seven-mile run across Limon Bay to Cristobal—Colon's port town which looked as if it had seen better days. Sibert protected the bay anchorage from Caribbean storms by building 11,000 feet of breakwater. Like an exposed barrier reef, it juts from the mainland to Toro Point where ships enter the bay.

The full transit of the canal took most of the day, the bus ride back to Panama City not ending until well after dark. The trip through the canal is essential to acquiring at least some understanding of what Sibert and his fellow engineers accomplished under the most trying of circumstances. For a really complete understanding of what those American engineers managed to carve from an unforgiving jungle, you had to be there, circa 1907-1914, and live through one of man's greatest engineering achievements of all times. [6]

As for Gatun Locks and Dam, a more fitting monument to the memory of Major General William Luther Sibert, U.S. Army Corps of Engineers, cannot be imagined. There are, of course, other memorials, both large and small, to the superb engineer. Even the ruins of the Woodbury Dam at Lock No. 4 on Green River make an impression when you realize they were pooling Green River water in 1840. And the only medal Sibert chose to wear in his official portrait, the Distinguished Service Medal, a tiny thing in comparison to the timber crib dam, celebrates, according to the citation: Sibert's "exceptionally meritorious and distinguished service to the Government of the United States in a duty of great responsibility during the World War, in the organization and administration of the Chemical Warfare Service, contributory to the successful prosecution of the war." (The Distinguished Service Medal is the Army's highest award for meritorious service rendered in a noncombatant role.) [7]

An even smaller memento of momentous service rendered by Sibert was—literally—paper thin. On the 24th anniversary of the *Gatun's* initial ascent and transit of the triple-decked Gatun Locks, September 26, 1937 (two years after Sibert's death), Sibert was recognized with his portrait gracing a 14-cent postage stamp issued as a part of the Canal Zone's permanent postal stamp array, the American enclave issuing its own stamps rather than using American domestic postage stamps. The paper-thin tribute to Sibert and his fellow ICC commissioners, along with Sydney B. Williamson, Pacific Division engineer, and John F. Stevens, chief engineer before TR accepted his resignation, was routinely used by Canal Zone postal authorities until the United States handed over control of the canal to the Republic of Panama. [8]

Hall of Fame? There are all kinds of those, even one at Bowling Green High School which recognizes graduates who manage some more or less notable achievements. There may even be a Miss America Hall of Fame, no doubt dominated in earlier years by those comely coeds from Ole Miss. Some fame sites are more serious than others and Sibert is enshrined in at least two of the serious variety. Simply identified as an "Engineer, Soldier" and, more effusively, as "one of the world's great engineers", General Sibert joined the Alabama Hall of Fame in 1961. He would feel comfortable sharing the honor with a fellow Alabaman of Panama Canal fame: Dr. William C. Gorgas. [9]

For Sibert, there is also a more specialized, and, at least professionally, a more meaningful honor residing in the State of Alabama Engineering Hall of Fame. William Luther Sibert was a member of the engineering elite's inaugural class of 10 (six of them deceased at the time) in 1989. With his storied Hessian lineage, he shared honors with another member of the class with undeniable Teutonic ties: Werner von Braun of rocketry fame on both sides of the Atlantic, late of Huntsville, Alabama. [10]

If Sibert were still around and if the accumulated honors happened to be mentioned in his presence, more likely than not, the old engineer-warrior would express wonderment at all the fuss and happily retell the story of Sooky's triumph in the 1929 National Field Trials at Nashville.

ENDNOTES

Prologue
[1] Sibert, Edwin Luther, Jr., personal interview, November 19, 2011. [Sibert, Edwin, Interview].

Chapter 1 – Aboard the Tugboat Gatun
[1] Ralph Emmett Avery, *America's Triumph in Panama* (Chicago: The L.W. Walter Company, 1913) 331, pp. 352-354, 356.

[2] Avery, pp. 140, 331, and map opposite p. 375.

[3] Jon T. Hoffman, *The Panama Canal, An Army Enterprise* (Washington Center for Military History, United States Army, 2009), pp. 16, 63.

[4] Avery, p. 355.

[5] Frederic J. Haskin, *The Panama Canal* (Garden City, New York: Doubleday, Page & Company, 1913), pp. 46-47, 78 and Avery, p. 78.

[6] Avery, pp. 78-79.

Chapter 2 – The Sibert Legacy
[1] Sibert, Edwin, Interview and Sibert family oral history [SFOH] and Vasco B. Sibert, *Crisis of Henry Sibert Whickerbill Jones Make (sic) A Million Dollars* (Vasco B. Sibert, 1974), pp. 34-35. Also see: Albert Bernhardt Faust, *The German Element in the United States* (Boston: The Riverside Press, 1909) pp. 346-347, 354 and *The Hessians: Mercenaries from Hessen-Kassel in the American Revolution* (Cambridge: Cambridge University Press, 1980).

[2] Allen D. Candler, *The Revolutionary War Records of the State of Georgia, Vol 2,* (Atlanta, The Franklin Turner Company, 1908), pp. 364-365 and *1790 Census* and Edward B. Clark, *William L. Sibert, The Army Engineer* (Philadelphia: Dorrance & Company, Inc., 1930), p. 19.

[3] Clark, pp. 17-20 and Thomas McDory Owen, *History of Alabama and Dictionary Of Alabama Biography, Vol. 4* (Chicago: The S.J. Clarke Publishing Company, (1921), p. 1556 and Letter to Franklin R. Sibert (Alabama Dept. of Archives and History, August 26, 1967).

Chapter 3 – *The Mathematical Farm Boy*

[1] *History of Alabama and Her People, Vol. 3* (Chicago: The American Historical Society, Inc., 1927), p. 716 [History Alabama] and Loyd Sybert, *Sibert Geneology* (Ft. Pierce, Florida) and *1860 Census.*

[2] Clark, pp. 21-23 and SFOH.

[3] James B. Sellers, *History of the University of Alabama, Vol 1* (Tuscaloosa, University of Alabama Press, 1953).

[4] Clark, pp. 23-24 and SFOH.

[5] Sellers and SFOH.

[6] Owen, p. 1556 and SFOH.

[7] Sellers, pp. 373, 440, 442, 447 and Clark, p. 25.

Chapter 4 – *West Point: David and Goliath*

[1] Clark, pp. 25-28.

[2] *Official Register of the Officers and Cadets of the U.S. Military Academy, 1881-1884* Register] and SFOH.

[3] See: Sibert's handwritten acknowledgement of commission and oath of office executed at Gadsden, Alabama, on July 14, 1884. *National Archives*, Record Group 77, pp. 2, 5 [RG77NA].

Chapter 5 – *Texas Belle and Kentucky River*

[1] *Galveston Daily News*, September 19, 1887.

[2] Eleano Russell Rentfro, "Cummings, Franklin", *Handbook of Texas Online*, (Texas State Historical Association, June 5, 2012).

[3] *Galveston Daily News*, September 19, 1887.

[4] See: Special Order No. 152, RG77NA, pp. 25, 27-28.

[5] *Annual Report, Army Corps of Engineers*, Vol. 1, 1888, p. 226 and Appendix EE, pp.1770-1772 [ARACE], and RG77NA, pp. 8, 11, 30.

Chapter 6 – *The Waters of Green River Valley*

[1] For excellent overview of Green River Valley's history from pioneer days to present see: Helen Bartter Crocker, *The Green River of Kentucky* (Lexington, The University Press of Kentucky, 1976).

[2] Sibert, Edwin, Interview.

[3] Crocker, pp. 27, 39-45 and ARACE, Appendix GG2, 1889, p. 1965.

[4] Crocker, pp. 7-8.

[5] Army Corps of Engineers, *Green and Barren River Navigation Charts*, Nos. 1-2, 1962 [GBRNC].

[6] GBRNC, Nos. 3-11.

[7] ARACE, Vol. 3, Appendix GG2, 1889, p. 1965.

[8] GBRNC, Nos. 12-18.

[9] ARACE, Vol. 3, Appendix GG2, 1889, pp. 1966-1969.

[10] GBRNC, No. 18.

[11] GBRNC, Nos. 19-20.

[12] ARACE, Vol. 3, Part 1, 1889, p. 263.

[13] SFOH.

[14] Agnes S. Harralson, *Steamboats on the Green and the Colorful Men Who Operated Them* (Berea, Kentucky: Kentucky Imprints, 1981), pp. 147-150.

[15] GBRNC, Nos. 21-27.

[16] GBRNC, Nos. 27A, 27B, 27C and *The Kentucky Encyclopedia* (Lexington: The University Press of Kentucky, 1992), p. 88.

[17] Donald R. Ball, "Useful But Impermanent: The Timber Crib Dam at Lock and Dam Number 4, Green River, Kentucky", *Journal of the Symposium on Ohio Valley Historical Archaeology*, Vol. 15, 2000: 53-65.

[18] GBRNC, Nos. 27-29, 31.

[19] ARACE, Vol. 3, Appendix GG2, 1889, p. 1963.

[20] GBRNC, No. 31.

Chapter 7 - Fixing Locks and Making Friends

[1] ARACE, Vol. 3, Part 1, 1889, p. 263.

[2] ARACE, Vol. 3, Part 1, p. 262 and Appendix GG2, p. 1965.

[3] ARACE, Vol. 3, Appendix GG2 and Part 1, Appendix JJ, 1890, p. 2259.

[4] ARACE, Vol. 1, 1891, p. 304.

[5] ARACE, Vol. 3, Appendix GG2, 1890, pp. 2256-2260 and ARACE, Part 1, 1891, pp. 309-310 and Appendix JJ2, 2478-2482.

[6] The voluminous ARACE accounts published by the Corps of Engineers reflect the projects listed herein and much more activity attributed to Lieutenant Sibert.

[7] ARACE, Vol. 1, 1893, p. 389 and RG77NA, p. 44.

[8] Mitchell, Blanche Overstreet, series of interviews, 1942-1950 [BOM] and SFOH.

[9] See: Loyd Sybert.

[10] *Parish Records, Christ Episcopal Church*, 1861-1919, copied from originals, 1942.

[11] *Minutes of XV Club*, 1892, Kentucky Library, Western Kentucky University.

Chapter 8 – Great Lakes, Little Rock and Willet's Point

[1] See: *History of the Soo Locks*, Detroit District, Army Corps of Engineers, history of navigation on St. Mary's River. Huron.Ire.usace.army.mil/SOO/lockhist.html.

[2] See:Paul Taylor, *Orlando M. Poe: Civil War General and Great Lakes Engineer* (Kent State University Press, 2009).

[3] ARACE, Vol. 1, 1893, pp. 389-393, and Appendix NN1, pp. 2962-2966; ARACE, Part 1, 1894, pp. 361-368 and Appendix MM, pp. 2261-2268, 2371-2375; ARACE, Part 1, 1895, pp. 397-402.

[4] RG77NA, p. 44.

[5] See: ARACE, Vol. 3, Appendix V, 1895.

[6] See: ARACE, Part 3, Appendix U, 1896.

[7] ARACE, Vol. 2, 1897, pp. 1650, 1677 and Part 3, Appendix V, pp. 1949-2000.

[8] Accounts of Sibert's accomplishments in the Little Rock District published in detail in the Army Corps of Engineers Annual Reports.

[9] RG77NA, pp. 45-57.

[10] Sibert's unsuccessful efforts to obtain a combat command are reflected in the *National Archives*. RG77NA, pp. 64-115.

[11] See: Order dated September 1, 1898 assigning Sibert command of engineer company at Ft. Totten. RG77NA, pp. 84-86, and Special Order 13, dated March 11, 1899, assigning Sibert to participate in planning long range development of Arkansas River. RG77NA, pp. 113-115.

Chapter 9 – To War by Pullman and Hobo Steamer

[1] James Trager, *The People's Chronology* (New York: Holt, Rinehart and Winston, 1979) pp. 662, 990.

[2] SFOH and Clark, pp. 39-45.

Chapter 10 – Philippines: Combat and Railroading

[1] RG77NA, p. 133.

[2] See: Letter from Marietta Sibert to her son dated September 3, 1899. SFOH.

[3] For excellent background on Army's innovative Krag-Jorgensen bolt action rifle, see: Tom Pearce's historical sketch on the Krag Collectors Association website: Kragcollectorsassociation.org/kca/home.htm.

[4] See: General Schwan's *Report of Cavite Expedition, October 7-14, 1899* and 8th Army's Special Orders Nos. 251 and 294. RG77NA, pp. 128-129 and 132 and Clark, pp. 47-60.

[5] See: Extract from General Otis' report of Luzon offensive, RG77NA, P. 136 [Otis Report] and Clark, pp. 48-51.

[6] Clark, pp. 51-55.

[7] Clark, pp. 53-55.

[8] Otis Report, p. 136 and Clark, p. 55-57.

[9] See: General Order No. 23, Office of U.S. Military Governor of Philippines dated February 10, 1900, RG77NA, p. 130, and Clark, pp. 68-70.

[10] Clark, pp. 70-73.

[11] RG77NA, pp. 129-130.

[12] See: Extract from Brigadier General Theodore Schwan's report of 2nd Cavite Expedition, January 4, 1900-February 8, 1900 and Schwan's letter dated February 11, 1900 to Chief of Engineers, RG77NA, pp. 122, 131, 135 and Clark, pp. 64-65.

[13] The Chief Engineer's Annual Report took pride in noting the accomplishments of the officers and men serving in combat in the Philippines. ARACE, 1900, Appendix KKK, pp. 5445-5448.

[14] RG77NA, pp. 117-120, 124-127.

[15] 1900 Census.

Chapter 11 – Deep Thinking and Dam Busting

[1] Leland R. Johnson, *The Falls City Engineers, A History of the Louisville District Corps of Engineers United States Army* (Washington: Army Corps of Engineers, 1974), pp. 47, 169, 308 [Falls City Engineers], and Clark, p. 81.

[2] Falls City Engineers, pp. 169, 188 and Clark, pp.9-80. Also see Leland R. Johnson, *The Ohio River Division, U.S. Army Corps of Engineers: The History of a Central Command* (Washington: Army Corps of Engineers, 1992) [Ohio Division] and *Proceedings of 36thAnnual Convention of Ohio Valley Improvement Association*, 1930.

[3] Ohio Division, pp. 54, 64 and Falls City Engineers, pp. 187-188 and Clark, pp. 80-81.

[4] Leland R. Johnson, *The Headwaters District: A History of the Pittsburgh District*, U.S. Army Corps of Engineers (Washington, Army Corps of Engineers, 1979) pp. 148-150 and Ohio Division, p. 47 and Clark, pp. 85-95.

[5] See: *Dam Busters* website and reference to UK Public Records Office, KEW-Air 27/2128 *Operations Record Book*, 1943

[6] See: Letter of appreciation dated January 26, 1907, from Heidenkamp Mirror Company to Corps of Engineers and letter dated January 30, 1907, from Chief of Engineers Commending Major Sibert for showing "ability and judgment of a high order" in a "difficult and dangerous matter." RG77NA, Pp. 40, 42-43.

Chapter 12 – America's Canal in Panama

[1] Hoffman, pp. 1-2.

[2] Forbes Lindsay, *Panama and the Canal Today* (Boston, L.C. Page and Company, 1912), pp. 23, 29, 31-34 and Hoffman, pp. 3, 6, 8 and Clark, p. 199.

[3] Lindsay, pp. 86-95, 99 and Hoff, pp. 8-9.

[4] Hoffman, pp. 11-14, 16.

[5] RG77NA, pp. 45-50.

[6] Avery, p. 95 and "Interesting Facts and Figures" tabulated on map opposite p. 374.

[7] Haskin, p. 30.

[8] Avery, p. 78 and Haskin, pp. 30, 139-143, 262-263 and Lindsay, p. 109.

[9] William Luther Sibert and John Frank Stevens, *The Construction of the Panama Canal*, pp. 196-199 and Avery, pp. 299-301.

[10] Haskin, pp. 32, 213 and Hoffman, p. 19 and Avery, pp. 135-138, 142 and Lindsay, pp. 125-126.

[11] Haskin, See color fold-out insert of The National Geographic Society's *Bird's Eye View of the Panama Canal* facing title page.

[12] Haskin, pp. 34-39 and Avery, pp. 140, 144-150 and Hoffman, pp. 60-61 and Lindsay, pp. 32, 125, 133.

[13] Haskin, pp. 31-35 and Hoffman, p. 60 and Avery, pp. 142, 144, 341-342.

[14] Avery, p. 153.

[15] Haskin, pp. 45-46.

[16] Sibert and Stevens, Chapter 12.

[17] Haskin, pp. 53-55 and Sibert and Stevens, pp. 43-44 and Avery, pp.63-165.

[18] Sibert and Stevens, p. 41.

[19] Sibert and Stevens, Chapter 13 and Haskin, pp. 82-87 and Clark, pp. 127-128.

Chapter 13 – Friction and Fun in Panama

[1] Hoffman, p. 9, 18-19 and Clark, pp. 118-120.

[2] Sibert and Stevens, pp. 28-29 and Clark, pp. 106, 108-113 and SFOH. While Sibert greeted Goethals' failure to speak with equally blunt silence, Gaillard pretended to ignore the artificial silences and continued to converse normally with the mute chief engineer—a much more subtle rejoinder than his ex-roommate's silence. SFOH.

[3] Within the *National Archives*, two sets of documents appear, the first indicating a September 1909 promotion date, the second documenting noting a December 30, 1909 promotion date. RG77NA, pp.5-50.

[4] Sibert and Stevens, pp. 18-22. Although generally frowned upon stateside, Sibert Declared that "the policy of extreme paternalism" worked well in the Canal Zone.

[5] *Canal Record*, Vol. 6, August 1912-August 1913.

[6] Clark, pp. 131-133 and SFOH.

[7] Sibert Geneology, p. 17 and SFOH.

[8] Clark, pp. 103-105.

[9] *Canal Record, Vol. 7*, March 18, 1914 edition.

[10] One known copy of the menu still exists, a part of the Sibert Collection, Kentucky

[11] *Canal Record, Vol. 7*, March 18, 1914 and April 1, 1914 editions.

Chapter 14 – China Service and 'Frisco Funeral

[1] William Luther Sibert and George Whitefield Davis, *Report of the Board of Engineers on the Huai River Conservancy Project in the Provinces of Kiangsu and Anhui, China* (Washington: American Red Cross, 1914).

[2] Clark, p. 155.

[3] Ohio Division, pp. 48, 64-65.

[4] RG77NA, p. 51 and Clark, p. 155-158.

[5] Trager, p. 709.

[6] See: *Brownsville News*, May 21, 1915, for report of Mamie Sibert's death.

[7] BOM.

[8] Records of Warren County Clerk, Warren County Courthouse, Bowling Green, Ky.

[9] Mary Elizabeth Sibert's photo appears in *Lamarada*, 1919, the yearbook of Mount Holyoke College, discovered in the extant portion of General Sibert's personal library, now in possession of the actor, Andy Stahl, and his mother, Mrs. Antoinette *Toni* Stahl at their home in Butler County, Kentucky.

Chapter 15 – Pershing and Gas

[1] See Frank E. Vandiver, *Black Jack, The Life and Times of John J. Pershing*, Vol. 1 (College Station, Texas: Texas A&M University Press, 1977) [Black Jack].

[2] *Pershing and the Anatomy of Leadership*, Frank E. Vandiver, Harmon Memorial Lecture No. 5, U.S. Air Force Academy, 1963 and John Keegan, *The First World War* (London, Alfred A. Knopf, Inc., 1998), p. 372 [Keegan] and Hew Strachan, *The First World War* (New York: The Penguin Group, 2003), pp. 225, 227-228 [Strachan].

[3] Clark, p. 159 and SFOH.

[4] Keegan, pp. 374-375 and Gary Mead, *The Doughboys* (The Overlook Press, 2000), pp. 8, 11-14 [Mead]. Also see Black Jack for explanation of what Army planners deemed President Wilson's premature commitment of untrained American troops to the trenches in France. Strachan, p. 228 and Mead, pp. 8, 11.

[5] James J. Cooke, *Pershing and his Generals: Command and Staff in the AEF*, (Westport, Conn: Praeger, 1997), pp. 18-19 and Clark, pp. 156-158.

[6] SFOH. The accounts of credible historians generally agree with the Sibert family's version of events surrounding General Pershing's relief of General Sibert as commander of the 1st Infantry Division. See Black Jack, Vol. 2, pp. 795-797 and Gene Smith, *Until the Last Trumpet Sounds* (New York: John Wiley & Sons, Inc., 1998) pp. 164-165 [Smith] and Jim Lacey, *Pershing* (New York: Palgrave MacMillan, 2008) pp. 115-116 [Lacey].

[7] Peyton C. March, *The Nation at War* (New York: Doubleday, Doran, 1932) pp. 266-269 [March].

[8] Black Jack, pp. 796-798, 809-810 and Smith, 164-165 and Lacey, pp. 115-116 and John J. Pershing, *My Experiences in the World War Vol. 1* (New York: Frederick A. Stokes Company, 1931) p. 217 [Pershing].

[9] The tone of the letters was caustic and referred to rumors that some ranking American officers (no names mentioned) doubted the AEF's ability to breach the German lines and defeat them in the open, pointing out that officers must radiate confidence to the troops and expect success against the Germans. Pershing's diary entry on October 24, 1917 suggests such tales lacked substance. Pershing, pp. 199-200.

[10] After seeing the 1st Infantry Division through the difficult training period and deploying its various units into the trenches for the first time, Sibert's removal was preordained because of his engineering *pedigree*, says Edward M. Coffman, a foremost student and historian of America's World War I generals. Pershing, according to Coffman, simply would not tolerate an engineer in command of his only infantry division. Telephone and e-mail discussions with Professor Coffman, June 2013. See also Edward M. Coffman, *The Hilt of the Sword* (Madison, Wisconsin: University of Wisconsin Press, 1966) and Edward M. Coffman, *Peyton C. March: Our Greatest Unsung General*, *Military History Quarterly*, summer, 2006.

[11] Clark, p. 159. Also see Christ Episcopal Church's World War I role of soldiers.

[12] Letter dated May 21, 1918 from General Sibert to his brother, Samuel Houston Sibert. Loyd Sybert.

[13] General Sibert's biographical sketch in the Archives of the Chemical Corps Regimental Association, Ft. Wood, Missouri, states: "After General Pershing persuaded the War Department to create a separate Chemical Warfare Service (CWS), Pershing was asked 'to name a general office of both ability and seniority'to command the CWS. General Pershing immediately sent the name of MG Sibert to the War Department to fill that position". Clark, p. 161.

[14] Clark, pp. 159-163. With dispatch, General Sibert created and fine-tuned the CWS. Major General Amos A. Fries, who succeeded Sibert as CWS commander, applauded Sibert's efforts to *gas* the Germans. See: Amos A. Fries and Clarence J. West, *Chemical Warfare* (New York: McGraw-Hill Book Company, Inc., 1921). One writer/historian strongly asserts that the CWS command was "imposed on him (Sibert) by Pershing" in order that Sibert's organizational and administrative skills would not be lost to the American war effort. Mead, p. 98.

[15] Clark, pp. 160, 163-164. For an overview of problems faced in organizing an efficient CWS, see *Origins of the Chemical Warfare Service,* Leo P. Brophy, *Military Affairs, Vol. 20, No. 4* (Winter 1956) pp. 217-226.

[16] Address by General Sibert upon dedication of new chemistry building at the University of November 1919.

[17] *New York Times*, April 7, 1920.

Chapter 16 – Home and Hounds

[1] *XV Club minutes*, 1920-1931, Kentucky Library, Western Kentucky University.

[2] Sibert Wedding, *Park City Daily News*, June 8, 1922.

[3] Census 1930.

[4] Clark, 9-10.

[5] Oral history as told by Dr. Jess Funk to David Garvin.

[6] Sibert and National Field Trials, *New York Times*, rotogravure section, November 2, 1924.

[7] National Field Trials, *Park City Daily News*, November 18, 20, 1924, p. 1.

[8] Foxhunting procedures and traditions, as recalled by Robert M. Coleman, Judge of Warren Circuit Court, Bowling Green, Kentucky.

[9] National Field Trials, *Park City Daily News*, November 17, 19, 21-22, pp. 1.

Chapter 17 – Boulder Dam and Mobile Docks

[1] Samuel L. Webb and Margaret Armbrester, *Alabama Governors: A Political History of the State* (Tuscaloosa: University of Alabama Press, 2001), p. 172 [Governors].

[2] See: Captain John Grant, *Improvement of the Harbor, Bay and River of Mobile* (Mobile: Henry Farrow & Co, Printers, 1872) and *Geometrical Proof of the Superiority of the Port of Mobile* (Mobile: The Commercial Club, 1890).

[3] *United States Ports*, February 1941, pp. 13, 24 and Earle L. Rauder, *The Alabama State Docks: A Case Study in State Development* (Atlanta: Federal Reserve Bank of Atlanta, 1945) pp. 2, 10-11 and *World Ports (Mobile Number)*, November 1930, p. 25 and *Mobile City Directories*, 1926-1928.

[4] Council of State Governments, *The Book of States, Vol. 6, p. 404* and Rauder, p. 10 and Webb and Armbrester, p. 172.

[5] Rauder, pp. vii, 11 and *United States Ports*, 24.

[6] Plans called for a colossal structure to be constructed of poured concrete in order to dam the Colorado River. Giant hydroelectric generators were designed to produce cheap power for three states. The dam exceeded 700 feet in height and was 1,244 feet wide. Trager, 923.

[7] John M. Barry, *Rising Tide* (New York: Simon and Schuster, 1997), p. 405.

[8] Clark, pp. 194-199, Trager, 923.

[9] SFOH and BOM.

[10] Editorials, *The Engineering News-Record*, December 13, 20, 27, 1928 and Clark, 199-204.

Epilogue

[1] *Park City Daily News*, October 16, 1935, p. 1 and *Louisville Courier Journal*, October 19, 1935 and Sibert, Edwin interview.

[2] Invasion of Samar, Philippine Islands, *Park City Daily News*, October 29, 1944, p. 1.

[3] Major General Edwin Luther Sibert, *Undated letter detailing his eye witness account (as G-2, 12th Army Group) of German garrison's surrender of Paris*, August 25, 1944.

[4] Sibert, Anne, multiple e-mail and telephone discussions, 2013.

[5] Author's recollections: General Sibert's service revolver and poison gas artillery shell.

[6] Author's observations: Full transit of Panama Canal, March 16, 2013.

[7] General Order No.8, Adjutant General's Office, U.S. Army, 1919.

[8] Sibert postage stamp issued, *Park City Daily News*, September 26, 1937. The Canal Zone stamp, a portrait of Sibert in blue, is listed as A44 in *Scott's Standard Postage Stamp Catalogue, Vol. I*, (1947), p. 96.

[9] Archives, *Alabama Hall of Fame*, 1961.

[10] Archives, *State of Alabama Engineering Hall of Fame*, Inaugural Class, 1989.

ABOUT THE AUTHOR

Robert W. (Bob) Dickey enrolled at Centre College of Kentucky, where a 160-pound interior lineman could play a little football, and stayed around to graduate. He also attended Western Kentucky University.

After a hitch in the U.S. Marine Corps, Dickey worked as a reporter and local news editor for the *Park City Daily News* in Bowling Green, Kentucky. Thereafter, he graduated from Vanderbilt University Law School and engaged in the practice of law in Kentucky for 40 years.

Photo by Tom Frost

Other books to his credit, all focused on historical subjects and personalities, include: *Near Misses*, a memoir of growing up during World War II; *Dynasty of Dimes*, a biography of a country amusement park entrepreneur; and *Greyhound to Vegas*, a biography of a Kentucky casino lady who was murdered in Las Vegas.

INDEX